Mark

Good News Commentaries

Mark

Larry W. Hurtado

A GOOD NEWS COMMENTARY

New Testament Editor

W. Ward Gasque

1817

HARPER & ROW, PUBLISHERS, SAN FRANCISCO

Cambridge, Hagerstown, New York, Philadelphia
London, Mexico City, São Paulo, Sydney

to Shannon
with love and gratitude

Mark: A Good News Commentary. Copyright © 1983
by Larry W. Hurtado. All rights reserved. Printed in
the United States of America. No part of this book may
be used or reproduced in any manner whatsoever
without written permission except in the case of brief
quotations embodied in critical articles and reviews.
For information address Harper & Row, Publishers,
Inc., 10 East 53rd Street, New York, NY 10022. Pub-
lished simultaneously in Canada by Fitzhenry &
Whiteside, Limited, Toronto.

FIRST EDITION

Designed by Design Office Bruce Kortebein

**Library of Congress Cataloging in Publication
Data**
Hurtado, Larry W., 1943–
    MARK.

    (A Good News Commentary)
    Bibliography: p.
    Includes indexes.
    1. Bible. N.T. Mark—Commentaries. I. Bible
N.T. Mark. English. Good News Bible. 1983.
II. Title. III. Series
BS2585.3.H87   1983   226'.307'7   82-48930
ISBN 0-06-064085-5

83 84 85 86 87 10 9 8 7 6 5 4 3 2 1

About the Series

This is the first major series to use the popular Good News Bible, which has sold in the millions. Each volume is informed by solid scholarship and the most up-to-date research, yet each is biblically faithful and readily understandable to the general reader. Features include:

Introductory material highlighting authorship, dating, background information, and thematic emphases—plus a map

Full text of each Good News Bible book, with running commentary

Special end notes giving references for key words and concepts and providing suggestions for further reading

Full indexes for Scripture and Subjects/Persons/Places

Series Editor W. Ward Gasque is Vice-Principal and Professor of New Testament at Regent College in Vancouver. A former editor-at-large for *Christianity Today*, he is the author of numerous articles and books and has edited *In God's Community: Studies in the Church and Its Ministry, Handbook of Biblical Prophecy, Apostolic History and the Gospel,* and *Scripture, Tradition, and Interpretation.* Dr. Gasque's major involvement is in the provision of theological resources and education for the laity.

Contents

Foreword

The Good News Bible Commentary Series

Although it does not appear on the standard best-seller lists, the Bible continues to outsell all other books. And in spite of growing secularism in the West, there are no signs that interest in its message is abating. Quite to the contrary, more and more men and women are turning to its pages for insight and guidance in the midst of the ever-increasing complexity of modern life.

This renewed interest in Scripture is found outside of, as well as in, the church. It is found among people in Asia and Africa as well as in Europe and North America; indeed, as one moves outside of the traditionally Christian countries, interest in the Bible seems to quicken. Believers associated with the traditional Catholic and Protestant churches manifest the same eagerness for the word that is found in the newer evangelical churches and fellowships.

Millions of individuals read the Bible daily for inspiration. Many of these lay Bible students join with others in small study groups in homes, office buildings, factories, and churches to discuss a passage of Scripture on a weekly basis. This small-group movement is one that seems certain to grow even more in the future, since leadership of nearly all churches is encouraging these groups, and they certainly seem to be filling a significant gap in people's lives. In addition, there is renewed concern for biblical preaching throughout the church. Congregations where systematic Bible teaching ranks high on the agenda seem to have no difficulty filling their pews, and "secular" men and women who have no particular interest in joining a church are often quite willing to join a nonthreatening, informal Bible discussion group in their neighborhood or place of work.

We wish to encourage and, indeed, strengthen this worldwide movement of lay Bible study by offering this new commentary series. Although we hope that pastors and teachers will find these volumes helpful in both understanding and communicating the Word of God, we do not write primarily for them. Our aim is, rather, to provide for the benefit of the ordinary Bible reader reliable guides to the books of the Bible, representing the best of contemporary scholarship presented in a form that does not require formal theological education to understand.

The conviction of editors and authors alike is that the Bible belongs to the people and not merely to the academy. The message of the Bible is too important to be locked up in erudite and esoteric essays and monographs written for the eyes of theological specialists. Although exact scholarship has its place in the service of Christ, those who share in the teaching office of the church have a responsibility to make the results of their research accessible to the Christian community at large. Thus, the Bible scholars who join in the presentation of this series write with these broader concerns in view.

A wide range of modern translations is available to the contemporary Bible student. We have chosen to use the Good News Bible (Today's English Version) as the basis of our series for three reasons. First, it has become the most widely used translation, both geographically and ecclesiastically. It is read wherever English is spoken and is immensely popular with people who speak English as a second language and among people who were not brought up in the church. In addition, it is endorsed by nearly every denominational group.

Second, the Good News Bible seeks to do what we are seeking to do in our comments, namely, translate the teaching of the Bible into terms that can be understood by the person who has not had a strong Christian background or formal theological education. Though its idiomatic and sometimes paraphrastic style has occasionally frustrated the scholar who is concerned with a minute examination of the original Greek and Hebrew words, there can be no question but that this translation makes the Scripture more accessible to the ordinary reader than any other English translation currently available.

Third, we wish to encourage group study of the Bible, particularly by people who have not yet become a part of the church but who are interested in investigating for themselves the claims of Christ. We believe that the Good News Bible is by far the best translation for group discussion. It is both accurate and fresh, free from jargon, and, above all, contemporary. No longer does the Bible seem like an ancient book, belonging more to the museum than to the modern metropolis. Rather, it is as comprehensible and up-to-date as the daily newspaper.

We have decided to print the full text of the Good News Bible—and we are grateful for the kind permission of the United Bible Societies to do this—in our commentary series. This takes up valuable space, but we believe that it will prove to be very convenient for those who make use of the commentary, since it will enable them to read it straight through like an ordinary book as well as use it for reference.

Each volume will contain an introductory chapter detailing the background of the book and its author, important themes, and other helpful information. Then, each section of the book will be expounded as a whole, accompanied by a series of notes on items in the text that need further clarification or more detailed explanation. Appended to the end of each volume will be a bibliographical guide for further study.

Our new series is offered with the prayer that it may be an instrument of authentic renewal and advancement in the worldwide Christian community and a means of commending the faith of the people who lived in biblical times and of those who seek to live by the Bible today.

W. WARD GASQUE

Acknowledgments

When I was asked to write this commentary in early 1978, I did not foresee the many things that would prevent me from finishing the task till now. The delay, however, has afforded me more time to read the voluminous scholarship on Mark and to reflect upon this Gospel and its message. I believe this book is the better for it, whatever its remaining faults. I have done my work with two main aims in mind: first to produce a study that reflects and is built upon scholarly investigation of the Bible; and secondly, to present the results so that the untrained person can follow the discussion and be helped thereby to receive both the benefits of biblical scholarship and a fuller appreciation of the Gospel of Mark. In view of the reader for whom this book is primarily intended, I have not included references to and discussion of the technical literature, restricting my references to works accessible to the general reader and capable of being used easily by the nonspecialist. My colleagues in New Testament studies will detect my indebtedness to many who cannot here be acknowledged.

I have concentrated here on helping the reader to see what Mark was trying to say, and what were his theological emphases. I hope, therefore, that in some modest way this commentary will be useful to the preacher and teacher interested in presenting the message of Mark, as well as to the general reader and layperson.

I cannot send this work from my desk without expressing gratitude to the many who have helped in bringing it to be. Foremost, thanks must go to my wife, to whom I dedicate the book, and who read or listened to most of it, offering countless valuable improvements in stylistic matters. She has also patiently discussed Mark with me over the last four years and has been constant in encouragement. Sandra and Alvin Esau also read large portions of the manuscript, and Adelia N. Wiens gave the whole a reading. Our department secretary, Jo Ann Beavington, patiently worked from both a very rough typescript and my own scribble in producing the final typescript. I remember fondly the congregation and pastor of McLaurin Baptist Church (Edmonton, Alberta) and the Anglican clergy of the Diocese of Rupert's Land (Manitoba), who allowed me to lead them in studies of Mark in which I was able to try out ideas and sharpen them. Finally, I am grateful to Professor W. W. Gasque for the invitation to write this volume and to colleagues in the Mark Seminar of the Society of Biblical Literature, from whose work I have learned much.

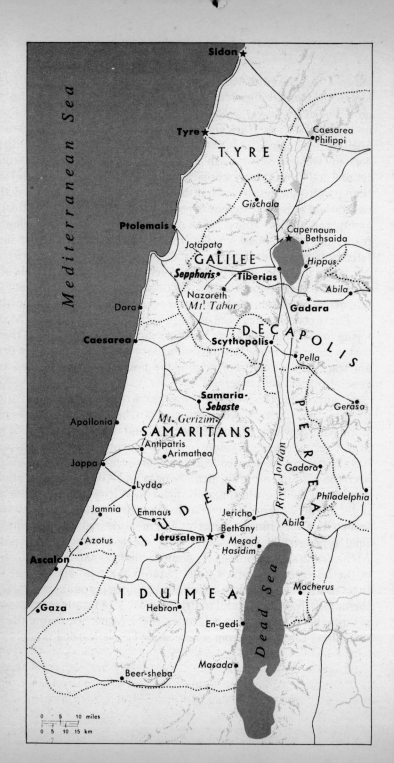

Mediterranean Sea

Sidon ★

Tyre ★

TYRE

Caesarea
Philippi

Gischala

Capernaum ★
Bethsaida

Ptolemais ●

Jotapata

GALILEE

Hippus

Sepphoris ●

Tiberias

Nazareth
Mt. Tabor

Abila

Gadara

Dora ●

DECAPOLIS

Caesarea ●

Scythopolis ●

Pella ●

Samaria-
Sebaste

Gerasa ●

Apollonia ●

Mt. Gerizim

SAMARITANS

P
E
R
E
A

Antipatris ●
● Arimathea

Joppa ●

Gadora ●

J
U
D
E
A

Philadelphia ●

Lydda ●

Jamnia ●
Emmaus ●

Jericho ●

River Jordan

Abila ●

Azotus ●

Jerusalem ★
Bethany ●
Meṣad
Hasidim ●

Ascalon

Dead Sea

Macherus ●

I D U M E A

Gaza ●

Hebron ●

En-gedi ●

Masada ●

Beer-sheba ●

0   5   10 miles
0 5 10 15 km

Introduction

Very possibly the oldest written account of Jesus' ministry that we possess, the Gospel of Mark is a vivid and fast-paced writing that holds the interest of the popular reader and the biblical scholar alike. When Christians first began discussions about drawing up a list of writings that would be regarded as authoritative for Christian faith (a discussion beginning perhaps in the middle of the second century) the Gospel of Mark was among the first writings selected for inclusion in this list and is today, of course, still regarded as one of the four "canonical," or authoritative, written portraits of Jesus in the New Testament. For these and other reasons (some of which will be discussed in the following pages) the Gospel of Mark is an important document and well repays the time spent in studying it.

The purpose of this new commentary is to encourage and make more profitable the study of Mark by readers with little or no formal training in biblical and theological subjects. The translation of Mark discussed in this commentary, the Good News Bible, was prepared in order to make the Bible available in easy-to-read but accurate English for the general reader, and this same reader is kept in mind in the present book. Before turning to the actual text of Mark, however, we shall, in this introductory section, look at some information gathered to orient the reader toward a more intelligent study of this lively story of Jesus.

Mark and the Other Gospels

Mark is one of four New Testament writings that we call Gospels, and there are still other writings from the ancient church that are described today by the same term. In order to appreciate properly the Gospel of Mark, it is helpful to see something of the relationship of this writing to these other Gospels. First, we shall look at Mark and the other *canonical* Gospels in the New Testament.

An examination of the four canonical Gospels will show that, though all four obviously have many features in common, Matthew, Mark, and Luke have many specific similarities, and John seems somewhat more distinctive. The similarities among the first three Gospels are so striking that most scholars think that some kind of literary dependence must be postulated. The majority of New Testament scholars believe that Mark was the first of these Gospels and that Matthew and Luke used Mark as a major source. This view has been disputed, especially in recent years, and the attempt to explain the similarities and differences among the first three Gospels is a continuing matter for scholarly activity among some

Bible specialists. The debate about the relationship of the Gospels of Matthew, Mark, and Luke (called the Synoptic Problem) need not detain us here. We are more interested in noting simply the basic similarities and differences between Mark and the other Gospel writings.

The characteristic that unites all four New Testament Gospels is the presentation of the ministry of Jesus, describing him in ways that accord with Christian faith. He is, for example, described as the fulfillment of Old Testament (OT) promises of a God-appointed figure (Messiah) who would represent and carry out salvation for Israel and for all nations. The Gospels use titles such as Son of God, Christ (Messiah), and Lord and consistently portray Jesus as sent by God. This sort of portrayal of Jesus means that writers of the Gospels present Jesus for the purpose of encouraging faith in him; they are not simply trying to give a documentary account for historical study.

Although emphasis on the ministry of Jesus characterizes all the canonical Gospels, Mark can be distinguished from the other Synoptic Gospels (Matthew and Luke) by the absence of a birth story and genealogy and by a smaller amount of material containing the teachings of Jesus. In the ancient church, Mark was frequently described as an abbreviated form of Matthew, and it is easy to see how this impression could have arisen.

In spite of these major differences (and several smaller ones) between Mark and the other Synoptic Gospels, nevertheless it is clear that all three are very much alike in certain respects. Scholars have shown, for example, that all three pursue basically the same narrative of Jesus' ministry. There are variations among the Synoptic Gospels in the ordering of incidents and sayings, and there are individual features in one or another of the Gospels that "interrupt" this basic narrative outline (such as Matthew's block of sayings material in chaps. 5–7, for example), but Mark represents, on the whole, the narrative of Jesus' ministry shared by all three Synoptics. So, although the scholars debate the question of whether Mark was the earliest Gospel written, it is plain that Mark represents the "basic" Gospel writing. Indeed, it is very fitting to recommend that one begin studying the Gospels by looking at Mark.

In a later section of this Introduction we shall examine more closely the distinguising characteristics of Mark over against the other canonical Gospels, but these are not the only writings that are called Gospels. Additional writings, usually called apocryphal Gospels, appeared in the early church but were not included in the New Testament (NT). These writings appeared later than the canonical Gospels and often seem to have been written to some degree in imitation of them. A number of these writings survive and are available in English translation, making comparison of them with the NT Gospels an easy and fascinating procedure.[1] Several of these apocryphal Gospels show a great concern with the childhood of Jesus and contain many accounts of miraculous deeds attributed to him during his infancy and childhood, accounts that are certainly pure invention. This concentration on the childhood of Jesus distinguishes several of the apocryphal Gospels from the canonical ones.

Another kind of apocryphal Gospel consists of sayings of Jesus with little or no narrative framework, and in such a writing as the Gospel of Thomas, one is given what are presented as revelations of Jesus spoken to his disciples after his resurrection. This sort of Gospel seems to have been popular among groups of Christians deemed heretical by the "great church" (the Christians who won the right to be called "orthodox") and seems to have been a vehicle for attributing to Jesus sayings that supported their religious views. Thus, characteristic features of this sort of writing—a preoccupation with the sayings of Jesus to the exclusion of narrative, the absence of a narrative of Jesus' death, the claim to be delivering (secret) revelations of the risen Jesus—all set these apocryphal "Gospels" apart from the canonical Gospels. Indeed, if one uses the NT Gospels as models of what qualifies a writing to be called by the description Gospel, it is questionable whether these documents really qualify for the same label.

In addition to studying the Gospels of the NT in comparison with one another and with the later, apocryphal Gospels, scholars also compare them with non-Christian writings of the ancient Greco-Roman world. This sort of study requires a great deal of specialized knowledge of the Gospels and ancient literature, and there is a continuing debate in recent times as to whether the Gospels are to be likened to biographical writings of the ancient period. We shall not attempt to review this complex discussion here, and we shall by no means try to formulate a judgment on the issue involved. It may be helpful for the reader to know, however, that even among those scholars who argue that the Gospels *are* a kind of ancient biographical writing, there is the admission that they are somewhat distinctive. The Gospels must certainly be distinguished from *modern* biographical writings by their lack of attention to the development of Jesus and by their close connection with the preaching and teaching activity and interests of the churches of their own time. The impetus for writing the Gospels did not spring from biographical interests, at least as we today would know them, but from a desire to encourage and shape faith in

Jesus. Therefore, while it is important for scholars to study the Gospels against the background of the ancient literature from the Greco-Roman world, it remains a fact that the most important context for understanding the Gospels is the life of the early church and the nature of its faith.

The Circumstances for Mark's Gospel

The opening verse of Mark's writing connects his work with the "gospel," the preaching of Jesus as the Christ and the Son of God. When speaking of the circumstances for Mark's Gospel writing, therefore, we must begin with the life of the early church, especially its presentation of Jesus in preaching and in the instruction of converts. Mark wrote his Gospel because first there was a church that built its life upon the ministry of Jesus.

This preaching and teaching activity of the early church provides not only the occasion for Mark's Gospel but also much of the explanation for the actual contents of his book. For several decades now, scholars have seen in all the canonical Gospels evidences of the earlier, and primarily oral, use of tradition about Jesus in the early church. Form criticism is the name given to the study of the Gospels conducted with a view to describing the kinds of tradition about Jesus that may have been used by the authors of the Gospels in preparing their own accounts. This line of study begins by noting the kinds of material in our present Gospels—for example, miracle stories, parables, and "pronouncement stories" (in which a short narrative leads to some pithy statement of Jesus); it then analyzes the individual units of material to describe how they may have been affected by the churches that transmitted and used this material. Though scholars who pursue this research are by no means in agreement on all points, all would concur that the Gospels contain material about Jesus that was used and transmitted in the early church primarily because this material was useful for the ongoing life of the church in such matters as proclamation of Jesus, instruction on ethical matters, and debates with other religious groups (such as Judaism).

The above remarks provide a brief description of the general circumstances for Mark's Gospel, but can we be more specific as to why, when, and where this particular early Christian writing came into being? The answers to these questions about Mark's Gospel are not easy to come by, primarily because the author does not directly give us information of this kind. The document itself gives no name for the author, no date of writing, and no place or reason for the writing. (Contrast this with the opening remarks in Luke 1:1–4.) This means that the attempt to supply this kind of information for Mark must, of necessity, involve a very close scrutiny of the document itself for any indirect clues, and as one might suspect, the interpretation of these clues involves both scholarly sophistication and a great deal of judgment. For this reason, scholars are not in agreement about *any* of the specific circumstances for this writing! In view of this, therefore, we shall have to remain tentative in suggesting answers to the questions here. It should be of no small comfort to the general reader and the scholar alike that the author did not apparently think that such specific information was essential for an understanding of his book, otherwise he surely would have included it.

Since at least the second century of the Christian era, it has been suggested that the author of Mark was John Mark, the relative of Barnabas (Acts 12:12, 25), and that he wrote his Gospel in Rome, basing it in some way on the preaching of the Apostle Peter. This is still the view of some scholars, though it must be admitted that the evidence is little more than early church tradition. Some have seen a very indirect reference to the author in the "young man" mentioned in Mark 14:51–52, but there is no hint within the document that the incident is intended to be taken this way. It may seem strange, or even disconcerting at first, but we shall probably never know for sure who penned this—perhaps the first—written Gospel. Because the name of the author is finally uncertain, most scholars today use the name Mark simply as a convenient way of referring to the author of this anonymous document, and in the commentary we shall do the same. In any case, far more important than the name of the author is what can be gleaned from the book about the author's purposes and emphases and, perhaps, the setting of this writing.

To begin with the obvious, the author wrote for Greek-speaking readers, for this is the language of the original text. More specifically, the first readers appear to have been unfamiliar with the Semitic languages of Palestine (Aramaic and Hebrew), because the writer pauses to interpret phrases in these languages when he employs them (see 5:41; 7:11, 34; 10:46; 15:22, 34). Further, the writer explains Jewish customs and religious groups to his readers, indicating that they were not residents of Palestine and were probably not Jews (see 7:3–4; 12:18; 14:12). All this is, however, only slightly helpful, telling us only what the intended readers were *not*. The only positive conclusion to draw is that Mark wrote for gentile Christians located somewhere outside of Palestine. Attempts to locate the Gospel more specifically have not won wide acceptance. This does mean, however, that the book's historical circumstance reflects the spread of Christianity among the Gentiles, the development that changed the Christian movement from what must have appeared at first as a Jewish sect into a separate religion.

The most direct information about this development in its early stages in contained in the Letters of Paul in the NT, and several scholars have pointed out in some detail the similarities between vocabulary and themes in Mark and in Paul's writing. It is not our purpose here to illustrate any direct connection between Mark and Paul but only to indicate that this Gospel was probably written for Christians like those addressed in Paul's Letters and that it is to be seen as part of the movement of Christianity out into the larger Greco-Roman world of the first Christian century.

Scholarly discussion of the date of Mark revolves around when and whether to place the book in relation to the revolt of the Jews against the Romans in A.D. 66–72. Mark 13:14–20 prophesies great turmoil in Judea in language borrowed from the OT—"You will see 'the Awful Horror' standing in the place where he should not be" (see Dan. 9:27). Some scholars are convinced that no such prophecy could have been uttered by Jesus, that the passage refers to the siege and capture of Jerusalem by the Roman army (A.D. 67–70), and that the passage was written in the form of a prophecy after the events had taken place. According to these scholars, the Gospel of Mark was probably written in A.D. 70 or shortly thereafter. Other scholars agree that the passage does not stem from Jesus but argue that its somewhat veiled language indicates that it was written shortly before the conquest of Jerusalem had been completed, placing Mark sometime during the A.D. 67–70 siege. Still other scholars find no good reason for doubting that such a prophecy of divine judgment by military destruction could have been uttered by Jesus some thirty-five to forty years before the Jewish revolt. Further, they argue that details in the passage may in fact indicate that the prophecy *did* originate well before the war in Judea. Such details include the fact that the turmoil prophesied is not described clearly but only in words borrowed from OT prophetic passage and the interesting fact that the advice given, to flee to the Judean hills, was not what refugees of the Jerusalem siege did, because the hills surrounding Jerusalem were controlled by the Romans. These scholars conclude that the date of the composition of Mark cannot be determined with any precision but that it is probably to be placed sometime between A.D. 50 and 70. It is probably best to avoid becoming overoccupied at this point with the question of exactly when or where Mark was written, since all discussion of these matters seems somewhat inconclusive and based upon intricate judgments about the Gospel and the whole history of the first century.[2] For our purposes, we shall allow for the writing of Mark anytime between A.D. 50 and 70, as I see no compelling reason to believe that the crucial passage, Mark 13, could not have been composed before the Jewish war.

Just as there is no direct indication of who the author was when he wrote, so there is no statement in the book as to why it was written. Here, also, conclusions about the author's purposes can be based only on a careful study of what the book contains. (Compare the explicit statements of intention in Luke 1:1–4 and in John 20:30–31.) More specifically, in their effort to discover the author's purposes in writing this Gospel, scholars try to determine the themes and emphases of Mark by looking for things that are repeated and matters to which large amounts of space are given in the book. This scholarly activity is usually called redaction criticism or sometimes literary criticism, depending on the exact nature of the procedure followed. Scholars also study Mark (or any of the Gospels) by comparing it with the other Gospels, and this comparison can be done in great detail when the same incident is recorded in Mark and in one or more of the others. For this kind of study a synopsis of the Gospels is very helpful. A handy tool is B. H. Throckmorton, *Gospel Parallels* (New York: Nelson, 1967), a synopsis that employs the RSV text of the first three (Synoptic) Gospels. We shall make many such detailed comparisons in the main body of this commentary, but here let us examine a few major emphases of Mark. It is not clear that we can always determine an author's purposes or occasion for writing by what seems to be emphasized, but the study of an author's emphases and themes has its own reward in helping us to become better acquainted with the writing we may be examining.

The Major Themes and Emphases of Mark

Although each of the four Gospels is a book about Jesus, each of them has particular things to say about him, and so we may begin this introduction to the themes and emphases of Mark by describing what in particular this Gospel seems to underscore about Jesus.

It is immediately apparent to the reader that Mark gives a picture of Jesus from the standpoint of Christian faith. The opening line shows this: "This is the Good News about Jesus Christ, the Son of God." In keeping with this, the book gives bits of information about Jesus' background only incidentally. We learn that he came from Nazareth (1:9), that his mother's name was Mary and he had four brothers and an undisclosed number of sisters (6:1–3), and that he had responded favorably to John the Baptist's ministry, undergoing baptism at his hands (1:9); but this is virtually all. Indeed, if Mark were the only Gospel writing, there would be a great mystery about Jesus' earthly origins. This relative silence about the birth and childhood of Jesus, when compared with the birth narratives of Matthew and Luke, has been understood often as indicating that the author of Mark knew of no such traditions; but this view is neither more nor less likely than the opposite view—that the author knew of a birth/childhood tradition and deliberately refrained from including it in his book. So, though we do not know with certainty the full reasoning, we can say that Mark is a book dealing with the adult *ministry* of Jesus and that the author regarded his information about Jesus' ministry as sufficient to portray his Good News about Jesus.

The lack of information about Jesus' background does, however, agree with the larger note of mysteriousness that hangs over the figure of Jesus in Mark. For although the reader is given the religious significance of Jesus in the opening line of the book, the author consistently portrays the human characters who encounter Jesus as seriously defective in their apprehension of him. This theme of mystery and secrecy is a well-known feature to students of Mark and has generated much interest. Some have described Mark as portraying a "messianic secret," the secret of Jesus' messiahship, that is kept hidden from the people who witnessed Jesus' ministry and revealed only in the preaching of the church. There is no denying the fact that, more than any of the other Gospels, Mark shows Jesus insisting on secrecy: silencing the demoniacs who acclaim him (e.g., 1:25, 34), commanding those healed not to publicize it (e.g., 1:44; 5:43), and ordering the disciples to keep revelations of his glory to themselves (8:27–30; 9:2–9). A debate continues among scholars as to whether this theme of secrecy stems from Jesus' own actions or is an editorial emphasis coming from Mark or his tradition. The writer of this commentary inclines to the view that Jesus did seek to suppress those who tried to make him a Messiah and that his own understanding of his task was modeled much more after the prophets of the Old Testament than after the messianic expectations for a powerful king like David. His crucifixion by the Romans as one claiming to be a king (15:26) shows that he did excite hopes and fears that he was a claimant of messiahship, in spite of his attempts to avoid such ideas.

But to return to the question of why the secrecy theme is so prominent in Mark, I suggest that its prominence is to be understood as part of a larger Markan theme. One of his major points is that Jesus' crucifixion was his key work and that all else—even the exorcisms, healings, and other miracles—was only an incomplete hint of Jesus' true nature and meaning. This is why no one is allowed to acclaim Jesus openly as Son of God or Messiah, for any acclamation uninformed by the crucifixion is misleading and invalid. This is why, also, the people and the disciples are presented in Mark (much more so than in the other Gospels) as bewildered and even stupid. In Mark's view, no one could understand the true meaning of Jesus and his work until Jesus had actually completed it by his death as a ransom for others (10:45). Thus, there is a theologically profound reason for the emphasis on secrecy, mystery, and the dullness of crowds and disciples.

This mysterious Jesus also acts with great authority (e.g., 1:27; 2:10, 28; 7:19; 11:15–19, 27–33), even doing things proper only to God, such as forgiving sins. He demonstrates the powers of God over nature (e.g., 4:35–41; 6:45–52), and receives the acknowledgment of demons (e.g., 1:24; 5:7) and of God himself (1:11; 9:7). All of this strongly indicates that Mark wished to emphasize that the one who offered his life as a ransom, whose greatest work was his humiliation and death, is in fact far more than a prophet, Messiah, or mere man of any category; he is the Son of God and is in some mysterious way divine. It is this concern with the person of Jesus that accounts for Mark's emphasis upon Jesus' conflict with demonic powers (also more emphasized in Mark than in the other Gospels). In Mark, Jesus actually brings the Kingdom of God into the world troubled by evil powers and disrupts their hold over people, and this direct conflict shows him to be the Divine Son who does God's work of expelling the powers ranged against him.

But not only is Mark a book about Jesus, it is also a book about being a follower of Jesus, a disciple. Mark was concerned to emphasize that the cross was not only the key work of Jesus but also the pattern for discipleship. As we shall see in the comments later, Mark 8–10, especially, is concerned with Jesus' description of his own coming sufferings as his essential duty, and his definition of discipleship as following his example (e.g., 8:27–38). Just as Mark wished to emphasize that the gospel is centered in Jesus' suffering for others, so he wished to correct the notion of discipleship as an easy, triumphant life. There is not only a profound theology of the gospel in this book but also a profound grasp of Christian life.

We have noted briefly the major emphases, and in the actual examination of the text we will discuss these and other themes more fully. Before we turn to the text of Mark, however, it will be helpful to describe briefly some features of his style, so that the reader is better prepared to follow what he writes.

Mark's Literary Style

To begin with basics, Mark's account is heavily narrative, conveying the feeling of fast-paced action. His Greek style is simple and unsophisticated, using many simple sentences connected by the word for "and." A comparison of events found in Mark and in the other Gospels will show that his version often seems wordy and less well constructed.

Yet, Mark did employ certain techniques that demonstrate some skill and literary intent. As we shall see, he sometimes quotes, but more frequently alludes to, the OT and seems to have expected his readers to be sufficiently familiar with it to appreciate these allusions. For Mark and his readers, the OT was holy Scripture and a prophetic foreshadowing of Jesus' work. Several times Mark connects two stories by enclosing one within another, his intent being to use the two stories to cast light on each other. Mark also groups stories together to make a sustained point (e.g., the conflict stories in 2:1–3:6), and this sometimes includes quite a large amount of material, as his handling of chapters 8–10 shows.

Above all, a comparison of Markan passages with parallels in the other Gospels shows that the writer was not carelessly relaying stories. He wrote with theological intentions and worked to make his material bring out his points forcefully. To understand and appreciate Mark's intentions, the reader must read the text closely and must give it the thought it deserves. In the commentary that follows, I hope the reader will find assistance and encouragement for this effort.

Basic Outline

Rather than attempt to justify a detailed outline here, I have thought it better to give only the most basic description of the structure of the Gospel of Mark.

1:1–13	Prologue and Setting
1:14–8:30	Ministry, Conflict, Rejection, and the Question of Jesus' Identity
8:31–10:52	Jesus' Mission and Discipleship
11:1–16:8	The Jerusalem Ministry, Jesus' Death and Resurrection

Notes

1. The standard English translation of many of these apocryphal Gospels is E. Hen-

necke and W. Schneemelcher, *New Testament Apocrypha*, 2 vols., trans. R. McL. Wilson (Philadelphia: Westminster, 1963).

2. Major reference works on questions about the date, authorship, and origin of the NT writings and related matters are the following: W. G. Kümmel, *Introduction to the New Testament*, trans. H. C. Kee (Nashville: Abingdon, 1975); D. Guthrie, *New Testament Introduction* (Downers Grove, Ill.: Inter-Varsity, 1970). A student-level discussion of the nature and origin of the Gospels is R. Martin, *New Testament Foundations: A Guide for Christian Students* (Grand Rapids: Eerdmans, 1975).

Note: A list of the abbreviations used in the commentary is found at the end of the book (see p. 279). See also For Further Reading (pp. 280–81); full bibliographical references for works referred to in short-form notes within the commentary are supplied there.

The Forerunner and Jesus

This is the Good News about Jesus Christ, the Son of God.[a] [2]It began as the prophet Isaiah had written:

"God said, 'I will send my
    messenger ahead of you to open
    the way for you.'
[3]Someone is shouting in the desert,
    'Get the road ready for the Lord;
    make a straight path for him to
    travel!' "

[4]So John appeared in the desert, baptizing and preaching.[b] "Turn away from your sins and be baptized," he told the people, "and God will forgive your sins." [5]Many people from the province of Judea and the city of Jerusalem went out to hear John. They confessed their sins, and he baptized them in the Jordan River.

[6]John wore clothes made of camel's hair, with a leather belt round his waist, and his food was locusts and wild honey. [7]He announced to the people, "The man who will come after me is much greater than I am. I am not good enough even to bend down and untie his sandals. [8]I baptize you with water, but he will baptize you with the Holy Spirit."

[9]Not long afterwards Jesus came from Nazareth in the province of Galilee, and was baptized by John in the Jordan. [10]As soon as Jesus came up out of the water, he saw heaven opening and the Spirit coming down on him like a dove. [11]And a voice came from heaven, "You are my own dear Son. I am pleased with you."

[12]At once the Spirit made him go into the desert, [13]where he stayed forty days, being tempted by Satan. Wild animals were there also, but angels came and helped him.

[14]After John had been put in prison, Jesus went to Galilee and preached the Good News from God. [15]"The right time has come," he said, "and the Kingdom of God is near! Turn away from your sins and believe the Good News!"

[16]As Jesus walked along the shore of Lake Galilee, he saw two fishermen, Simon and his brother Andrew, catching fish with a net. [17]Jesus said to them, "Come with me, and I will teach you to catch men." [18]At once they left their nets and went with him.

[19]He went a little farther on and saw two other brothers, James and John, the sons of Zebedee. They were in their boat getting their nets ready. [20]As soon as Jesus saw them, he called them; they left their father Zebedee in the boat with the hired men and went with Jesus.

a. *Some manuscripts do not have* the Son of God.
b. John appeared in the desert, baptizing and preaching; *some manuscripts have* John the Baptist appeared in the desert, preaching.

1:1-8 / In this brief but fully packed introductory section, Mark first describes Jesus by titles that summarize for the author the proper significance of Jesus and then links him with Old Testament prophetic themes and with the historical figure John the Baptist. It is interesting that, although Mark presents the human characters in his story, even the disciples, as largely unable to perceive properly who Jesus really is until his resurrection, the reader is given in the opening line the titles that prove to be Mark's favorite terms for communicating Jesus' true dignity—**Christ** (Messiah), and **Son of God.** There is a certain secrecy surrounding Jesus in the book, but the reader is let in on the secret right at the beginning. The effect of this is that the reader is prepared to feel how tragic and grievous were the rejection of Jesus by his enemies and the misunderstanding of Jesus by his disciples. The introduction of Jesus by these titles also immediately shows that the writer proceeds out of adoration for Jesus, and that the work is not written from the standpoint of unconcerned historical observance but with deeply religious interests in mind.

The Old Testament (OT) passages (Mal. 3:1 and Isa. 40:3; see the notes on 1:2, 3) are furnished to show that John the Baptist and Jesus are to be understood in the context of the prophecies regarded by ancient Jews and Christians as holy Scripture and divine revelation of God's purposes. That is, in the writer's view, neither Jesus nor John appeared "out of the blue" but, rather, as fulfillment of God's plan of redemption. This attitude, that the OT is a record of God's work and plan and that Jesus must be interpreted as fulfillment of the work and word of God in the OT, is reflected throughout the New Testament (NT) writings and received continuing expression as the church used the OT writings as Scripture in its subsequent history. This view is, of course, formally reflected in the inclusion of the OT as part of the Christian Bible—a decision still accepted by all the major branches of Christianity today. The early Christians not only saw Jesus pre-figured in certain OT prophecies of a coming redemption, but more deeply, they regarded Jesus as the culmination of all God had done in the OT. In this sense, virtually everything in the OT seemed to have anticipated and pre-figured Jesus and thus gained its "fulfillment" in him.

The passages quoted here in Mark seem to relate specifically to John the Baptist. He is seen as the **messenger** sent **to open the way** for Jesus; he is the one **shouting in the desert**, urging Israel to **get the road ready for the Lord**. This role is made clear by Mark's description of John as working **in the desert** (v. 4), calling Israel to repentance and announcing one who would come after him (vv. 7–8) with an even more significant ministry.

The passage from Malachi 3:1 (quoted in 1:2) seems to have been understood by many ancient Jews and Christians as predicting a prophet-like figure of the end time, and this figure was understood, in the context of

Malachi 4:5–6, as like Elijah, the OT prophet (see 1 Kings 17–21; 2 Kings 1–2). Mark's description of John's attire (v. 6) seems intended to recall for his readers the image of Elijah, who is similarly attired in the OT (2 Kings 1:8). Indeed, the expectation of an Elijah figure and the connection between John and Elijah is made more explicit elsewhere in Mark (see the comments on Mark 6:15).

Although this connection of John with the expectation of an Elijah figure in ancient Judaism is implied here, Mark's main intent in this section and the following verses is to relate John to Jesus. In the following verses Mark tells us that Jesus was baptized by John (1:9), at that time receiving his calling to his ministry (1:10–11), and that Jesus' ministry in Galilee began after John's arrest (1:14). In the present passage John is presented as a forerunner to Jesus. This means that Mark wishes to make John's ministry the immediate historical setting for Jesus' ministry, and in the process, he wishes to make John's prediction of a greater one to follow a prediction (and endorsement) of Jesus.

This connection of Jesus with John is well attested in the NT. All four Gospels describe the beginning of Jesus' ministry by referring to John (cf. Matt. 3:1–17; Luke 3:1–22; John 1:6–35); and the accounts of the early church in the Acts of the Apostles likewise trace Jesus' ministry from John's work (Acts 1:21-22; 10:36–38). Elsewhere in Mark there is the reported rumor that after John's execution Jesus was viewed by some (especially Herod Antipas, the ruler of Galilee) as perhaps a reappearance of the martyred prophet! This must imply that there were sufficient similarities in the ministries of Jesus and John to make such ideas worth considering in the minds of some. Further, in Mark's account of the temple-cleansing controversy between Jesus and the priestly authorities (11:27–33), we are told that Jesus demanded an evaluation of John's ministry as a condition for defending his own deeds, implying perhaps that the two ministries were to be seen as connected in some way.

John the Baptist is also referred to by Josephus,[1] the Jewish historian who wrote in the latter part of the first century A.D. His reference to John is in connection with a description of the rule of Herod Antipas, who had John executed. Josephus describes John as a popular figure with the masses, highly respected for his godliness and his strong call to righteousness, and this evidence of John's impact in first century Palestine may help us to see why the Gospels connect Jesus explicitly with John. To do so was to associate Jesus with a highly respected religious figure of first-century Judaism, and to claim John's prophetic endorsement of Jesus was both to define somewhat Jesus' ministry by association and to distinguish Jesus as even greater than John.

From the descriptions of John the Baptist in the NT writings and in Josephus, we learn that he was a prophet-like preacher calling Israel to repentance and to preparation for the coming day of God's manifestation of salvation (for those prepared) and judgment (see Matt. 3:1–12). Part of his ministry involved immersing repentant Jews in the river Jordan, and from this practice we derive his designation as John the Baptist (or Baptizer). This ritual seems to have been a somewhat new practice in Jewish religion. It appears that the Jewish sect at Qumran (site of the Dead Sea Scrolls) may have practiced ritual immersions daily to symbolize (and effect?) daily cleansing from religious impurity. It may be that Gentiles who became proselytes (converts to the Jewish religion) underwent a ritual immersion (baptism) as part of their conversion requirements (though scholars disagree as to when baptism of proselytes began). John's baptism rite was different. For one thing, it appears that John administered baptism only once to each repentant sinner, which is unlike the daily immersion rite at Qumran but similar to the practice of proselyte baptism. For another, John sought to bring Israel (Jews) to repentance and baptism, whereas proselyte baptism was only for non-Jews who wished to take up Judaism. So, there is no clear analogy for John's rite. The Christian rite of baptism, which dates from a slightly later time than John the Baptist, may have been patterned after John's rite in that, in this case as well, baptism was administered once to each person and the rite was required of all, Jew or Gentile, who sought to become Christians.

The final feature about John mentioned in this part of Mark is that John heralded one greater than he, who would have a still greater ministry (vv. 7–8). Whereas John baptized in water, the one coming would baptize **with the Holy Spirit**. This statement is to be seen against the background of the OT promises of a time when God would bestow his Spirit on all his people, giving them all special closeness with Him and, thereby, the blessings of salvation. (See Joel 2:28–32; Ezek. 36:22–32; Jer. 31:31–34.) Obviously the Holy Spirit is not a liquid, and the language of "baptizing" with the Holy Spirit is an image intended both to associate the coming salvation with John's own ministry of baptizing and at the same time to show the superiority of one to the other by the contrast of Holy Spirit and water.

---

1. Josephus, *Antiquities of the Jews*, bk. 18, pars. 116–19. A convenient translation of Josephus is L.H. Feldman, *Josephus*, Loeb Classical Library (Cambridge: Harvard University Press, 1969), vol. 9, pp. 81–85. Note also the articles on John the Baptist in *IDB*, vol. 2, pp. 955–62, and *IDBSup*, pp. 487–88.

This opening of this book by reference to John the Baptist means that we are introduced immediately into the time of the adult ministry of Jesus, with no information on Jesus' childhood. Though Matthew and Luke have birth and childhood stories, Mark plunges the reader into the thick of Jesus' ministry almost immediately. Scholars disagree as to whether Mark was uninformed about Jesus' childhood or whether it was simply not a part of his interest to write about that period of Jesus' life. Whatever the reason, the absence of material on Jesus' childhood, together with the fast-paced narrative content of the book throughout, makes Mark's Gospel an arresting summary of Jesus' ministry.

1:9-13 / In this passage Jesus appears for the first time in the narrative, and the direct relevance of the introduction of John the Baptist earlier in the story becomes clear, for here Jesus is baptized by John. This of course means that Mark's narrative not only associates John with Jesus as an endorser of Jesus but also associates Jesus with John as one who accepted John's message and obeyed his call to be baptized.

A relationship of Jesus and the Baptist is attested in all the four Gospels, but in the Gospel according to John many scholars see evidence that the writer attempted to make it very clear that Jesus was fully superior to the Baptist, perhaps to counter any suggestion that Jesus was a follower of the Baptist and therefore inferior to him. It is interesting, by comparison, that the fourth Gospel does not actually say that Jesus was baptized by John (John 1:29–34) but includes a lengthy passage where the Baptist explicitly describes Jesus' superiority (John 3:22–30). In the passage before us, there is no such reluctance to associate the beginnings of Jesus' ministry with the Baptist.

In connection with his baptism, Jesus experiences a vision that Mark apparently presents as Jesus' call to his own ministry. The **opening** (Greek, "splitting apart") of **heaven** (Greek, "the Heavens") apparently signifies both that God is about to act directly and that Jesus is given an intimate glimpse of divine purpose. The action may allude to Isaiah 64:1, where the prophet prays for God to "tear the sky open and come down," in a passage appealing for divine salvation for the people of Israel (64:1–12). The point of the allusion would be that Jesus' calling by God is to be seen as the fulfillment of the prayer and hope for God's new deliverance and revelation that Isaiah 64 reflects.

The descent of the Spirit of God upon Jesus **like a dove** is an action intended to show that Jesus is commissioned by God. This reminds the reader of Isaiah 61:1, where God's servant describes his calling as involving God's spirit being upon him. ("The Sovereign Lord has filled me with his spirit": lit., "the Spirit of the Lord is upon me.")

The voice from heaven is clearly God's, and the statement alludes to several OT passages, identifying Jesus with revered figures from the passages in question. **You are my . . . Son** echoes Psalm 2:7, a psalm originally addressed to the ancient Jewish kings. **Dear** son echoes Genesis 22:2, where God addresses Abraham, telling him to offer his son Isaac ("your only son, whom you love so much"). **I am pleased with you** reflects Isaiah 42:1, where God points to his servant as one chosen to speak for him.

It appears that Psalm 2 and Isaiah 42, and perhaps Genesis 22:2, were understood by some in Mark's time as foreshadowing the Messiah (the anointed one, the Christ), and so the allusion to these passages implicitly designates Jesus as the one foreshadowed. As we will see in subsequent passages, Mark wishes to enchance and enlarge the significance of Jesus beyond his simply being the Messiah, but the allusion to these verses from the OT means that Mark wishes also to claim for Jesus the honor attached to the Messiah figure of Jewish hope.

This vision and the accompanying voice from heaven are similar to the OT accounts of prophets who were called by God to speak to Israel. Isaiah (6:1–13) and Ezekiel (1:1–2:10) give extended descriptions of such experiences, but such visions and accompanying experiences of being called by God seem to have prompted the ministry of several other prophets as well (e.g., Amos 7:1–9:1). Certainly Mark saw Jesus as more than a prophet, but this account seems intended to describe the beginning of Jesus' ministry as provoked by a prophetic calling experience. It is worth noting that Jesus elsewhere likens himself to a prophet (6:4) and that some people so regarded him (6:15; 8:28). But though the form of the calling here is like that of OT prophets, the substance of the call is to serve as God's chosen Son!

All the Synoptic Gospels describe Jesus undergoing a period of temptation in a desert area shortly after his baptism, but there are interesting peculiarities to the account in Mark. For one thing, although the accounts in Matthew (4:1–11) and Luke (4:1–13) describe the Spirt *leading* Jesus into the desert, Mark says that the Spirit **made him go into the desert** (1:12). Though we do not really know what was behind Mark's choice of words here, the effect is to make the temptation seem more of an unsought and uncomfortable experience, an ordeal. The fact that it is the **Spirit** who drove him into the desert means that the testing there was God-ordained, part of the necessary preparation for God's chosen Son. For another thing, Mark alone refers to **wild animals** in the desert experience (1:13), and his intention, apparently, is to show the dangers of the scene. Some scholars suggest that the writer alludes here to the creation accounts, in which Adam in the garden names the animals (Gen. 2:18–19), the significance of the possible allusion being that Mark may be portraying Jesus as a new Adam signifying a new beginning for the human race. (I am not persuaded by this suggestion, however.)

All three Synoptic Gospel accounts describe the temptation as lasting forty days, and we should note two things about this figure. First, it is a round number and therefore probably not intended as an exact description of the chronological length of the temptation period. Secondly, it is worth noticing that the forty days of Jesus' temptation in the desert seem intended to echo the traditions that Israel spent forty years in the desert (Deut. 29:5) and that Moses spent forty days on Mount Horeb waiting to receive the Law (Exod. 24:18). The point of the probable allusions to these traditions is to make Jesus' desert period a time of new revelation and salvation equivalent to the revelation given to Moses and Israel in the classical, Exodus time.

Acclaimed by God at his baptism, gifted with the Spirit of God, and directed by the Spirit into this testing, Jesus is also helped by angels (v. 13). Matthew (4:1–11) and Luke (4:1–13) both devote greater space to the temptation scene, but even the briefer Markan account makes it clear that this episode is the testing and preparation for the one just called to do the work none other was called to do. Early here in the Gospel story Jesus encounters Satan (v. 13) under adverse circumstances and, as the narrative implies, wins against him, setting the tone for the theme of Jesus' conflict with demonic powers so prevalent throughout the rest of the book.

1:14-20 / Linking the beginning of Jesus' ministry with the arrest of John here has the effect of associating Jesus with John's ministry still more clearly than indicated in the preceding passages. This is especially so in view of the partial similarity of their messages. In 1:4 John proclaims, "Turn from your sins," and here in 1:15 Jesus utters a similar message.

There are, however, important differences between Jesus and John given in the passage before us. Here Jesus is said to proclaim that the Kingdom of God has drawn near and that the day of fulfillment (**the right time**) has come. This conviction that God's chosen time had come is similar to the Baptist's sense of urgency and his belief that he was called to prepare Israel for the day of God's salvation (1:4–8), but Jesus' words reflect the conviction that the day of God's rule has come even nearer than

John knew. In Mark, Jesus' message is called **the Good News from God,** but this is not said of John's words; this seems intended to give Jesus' message a special significance above the message of John.

The urgent conviction reflected in Jesus' words sets the tone for the rest of the story of his ministry and, together with his acclamation as God's Son, marks his work with momentous significance. **"The Kingdom of God"** here means the rule of God, and Jesus' message signifies that God has begun to establish his rule in a world viewed by many religious Jews as under the tyranny of Satan and evil. The Kingdom of God thus represents the triumph of God's plan of salvation over human sin and demonic opposition. An ancient Jewish prayer reads, "May God establish his kingdom in our lifetime," and Jesus' announcement is to be heard in the context of the hope reflected in that prayer. The reader must not underestimate the central importance of this message of the approaching Kingdom of God for understanding properly Jesus' ministry. Virtually everything in his behavior and teaching was based on this conviction about his day as the time of the approach of God's rule, and the accompanying conviction about his role as its herald and, indeed, its dramatic vehicle.

Jesus' summoning of the four men to be his disciples has the effect immediately of widening the circle of attention to include Jesus and the men chosen to accompany him. Elsewhere in the book we will see evidence that Mark intended to address the topic of Christian discipleship, and here in this account we see what must be role models in the immediate response of the four men to Jesus' authoritative call.

Jesus' summons to discipleship includes the promise that the men will **catch men**; that is, they are called to enter into his mission and not to be observers. Later, we learn of twelve men thus called, and we are told specifically that they were given a ministry modeled after Jesus' own (3:13–19). The effect of this episode is to give the readers followers of Jesus with whom to identify themselves. The readers are thereby drawn into the story, and the Christian reader especially is intended to follow the calling and duties, the trials and failures, of the disciples with a view to drawing lessons for living.

Additional Notes

1:1 / **Good News** is a term in Greek (*evangelion*) that was used in the contemporary world to refer to a message of good news but that seems to have acquired a special significance for early Christians as a technical term for the message of salvation through Jesus. (See, e.g., Mark 1:14–15; 8:35; 10:29; 13:10; 14:9; Rom. 1:1, 16–17; 1 Cor. 4:15.) Here too the term refers to the *message* about Jesus, not the book. The term *Gospel* was not applied to books until the second century, when we have references to the "four Gospels," meaning the canonical writings attributed to Matthew, Mark, Luke, and John.

The Son of God. These words are missing in some important early witnesses to the NT text. The claim that Jesus is Son of God appears at several points in Mark, indicating that Jesus' divine sonship is an important part of Mark's portrait (cf. 1:11; 3:11; 5:7; 9:7; 14:61–62; 15:39), and this causes most scholars to believe that the title was originally here in the opening of the book and that it was accidentally omitted in some copies. It is very significant that Jesus is called the Son of God only by God (1:11; 9:7), by demons (3:11; 5:7), and by one man, the centurion at the cross (15:39), illustrating Mark's emphasis upon the blindness of people to Jesus in his own ministry. (See "Son of God," *NIDNTT*, vol. 3, pp. 634–48.)

1:2 / **It began as the prophet Isaiah had written** is literally "as it is written in Isaiah the prophet." This is the wording in the earliest manuscripts, but in many later ones the reading is "as it is written in the prophets." Most scholars suspect that the latter reading arose because the quotations given in vv. 2–3 are in fact from Mal. 3:1 and Isa. 40:3, and so some copyists may have felt it necessary to avoid the impression that the writer had mistakenly credited Isaiah with a statement from another prophet. We do not know for sure why the writer attributes this composite quote to Isaiah alone, but it may be that he was using a list of OT prophecies prepared as a teaching aid and that the passages cited here were listed under the name of Isaiah.

Ahead of you to open the way for you: The quote is not exactly the same as the Hebrew text of Mal. 3:1. It is especially interesting that in Hebrew we read "to prepare the way for *me*." Here in Mark the prophecy seems to be addressed to Jesus—the *you* here in v. 2.

God said is not in the Greek text but supplied by the English translator here to make clear who seems to be speaking.

1:3 / **Someone** is literally "a voice."

The Lord: Here this probably refers to Jesus, who is given this title elsewhere in the NT (in Mark cf. 5:19; 11:3; also, e.g., 1 Cor. 8:6; Acts 9:1–29).

1:4 / **Turn away . . . your sins:** This whole sentence is a paraphrase attempt to render the Greek phrase, which speaks of "a baptism of repentance for [unto?] the remission of sins." The point is that his baptism was intended to be the immediate demonstration of repentance, just as responding to an evangelistic invitation is seen in some church circles.

1:5 / **Many people . . . Jerusalem** is literally "all the area of Judea and Jerusalemites went," but of course Mark probably does not mean that everyo from these areas went!

1:6 / John's dress and diet seem to reflect the strict life of a desert monk. From other references (Matt. 11:7-8, 16-19) we get the impression that John lived by strong ascetic standards, perhaps modeled somewhat after the Nazarite vow described on the OT, involving abstinence from wine among other rules (see Num. 6:2-21; Judg. 13:5-7; 16:17; Amos 2:11-12).

1:8 / The Holy Spirit: The accounts of John's message in Matt. 3:11 and Luke 3:16 say that the one coming will baptize with "Holy Spirit and fire." The "fire" is probably a symbol of the coming judgment mentioned in those passages. Here (and in Acts 1:5) there is no reference to judgment, and so only the Holy Spirit mentioned, referring to the coming salvation.

1:9 / Nazareth: It is the uniform Gospel tradition that Jesus' hometown was Nazareth, a small town in central Galilee otherwise of no importance in history. (See *MBA*, 228; *IDB*, Vol. 3, pp. 524-26.)

1:10 / Like a dove: Though paintings of the scene often show the Spirit in the form of a dove alighting upon Jesus' head, the comparison refers to the gentle way that the Spirit came upon Jesus, and no conclusion about the visible form of the Spirit is intended.

1:12 / The desert: The area in view here is probably the barren area near the northern shore of the Dead Sea. In 1:4 we have been told that "John preached in the desert," and the fact that he was arrested by Herod (Antipas) probably means that John's ministry was centered near the southern end of the Jordan River.

1:14 / John . . . put in prison: Mark does not explain John's imprisonment and he does not give the outcome here. In 6:14-29 he gives a rather full account of these matters.

Galilee is the name given to the part of ancient Palestine north of Samaria. Jesus seems to have made Galilee (his home area) his major area of ministry. The area was administered by Herod Antipas, a client ruler for the Romans, while Judea in the south was administered by a Roman military governor.

1:16 / Simon . . . Andrew: These two are described as brothers in other Gospel traditions (Matt. 4:18; 10:2; Luke 6:14; John 1:40), as are James and John Zebedee (Matt. 4:21; Luke 5:10). It is interesting to note that Simon (Peter, cf. 3:16) and John became much more frequently mentioned in Christian tradition than Andrew or James (mentioned as martyred in Acts 12:2).

Simon Peter is prominent among the disciples in all the Gospels and in most Christian tradition is regarded as the representative and chief of the twelve apostles.

Catching fish: Fishing was a major industry in Roman times around Lake Galilee, and the impression one gets here is that these four men were partners of small (or perhaps large!) businesses. They were in all likelihood "middle class" economically, for the Zebedee brothers, at least, had employees in their family business (1:20).

1:17 / Catch men: Many scholars think that we have here an allusion to Jer.

16:16 where God promises "fishermen" to find the Israelites so that they may be brought to judgment and ultimate restoration. Jesus' words here may be intended to hint that Jesus' ministry marks the time of the fulfillment of this prophetic promise. Of course, Mark does not restrict the disciples to "catching" Israelites, for he knows that the prophet's words took on larger meaning in the international mission of the church.

2

The Ministry Begins

Jesus and his disciples came to the town of Capernaum, and on the next Sabbath Jesus went to the synagogue and began to teach. [22]The people who heard him were amazed at the way he taught, for he wasn't like the teachers of the Law; instead, he taught with authority.

[23]Just then a man with an evil spirit came into the synagogue and screamed, [24]"What do you want with us, Jesus of Nazareth? Are you here to destroy us? I know who you are—you are God's holy messenger!"

[25]Jesus ordered the spirit, "Be quiet, and come out of the man!"

[26]The evil spirit shook the man hard, gave a loud scream, and came out of him. [27]The people were all so amazed that they started saying to one another, "What is this? Is it some kind of new teaching? This man has authority to give orders to the evil spirits, and they obey him!"

[28]And so the news about Jesus spread quickly everywhere in the province of Galilee.

[29]Jesus and his disciples, including James and John, left the synagogue and went straight to the home of Simon and Andrew. [30]Simon's mother-in-law was sick in bed with a fever, and as soon as Jesus arrived, he was told about her. [31]He went to her, took her by the hand, and helped her up. The fever left her, and she began to wait on them.

[32]After the sun had set and evening had come, people brought to Jesus all the sick and those who had demons. [33]All the people of the town gathered in front of the house. [34]Jesus healed many who were sick with all kinds of diseases and drove out many demons. He would not let the demons say anything, because they knew who he was.

[35]Very early the next morning, long before daylight, Jesus got up and left the house. He went out of the town to a lonely place, where he prayed. [36]But Simon and his companions went out searching for him, [37]and when they found him, they said, "Everyone is looking for you."

[38]But Jesus answered, "We must go on to the other villages around here. I have to preach in them also, because that is why I came."

[39]So he traveled all over Galilee, preaching in the synagogues and driving out demons.

[40]A man suffering from a dreaded skin disease came to Jesus, knelt down, and begged him for help. "If you want to," he said, "you can make me clean."[c]

[41]Jesus was filled with pity,[d] and reached out and touched him. "I do want to," he answered. "Be clean!" [42]At once the disease left the man, and he was clean. [43]Then Jesus spoke sternly to him and sent him away at once, [44]after saying to him, "Listen, don't tell anyone about this. But go straight to the priest and let him examine you; then in order to prove to everyone that you are cured, offer the sacrifice that Moses ordered."

[45]But the man went away and began to spread the news everywhere. Indeed, he talked so much that Jesus could not go into a town publicly. Instead, he stayed out in lonely places, and people came to him from everywhere.

c. MAKE ME CLEAN: *This disease was considered to make a person ritually unclean.*
d. pity; *some manuscripts have anger.*

1:21-28 / It is significant that the first scene of Jesus' ministry (after the calling of the four disciples) is one in which Jesus teaches and performs an exorcism. Both actions are emphasized in Mark's Gospel as characteristic aspects of Jesus' ministry, and by placing this account here in the opening of Jesus' ministry, Mark appears to have intended to show the reader immediately a representative scene.

Although Mark says that Jesus "preached" (1:4), more characteristically he describes Jesus as teaching, as here in the present scene. We are not told what he taught here; instead the author emphasizes the *manner* of his teaching—**with authority** (v. 22). We must note that this term is used several times in Mark's story of Jesus, and that it was apparently a major object in his writing to deal with the issue of Jesus' authority. The topic surfaces in verse 21 and verse 27, but Mark raises the matter of Jesus' authority again in 2:10 (authority to forgive sins), in 3:15 and 6:7 (authority given to his apostles to exorcise demons), and in connection with Jesus' attack upon the money changers in the Temple (11:28–33; here the same Greek word is translated in GNB "right"). In these passages cumulatively, Jesus is shown *(a)* exhibiting authority in his teaching, *(b)* exercising authority over the demons, *(c)* demonstrating his authority to forgive sins, *(d)* taking authority over the Temple and its administration, and *(e)* conferring authority upon his apostles to expand his attack upon demonic power.

Here in verse 22, the crowds contrast the authority affirmed in his teaching with **the teachers of the Law** (the Greek term is often translated "scribes"; see the note on v. 22). These were men who had studied the OT with the particular interest of teaching the proper interpretation and application of the many commandments of religious law attributed to Moses. Mark's point here is that Jesus' teaching was not seen as simply another example of the learned activity of placing of his opinion alongside that of other teachers on religious matters. Rather, the people are pictured as sensing in Jesus' manner an authority beyond any they were accustomed to see exhibited in these other teachers.

It is interesting that the response of the people in verse 22 and verse 27 involves surprise and wonder but not faith. They notice the demonstration of authority but seem unable to identify its source and nature. We will note in subsequent passages that Mark mentions such wonder and astonishment frequently (e.g., 2:12; 7:36), but in all these instances these responses are clearly meant to be seen as something less than Christian faith and true illumination about Jesus' significance.

This account of Jesus' teaching includes the striking story of the man

13

with an **evil spirit** (see note on v. 23), and Mark clearly intends this part of the episode as an illustration that Jesus was much more than simply another teacher, and that the authority claimed in his teaching represented a real authority and not simply an empty claim. We are to understand, then, that the news about Jesus spread so quickly (v. 28) particularly because of this kind of deed.

The theme of Jesus' expulsion of **evil spirits**, or demons, from people is certainly a major part of Mark's story. We shall encounter numerous examples of this theme in subsequent episodes, and so the reader is here prepared to view Jesus' ministry as an attack upon these evil powers. We see in this that the "Kingdom of God" that Jesus announces in verse 15 involves the deliverance from demonic forces of people like the man in this episode. This gives to the phrase "Kingdom of God" a dynamic and material reality, making it far more than simply an ethical concept. As this scene shows, the Kingdom (or Reign) of God is God's power (authority) in action.

In the story of the exorcism here we are introduced to another important theme running through Mark, the acclamation of Jesus by the demon-possessed man and Jesus' command of silence (vv. 23–25). Elsewhere, also, the demons acclaim Jesus (3:11; 5:7), and we are told that the demons "knew who he was" (1:34). Characteristically, Jesus silences them (1:25, 34; 3:12), rejecting their acclamation even though they seem to use titles that do reflect Jesus' true significance. Of course, this rejection of demonic acclamation counters the charge made by his opponents that Jesus was a sorcerer and manipulated the demons to bring himself glory (see 3:22–30). Jesus strikes no truce and offers no terms; he expels the demons with great authority.

We should note that this silencing of the demons, together with the astonishment of the synagogue congregation, form part of the larger emphasis in Mark on the identity or true significance of Jesus. At several points in the narrative that follows, Mark shows the crowds (2:12; 6:2–3; 7:36) and the disciples (4:41; 6:49–52; 8:17–21, 32–33) wondering who Jesus really is and unable to perceive him and his task properly. Also, Mark tells us of the various (incorrect) estimations of Jesus circulating during his ministry (3:20–22; 6:14–16; 8:27–28). All of this creates a great tension in the narrative, for the reader knows Jesus' real significance and identity, and this makes the fumbling efforts to perceive Jesus by the human characters in the story all the more disappointing. The suppression of the demonic acclamations of Jesus also shows that Jesus was not interested in mere acclamation, and at the same time, these acclamations are intended to help establish for the reader the validity of the claims about Jesus that are made in the opening of this book (1:1) and that are integral to Christian faith.

We shall note in the examination of the subsequent sections of Mark that no human character accurately perceives Jesus until the crucifixion and resurrection. Even Peter's acclamation of Jesus as "Christ" is shown to reflect a faulty grasp of God's purposes (8:28–33). The **news about Jesus** (v. 28) that spreads quickly is, in Mark's view, not true faith but only notoriety. This immediately begins something of a tragic note in the story, while it sets the scene for the ensuing accounts of Jesus' further ministry.

1:29-34 / In this episode Jesus is shown healing a particular person, Peter's mother-in-law, which seems to illustrate and document the summary reference to Jesus' healing miracles in 1:32–34. The disciples mentioned with Jesus, Simon (later called Peter, 3:16), Andrew, James, and John, are the same ones already named in 1:16–20 and are all from Capernaum; mentioning them by name in this very specific and homey account gives the scene a certain realism.

We are probably intended to see in the simplicity of Jesus' healing action, his merely taking the woman by the hand, another indication of Jesus' power and authority—this time in the face of illness. Her response is probably intended by Mark as illustrative of the proper response of his readers, who also have been "touched" by Jesus. Elsewhere Mark shows Jesus as commanding service to one's fellow disciples as the proper response to the Gospel (9:33–35; 10:42–45).

In verses 32–34, then, Mark gives one of several "transitional summaries" in the early chapters of his account (other examples are 1:39; 3:11–12; 4:33–34; 6:6, 56). These are places where Mark both summarizes aspects of Jesus' ministry and makes a transition to another account. These passages are also interesting as indicators of the editorial interests of Mark, since they are clearly his own direct comments upon the tradition of Jesus with which he is working. In the present passage, Jesus is shown working **many** wonders of healing and exorcism, and there is renewed emphasis that Jesus characteristically silenced the demons precisely because **they knew who he was**. This must be read in the context of the confusion and wonder of the synagogue crowd (1:27), and the result is to create tension and irony in the narrative—demons know him, but the people cannot perceive his real significance.

1:35-39 / Here, the one who in previous episodes is shown exercising such great power and authority is described as seeking a quiet place of prayer. Since we are not told what Jesus' prayer was, it must be the mere fact that Jesus prayed that fits Mark's narrative purpose here.

Mark mentions Jesus praying only two other times, in 6:46, after the feeding of the five thousand, and in 14:32–39, in Gethsemane just before his arrest. By contrast, Luke mentions Jesus praying on eight occasions (3:21; 5:16; 6:12; 9:18, 28; 11:1; 22:32, 41), though he does not mention Jesus praying in his account that parallels the present one (cf. Luke 4:22–43). The fact that Jesus expresses a conviction as to the direction of his ministry in the discussion immediately following (v. 38) may mean that his prayer is to be taken as his effort to determine God's direction for his ministry. Mark's account shows the source of Jesus' power against illness and demons and also provides in Jesus' behavior an example for his readers in Jesus' earnest and dedicated pursuit of God in prayer.

The reference to the people seeking Jesus is not explained by Mark, but the Lucan parallel says that the people "tried to keep him from leaving" (Luke 4:42). Does this suggest that they may have wanted to make him the head of a popular movement, as in the episode in John 6:14–15? If so, then Jesus' prayer may have been a petition to God to give him guidance in the face of such a reaction among the crowd.

In the summary that concludes this episode (v. 39), we should note what we pointed out in our discussion of 1:21–28—that Mark's characteristic description of Jesus' ministry involves teaching/preaching and the expelling of demons.

1:40-45 / Here we encounter another type of illness and Jesus' power in the face of it. This time it is a person who has **a dreaded skin disease** (see the notes for discussion of the term used). Such an illness rendered the person ritually and socially "unclean," according to OT Law (Lev. 13–14), meaning that he or she was not allowed in the Temple or at any social or religious gathering. What is more, anyone who touched a person in such a condition became unclean also. This is why the man here (1:40) asks to be made **clean**. To have such a condition was not just a health liability; it made one a prisoner, cut off from all normal life.

It is not to be overlooked that all the parallel Gospel accounts agree that Jesus **touched** the man (1:41; Luke 5:13; Matt. 8:3). The point of mentioning this seems to be to show that Jesus not only healed the man but also established immediate social contact with him. In doing this, Jesus could be seen as actually violating the laws about ritual purity for the sake of healing the man. No doubt Mark intended his readers to see the similarity of this action to Jesus' welcome of other "outcasts," such as tax collectors.

The uncertainty expressed in the man's plea, **If you want to**, is answered by Jesus' firm, **I do want to**, and the reader is intended to see in this exchange a revelation of the heart of Jesus. Mark is unique in attributing to Jesus directly an emotion in connection with this healing—**Jesus was filled with pity** (v. 41). Though there is some uncertainty about the reading here (see the notes), this is probably the correct one, and so Jesus' compassion is emphasized in Mark's account.

It is curious that Mark says Jesus **spoke sternly** to the man, ordering him not to generate a great deal of publicity. The parallels in Matthew 8:4 and Luke 5:4 include the command to silence, but Mark's term is more severe in connotation than the language used by the other evangelists. This is probably a part of the larger Markan emphasis upon Jesus' desire for secrecy, but it must be noted that Jesus' desire is frustrated, according to Mark, and his account emphasizes the difficulties that resulted for Jesus (1:45).

Although the man is commanded not to generate publicity, he is told to follow the prescribed OT ritual requirements to certify his healing (v. 44). This means that Jesus is shown making a distinction between a (shallow?) publicizing of his powers, on the one hand, and a proper "witness," on the other. **To prove to everyone** translates a phrase reading literally "for a testimony to them," and this resembles Mark's use of the term "testimony" in 6:11 (translated "warning" in the GNB) and 13:9 (see notes on this verse). In this passage, then, the reader is to see a lesson in which proper "testimony" based on obedience to Jesus is contrasted with sensationalized and shallow publicizing of Jesus as a wonder-worker. Though the man has been cured by Jesus and owes him obedience, he shows himself disobedient and devoid of genuine insight into Jesus' significance. His going to the priest would have shown his healing to be not only a release from the power of illness but *also* a sign of the new day of God's mercy surpassing the old order (represented by the Temple, the Law, and the priest). For, whereas the Law of Moses and its institutions could only certify disease or health, Jesus displays the power to *heal*, effecting a release from the verdict of the Law that a person with the disease mentioned here was "unclean."

Additional Notes

1:21 / **Capernaum**: A fishing town on the west shore of Lake Galilee. The name is Hebrew, meaning "village of Nahum." It was the home of Peter and other members of the twelve disciples (1:29). Jesus apparently made the town his headquarters and home during his ministry (Matt. 4:13).

Matt. 11:23–24 and Luke 10:15 record Jesus' condemnation of Capernaum along with other Galilean towns for their poor response to his message. The site known as Tel Hum is now identified with Capernaum by the Israeli government and many archaeologists. (See *IDB,* vol. 1, pp. 532–34; *MBA,* 228.)

1:22 / **Sabbath ... synagogue**: The command to observe the seventh day of the week as a day of rest from labor and a time of religious reflection appears in the OT law codes (Exod. 10:8–11; Deut. 5:12–15), and obedience to this command became a major distinguishing feature of Jewish life. By the time of Jesus there was already great symbolical importance attached to the Sabbath. The longed-for Kingdom of God was regarded as the Sabbath of human history, and sometimes history was pictured as divided into seven periods, the last being the appearance of the promised millennial time of bliss and righteousness often associated with the appearance of the Messiah.

By Jesus' time the synagogue had become a familiar Jewish institution, though it is not mentioned in the OT. It appears that during or after the Babylonian exile religious Jews began to meet on the Sabbath for prayer and religious instruction, and from this practice the fully developed synagogue institution arose. The term is Greek, meaning "a gathering," but was adopted as a loanword into Jewish speech. Ten adult males were the required minimum for a proper synagogue. Already by Jesus' time the term was being applied to the buildings used for the gatherings, and it appears also that a somewhat standardized order of service was followed, consisting of prayers (including recited, set prayers), readings from the OT, and a sermon of some sort. In Jesus' time synagogues were not led by a professional rabbi as in modern times. Instead, there were lay leaders who supervised the meetings. If the synagogue meeting included someone known as a teacher of religion, that person would be invited to give the sermon. In the present episode, Jesus is apparently shown giving the sermon, having been invited to do so on account of his growing reputation. (See "Synagogue," *IDB*, vol. 4, pp. 476–91.)

1:22 / **Teachers of the Law**: These men (sometimes called scribes and lawyers) were a recognized body in Jesus' time, having emerged sometime during or after the Babylonian exile (sixth century B.C.). They included perhaps priests and many others not from priestly descent, and their main activity was the study, discussion, and teaching of the religious law of ancient Judaism based on the OT Law attributed to Moses. Their expertise gave them great respect among the people, and they appear to be an early stage of the modern office of the rabbi in Judaism. Their discussions of the requirements of the Jewish Law were often quite complex and involved detailed arguments about the meaning of OT passages. In their zeal to make the Jewish law applicable to all areas of life, they produced a large body of oral law, collections of precedents and judgments by revered teachers, that came to be regarded as of equal weight as the written commandments of the OT. (See note on 2:6).

1:23 / An evil spirit: The term used here is literally "an unclean spirit," and it appears several times in Mark (e.g., 3:11; 5:2; 6:7). In other places Mark uses the term "demon" to indicate the same phenomenon (e.g., 1:34, 39; 3:22). Elsewhere the literal expression "evil spirit" is used as another synonymous description (e.g., Luke 7:21; 8:2). All these terms refer to the belief, common in ancient Jewish life, that there are evil powers, understood as actual beings of which the chief is Satan (see 3:22–26). Mark's description of them as "unclean" means that they are associated with evil and with things regarded as impure from a religious perspective. People afflicted with such spirits in Mark are usually described as if they are under the control of a will and purpose not their own (e.g., 5:1–20; 9:14–27). The accounts resemble descriptions of certain kinds of behavior labeled in modern medical language as particularly severe mental disorders. Though it is certainly true that the Gospel writers employ the descriptive language of their day for such conditions and that moderns may be uncomfortable with ideas of "demon possession," we must not allow the medical question to overshadow the fact that the Gospel accounts show Jesus as bringing deliverance and health to such afflicted people as part of God's manifestation of his rule. That Jesus is shown taking pity on such people and releasing them, rather than condemning them or superstitiously avoiding them, is significant as a role model of care for such troubled persons today.

1:30 / Simon's mother-in-law: In 1 Cor. 9:5, Paul refers to Peter as married. In 10:28 Peter speaks of having "left everything" to follow Jesus. This may mean that Peter (and others of the disciples?) left a wife and other responsibilities to answer Jesus' call, though this probably did not involve desertion of the marriage but prolonged time away from home.

1:35 / A lonely place: The description of the place in the Greek original resembles the description of the place of Jesus' temptation (1:12), and this may mean that Mark sees some connection between the two episodes, perhaps because in both cases Jesus is shown preparing for his further ministry.

1:36 / Simon: Note here the prominence given to Simon Peter among the disciples. This is, of course, characteristic of the whole Gospel tradition, in which Peter occupies very much a representative role among the others.

1:40 / A dreaded skin disease: The Greek term *lepros* (from which our term *leprosy* comes) is used in the ancient Greek translations of the OT to cover a whole variety of skin disorders and here probably does not represent the modern medical usage of "leprosy." The OT account (Lev. 13–14) seems to reflect the ancient difficulty in dealing with such diseases and the difficulty in diagnosing people in primitive situations. We simply do not know the exact medical definition of this man's problem. (See "Leprosy," *IDB*, vol. 3, pp. 11-13.)

1:41 / **Filled with pity**: A few ancient manuscripts read here "moved with anger." It is possible that this is the original reading, of course, but in view of its weak support among manuscripts and in view of the fact that it may have been introduced to make Jesus' emotion here seem more compatible with his stern command in v. 42, it is probably wiser to regard the reading accepted in the text here as the original reading.

1:43 / **Jesus spoke sternly to him**: The stern command described here may seem strange to the reader, but Mark apparently intends to emphasize that the man's actions were in violation of Jesus' emphatic instructions. Although Mark says the man **spread the news everywhere**, and although Mark uses the language of Christian proclamation to describe the man's actions (lit., "he began to proclaim greatly and to circulate the word," v. 45; cf. 1:39, where the same word is used), we are to see the man as disobeying Jesus and probably as simply publicizing Jesus' miracle rather than really giving the proper witness to Jesus' significance.

1:45 / **Lonely places**: Again, as in 1:12 and 1:35, Mark sets Jesus in the uninhabited areas. And again Mark probably intends to show Jesus retreating from the shallow glory of publicity, avoiding its temptations that he might concentrate on God's will for him. As crowds come to hear John the Baptist in the "desert" (1:4–5), so here the people come to Jesus in the **lonely places** (same word in Greek, *erēmos*).

3

Blasphemy and Bad Company

MARK 2:1–17

A few days later Jesus went back to Capernaum, and the news spread that he was at home. ²So many people came together that there was no room left, not even out in front of the door. Jesus was preaching the message to them ³when four men arrived, carrying a paralyzed man to Jesus. ⁴Because of the crowd, however, they could not get the man to him. So they made a hole in the roof right above the place where Jesus was. When they had made an opening, they let the man down, lying on his mat. ⁵Seeing how much faith they had, Jesus said to the paralyzed man, "My son, your sins are forgiven."

⁶Some teachers of the Law who were sitting there thought to themselves, ⁷"How does he dare talk like this? This is blasphemy! God is the only one who can forgive sins!"

⁸At once Jesus knew what they were thinking, so he said to them, "Why do you think such things? ⁹Is it easier to say to this paralyzed man, 'Your sins are forgiven,' or to say, 'Get up, pick up your mat, and walk'? ¹⁰I will prove to you, then, that the Son of Man has authority on earth to forgive sins." So he said to the paralyzed man, ¹¹"I tell you, get up,

pick up your mat, and go home!"

¹²While they all watched, the man got up, picked up his mat, and hurried away. They were all completely amazed and praised God, saying, "We have never seen anything like this!"

¹³Jesus went back again to the shore of Lake Galilee. A crowd came to him, and he started teaching them. ¹⁴As he walked along, he saw a tax collector, Levi son of Alphaeus, sitting in his office. Jesus said to him, "Follow me." Levi got up and followed him.

¹⁵Later on Jesus was having a meal in Levi's house.ᵉ A large number of tax collectors and other outcasts was following Jesus, and many of them joined him and his disciples at the table. ¹⁶Some teachers of the Law, who were Pharisees, saw that Jesus was eating with these outcasts and tax collectors, so they asked his disciples, "Why does he eat with such people?"

¹⁷Jesus heard them and answered, "People who are well do not need a doctor, but only those who are sick. I have not come to call respectable people, but outcasts."

e. in Levi's house; *or* in his (*that is*, Jesus') house.

2:1-12 / Up to this point Mark has introduced us to Jesus and given us samples of his ministry, showing us the effect of his teaching (1:21–22, 39) and his powerful works of exorcism (1:23–27, 34) and healing (1:29–34, 40–45). In chapter 2 we have further glimpses of Jesus' ministry of miracles and teaching, but we should really think of Mark 2:1–3:6 as a single unit of the narrative, for each of the incidents described here involves some controversy between Jesus and various critics. The incidents in Mark 1 all indicate how Jesus' fame grew (1:28, 32–34, 37–39, 45). The incidents in 2:1–3:6 all indicate how Jesus encountered opposition, and so a certain somber tone appears in this section of the story, culminating in the sinister events mentioned in 3:6. We have, then, in 2:1–3:6, Mark's description of the issues of conflict between Jesus and many of the religious leaders of his day. At the same time, because Mark clearly supports Jesus against his opponents, he portrays in these events the claims and powers of Jesus, telling us more of the nature of his ministry.

In the first incident, Jesus is shown again at Capernaum, which probably functioned as the home base of his Galilean ministry (see note on 1:21). While Jesus is speaking to a crowd gathered, apparently, in and around a house where he is staying, a paralytic is brought by friends for healing. Determined to get Jesus' attention, they make an opening in the roof and lower the disabled man on his mat right in front of Jesus! Our interest and perhaps even our amusement grows as we read how these (anonymous) men literally overcome the crowd to get to Jesus on behalf of the paralytic.

The story is full of color. Imagine a crowd of villagers refusing to give way to the friends and their burden. Picture the four climbing up to the roof, hoisting up the paralyzed man on his cot and boldly attacking the roof to make a hole in it (see the notes) big enough for their friend!

The four men are the center of attention and it is *their* faith that Jesus notices (v. 5). Yet, as soon as their work and faith are mentioned, they disappear from the narrative. Our attention is directed to Jesus, the paralyzed man, and **some teachers of the Law** who take offense at Jesus' words.

The boldness of the four friends is matched by the strangeness of Jesus' first statement. We expect him to heal the disabled man, but instead he gives forgiveness for the man's sins. And this introduces what is clearly the main value of the story for Mark. What appears at first to be a miracle story with interesting color suddenly develops into a major controversy story regarding Jesus' authority to forgive sins. The paralytic's response to Jesus' word of forgiveness is not given, but **teachers of the Law** (lit., "scribe," see note) regard Jesus' action as **blasphemy** (v. 7), and the fat is in the fire!

Blasphemy is usually regarded as the worst sin among religious people, and so the issue is by no means a small one. Contrast John the Baptist's words in 1:4 ("God will forgive your sins") with the direct forgiveness given by Jesus here in 2:6, and we understand better the theological complaint of these teachers in 2:7 that **God is the only one who can forgive sins**. We should note also that the charge of blasphemy anticipates the condemnation of Jesus in 14:63–64, and it seems likely that in this first controversy scene in his Gospel, Mark intended to give the reader a foretaste of the final opposition and the issue that would lead to Jesus' execution.

These teachers were devoted to the study and application of the Law of Moses to all of life, and function here and elsewhere in Mark as representatives of the Jewish religion who find fault with what they regard as the dangerous and improper conduct and teaching of Jesus. They see themselves as defending the exclusive honor of God in this incident against the suggestion that a mere man could forgive sins. At first glance, they appear to be in the right, for God is the true judge of all conduct and it does seem strange for a human being to grant forgiveness as if he were God. The forgiveness here mentioned is not the forgiving of an offense against one's own person but the granting of full pardon from divine judgment against sins.

Jesus, sensing their thoughts, engages them in an argument designed to justify his action. The starting point of Jesus' argument is the implication in the thought of the teachers that, though Jesus may *talk* as if he can forgive sins, in fact only God can actually confer forgiveness (v. 7:**How does he dare talk like this?**). So Jesus seems to say, "Do you think that this is merely talk and that it is easy to pretend to have such authority? Allow me to give a tangible demonstration of the authority involved" (2:8–11). The healing of the paralytic is, however, not just a display of authority but also an illustration of the forgiveness with which it is linked. The man imprisoned by his paralysis, confined to his bed, seems a fitting picture of the bondage of sins, and his release from the paralysis, a vivid picture of release from sins and guilt.

Now, it should be noted that the word **authority**, already mentioned as important in Mark, reappears in this story (see 1:21, 27 earlier and comments on these verses). Here again this question is whether Jesus has the right to act as he does, and in this case it is matter of acting as God—no small matter!

In verse 10 we encounter for the first time in Mark the term **the Son of Man**, a term used *only* by Jesus as a self-descriptive title and, indeed, the only self-descriptive title used directly by Jesus in the Gospel. Before we proceed further, we must note that biblical scholars have devoted intense effort to the investigation of this term, in scores of books and articles, and that there remains, to this point at least, considerable disagreement about the full meaning of the term. The evidence and arguments involved in this scholarly controversy are complex and require familiarity with several ancient languages and numerous documents not widely known among the general readers of the Bible (see the notes on v. 10). In what follows I shall offer a view built upon a study of the wider evidence and arguments referred to above, but in the present discussion we shall give our attention to the use of the term as we meet it in the Gospel of Mark.

As shown in the notes below, the term *son of man* is used in the OT characteristically to mean "a human being," and in this passage before us it seems that something of this basic meaning remains prominent. The teachers of the Law say that only God can forgive sins (v. 7), but Jesus wishes to show that the Son of *Man* has such authority **on earth** (v. 10), and the contrast between **God** and **the Son of Man** is evident and intentional. At the same time, we get the impression that the point of the story here is not that *any* human can exercise God's authority, but rather that *this particular* human can do so. This seems to be the significance of the definite article, *the* **Son of Man**, which functions here almost as a demonstrative pronoun, "this." So, the term is used as a title for Jesus and seems to carry a certain ironic significance. This son of man, this human, is in fact not just another human, but exercises divine authority. The usage of the term reflects the whole message of Mark, that the man Jesus is in fact the Son of God (1:1; 15:39). Without attempting to deal here with all the issues concerning the history of the use of the term, we may safely conclude that the term as used in Mark describes Jesus as a human being who is not recognized for who he really is. The term **the Son of Man** is the "outward" or "public" title, which expresses no special or obvious dignity in itself. But, because we have been informed already (1:1) what Jesus' real significance is (the Son of God), we see the irony of the title. The title conveys the scandal of Jesus, that this mere man (in the eyes of his uncomprehending contemporaries) should teach and act with such radical and shocking authority.

The response of the crowd is amazement and the recognition that something new has happened. This is on the whole a favorable response, but it is not fully intelligent faith, and this represents Mark's consistent emphasis that Jesus' miracles produced fame and interest but not true faith or proper recognition of Jesus' true significance. (See the note on v. 12).

The main point of the story seems to be to show the authority of Jesus and the criticism and opposition he generated. The following stories supply more examples of these themes.

2:13-17 / Mark introduces a second example of conflict, in this section devoted to the theme, by means of this story of Jesus' call of a tax collector and Jesus' social association with such people. There are two incidents mentioned here, the call of Levi (vv. 13–14) and the eating with **outcasts** (vv. 15–16), and the connection between them is that they both show Jesus associating closely with people deemed unacceptable by the religious purists of his day.

In the one case, a tax collector, an employee of the Roman-installed-and-supported government of Herod Antipas, is invited to become a personal disciple of Jesus. Such people were disliked by many as religiously impure or even as collaborators with the Romans (see note). By calling Levi (see note) to personal fellowship and service, Jesus would have offended many, raising questions in their minds about his own judgment, loyalty, and purity.

The next incident involves Jesus and his disciples eating with **a large number of tax collectors and other outcasts** (v. 15). These **outcasts** ("sinners," see note) were people known publicly as failing to live by the religious law of Judaism, apparently in some major matters. We must understand that generally in the ancient Near Eastern lands sharing a meal was considered a significant and even an intimate social contact, establishing a bond among those who partook. Among ancient religious Jews, eating with a person implied religious acceptance of that person, and there is every reason to believe that Jesus shared this view and that his eating with these "sinners" was intended to signify and to communicate acceptance of them and forgiveness of their sins. Jesus' reply to the criticism of his action shows that his association with such sinners was a studied policy (v. 17). Most scholars believe that the early Christian practice of a common meal as the chief symbol of their fellowship (upon such a common meal our modern Lord's Supper, or Eucharist, practices are based) derived not only from a Last Supper (such as is described in 14:12–26) but also from Jesus' practice of eating with sinners as a sign of their acceptance.

In the narrative, the **teachers of the Law** are joined with **Pharisees** (see note), and the complaint is that Jesus sets a bad example as a holy man by welcoming known sinners into his circle. In the minds of these critics, Jesus should have disassociated himself publicly from such sinners and should have summoned them to repentance and study of the religious law as a precondition for any social acceptance. These critics were desirous of upholding a religious standard and of chastening and perhaps reforming transgressors. Jesus' mission was the proclamation and bestowal of God's new salvation and merciful welcome. These critics probably believed that obedience to the religious law was a precondition for the arrival of the Kingdom of God. Jesus was convinced with prophetlike assurance that God's Kingdom would come to a sinful Israel by God's free and gracious initiative and that he was the herald of its imminent arrival. Indeed, he probably saw his own ministry as the opening event of this divine initiative. What better way, in Jesus' mind, to demonstrate that God's Kingdom comes by divine grace and initiative and does not wait for a program of religious reform of Israel than by going to those well known as sinners and welcoming them to divine favor?

But, of course, Jesus' prophetic conviction that God's new salvation was at hand and that he was chosen to demonstrate it was not shared by many religious leaders, and so his conduct only generated disgust and offense among these opponents. This story and the preceding one in 2:1–12 are linked together in showing how Jesus' striking actions generated great opposition. The actions in view are really very similar, the forgiveness of sins and the welcome of sinners, and both are based upon Jesus' fundamental conviction about what he has been chosen to do—to demonstrate the arrival of God's Kingdom. There is probably intended sarcasm in Jesus' statement in verse 17; otherwise Jesus is made to speak like a "do-gooder" or a social reformer himself. The critics probably saw themselves as **well** and in no need of a **doctor**, as **respectable** (lit. "righteous") and not **outcasts** ("sinners"), and Jesus in effect says, "If you have no need of God's mercy (tongue in cheek here!), then, excuse me, I would like to get on with my work!"

No doubt, in the gentile churches among which Mark circulated, this kind of story was seen as precedent for the ingathering of Gentiles (who were also seen as sinners/outcasts by religious Jews) and showed Jesus as the pioneer of this welcome of religiously unacceptable people.

Additional Notes

2:1 / **At home**: The phrase in Greek implies that Jesus used a residence in Capernaum as a home base for his travels.

2:2 / **The message**: Probably here the words mean the message described in 1:14–15, and we are to understand that Jesus was elaborating upon this summary.

2:4 / **A hole in the roof** is literally "they dug through the roof," perhaps reflecting Palestinian peasant homes in which walls and roof were made of sun-baked earth. Luke 5:19 describes a tile roof, reflecting house construction in many ancient Mediterranean areas. Matt. 9:1–8 omits any reference to the paralytic being lowered through the roof.

2:6 / **Teachers of the Law** is literally "scribes"; these were people trained in the religious law of Judaism, experts in opinion of proper conduct. They appear several times in Mark as critics of Jesus, often with people called Pharisees (e.g., 2:16; see notes on this verse), during Jesus' Galilean ministry, and in Jerusalem with the priests of the Jewish Temple (e.g., 11:18, 27). The scribes were a professional class and not a religious sect or party (see note on 1:22).

2:10 / **The Son of Man**: It is striking that this is the only term used of himself by Jesus in Mark, and yet it is never used by others as a title for him. The term "a son of man" or "sons of men" appears in the OT often as a Hebraic way of saying "human being(s)" (e.g., Pss. 8:4; 144:3; 145:12; often translated "mere man" in the OT in the GNB). In Ezekiel the term "son of man" is used by God to address the prophet (e.g., 2:1, 3, 6, 8). Many scholars have argued that the term became a title for a heavenly figure who was expected to appear in the end of history to judge the world on God's behalf and have found echoes of this supposedly pre-Christian usage in the NT, in Mark 8:38, for example. But to other scholars, including the present writer, the absence of any clearly pre-Christian evidence for usage of the term as a title, together with what they regard as superior interpretations of the NT usage combine to make this theory unacceptable. Instead, they regard the term "the Son of Man" as probably first used as a title by Jesus, and understand the title as deliberately ambiguous or oblique in meaning. In this view, Jesus described himself as "this mere man" with the term, and thereby expressed his obedient and humble position before the world and God. There have been elaborate attempts to classify the ways the term is used in sayings attributed to Jesus, and intense arguments as to how many reflect the authentic words of Jesus. The position adopted in this commentary is that Jesus did use the term as a self-description, though the variations in the sayings of Jesus between "the Son of Man" and "I" show that the term may have been inserted in some sayings by the Gospel writers in imitation of Jesus' own general usage (compare, e.g., 8:27 and Matt. 16:13).

2:12 / **They were all completely amazed**: Mark frequently describes people as amazed after Jesus' miracles but seems to regard it as far short of true recognition of him (see, e.g., 1:22, 27; 5:20, 42).

2:12 / **We have never seen anything like this**: Similar words appear in the parallel in Luke 5:26, but the Matt. 9:8 parallel says that the crowd "glorified God who had given such authority to men." This probably indicates that Matthew sees the story as precedent and example of the ministry of the church, which he describes as authorized to "bind" and "loose" (Matt. 16:19), that is, to assure judgment or forgiveness to people depending on their response to the Gospel. In the passage before us, Mark restricts the issue to the legitimacy of *Jesus* forgiving sins. The effect of the crowd's exclamation is to underline the unprecedented authority shown by Jesus in the healing and in the forgiving of sins, so that the reader is forced to choose between seeing Jesus as simply audacious or as truly acting with divine authority.

2:14 / **A tax collector:** The figures mentioned here and in vv. 15–16 were Jews who raised taxes for Herod and the Romans. They were accused popularly of greed, for they obtained their jobs by bidding how much money they could raise, and their own reward was determined by their diligence in squeezing the utmost from the tax-paying public. Luke 19:1–10 tells of another tax collector and hints at crooked measures employed in securing the tax receipts (Luke 19:8). Among the zealous Jews who sought to throw off the Roman yoke, these tax collectors were hated as traitors. We see something of the explosive nature of the religious objections to paying taxes to gentile conquerors in Mark 12:13–17.

Levi son of Alphaeus: In the Luke 5:27 parallel the man is called simply Levi, but the Matt. 9:9 parallel calls him Matthew. This "Matthew the tax collector" reappears in the list of the twelve apostles in Matt. 10:3, but though both Mark (3:18) and Luke (6:15) mention a Matthew in their list, he is not called a tax collector, and without the evidence from Matthew's Gospel we would not necessarily link the Levi of Mark 2:14 with the Matthew of the list of apostles. Another interesting point is that Mark describes this Levi as **son of Alphaeus** (2:14), though neither of the parallels in Matthew and Luke include this information. In the list of apostles (3:18; Matt. 10:3; Luke 6:15), there is a "James son of Alphaeus," leading some to suggest that this Levi (Matthew) and this James were brothers among the apostles. The curious thing is that Mark shows no interest in drawing connections among the Levi of 2:14 and the Matthew and James of 3:18, and so we are left to draw our own conclusions. It is obvious that Mark had more interest in telling his story of Jesus than in dealing with such matters. In church tradition, however, this Levi and the Matthew of 3:18 are regarded as the same man (there being precedent for a person to be known by more than one name, e.g., Simon/Peter/Cephas), and this figure is traditionally credited as the author of the Gospel of Matthew, although the book is actually anonymous and many scholars doubt this traditional claim for its authorship.

2:15 / **Levi's house**: The text has literally "his house," and in the context it could well mean either Levi's house or Jesus' house. The Matt. 9:10 parallel also is ambiguous, describing Jesus as eating in "the house," but the Luke 5:29 parallel identifies the place as Levi's. Mark 2:1 appears to imply that Jesus kept a home in Capernaum, at least for a while, and some scholars believe that Mark understood this dinner with the tax collectors and outcasts as taking place at Jesus' residence. If indeed Jesus acted as host of the meal, it would have dramatized all the more that it was an invitation to salvation and fellowship with Jesus.

Outcasts were people probably publicly known by their failure to observe religious practices and so, in the minds of the Pharisees (and the general Jewish public as well), were perceived as irreligious and disgraceful. The Greek term used here literally means "sinners," and reflects the cause of their rejection by the religiously upstanding people. Their sins may have included not only a lack of observance of religious scruples but also such things as fraud or adultery, as is shown in the case of Zacchaeus (Luke 19:1–10), who was probably guilty of cheating, and that of the woman of Luke 7:36–50. The translation of the term by the word **outcast** reflects the way such people were treated by religious people and also hints at the breach of religious convention in Jesus' welcome of and association with such people.

2:16 / **Pharisees**: The most well known sect of ancient Judaism, mainly because of their prominence in the Gospels. The first-century Jewish historian Josephus tells us that there were about six thousand members, and that they were highly respected for their devotion to the religious law. In the NT they most frequently appear as opponents and critics of Jesus, though there are exceptions. Nicodemus (John 3:1) is credited with helping to bury Jesus in John 19:38–42 and seems to be described as a secret follower of Jesus. Acts 5:33–39 pictures an important Pharisee, Gamaliel, urging a cautiously mild treatment of the Christians by the Jewish high council. But perhaps the most influential passage upon popular use of the term "Pharisee" today is Matt. 23:1–36, where Pharisees are accused of hypocrisy.

We should recognize that there were no doubt hypocritical and self-righteous Pharisees, as there are similar individuals among perhaps any religious group. But we should also recognize that the opposition of the Pharisees to Jesus was probably not uniform and was not prompted totally by such unworthy traits among them. No doubt some Pharisees, perhaps most, were simply unable to accept Jesus' striking prophetlike authority and were unconvinced that Israel could be saved by any means other than strict observance of religious law, so these Pharisees would have opposed Jesus from what were to them the highest of motives. The later opposition to Christianity by Saul the Pharisee, who became the Apostle Paul (Acts 9:1–31; Phil. 3:4–6; Gal. 1:13–14), was probably motivated by this kind of religious conviction. It is an unfair slur to portray all Pharisees as hypocrites and to account for their opposition to Jesus on the basis of bad character, as has regrettably happened in much Christian tradition. The Gospels give us the language of heated religious conflict and show us only one side of the conflict. The true pathos of the conflict between Jesus and Pharisees is recognized only when one understands that theirs was a case of deeply religious and sincere people, not just hypocrites, who (from a Christian standpoint) were unable to recognize and submit to the new message of God's gracious salvation apart from observance of religious law.

4

More Controversies

On one occasion the followers of John the Baptist and the Pharisees were fasting. Some people came to Jesus and asked him, "Why is it that the disciples of John the Baptist and the disciples of the Pharisees fast, but yours do not?"

[19]Jesus answered, "Do you expect the guests at a wedding party to go without food? Of course not! As long as the bridegroom is with them, they will not do that. [20]But the day will come when the bridegroom will be taken away from them, and then they will fast.

[21]"No one uses a piece of new cloth to patch up an old coat, because the new patch will shrink and tear off some of the old cloth, making an even bigger hole. [22]Nor does anyone pour new wine into used wineskins, because the wine will burst the skins, and both the wine and the skins will be ruined. Instead, new wine must be poured into fresh wineskins."

[23]Jesus was walking through some wheatfields on the Sabbath. As his disciples walked along with him, they began to pick the heads of wheat. [24]So the Pharisees said to Jesus, "Look, it is against our Law for your disciples to do that on the Sabbath!"

[25]Jesus answered, "Have you never read what David did that time when he needed something to eat? He and his men were hungry, [26]so he went into the house of God and ate the bread offered to God. This happened when Abiathar was the High Priest. According to our Law only the priests may eat this bread—but David ate it and even gave it to his men."

[27]And Jesus concluded, "The Sabbath was made for the good of man; man was not made for the Sabbath. [28]So the Son of Man is Lord even of the Sabbath."

[1]Then Jesus went back to the synagogue, where there was a man who had a paralyzed hand. [2]Some people were there who wanted to accuse Jesus of doing wrong; so they watched him closely to see whether he would heal the man on the Sabbath. [3]Jesus said to the man, "Come up here to the front." [4]Then he asked the people, "What does our Law allow us to do on the Sabbath? To help or to harm? To save a man's life or to destroy it?"

But they did not say a thing. [5]Jesus was angry as he looked around at them, but at the same time he felt sorry for them, because they were so stubborn and wrong. Then he said to the man, "Stretch out your hand." He stretched it out, and it became well again. [6]So the Pharisees left the synagogue and met at once with some members of Herod's party, and they made plans to kill Jesus.

2:18–22 / Here, another issue surfaces between Jesus and his critics, in this case the question of why his disciples do not observe fasts like those of the other religious groups named. The translation **on one occasion** could give the incorrect impression that the fasting referred to here was a one-time event, but actually the fasting in question was a weekly exercise (for the Pharisees, on Mondays and Thursdays) and seems to have been intended as an expression of mourning over the sins of Israel and over the fact that the longed-for salvation of prophetic hope had not appeared (on fasting in Mark, see note). The fact that the question emerged indicates that these fasts were publicly known, and that they were probably intended as symbolic rebukes of the sinful among Israel and weekly reminders to all to participate in religious reform and repentance.

Matthew 6:16–18 criticizes this publicizing of fasts as all too prone to become a device for self-exaltation, but the original intent was certainly more noble. From later tradition of rabbinic Judaism we know that the dominant opinion among the descendants of the Pharisees was that the Messiah and the long-awaited salvation would come when Israel had made herself ready and worthy by observance of religious law. John the Baptist certainly urged repentance as preparation for the coming day of judgment and salvation, and the fasting of his followers and the Pharisees was no doubt, therefore, related to the hopes for such a day.

The puzzlement of those who questioned Jesus on this issue was caused by the fact that Jesus proclaimed the near arrival of the Kingdom of God, the day of salvation, but was not showing what his critics regarded as proper preparation by mourning over its delay. Jesus' response (2:19–22) indicates that he shared neither their view that the Kingdom of God would not come until Israel was ready for it nor their understanding of the present as a time for mourning in the absence of the Kingdom. His image of a **wedding party** (see note), a joyous, exuberant occasion in ancient Israel, to describe the moment means that he saw the Kingdom of God already approaching and that the time was ripe for joy and celebration. But, if the Kingdom of God is seen as approaching a sinful Israel without her being worthy, this means that the Kingdom of God is based on God's gracious design to save even the unworthy. This in turn explains both why Jesus' disciples are not fasting to bring the Kingdom *and* why Jesus welcomes the unworthy, the outcasts, along with the rest, as in the preceding passage (2:13–17).

The imagery of 2:21–22 seems intended to show how inappropriate the beliefs and practices of the past are now when the Kingdom of God is already approaching. The illustrations are relatively easy to understand. New cloth when washed will shrink much more than previously-washed cloth, and so it is not wise to try to patch the latter with the former. **New wine** here is wine not fully fermented, and so putting it into previously used wineskins which have already been stretched by the fermentation of their previous contents will cause the skins to burst as the new wine continues to ferment. The two things common in this imagery are the contrast between **new** and **old** or **used**, (the same word in the Greek here) and the fact that both new cloth and new wine possess "life," that is, dynamism or power. They are fitting symbols, not only of the newness of the present moment, which marks the approach of the Kingdom of God, but also of the dynamic effect of the Kingdom of God upon the structure of established religious practice.

It is difficult to tell whether the comment in 2:20 is to be understood as one attributed to Jesus or as an editorial aside by our author. In any case, it means that Jesus is seen as the **bridegroom**, the immediate cause for joy, and the statement anticipates his approaching death and the mourning of the disciples. In other words, the statement is not to be taken as a reference to later Christian fasting practices but rather as a note of solemnity in anticipation of the crucifixion of Jesus, so important in Mark.

It should not be ignored that whereas the center of attention in the first two controversies (2:1–12, 13–17) is Jesus and his actions, in the present and following passages (2:18–22, 23–28) it is the behavior of Jesus' disciples that is in dispute. If the widely held scholarly opinion is correct that the Gospel authors wrote their accounts with a view to the needs and activities of the churches for whom they wrote, then these controversy stories were intended to show Jesus defending not only his own authority and message (as in 2:1–17; 3:1–6) but also the "lifestyle" or religious practices of his disciples, with whom the readers would naturally identify themselves. So, in the present and following incidents, the first readers would see Jesus giving a justification for practices that they saw as precedents for their own behavior. The gentile Christians for whom this Gospel was probably written, who no doubt did not observe Jewish fasts, would have seen that Jesus and the Twelve began the precedent— and for very good theological reasons, not simply as an indication of religious laxness.

2:23–28 / In this passage the author gives a fourth controversy story, this time dealing with the matter of Sabbath observance, the issue in the next story also (3:1–6). When reading this passage we must remember that the observance of Sabbath rest from labor is a command from the OT (indeed, one of the Ten Commandments, Exod. 20:1–17) and in Jesus' day was perhaps the supremely important demonstration of a Jew's loyalty to God and to his nation. Some later rabbis said that the Messiah would come if all Israel kept the Sabbath twice! The issue of Sabbath observance was therefore by no means a minor one, and Jesus' apparent breach of the commandment was a serious matter.

Again, the controversy is described as concerning especially the conduct of Jesus' disciples, but of course he and they are really involved together. To understand what they were doing wrong in the eyes of the Pharisees, we must realize that the simple command about doing no labor on the Sabbath had of necessity been elaborated into a whole complex body of religious customs. In the later collection of rabbinic discussion of this commandment (the tractate "Sabbath" in the Talmud) there are thirty-nine types of activity discussed and regulated. The regulations, no doubt already in Jesus' day, covered such things as regular work and also such matters as traveling and even preparing and eating food.

In the present case, Jesus and his disciples are seen traveling (not just out for a stroll), no doubt in the course of their itinerant mission around Galilee (1:38-39). In the process of their travels, they enter a grainfield to get some quick nourishment by picking heads of ripe grain, rubbing off the chaff, and eating the grain (a tasty snack, as those growing up near grainfields can attest). On the one hand, the OT Law allows the poor and hungry to do this (Lev. 19:9-10), and the mission instructions given by Jesus to his disciples in 6:7-11 may reflect his own practice, meaning that they would have carried no supplies with them and would have been constantly dependent on the hospitality of others and provision from God (cf. Matt. 5:25-33). On the other hand, the Pharisaic understanding of the Sabbath was that almost everything else was to give way to observe this command (see note). So, in the Jewish Maccabean revolt against the Syrians (168 B.C.), and in subsequent wars, many Jews refused to fight on the Sabbath, even to save their lives. From the viewpoint of the Pharisees, Jesus and his disciples were breaking the Sabbath by their traveling and by gathering food; and there was no need for this bad example of religious conduct, for Sabbath law came ahead of the desire to travel in the conduct of one's business.

Jesus' reply seems at first unrelated to the Sabbath issue (2:25-26), or else seems to justify breaking one commandment merely by citing the precedent of David violating another; but there is more to the reply than this. The reference to David's action here is better understood if we keep in mind that the actions of Jesus and his disciples in 2:23-24 are to be seen as happening in the context of their itinerant ministry, in which they proclaimed with prophetic urgency the approach of the Kingdom of God. There is then a valid analogy between Jesus' situation and David's, for in both cases we have a bank of men who represent a new, as yet unrecognized, "regime" in emergency circumstances. The Davidic incident referred to (1 Sam. 21:1–6) here is part of the narrative of David's wanderings with a group of men, in which he tries to avoid King Saul's wrath and is all the time himself the rightful future king of Israel. In the context, David's breach of religious rules was necessitated by the urgent situation, and Jesus is saying that the urgency of his mission demands that he too must violate religious custom by traveling and foraging even on the Sabbath. The point is that the actions of Jesus and his disciples are closely connected with their mission, and the analogy with David is one of situation and not exact conduct.

This, however, means that the issue boils down to the question of whether in fact Jesus' message and mission come before the observance of such an important commandment as Sabbath. The OT says David was chosen by God to replace Saul as the rightful king, and the description of David's action without comment in 1 Samuel 21:1–6 implies that the divine appointment of David justified his action. Jesus' reference to this incident in defense of his actions means that the Pharisees, and the readers, are forced to decide whether Jesus too has a calling that justifies his actions. The context for the dispute is the mission of Jesus, and the real issue, from Jesus' perspective, is whether he has the authority to violate Sabbath convention by virtue of his calling and mission. In other words, the text presents us with a decision about the person of Jesus.

This explains why, after giving the statement in 2:27 that the Sabbath is **for the good of man**, Mark goes on to the real point he wishes to make, that Jesus has authority over the Sabbath by virtue of his calling: **The Son of Man is Lord even of the Sabbath** (2:28). That is, Mark's point is not some generalizing principle like "people are more important than rules" (which sounds so congenial to the modern reader). Rather, by virtue of Jesus' authority and the urgency of his mission, he is presented as free to judge how to employ even the Sabbath day in the pursuit of his task, in which he heralds the arrival of the ultimate "good" for man, symbolized in the gift of the Sabbath rest.

3:1-6 / This is the last of the five conflict stories that run from 2:1 to 3:6, and it is intended as the climactic one, ending as it does with the reference to a plot to kill Jesus (3:6). As in the preceding story, the issue concerns the Sabbath regulations and Jesus' authority to violate them in the pursuit of his ministry. In the previous story, the actions of the disciples drew criticism, but here it is Jesus' action that is the center of controversy.

The setting for this story is a synagogue (see note), and the phrase **back to the synagogue** reminds us of the first mention of a synagogue in 1:21–27, the first story about Jesus' ministry. The synagogue—the most frequently encountered religious institution of Judaism in ancient or modern times—used as the setting for this story is intended to portray Jesus as addressing the religion of his day, confronting it with his claims and his message.

This controversy story concerns the healing of a man with a paralyzed (lit. "withered") hand (see note), and the account shows the characteristic simplicity of Jesus' healing actions as well. The literature of the ancient world furnishes numerous examples of healers and exorcists, but usually they involve elaborate steps, including incantations, the production of loud noises, pungent odors, and other "techniques" of a quasi-magical nature. Here Jesus merely commands the man to extend his arm, whereupon the man's hand is restored; this kind of account seems intended to show the tremendous authority of Jesus, who, like God in the creation account in Genesis 1, needs only to speak to work a miracle. But the significance of this healing is more fully seen when one realizes that, by OT Law (Lev. 21:16–24), cripples, lepers, and such were forbidden to enter the Temple and so could not participate fully in the religious life of their people. Therefore, to heal such a person was to bestow both health and new religious and social acceptance.

The chief question in this story, however, is whether it is proper for Jesus to heal on the Sabbath day. That such a question would arise may seem strange to moderns, accustomed to treat all days pretty much the same, but the fact of such an issue is clear indication of how important scrupulous observance of the Sabbath was for Pharisees and other dedicated Jews. The question of what was necessary and legitimate activity on the Sabbath was already a much-discussed matter. It seems to have been agreed that circumcision of infant boys could be performed on the Sabbath, when necessary, to fulfill the commandment that it be done on the eighth day after the baby's birth (Lev. 12:1–3). Also, Pharisees seem to have permitted the saving of the life of a human or an animal when endangered on the Sabbath (cf. Matt. 12:11–12 and Luke 14:5), but the early Jewish religious community known to us in the so-called Dead Sea Scrolls forbade even this kind of activity. In the present setting, the man's life was not in danger, and so the scrupulous question about the legitimacy of healing him, and thereby breaking a commanded Sabbath rest, presents itself.

We must beware of reading Jesus' challenge to the synagogue critics as merely the posing of an abstract principle (3:4). To be sure, it is likely that the question Jesus asks has as part of its background the discussions described above about rescuing a human or an animal on the Sabbath. But more than this, the urgent ministry and message of Jesus about the approaching Kingdom of God is the immediate context of this story. Mark 3:1–2 suggests that his critics already suspected what he would do (see note), and the Gospels contain other accounts of Sabbath healing by Jesus (Luke 14:1–6; 13:10–17; John 5:2–18; 7:22–24; 9:1–17), leading us to suspect that Jesus may have deliberately healed on the Sabbath as a sign of the significance of his works. That is, his healing on the Sabbath linked his miracles with a day that symbolized for ancient Jews the future Kingdom of God, when bondage would cease and the time of joy and messianic celebration would begin (see note). His Sabbath healings then were to be seen as foretastes and signs of the Kingdom he confidently announced. Further, of course, by healing on the Sabbath Jesus forced people to make a decision about his works and message; for if he had not been called by God to herald the coming Kingdom, if he was not what his Sabbath healings claimed him to be, then he was a Sabbath-breaker. In any case, he could not be written down as simply another harmless religious healer. He prevented that by the way he conducted his healings, making them an issue.

Indeed, from one standpoint, all Jesus was doing was helping a man; but Jesus' point in 3:4 is not that people should be free to give medical attention even on religious holy days. Rather, his question constitutes a challenge to his audience to decide whether his treating the Sabbath as a day for conducting his ministry is good or not. This is why the response of his critics is a sullen refusal to answer (3:4b–5). The real issue is not the principle of humanitarian aid on the Sabbath but the validity of Jesus' message and implicit claim for himself.

Mark's reference to the critics (3:5) as **stubborn and wrong** (see note) describes them in terms taken from the OT that always connote disobedience to God's revelation. Thus, the significance both of the event and of their response is made clearer. This is no simple disagreement, but (in literal translation) "hardheartedness" against the revelation of God's prophetic voice coming to them through Jesus.

The murderous plot of 3:6 involves a collusion between Pharisees and **members of Herod's party** (see note), and is a strange alliance. What may be referred to is a plan to have Jesus arrested by Herod Antipas (ruler of Galilee), involving cooperation by Pharisees in implicating and accusing Jesus. This seems a bit strange, however, because elsewhere we learn of Pharisees who warn Jesus of Herod's desire to arrest him (Luke 13:31). Whatever the historical explanation, the plot functions in Mark's narrative both as a sudden indication of the severe nature of the crisis Jesus brought to the Judaism of his day and as a sobering preview of the coming crucifixion that lay ahead.

In the five conflict stories of 2:1–3:6, Mark describes major points of controversy between Jesus and his critics, and these controversies give major indications of Jesus' significance. He is presented to the readers as authorized to forgive sins and to welcome even great sinners into his fellowship (2:1–17), and both he and his followers are free to ignore religious conventions in the executing of their mission, making obedience to his message of more significance than observance of Jewish religious law (2:18–3:6). By this early point in the narrative, we already know that Jesus' message both demands decision on major issues and provokes a crisis for those who hear him.

Additional Notes

2:18 / Fasting: The practice is well attested in the OT as an expression of mourning and repentance (e.g., 2 Sam. 1:12; 12:21–23); it does not seem to have been done in a regularly scheduled way but only when the occasion demanded it. In Jesus' time, Pharisees and others regularly fasted as a sign of religious devotion to the Law of God (e.g., Luke 18:12). There is ample evidence for fasting among early Christians as well (e.g., Acts 13:2–3; 14:23; 1 Cor. 7:5; 2 Cor. 6:5; 11:27). Again, it does not appear to have been a regularly scheduled practice but, rather, something done when it was deemed appropriate. In Mark, in addition to this passage, there is a reference to fasting in some manuscripts at 9:29, where the words "and fasting" are placed after "prayer." This is no doubt a later insertion, however, and for this reason does not appear in the Good News translation of the verse. The only genuine reference to Christians fasting in Mark is therefore 2:20, which seems to refer to the mourning of the disciples after Jesus' crucifixion. This should be understood in the context of the emphasis on food and eating in Mark, where Jesus is pictured as bestowing participation in the Kingdom of God to sinners by eating with them (2:15–17), where "food" (lit. "bread") is used to symbolize Jesus' ministry (7:27–28), and where *two* feeding miracles are given (6:30–44; 8:1–10), suggesting that the author presents Jesus' ministry as the occasion for enjoying God's "food" of salvation, and that he uses fasting as a symbol of the barrenness and joylessness of those who fail to recognize the approach of God's Kingdom. (See "Fasting," *IDB*, vol. 2, pp. 241–44.)

2:19 / Wedding party: The translation attempts to remove the repetitiousness of the literal Greek wording here, which emphasizes that fasting is inappropriate while the bridegroom is present with his friends (cf. the RSV here).

The imagery of a wedding celebration may have its roots in the OT description of God's relationship to Israel as a marriage (e.g., Jer. 3:1–14; Ezek. 16:1–62; Hosea). In keeping with this imagery, the sins of Israel were seen by the prophets as adulteries, and the exile in Babylon (approximately 586–450 B.C.) as a divorce. But they held out the hope for a renewal of God's mercies and a re-establishment of the relationship. This was seen as partially fulfilled in the return of the nation from exile (fifth century B.C.), but in Jesus' time there was alive still a fervent hope for a richer display of God's power on behalf of the nation. When Jesus used the image of a wedding celebration to symbolize his ministry here, it may very well have been intended not just as a symbol of joy but more specifically as a sign that the hopes of the prophets were being realized. The imagery of a wedding celebration in connection with the Kingdom appears also in Matt. 22:1–14; 25:1–13; and in Rev. 19:7–9 the final victory of Christ and his everlasting union with his saints is likened to a marriage feast, showing how the OT imagery was transferred to Christian hopes.

2:23 / **Sabbath** is the seventh day of the week (Saturday); but in Jewish reckoning the days begin at sundown, so the Sabbath begins Friday evening and runs till sundown Saturday. The command to observe Sabbath rest from all labor forms part of the Ten Commandments (Exod. 20:8–11) and became, by Jesus' time, one of the most important symbols of obedience to God's Law and loyalty to the Jewish people. Severe punishment was prescribed for Sabbath violation—death (Exod. 31:12–17; 35:1–3)! The matter in dispute here is thus no petty regulation but a crucial command of God, and Jesus' action cannot be accepted apart from an acceptance of his significance as the divinely assigned vehicle of the Kingdom of God and, therefore, as the Lord of the Sabbath.

2:25 / **David** was the great King of ancient Israel, and the one from whom it was expected that the Messiah would be descended (see, e.g., Jer. 23:5; Ezek. 34:23–24; 37:24–25). In Mark 11:6–10 Jesus is hailed as the one who brings the kingdom of David and in 10:46–48 is called son of David. In 12:35–37, Jesus appears to question the validity, or better, the adequacy, of the term "son of David" as a description of the Messiah; but in Mark overall Jesus is presented as the Messiah or "Christ" (1:1), and so here the reference to David probably means not only that Jesus is in a situation like David's but that Jesus is to be seen as a new and even greater "David." The reference to David is, in short, another hint of Jesus' messianic status.

2:26 / **When Abiathar was the High Priest**: This is a problem, for the 1 Sam. 21:1–6 account says that it was Ahimelech who was the priest who gave David the sacred bread. It is possible that the Markan account is confused here, for the OT itself is not easy to follow in its references to Ahimelech and Abiathar. In 1 Sam. 22:20, Abiathar is described as son of Ahimelech; whereas 2 Sam. 8:17 and 1 Chron. 24:6 refer to an Ahimelech as son of Abiathar and as high priest under David. Elsewhere Abiathar is referred to as David's high priest with Zadok (2

Sam. 15:16–29, 35–37; 20:23–26; cf. 1 Kings 2:26–27, 35). The parallel accounts in Matt. 12:1–8 and Luke 6:1–5 omit this reference to Abiathar, as do a few manuscripts of Mark—in the latter case no doubt because the mention of him seemed incorrect and embarrassing to some scribes. It is possible that the Greek phrase here translated **when Abiathar was the High Priest** may mean simply "in the time of Abiathar the [later] high priest" and not that Abiathar was high priest at the time of the incident.

The bread offered to God is the sacred bread (lit. "bread of the presence") that was to be prepared for the sanctuary and set on a sacred table, after which it was food for the priests, but for them only (Exod. 25:30; Num. 4:7).

Gave it to his men: Here the analogy extends beyond Jesus and David to include Jesus' disciples too. That is, the issue includes not only Jesus but also the actions of his disciples in mission with him and in his name, and Jesus here defends their action by saying that he, like David, is authorized to involve his followers in his controversial actions. Again, we should assume that this was seen by early Christians as justification for their conducting of their ministry even if it meant Sabbath violation.

2:28 / **Son of man**: the second use of this term (cf. 2:10 and the comments and note on that verse). Here again, the term is to be seen as an intended contrast with the authority of the one to whom it refers. This "mere man" is **Lord** even of the Sabbath.

Lord: This term in Hebrew, Aramaic, and Greek can be used to mean simply "master," or as a title for God, and was certainly used by early Christians as a title for Jesus connoting reverence for him as quasi-divine (eg., Rom. 10:9; 1 Cor. 8:6; Phil. 2:9–11; John 20:28). Now the question here is whether we are to read the term in Mark 2:28 in the full sense of Christian devotion, or in the more general sense of "the one in charge." The capitalizing of the word by the translators implies that they took it in the fuller sense, and that judgment is probably correct as far as how it was read by early Christians. It is another matter as to whether Jesus is to be seen as using the term in this way of himself, or whether the whole of 2:28 is to be understood as another Markan editorial comment (e.g., 3:30; 5:8; 7:3–4; 13:14b) to help the reader see the significance of Jesus' actions. I am inclined to think the latter is more likely.

3:1 / **The synagogue** may imply the same synagogue as mentioned in 1:21, but not necessarily. It should be noted that **the** is not attested in the best Greek manuscripts and may have been introduced by scribes, thereby connecting this synagogue with the one in 1:21, though the author may not have intended this connection. (On synagogues, see note on 1:21).

A paralyzed hand, lit., "a withered hand," probably means simply a hand in which there is no power, movement, or "life," and so **paralyzed** is a good translation. There is earlier the account of the paralytic in 2:1–12, who seems to have been more severely disabled.

3:2 / For **Sabbath**, see note on 1:21. In the Matt. 12:10 parallel, the critics ask Jesus directly about Sabbath healing.

3:5 / **Angry . . . felt sorry for them**: This is the only direct reference to anger in Jesus, though there is a chance that Mark referred to Jesus' anger in 1:40 (see note there). Elsewhere Mark refers to Jesus' rebuke of his disciples (8:33), which may also have involved heated feelings, and the sharp words against Pharisees (7:6–8; cf. Matt. 23:13–39) seem to reflect strong emotions as well. The phrase translated **felt sorry for them** may rather mean that he was grieved or deeply disappointed and hurt at their sullen refusal to decide.

Stubborn and wrong: Literally, Jesus was upset at their "hardness of heart," and this term is borrowed from such passages as Exod. 7:14, 22; 8:19; 9:35, where equivalent terms are used to describe the pharaoh's resistance to Moses' demand that Israel be set free. Mark, in using this language, thus likens Jesus' critics to Pharaoh. The language reappears in 6:52 and 8:17, describing even the disciples in their lack of perception about Jesus. Similar terms appear in 10:5 and 16:14 (see comments on those verses.) The use of this language, influenced by the OT, shows that Mark wished to describe the unresponsiveness to Jesus in serious terms, as disobedience to God's revelation and not simply innocent misunderstanding.

3:6 / Very little is known of the group referred to as **members of Herod's party** (lit., "Herodians") outside the Gospel references. Elsewhere they appear only in connection with the question about paying tribute to Caesar (12:13 and Matt. 22:16; also see note on Mark 8:15), and they appear to be supporters of the Herodian dynasty and/or members of court or civil servants of Herod Antipas. They do not seem to be a religious party but rather more a political group.

5

The Ministry Widens

[7]Jesus and his disciples went away to Lake Galilee, and a large crowd followed him. They had come from Galilee, from Judea, [8]from Jerusalem, from the territory of Idumea, from the territory on the east side of the Jordan, and from the region around the cities of Tyre and Sidon. All these people came to Jesus because they had heard of the things he was doing. [9]The crowd was so large that Jesus told his disciples to get a boat ready for him, so that the people would not crush him. [10]He had healed many people, and all the sick kept pushing their way to him in order to touch him. [11]And whenever the people who had evil spirits in them saw him, they would fall down before him and scream, "You are the Son of God!"

[12]Jesus sternly ordered the evil spirits not to tell anyone who he was.

[13]Then Jesus went up a hill and called to himself the men he wanted. They came to him, [14]and he chose twelve, whom he named apostles. "I have chosen you to be with me," he told them. "I will also send you out to preach, [15]and you will have authority to drive out demons."

[16]These are the twelve he chose: Simon (Jesus gave him the name Peter); [17]James and his brother John, the sons of Zebedee (Jesus gave them the name Boanerges, which means "Men of Thunder"); [18]Andrew, Philip, Bartholomew, Matthew, Thomas, James son of Alphaeus, Thaddaeus, Simon the Patriot, [19]and Judas Iscariot, who betrayed Jesus.

3:7-12 / This portion of the narrative gives an account of Jesus' ministry to a crowd at Lake Galilee (see note) together with one of several summaries of Jesus' Galilean ministry (3:11–12; cf. 1:39; 4:33–34; 6:6, 56), and seems to function as a transition from the preceding collection of conflict stories (2:1–3:6) to a new section that may be thought of as extending to 6:6 (where Jesus is rejected in Nazareth) or even to 8:30 (the confession at Caesarea Philippi). The section 3:7–6:6 shows Jesus teaching (e.g., 4:1–34) and working miracles in both gentile (5:1–20) and Jewish (5:21–43) settings and concludes with his rejection by the people of Nazareth (6:1–6). This section seems designed to give further samples of Jesus' ministry and more indication of the polarizing effects it h upon the people who witnessed it. Earlier (1:45), we have been told Jesus' increasing fame, but now Mark paints a scene of people from various areas (see notes) to show the results of his fame. His deeds, no doubt primarily his miracles (3:8, **the things he was doing**), caused many to come to see him, including many sick (3:10).

The scene would have been one of frantic commotion, as viewers of newsfilms of religious excitement in Near East countries can easily imagine. Regarding him as a holy man with healing powers, the sick struggled to touch him, hoping that the mere touch of such a person might cure them. (Note the well-known story of the sick woman, 5:25–34).

The mention of a boat in 3:9 is the first of several references to a boat being used in Jesus' ministry (see note), and here the boat serves as a getaway vehicle and/or perhaps a safe platform from which to deal with the frantic and dangerous crowd. This mention of the potential danger of the crowd (3:10) suggests that the results of Jesus' growing notoriety were not all good (cf. 1:45; 3:20), and the crowd is portrayed as more interested in satisfying their curiosity and physical needs than in becoming true followers.

The reference to the **evil spirits** (3:11–12) again shows Jesus' authority over these demons and his unwillingness to accept their acclamation (cf. 1:23–25, 34). Both the crowd and the evil spirits, then, attest for the reader the significance of Jesus, but also show inadequate responses to him.

The cry of the demons is very significant, **You are the Son of God!** Elsewhere in the narrative, only God (1:11; 9:7), other demons (5:7), and the centurion at the cross call Jesus by this title (15:39). Mark 1:1 and these references indicate that **Son of God** is a key title for expressing Jesus' significance; but the present passage shows Jesus rejecting the demonic acclamation, for it does not proceed from commitment and discipleship.

This command to silence is one of several similar commands given to demons (1:25, 34), a leper (1:44), and the disciples (8:30, 9:9) and reflects a major theme in Mark. There have been various attempts to interpret these commands to silence, including the theory of W. Wrede that they are fictitious incidents made up by Mark to explain why Jesus was supposedly not recognized as Messiah during his earthly ministry. Wrede's theory ("the messianic secret") does not account for the fact that Jesus was crucified as a messianic pretender ("King of the Jews," 14:61—63; 15:2–31, showing that at least his enemies saw him as more than merely another teacher!), and for this and other reasons this theory must be rejected. Instead, the emphasis on secrecy in Mark is linked with Jesus' crucifixion and resurrection (9:9; see comments on this verse) and seems intended to show that no proclamation of Jesus as Christ was proper until these decisive events took place that disclosed the meaning of his person and work in sufficient fullness.

3:13-19 / Clearly one of the major features of Mark's Gospel is an interest in the twelve disciples and the associated theme of discipleship. Already Mark has told us of the calling of four disciples (1:14–20) and of controversy over the conduct of Jesus' disciples (2:18–28), and he has pictured these men as close associates of Jesus in his ministry (1:21, 29, 36–38; 3:7). Here, Mark describes twelve men as chosen by Jesus for a special role in which they are assigned essentially the same activities as Jesus himself: preaching and driving out demons (v. 15). As Mark's Gospel continues, we will see that these men are depicted surprisingly often in an unfavorable light (e.g., 4:10, 35–41; 6:45–52; 7:17–19; 8:14–21, 31–33), and some scholars have argued that Mark in fact intended to present the Twelve as examples purely of how not to behave as a disciple or as representatives of Christians in the early church with whom he disagreed. This interpretation, however, does not do justice to all that Mark says about these men; and to anticipate our study of the rest of the book, it seems closer to the truth to say that Mark presents the Twelve in an ambivalent light, as men who, in spite of their own weaknesses, were chosen by Jesus to be the foundation of the church. (We shall take up the question of how Mark presents the disciples at several later points when they are featured in the text).

In the present passage Jesus is pictured as ascending **a hill** (lit., "the hill/mountain"), and it is a reasonable suggestion that this setting is intended as a clue that the appointment of the Twelve is an important event that reveals something of Jesus's mission, for the Gospel writers frequently use a mountain setting for events that are important revelations (see note). Further, the fact that the number chosen was twelve seems to have as its explanation the symbolic importance of this number in the OT. There were twelve sons of Jacob who are seen as the fathers of the twelve tribes that made up ancient Israel (e.g., Gen. 35:22–26; 49:28; Exod. 28:21), and elsewhere (Matt. 19:28) the twelve disciples are promised a role as leaders in the future people of God. The choice of twelve, therefore, is intended to portray Jesus as the founder of a reconstituted Israel; thus, Jesus and the Twelve are distinguished as more than simply another rabbi and his followers. This event is narrated, not simply as a historical detail, but as an important step in the preparation for the Kingdom of God, in which the chosen disciples appear as prospective princes. (The question of the disciples in 10:35–37 becomes more understandable in this light; cf. also 10:28–31).

Whatever conclusion we reach about Mark's presentation of the Twelve, it is clear that they were seen collectively as a special group in the early church at the earliest date (see note), and Mark at least shows that he is familiar with this tradition. In light of this importance assigned to the Twelve, it is natural that a list of names is included, even though some of those names do not receive special attention elsewhere in the story. The name lists in the Gospels (cf. Matt. 10:1–4; Luke 6:12–16) show curious variations (see note), but some of those named have special significance in all the lists.

Pride of place goes to Peter, whose given name was actually Simon. The Greek word *petros*, rendered **Peter** here, means "rock," and is a translation of the Aramaic word *cephas* ("rock"), the word actually used by Jesus, which is retained elsewhere in the NT (cf. John 1:42; 1 Cor. 1:12; 3:22; 9:5; 15:5; Gal. 2:9). The famous saying in Matthew 16:18 is a pun based on the meaning of Peter's name. In Mark, as in the other Gospels, Peter is treated as the leader or spokesman of the Twelve and is the most familiar figure besides Jesus to readers of these narratives. We shall have much more to note about Peter in later mention of him in Mark.

James and John Zebedee are also important, having been mentioned once already (1:19–20), and they reappear as a kind of inner circle with Peter (cf. 5:37; 9:2; 14:33, and note on 3:16). They too are described as having been given a new name (a nickname?) by Jesus, **Boanerges**, which Mark translates **Men** (lit. "sons") **of Thunder** (the exact Hebrew or Aramaic term translated here is still debated by scholars). Unfortunately, no explanation is given for this intriguing term, though this has not stopped commentators from offering speculations, such as that these two had volatile dispositions. This kind of suggestion is best taken with a grain of salt. It is at least as likely that **thunder** is a symbol for the appearance of the Kingdom of God (thunder, earthquakes, etc., are mentioned in the OT in connection with manifestations of God's power, e.g., Exod. 19:16; 1 Sam. 7:10; Ps. 104:7; Isa. 29:6; also Rev. 4:5; 8:5; 11:19). If so, then these two are described here simply as supporters or participants in the events of Jesus' ministry, which is thus portrayed as a manifestation of God and an anticipation of the future Kingdom of God.

The other disciple who figures prominently in the Gospel accounts is Judas Iscariot **who betrayed Jesus** (v. 19). There are many quite natural questions provoked by the mere mention of his name. For one thing, it is not entirely clear what **Iscariot** signifies, perhaps his geographical origin, or something else (see note). More importantly, we want to know why one of Jesus' own close disciples would have betrayed him, but no explanation is given either here or later in Mark when the deed is recounted (14:10–

11, 43–45, and the comments on these verses later). The only thing Mark wishes to emphasize here is the gripping fact that, in addition to the plot against Jesus by his critics (3:6), there was also this even more grievous betrayal by one of those called to follow Jesus. By this reference to Judas, Mark makes his story of Jesus' ministry and the responses it generated more complex and engaging. It prepares us for a story involving not only a division between critics and supporters of Jesus but also a testing and crisis for those who became his followers. The rest of the narrative will show just how much Mark emphasizes this latter point.

Additional Notes

3:7 / **Lake Galilee**: a large lake formed from waters flowing out of the mountains to the north, such as Mount Hermon. This body of water is about thirteen miles north to south and about seven miles east to west, and is in a deep basin, about 695 feet below sea level at the surface. The river Jordan flows out the south end toward the Dead Sea. There is a plain on the western shore, varying in width, and sharp cliffs on the eastern side. On this plain in Jesus' time were flourishing towns—Capernaum, Bethsaida, Tiberias—where Jesus frequently ministered. The lake teemed with fish and supported a good export business. (See *IDB*, vol. 2, pp. 348–50.)

Galilee: the northern district of ancient Palestine, in Jesus' day governed by Herod Antipas, a descendant of Herod the Great. Galilee was and is a rich agricultural area.

Judea: the southern part of Jewish Palestine, hilly and drier than Galilee and less suitable for farming. Jerusalem was the chief city and the area was under direct Roman control through a Roman-appointed governor (procurator) in Jesus' time.

3:8 / **Jerusalem**: the sacred city of the Jews and chief city of Palestine, where the Temple was located. (See Joachim Jeremias, *Jerusalem in the Time of Jesus* [London: SCM, 1969] for detailed study on this city in ancient times; *IDB*, vol. 2, pp. 843–66.)

Idumea: This area lay to the south of first-century Judea and included many inhabitants of non-Jewish descent who had migrated from the area known in the OT as Edom. In the time of the Jewish revolt against the Seleucids (168 B.C.–142 B.C.), Judas Maccabee and subsequent Jewish leaders conducted military campaigns in the area, and in about 126 B.C. John Hyrcanus (the Jewish ruler and descendant of the Maccabee family) subdued the area, placing it under Antipater (the Idumean grandfather of Herod the Great) as governor responsible to Hyrcanus, and forcing the inhabitants to convert to the Jewish religion.

The east side of the Jordan: The vague reference is probably to the area known as Peraea (modern-day Jordan) in the time of Jesus, roughly corresponding to the Gilead of the OT. In the early first century, the area was part of Herod

Antipas' domain and was occupied by Jews.

Tyre and Sidon: Both of these cities were originally Phoenician seaports and remained essentially gentile cities in Jesus' time, though Jews were living in them. The mention of the region around these cities suggests that non-Jews are presented here as coming to see Jesus, and elsewhere (7:24–31) we read of Jesus healing the daughter of a gentile woman from this area. In addition, in Luke 10:13–14 and Matt. 11:21–22 Jesus refers to both Tyre and Sidon favorably in comparison to Israelite towns. No doubt these people were seen by Mark's first readers as the initial Gentiles who foreshadowed the later reception of the Christian gospel by Gentiles in the church. (For historical background, see "Tyre," *IDB*, vol. 4, pp. 721–23.)

3:9 / **A boat**: No doubt this was a lake fishing craft such as at least some of his disciples were used to handling. A boat reappears at several points in the following narratives (cf. 4:1–2, 35–41; 5:1–2, 18–21; 6:30–36, 45–56; 8:10–15) and is so characteristic an item in the stories of Jesus and his disciples that the image of a boat early became a favorite Christian symbol for the Christian fellowship.

3:13 / **A hill**: The Greek original says "*the* hill" or "*the* mountain" (the word can mean either), and this construction is strange, for there is no hill mentioned previously in Mark. Mountains or hills are well-known sites for divine revelations and for important events in the Bible. Importantly, we should note the giving of the Law and the covenant to Israel under Moses (Exod. 19:1–25; 20:18–20). This setting in Mark may be intended to signify that the choice of the Twelve is a new event in the sacred history of redemption, like the original constitution of Israel as God's chosen nation. The Luke 6:12 parallel describes Jesus praying in the hills before this choice of the Twelve, and this is intended to make it clear that the choice is part of the divine plan for Jesus' ministry. For other examples of events in the Gospels connected with hills, note 9:2–9 and Matt. 17:1–8 and Luke 9:28–36 (the transfiguration); 13:3–37 and Matt. 24:3–44 (the discourse on the future); Matt. 5:1 (the Sermon on the Mount); and Matt. 28:16–20 (the Great Commission).

3:15 / **Authority**: This term is an important one in Mark (cf. 1:22, 27; 2:10; 11:28–33, and comments on these verses), and it is clear that one of his emphases is that Jesus carried divinely ordained authority in doing his work. Here the striking thing is that Jesus confers this authority on the Twelve, which can only mean that they are described here as co-workers in the deeds of Jesus, though theirs is an authority derived from Jesus. Notice further how Mark summarizes this divine authority as power against demons. We noted already that the first miracle in Mark's narrative of Jesus' ministry is an exorcism (1:23–26), and that the expulsion of demons figures prominently in the summaries of Jesus' deeds (1:34; 3:11). It seems that the defeat of evil spirits was for Mark *the* representative deed showing the authority of Jesus and the nature of the Kingdom of God in action.

Apostles: The term means "commissioned" or "sent out with a commission." It is used in Acts to refer to the Twelve (cf., e.g., Acts 1:15–26; 2:43), but it is also used by Paul to describe himself (e.g., Rom. 1:1) and others (1 Cor. 15:5–7). From these and other references, we get the impression that apostles were seen as leaders who had special authority in the church (e.g., 1 Cor. 9:1–7). To call the Twelve **apostles** here means that they are to be seen as specially commissioned by Jesus to work in his name. (See "Apostle," *NIDNTT*, vol. 1, pp. 126–39; *IDB*, vol. 1, pp. 170–72.)

3:16 / **The twelve**: All four Gospels refer to a group of twelve disciples as a kind of core group. In numerous references, including the very earliest (1 Cor. 15:5, dated about A.D. 51), they are referred to as "the twelve" (cf., e.g., Mark 4:10; 6:7; 9:35; 10:32; 11:11; 14:10, 20, 23; Acts 6:2), indicating probably that the group collectively had a special place in the earliest church. The parallel list of names (Matt. 10:1–4 and Luke 6:12–16; cf. Acts 1:12–13) have curious variations. Aside from variations in the order of the names, we note that a Thaddaeus, listed in Mark 3:18 and Matt. 10:3, does not appear in Luke 6:14–16, and that the "Judas son of James" of the latter account is not mentioned in the parallels in Mark or Matthew. Of course, there are speculations about these being the same man, but we cannot be sure. The **Matthew** of 3:18 is described in Matt. 10:3 as a tax collector and seems to be presented there as the Matthew of Matt. 9:9, called Levi in Mark 2:14! Is this again a case of a man with two names?

Some of the other names are interesting for what they mean. **Bartholomew** means "son of Talmai" in Aramaic (cf. Mark 10:46, "Bartimaeus son of Timaeus"). Many have identified him with the Nathaniel of John 1:45–49; 21:2, who is not mentioned elsewhere! **Thomas** comes from an Aramaic word meaning "twin" (John 11:16; 20:24; 21:2, use the Greek translation "Didymas"), but whose twin he was we cannot say with any certainty. The Simon of 3:18 is called **the Patriot** and this translates an Aramaic term that is transliterated here in Mark "Cananean" (not to be confused with "Canaanite"!). The term translated "patriot" in the GNB in Luke 6:15 is a translation of the Aramaic term into Greek, literally, "the Zealous" or "the Zealot." This man may have been a member of some religious resistance group, such as certainly appeared slightly later, working to free the Jews from Roman rule. If so, this might mean that in the same band of disciples there were both a former tax collector (Matthew/Levi?) who had worked for the Roman puppet government of Herod Antipas and a former religiously dedicated resistance fighter against that same government.

The Levi of 2:14 is described as "son of Alphaeus," causing some to wonder if this Levi and **James son of Alphaeus** (3:18) were brothers. Among the Twelve, Peter and Andrew (Matt. 10:2 and Luke 6:14), James and John Zebedee, and possibly Philip and Bartholomew (Nathaniel?), were other pairs of brothers. And was Thomas ("the twin") a twin brother of another member of the group? (In the apocryphal writing known as The Acts of Thomas, he is depicted as the twin brother of Jesus, but in spite of the popularity of this writing even among orthodox circles of Syriac Christians, this idea must be regarded as a peculiar example of pious imagination. For information on the writing, and an English translation, see E. Hennecke, W. Schneemelcher, *New Testament Apocrypha*, trans. R. McL. Wilson [Philadelphia: Westminster, 1965], vol. 2, pp. 425–531.)

Judas Iscariot is called son of Simon Iscariot in John 6:71; 13:26, and many suggest that **Iscariot** is a transliteration of a Hebrew term meaning "a man from Kerioth," a place-name in the area called Moab (cf. Jer. 48:24, 41; Amos 2:2) but also a village in ancient Idumea south of Hebron (Josh. 15:25). (See also, e.g., "Twelve, the," *IDB*, vol. 4, p. 179.)

Critics, Family, and Followers

MARK 3:20–35

Then Jesus went home. Again such a large crowd gathered that Jesus and his disciples had no time to eat. [21]When his family heard about it, they set out to take charge of him, because people were saying, "He's gone mad!"

[22]Some teachers of the Law who had come from Jerusalem were saying, "He has Beelzebul in him! It is the chief of the demons who gives him the power to drive them out."

[23]So Jesus called them to him and spoke to them in parables: "How can Satan drive out Satan? [24]If a country divides itself into groups which fight each other, that country will fall apart. [25]If a family divides itself into groups which fight each other, that family will fall apart. [26]So if Satan's kingdom divides into groups, it cannot last, but will fall apart and come to an end.

[27]"No one can break into a strong man's house and take away his belongings unless he first ties up the strong man; then he can plunder his house.

[28]"I assure you that people can be forgiven all their sins and all the evil things they may say.[f] [29]But whoever says evil things against the Holy Spirit will never be forgiven, because he has committed an eternal sin." ([30]Jesus said this because some people were saying, "He has an evil spirit in him.")

[31]Then Jesus' mother and brothers arrived. They stood outside the house and sent in a message, asking for him. [32]A crowd was sitting around Jesus, and they said to him, "Look, your mother and your brothers and sisters are outside, and they want you."

[33]Jesus answered, "Who is my mother? Who are my brothers?" [34]He looked at the people sitting around him and said, "Look! Here are my mother and my brothers! [35]Whoever does what God wants him to do is my brother, my sister, my mother."

f. evil things they may say; *or* evil things they may say against God.

3:20-30 / Although this passage is separated from the following passage (3:31–35) in the GNB, the two really must be read together, for we appear to have here the first example of a narrative technique used frequently in Mark: beginning one story and then inserting another before bringing the first to a conclusion. Here, Mark begins telling us about the **family** of Jesus in 3:21 (see note), interrupts this story by telling us about Jesus' conflict with certain critics over his exorcisms in 3:22–30, and returns to the story of Jesus' family in 3:31–35. (Other examples of this technique are 5:21–42; 6:7–32; 11:12–25.) When Mark "sandwiches" stories in this manner, it seems that he presents the two stories as related in some way; and this is probably the case here. Briefly put, there are three groups in

3:20–35: (1) Jesus' family, who seem to misunderstand him and try to take him home for enforced rest; (2) critics, who accuse Jesus of being a sorcerer in league with Satan (**Beelzebul**; see note); and (3) those who do **what God wants** and who are treated favorably as Jesus' true "family" (3:33–35). This third group is not directly named, but the impression given is that it is made up of Jesus' disciples. Thus, the overall point of 3:20–35 is to contrast these three responses to Jesus' ministry, highlighting the third as the only correct one. This third response, shown by those who sit at his feet as disciples (**the people sitting around him,** 3:34), is **what God wants** (3:35).

It is worth noting that in 3:20 the disciples are shown working alongside Jesus and experiencing the costs of ministry with him (**no time to eat**), and this is further evidence of who those are to whom Jesus points in 3:35 as his new family. We should also remember that in 3:13–19 we have been presented with the Twelve as those who share in Jesus' authority and ministry. The incidents in 3:20–35 are connected with the preceding passage in that those named in 3:13–19, with whom Mark's Christian readers are to identify themselves, are shown as being given a relationship with Jesus that transcends and replaces his earthly ties. We shall return to this matter when we deal with 3:31–35 in the next section.

In 3:20–30, Jesus is shown heavily burdened in ministry with his disciples. The location is not entirely clear (see note). Next, Jesus' relatives (see note) set out to seize him out of concern for him. The Greek wording here is not quite as precise as the GNB translation, and it is not clear whether it is **people** or perhaps Jesus' family themselves who express doubts about his sanity. In recent years we have heard stories of other families who have attempted to dissuade family members (usually young adults) from fervent religious or political associations, sometimes forcibly in what is popularly called deprogramming, usually in the belief that their loved ones have been "brainwashed" and are not in control of their minds. Seen in this light, the passage before us has a familiar human ring to it.

The interruption of this story with the account of the accusation by some **teachers of the Law** seems designed to show that the attitude of Jesus' family, however understandable in one sense, is to be seen as a response like that of these critics. Although the charge **He's gone mad!** (3:21) is perhaps slightly less malevolent than **He has an evil spirit in him** (3:30), Mark presents them both as wrong responses to Jesus.

The charge against Jesus in 3:22 is that he is a sorcerer who does his exorcisms by evil power, a charge echoed in the Gospels and elsewhere (see note on **Beelzebul**). What is being contested is the *meaning* of Jesus' power and works. The reality of the miracles is not denied, but the charge that they are devilish negates them as signs of God's kingly power. Jesus' response is a series of quick **parables** (see note) to the effect that it is illogical to think that Satan would empower Jesus to destroy Satan's own **kingdom** exhibited in the demonized (3:23–27). The last parable (3:27), about taking the loot of a **strong man**, may be an allusion to Isaiah 49:24–25, where God describes his future salvation in the same imagery. The **strong man** of 3:27 is Satan, no doubt, and Jesus' exorcisms are the plundering of Satan's goods. If the allusion suggested is valid, then the plundering of Satan is also to be understood as a sign that the future rule of God promised in the prophets is being exhibited already. This connection of the exorcisms with the Kingdom of God is made more explicit in the parallel passages in Matthew 12:28 and Luke 11:20, but is intended here as well.

The saying in 3:28–29 distinguishes between saying **evil things** against the Holy Spirit and all other sins, in that there is no forgiveness for the former. The idea of an unforgiveable sin has haunted the minds of sensitive people in all Christian centuries, but all such anxiety is misdirected. As the context makes plain, Jesus' warning is against disregarding his message by calling it Satanic (see esp. 3:30), a quite specific deed. A person doing such a thing would have no concern about Christ's forgiveness for it. So, the very anxiety lest one may have done something that cuts one off from Christ's forgiveness is, ironically, evidence that one believes Christ to be sent from God, and thus proof that one cannot have committed the sin warned against here.

The reference to the Holy Spirit in 3:29 reminds us that in 1:10 Mark has told us that Jesus was empowered by the Spirit of God for his ministry. The point of the saying is that it is the Holy Spirit, God, who is the source of Jesus' miracles.

3:31-35 / This episode is directly connected with the preceding one (3:20–30), as explained in the comments on that portion, and is also part of a larger section that includes the calling of the Twelve (3:13–19). The Twelve are introduced in 3:13–19, and in 3:20–35 they are contrasted with "teachers of the Law" and with Jesus' family. Although the disciples fail in many ways in later episodes, here they are presented as specially favored by Jesus for their willingness to follow him. As mentioned before, the disciples are major characters in Mark and what is said about them is both positive and negative. The reader is supposed to identify with the Twelve and is supposed to learn from what is said to them and about them the high privilege and duties of discipleship, on the one hand, and, on the other hand, the difficulties and temptations to failure.

In the present passage, Jesus says of his disciples that they have become his true family. Though it is fairly clear that the Twelve are the ones referred to, the more general description of those Jesus commends as **the people sitting around him** (3:34) has the effect of leaving the circle open for others to join. The Christian readers are to identify themselves with those who do **what God wants** (3:35) and so are to see themselves included among those given this special closeness to Jesus.

It is not stated in this episode what Jesus' family wanted (3:31), but since it appears that they are mentioned in 3:21 as trying to "take charge of him," their intent here is no doubt the same—that is, this is not simply a friendly visit from relatives! This makes Jesus' sharp rejection of them in favor of his followers a little easier to understand. There is other evidence that Jesus did not enjoy the support of his own family during his ministry (e.g., John 7:1–9). There is the mention of Jesus' mother at the crucifixion in John 19:25–27, but little is said to indicate her own position among the disciples. Acts 1:14 mentions Mary, his mother, as among the disciples after Jesus' resurrection; and James, his brother, is mentioned as a leader in the early church (e.g., 1 Cor. 15:7; Ga. 1:19; 2:9). It is not made clear how Jesus' family moved from misunderstanding (and perhaps rejection) to faith and commitment.

In the light of this tension between Jesus and his family, the famous words of Jesus about discipleship involving the cost of one's family (Matt. 10:34–39) can be seen as reflective of his own personal experience (see also Luke 12:49–53). That is, Jesus can call others to sacrifice because he too has had to sacrifice to follow God's call.

It is remarkable that this somewhat negative treatment of Jesus' family survived, in view of the veneration of the mother of Jesus and the general high respect for his family in later church tradition. In the Roman Catholic tradition there is a special difficulty with the references to Jesus' family because of the official dogma that Mary remained perpetually a virgin and thus did not have children other than Jesus (see note). Of course, this information about Jesus and his family was not preserved for curiosity's sake but to demonstrate by Jesus' example the cost of discipleship and—by Jesus' words in 3:35—its reward.

Additional Notes

3:20 / **Home**: The Greek phrase here could mean either that Jesus went "into a house" or that he went "home." If the latter is the correct translation, it is not clear whether the intended location of the story is Capernaum, Jesus' headquarters during his Galilean ministry (see note on 1:21), or Nazareth, where he grew up and where his family probably lived.

3:21 / **His family**: The Greek phrase used here could be taken to mean anyone connected with Jesus, but in the context of 3:31-35 is probably a reference to Jesus' immediate family. Some Greek manuscripts of Mark have variations in the wording of this passage designed to remove the idea that Jesus' family or friends might have tried to seize him and might have thought him to be mad. Such an idea was no doubt embarrassing to some Christians in centuries when reverence for the family of Jesus was becoming prominent. (See also note on **Jesus' mother and brothers**, under 3:31.)

3:22 / **Beelzebul** is a name for Satan in the Gospels and is probably derived from the ancient name for a Canaanite god (Baalzebul), which meant "lord of the high place." This god is referred to in 2 Kings 1:2-6, 16, where he is called Baalzebub, which means "lord of the flies," probably a Jewish pun on the actual name. The name spelled as Beelzebub appears in the Gospels in ancient manuscripts written in Syriac and Latin, and thus in some English translations.

The charge that Jesus was a sorcerer is echoed in the parallels to this passage in Matt. 12:24 and Luke 11:15 and in Matt. 9:34; John 7:20; 8:48, 52; 10:20. The idea appears also in the ancient Jewish tradition known as the *Toledoth Jesu* and was a widespread Jewish interpretation of Jesus until modern times. It should be mentioned that in the twentieth century, especially, there is a widely supported effort among Jewish scholars to present Jesus in a more favorable light. I can adduce here such examples as Martin Buber, Joseph Klausner, G. Vermes, and Samuel Sandmel, to name a few.

3:23 / **Parables**: The word is derived from a Greek word (*parabolē*) that means a "comparison" or "analogy." Such teaching devices were widely used by ancient Jewish teachers especially, and they are thoroughly characteristic of Jesus' style of teaching. Mark 4:1-34 is wholly devoted to a collection of Jesus' parables, and there are similar collections in Matt. 13:1-52 and Luke 8:4-18; 10:25-37; 12:13-21; 13:6-30; 15:1-16:31. The parables of Jesus range from short statements to lengthy stories, and some of the latter have become justly famous, such as the parables of the Good Samaritan (Luke 10:25-37), and the Lost Son (Luke 15:11-32). Jesus' parables have generated a great deal of scholarly activity in recent decades. There is not space here to try to describe it all, but two major conclusions have been confirmed abundantly by this research and are vital for understanding Jesus' parables.

First, the parables of Jesus are all connected with this central message that God had begun to assert his kingly power against evil and that the promised time of salvation was at hand. That is, the parables are all closely connected with Jesus' proclamation of the Kingdom of God (e.g., 1:14-15); they are not simply stories illustrating general moral truths.

Secondly, the parables of Jesus embody the very nature of Jesus' ministry in that they are not fully obvious and transparent, unlike most sermon or lecture illustrations. The parables require the hearer or reader to use some effort to get their point, and to perceive their meaning truly involves not just mental effort but also a moral or spiritual readiness to accept the view of God and the world that the parables embody. In other words, the parables challenge and seek to provoke the hearer or reader to a response of repentance or rejection. The parables in this episode, for example, present the claim that Jesus' exorcisms represent the divinely sponsored attack upon Satan, and this can only mean that Jesus is in fact the vehicle of the promised Kingdom of God, and not just another exorcist or trickster.

3:28 / **I assure you**: The Greek phrase here is a solemn assurance with the force of an oath (lit., "Truly I say to you") and appears also in 8:12; 9:1, 41; 10:15, 29; 11:23; 12:43; 13:30; 14:9, 18, 25, 30, and numerous times in the other Gospels as well. Normally the word "truly" (Hebrew, *amen*) was used by a Jew in response to the words of someone else, to indicate assent. Jesus' use as a preface to his own statement seems unique. (See "Amen," *NIDNTT*, vol. 1, pp. 97–99.)

Evil things: The technical English term *blasphemy* is derived from the Greek word translated here by **evil things**. The verb form "to blaspheme" appears in 3:29, **whoever says evil things**. In 2:7 Jesus' critics accuse him of blasphemy in forgiving sins, for they believe it improper for a mere man to act as God (see comments on that passage). In the account of Jesus' trial (14:63–64) Jesus is accused of blasphemy, and for this reason is condemned to die. Of course, in Mark's view this charge against Jesus is wrong, and here he shows Jesus warning his critics not to commit the very sin they accuse him of by dismissing his power as devilish. From Mark's point of view, the ironic fact is that Jesus' critics committed the very sin for which Jesus was unjustly condemned.

3:31 / **Jesus' mother and brothers**: Sisters of Jesus are referred to in 3:32, though they are not mentioned in some important early manuscripts of Mark. Mark 6:1–3 unquestionably mentions sisters of Jesus among his family and names four brothers: James, Joseph, Judas, and Simon. The most natural reading of these references is to understand that Jesus' parents had several children. However, Roman Catholic dogma and Eastern Orthodox tradition include the teaching that Mary, Jesus' mother, was not only a virgin at Jesus' conception (the doctrine received by Catholic, Eastern, and Protestant wings of Christianity) but remained perpetually a virgin, never having sexual relations with her husband and, therefore, never having children other than Jesus. This tradition arose in the early centuries of Christianity when the emphasis on asceticism (celibacy, poverty, etc.) was developing into a movement in the church and became official teaching of Roman and Eastern bodies centuries later.

According to this view of Mary's "perpetual virginity," the brothers and sisters of Jesus in the Gospels are interpreted as being either children of Joseph, Jesus' father (Matt. 1:16, 18, and elsewhere), from a previous marriage or cousins of Jesus. Particularly in the latter interpretation, the force of this passage in which Jesus describes his followers as his true family seems weakened, for comparing disciples with cousins is not as striking as comparing them with one's own brothers and sisters.

The final decision about how to understand the references to Jesus' natural family will, of course, depend on whether one feels constrained to respect the particular church traditions mentioned here.

7

He Spoke in Parables

MARK 4:1–34

Again Jesus began to teach beside Lake Galilee. The crowd that gathered around him was so large that he got into a boat and sat in it. The boat was out in the water, and the crowd stood on the shore at the water's edge. [2]He used parables to teach them many things, saying to them:

[3]"Listen! Once there was a man who went out to sow grain. [4]As he scattered the seed in the field, some of it fell along the path, and the birds came and ate it up. [5]Some of it fell on rocky ground, where there was little soil. The seeds soon sprouted, because the soil wasn't deep. [6]Then, when the sun came up, it burned the young plants; and because the roots had not grown deep enough, the plants soon dried up. [7]Some of the seed fell among thorn bushes, which grew up and choked the plants, and they didn't bear grain. [8]But some seeds fell in good soil, and the plants sprouted, grew, and bore grain: some had thirty grains, others sixty, and others one hundred."

[9]And Jesus concluded, "Listen, then, if you have ears!"

[10]When Jesus was alone, some of those who had heard him came to him with the twelve disciples and asked him to explain the parables. [11]"You have been given the secret of the Kingdom of God," Jesus answered. "But the others, who are on the outside, hear all things by means of parables, [12]so that,

'They may look and look,

yet not see;
they may listen and listen,
yet not understand.
For if they did, they would turn to God,
and he would forgive them.' "

[13]Then Jesus asked them, "Don't you understand this parable? How, then, will you ever understand any parable? [14]The sower sows God's message. [15]Some people are like the seeds that fall along the path; as soon as they hear the message, Satan comes and takes it away. [16]Other people are like the seeds that fall on rocky ground. As soon as they hear the message, they receive it gladly. [17]But it does not sink deep into them, and they don't last long. So when trouble or persecution comes because of the message, they give up at once. [18]Other people are like the seeds sown among the thorn bushes. These are the ones who hear the message, [19]but the worries about this life, the love for riches, and all other kinds of desires crowd in and choke the message, and they don't bear fruit. [20]But other people are like the seeds sown in good soil. They hear the message, accept it, and bear fruit: some thirty, some sixty, and some one hundred."

[21]Jesus continued, "Does anyone ever bring in a lamp and put it under a bowl or under the bed? Doesn't he put it on the lampstand? [22]Whatever is hidden away will be brought out into the open, and whatever is covered up will be uncovered. [23]Listen, then, if you have ears!"

²⁴He also said to them, "Pay attention to what you hear! The same rules you use to judge others will be used by God to judge you—but with even greater severity. ²⁵The person who has something will be given more, and the person who has nothing will have taken away from him even what little he has."

²⁶Jesus went on to say, "The Kingdom of God is like this. A man scatters seed in his field. ²⁷He sleeps at night, is up and about during the day, and all the while the seeds are sprouting and growing. Yet he does not know how it happens. ²⁸The soil itself makes the plants grow and bear fruit; first the tender stalk appears, then the head, and finally the head full of grain. ²⁹When the grain is ripe, the man starts cutting it with his sickle, because harvest time has come.

³⁰"What shall we say the Kingdom of God is like?" asked Jesus. "What parable shall we use to explain it? ³¹It is like this. A man takes a mustard seed, the smallest seed in the world, and plants it in the ground. ³²After a while it grows up and becomes the biggest of all plants. It puts out such large branches that the birds come and make their nests in its shade."

³³Jesus preached his message to the people, using many other parables like these; he told them as much as they could understand. ³⁴He would not speak to them without using parables, but when he was alone with his disciples, he would explain everything to them.

4:1-9 / This passage begins a longer section dealing with the parables that runs through 4:34. Careful reading shows, however, that the passage is not only about parables but also about the necessity for the Twelve's understanding the parables and their difficulty in doing so. Note that this parable is given an explanation in 4:13–20, something not done for most of the parables in the Gospels. Though Mark says (4:34) that Jesus explained other parables to the disciples, this one is the only parable for which Mark records an explanation. This, plus the fact that this parable heads the list here, suggest that it has special significance and is perhaps the chief representative parable for Mark.

We will be able to discuss in more detail the meaning of the parable when we look at the explanation given in 4:13–20. Here we need only make some preliminary observations, for this passage really must be studied together with 4:10–20.

First, we note that the **again** of 4:1 puts Jesus in a scene similar to 3:7–12, where Jesus teaches at the shore of Lake Galilee from a fishing boat. As we noted before, a boat is featured often in Mark's narrative, being a kind of symbol for the fellowship of Jesus and the Twelve in the Galilean ministry.

Secondly, the sowing action here is that of ancient Palestinian agriculture, the sower walking through a field and throwing seed by hand over the ground, which was then plowed to bury the seed. This explains how seed in the parable seems to go everywhere. It was not put in neatly prepared furrows, as in modern agriculture; thus, the seed that fell on the path (4:4) or on rocky ground (4:5) or among thorn bushes (4:7) was not deliberately placed there but fell on these places in the scattering over the broad field. In an actual field, of course, comparatively little of the seed would land in such places. So, even though much space is devoted to listing these places, this does not imply that the bulk of the work of the sower is wasted.

Thirdly, it is important to note that there are not really four kinds of soils, as it might appear at first, but only two. There is unproductive soil, three examples given, and productive soil, again with three examples (4:8). The figures thirty, sixty, one hundred, refer to three examples of productive soil, and the translation **thirty grains** is a bit inaccurate. The numbers indicate, rather, the increase in grain harvested over grain sown in a field. Studies of the yield in Palestinian grainfields where the ancient agricultural methods were followed show that a tenfold harvest was a good yield and that the average was about seven and a half. This means that all three of the numbers in the harvest in this parable are intended to depict not a normal harvest, but a miraculously abundant one. This substantiates the point made earlier that the emphasis is not on how much seed is lost but on the abundant results of the sowing. Also, these figures hint that the harvest is a symbol for divine activity. That is, the abnormally high harvest figures cry out, "Look closer. This harvest story describes God's work."

The final statement (4:9) confirms this symbolic significance of the story, warning and encouraging the listeners to give serious attention to what they have heard. The statement reappears in 4:23, and it reflects the emphasis of the whole section on the parables (and indeed the emphasis of all of Mark) that one must exercise care to perceive Jesus properly.

4:10-12 / Although this passage introduces Jesus' interpretation of the preceding parable (4:13–20), Mark has the disciples asking Jesus about **the parables**. That is, Mark intends Jesus' statement in 4:11–12 to be a general statement on the use of parables in Jesus' ministry. In Jesus' statement, a clear distinction is made between those **outside** and the disciples, to whom is given **the secret of the Kingdom of God** (4:11). This same division is reflected in 4:33–34, where the disciples get explanations, but the crowds do not. We have seen already the note of secrecy in Mark's account of Jesus' ministry (e.g., 1:34, 43–45; 2:12), and this idea that the disciples are given special teaching seems to be a related matter.

The disciples are given **the secret of the Kingdom of God** (4:11), and this appears to mean not simply the interpretation of a few parables (see note) but, more profoundly, that they have been chosen to participate in the proclamation and advance of the Kingdom of God. That is, to be given **the secret** is not just to be given some information but is to be made a part of the secret operation of God's Kingdom. The Kingdom of God is a secret, not because nothing is said about it, but because the real significance of what is said and done in the name of the Kingdom is not perceived by many. The disciples here do not themselves understand fully the meaning of the parables (4:10, 13), yet they are given **the secret**. Obviously then, this must imply that to be given the secret is roughly the same as being called to follow Jesus and to participate with him in his ministry. Earlier, in 3:33–35, Jesus describes his disciples as his true family, and here another very positive privilege is theirs as well.

The distinction between those **outside** and those given the secret may sound offensive to modern readers with a sympathy for fairness to all and a dislike for favoritism. Two points must be made. First, the idea of certain people being chosen has roots in the OT presentation of Israel as a chosen nation and the prophetic teaching that God would select a "remnant" of Israel for future salvation and restoration. The point of these OT themes and the meaning of disciples being specially chosen to share **the secret** here is not to say that some are favored at the expense of others but that God sees to it that there are those who can serve as vehicles of his purpose. That is, the fact that the disciples have been divinely enabled to participate in the activity of the Kingdom of God is intended as good news, encouragement, to them. At the same time, the fact that they have been given **the secret** connotes sacred responsibility.

Secondly, the apparently harsh words in 4:12, suggesting at first glance that those **outside** are deliberately kept in confusion, in fact are not quite so cruel. They are an allusion to Isaiah 6:9–10, where the prophet Isaiah is called to proclaim God's message to ancient Israel, and where he is told by God that, though his message of warning will not be heeded, he is to give it anyway. Isaiah 6:9–10 is an indication of divine sovereignty and foreknowledge intended to say that the apparent failure of the messenger is no argument against his divine call. In its form, it is an ironic statement, giving the foreseen net result of the prophet's ministry as if it were all intended, when this is of course not the case. The fact that Mark 4:12 is an allusion to Isaiah 6:9–10 suggests that this too is prophetic irony.

Thus, the parables are described as producing no insight because that is their prophetically foreseen result. Stating the result of the parables in this ironic fashion suggests that the lack of response by the crowds is not something to crow about but is sad and lamentable, and reflects frustration, not joy. Seen in this light, the word that some *have* been given the secret is a word of consolation and encouragement.

Finally, to anticipate later passages in Mark, we will see that, even though the disciples are described here as having special access to God's purposes, they too show very dim perception of Jesus' true significance and little ability to accept what he knows must be his path through rejection and death in the will of God.

4:13–20 / In this passage Jesus explains the parable given in 4:1–9, making it clear that the parable concerns the proclamation of the message of the Kingdom of God and its reception by various kinds of listeners. Before giving the explanation of the parable, Jesus comments on the disciples' inability to understand his parables (4:13). This comment is the first of several in Mark that describe the disciples as themselves somewhat dull in understanding what Jesus is really up to (cf. 4:40–41; 6:51–52; 7:17–19; 8:14–21, 31–33; 9:30–32), and it is interesting that no similar statement appears in the Matthew 13:16–23 and Luke 8:11–15 parallels (see note). This illustrates that Mark seems to describe the disciples in a more critical fashion than the other Gospels. Still, it is a mistake to conclude (as even some scholars have) that Mark's intention is simply to attack the Twelve. Everything written about them to this point in Mark has been favorable and is designed to encourage Christian readers to identify themselves with the Twelve, seeing them as the first Christians, so to speak. If Mark shows the failures of these disciples, then it is because he wishes to emphasize that Jesus' message is a great challenge to any hearer, even to his followers. Mark's purpose seems to be to say to his readers, "Are you sure that *you* really understand what it is you profess to have accepted?"

The "seed" is **God's message** in 4:14; yet in 4:15–20 what happens to the seed when sown is likened to what happens in those who hear the message. Probably it is best to see the various soils as the various kinds of hearers, and for this reason some scholars have proposed that this parable should be titled The Parable of the Soils.

The explanation of the meaning of the various soils is relatively clear. Some who become adherents of the message fail under persecution (4:16–17). Some are so tied to materialist priorities that they cannot really surrender to the message (4:18–19). It is perhaps the first group, the ones from whom Satan takes the message, that requires some comment. These are quite probably those who never even begin to receive the message properly, those who in fact turn against it or ignore it. The reference to Satan reflects the view that this message about the Kingdom of God is an attack upon Satan and the power of evil, and that rejection of the message is a result of Satan-inspired opposition. Jesus has already described his ministry as an attack upon Satan's domain (3:23–27), and this reference to Satan reinforces the idea that the battle is one not just of earthly forces but of spiritual powers as well.

It is worth noting that the two major groups of earthly causes for failure among those who do not persevere (4:16–19) are, first, persecution and such troubles and, second, material care for riches and possessions. Warnings to be ready for persecution reappear in Mark at several points (e.g., 8:34–38; 10:35–40; 13:9–13), as do strong words about the danger of concern for possessions (10:17–31). Clearly Mark wishes to remind his readers that Jesus' message is no easy pill to swallow and no mild word of spiritual uplift but a declaration of war upon the power of evil and thus, as is true in any war, demands preparedness for opposition and sacrifice.

The emphasis in the explanation of the parable is twofold. First, there is a description of the things that prevent full obedience to Jesus' message, and secondly, there is the encouraging assurance that there are those who receive the message and that an abundant "harvest" will come. This means that the parable truly reflects the situation of Jesus' ministry and arose originally out of reflection on the response to his work. We catch some of the excitement of the fervent ministry of Jesus and the Twelve still shining through the story and its interpretation.

4:21-25 / In these verses there is a collection of sayings that all seem to be governed by exhortations to perceive properly God's presence in Jesus' ministry (4:23, 24). These same sayings appear in the other Gospels at various points, indicating that Mark has probably constructed chapter 4 from various sayings of Jesus (see note). The sense of 4:21–23 has to do with the note of secrecy sounded in 4:11, where the Kingdom of God is described as a secret that is not perceived by some in its present appearance in Jesus' ministry. The point of these sayings is that this present hidden form of the manifestation of the Kingdom will give way to a future openness and clarity, which is probably a reference to a promised time when God will fully manifest his truth and power and when Jesus' ministry will be vindicated as truly the foretaste of God's Kingdom. The GNB translation of words in 4:21 requires some comment (see note), but the basic idea is clear. In the same way that a lamp is not to be kept covered up, so the Kingdom, difficult for many to see in Jesus' ministry, will one day be brought fully to light. In view of this promise, the hearers are urged to perceive the truth of Jesus' message now (4:23).

In the present context, the sayings in 4:24–25 do not refer to judging others. The GNB translation is misleading here, for there is no mention of judging in the Greek original (see note). Rather, every saying has to do with recognizing and receiving the Kingdom of God making its appearance in Jesus' ministry. Thus, 4:24 urges attention to Jesus' words and warns that disobedience and rejection of his words will lead one to rejection by God. The riddlelike saying in 4:25 means that a positive response to the present, **hidden** manifestation of the Kingdom in Jesus will entitle one to still more of light and the blessings of the future salvation, whereas those who show no readiness to perceive God at work in Jesus now will suffer rejection at the judgment to come.

4:26–29 / This parable and the one following (4:30–32) both make use of the imagery of **seed** and agriculture, and in this way are similar to the parable that opens this chapter (4:1–9). No doubt the term **seed** acted as a memory device for early Christians, enabling them to link these parables.

When examining the parable in 4:1–9 we noted that it is probably to be seen basically as a parable of encouragement, with emphasis on the incredibly rich harvest. That is, though the crowds might take warning from the examples of bad soils, the disciples would find encouragement for their less-than-glamorous itinerant preaching in the assurance of great results. The parables here in 4:26–32 are likewise positive in tone and were probably directed originally to the disciples to raise morale for their work.

In 4:26–29, the emphasis is the contrast between the puny action of the sower who merely **scatters seed in his field** (4:26), and the development of the harvest. The grain grows whether he is awake or asleep (4:27), and **he does not know how it happens**. An ancient Jewish prayer says, "Blessed are you O God, King of the world, who brings forth bread from the earth," and this prayer reflects the basic attitude of wonder over the growth of crops that lies behind this parable. Jesus' point is that the Kingdom of God begins with the apparently insignificant action of "sowing" the message, but will finish as a great harvest. God, who gives the grain harvest, will also give a great result to the present ministry of Jesus and his disciples.

Mark's Christian readers, who did not yet see the great **harvest** themselves, were intended to apply Jesus' assurance in their own lives and mission of proclaiming God's message. The reference to the stages of growth (**the tender stalk . . . the head . . . the head full of grain**) is not intended to refer to stages of church growth but simply to elaborate the wonder of the mysterious, God-given result of the sower's work.

We may note, finally, that this is one of the few passages in Mark that does not appear in the other Gospels.

4:30-34 / This parable concludes the list, and it has the most elaborate introduction (4:30). In addition, there is the concluding statement (4:33–34) about the parables. But let us look at the parable itself before we turn to this statement.

First, we should emphasize that the point of the parable is the *contrast* between the insignificant mustard seed and the fully grown plant that it produces, not the *process* involved. So, the lesson is not that the Kingdom of God comes by quiet, prolonged growth, but rather that, though many might think the manifestation of the Kingdom in Jesus' ministry insignificant, they would be proven wrong in the day of its full appearance. And the disciples, for whom the parable was originally intended, were to have confidence that their humble ministry was to have great results.

Like all Jesus' parables examined in this chapter, this one too asserts the hope for a future vindication of his ministry. As we have noted before, it is important to understand that Jesus' whole message and work were centered around the conviction that the future time of divine salvation was already making its appearance in his activities, for those with eyes to see it. These parables have to be read with the excitement and urgency of this idea in view, or else, for modern readers, they can become only quaint little stories with harmless moral lessons.

In 4:33–34, we have a summary statement on Jesus' use of parables, which describes them as his characteristic form of teaching and which reaffirms the special place of the disciples. Here the parables are described as suited to the crowd's level of understanding, and this tends to verify our suggestion that 4:12 is to be taken as irony. That is, the parables are not really intended to confuse the crowds, but they *are* veiled communication forms, requiring active listening and the desire to understand. A major theme in Mark is that the true significance and meaning of Jesus were not really clear until after his crucifixion and resurrection. The parables are seen as the appropriate form of speech during the period when the full meaning of Jesus had not been shown and, indeed, *could not* be shown.

Additional Notes

4:9 / **If you have ears**: This formula-like statement reappears at 4:23 and at Matt. 11:15; 13:9, 43; Luke 8:8; 14:35, and is thus a well-established feature of Jesus' speech. In addition, we may note the statements in 4:12 about failing to listen with understanding and in 8:18 about the disciples having unperceptive ears. There are also two accounts of Jesus healing deaf individuals in 7:31–37 and 9:14–29, and for Mark these events serve not only as straight miracle stories but also as symbolical accounts dramatizing the spiritual deafness that must be cured to perceive Jesus' message properly.

4:11 / **You have been given the secret of the Kingdom of God**: A comparison of this passage with the parallels in Matt. 13:11 and Luke 8:10 yields some interesting observations. First, the Matt. 13:11 parallel has "the Kingdom of heaven," the synonymous term used often in Matthew. More significantly, both Matthew and Luke describe the disciples as given "the *knowledge* of the *secrets* of the Kingdom.*" That is, both of these writers refer to what the disciples are given as "knowledge" of "secrets," and these small verbal differences from Mark suggest that Matthew and Luke mean simply that the disciples are given explanations of the parables, whereas Mark's **given the secret** seems to suggest the broader idea that the disciples are made a part of the operation of the Kingdom.

4:12 / **So that**: This phrase read literally appears to mean that the parables were deliberately intended to confuse the crowds, but we have suggested above that it is to be taken as irony. The phrase appears also in the Luke 8:10 parallel, though Matt. 13:13 suggests that the parables are used *because* the people show little perception. In all these passages we see the idea that Jesus' parables are not simply teaching aids, like charts, diagrams, or other such devices. Though they are intended to present the Kingdom of God in story form and analogy, the Kingdom of God they describe does not conform to general expectation but makes its appearance in "secret" form in the ministry of Jesus and his disciples. Thus, the parables are difficult, challenging, because they embody and testify to a reality not easily recognized and received for what it really is.

4:13 / **Don't you understand?** This statement does not appear in the parallels in Matt. 13:16–23 or Luke 8:11–15. Instead, in Matt. 13:16–17 there is a very positive word about the privilege of the disciples, which appears also in Luke 10:23–24, and which seems similar in content to Mark 4:11–12 and the parallels (Matt. 13:11 and Luke 8:10). In general, both Matthew and Luke are less severe in their treatment of the Twelve. The reason is probably that, whereas Mark emphasizes the failure of the disciples as a warning to his readers, the other Gospel writers had emphases and purposes of their own. It is not so much a matter of disagreement as it is a difference of editorial emphasis. But to elaborate the differences would require more discussion than there is space for here.

4:21–25 / These sayings appear in scattered form at various other places in the

Gospels (Matt. 5:15 and Luke 11:33; Matt. 10:26 and Luke 12:2; Matt. 7:2 and Luke 6:38; Matt. 25:29 and Luke 19:26; Matt. 13:12 and Luke 8:16–18). This is evidence that the words of Jesus were treasured and used in various settings and ways in the presentation of his ministry by the early church.

4:21 / **Does anyone ever bring in a lamp**: The Greek reads literally "Does *the* lamp ever *come*," and because it seems strange to speak of a lamp "coming," the verb is translated here **bring**. But it is possible that Mark's wording is intended to be an allusion to Jesus as "the lamp" who "comes," now somewhat covered, but one day to be manifested openly. The actual lamp used as a figure here was a small clay lamp that burned olive oil. It was an item only a few inches high and so was usually placed on a stand to cast its light far enough to be useful.

Under a bowl or under the bed: The word translated here **bowl** really refers to a basket measure that contained about a peck. The **bed** here is very likely a couch on which people reclined during banquets after a style of dining introduced by the Greeks.

4:24 / **The same rules . . . to judge you**: Literally, the Greek text reads "With what measure you measure, it shall be measured to you." As indicated above, the context shows that this saying, somewhat in the form of a riddle, is a warning about being careful in responding to Jesus' message properly, for there will be consequences. The same saying appears in Matt. 7:1, but the context indicates a different application there (see also Luke 6:37–38).

4:31–32 / **The smallest seed . . . biggest of all plants**: The mustard seed was frequently referred to by ancient Jews as the proverbial picture of smallness. There are in fact smaller seeds in the world, but that is irrelevant, in that Jesus' words here are not botanical conclusions but the reflection of popular speech. The term **plants** here means mainly cultivated plants, such as vegetables, and the Greek word does not include a reference to trees.

The birds come and make their nests: The words are drawn from OT passages (see Ezek. 17:23; 31:6; Dan. 4:12). There, great nations are described as large trees, and the nesting of birds in the branches is a symbol of the formation of imperial control over many peoples. Because of this OT imagery, some have suggested that the **birds** here refers to the inclusion of many nations into the future of the Kingdom of God. That is, the parable may be taken as an allusion to the worldwide mission and growth of the Gospel.

8

Power over Sea and Spirits

MARK 4:35–5:20

On the evening of that same day Jesus said to his disciples, "Let us go across to the other side of the lake." ³⁶So they left the crowd; the disciples got into the boat in which Jesus was already sitting, and they took him with them. Other boats were there too. ³⁷Suddenly a strong wind blew up, and the waves began to spill over into the boat, so that it was about to fill with water. ³⁸Jesus was in the back of the boat, sleeping with his head on a pillow. The disciples woke him up and said, "Teacher, don't you care that we are about to die?"

³⁹Jesus stood up and commanded the wind, "Be quiet!" and he said to the waves, "Be still!" The wind died down, and there was a great calm. ⁴⁰Then Jesus said to his disciples, "Why are you frightened? Do you still have no faith?"

⁴¹But they were terribly afraid and began to say to one another, "Who is this man? Even the wind and the waves obey him!"

¹Jesus and his disciples arrived on the other side of Lake Galilee, in the territory of Gerasa. ²As soon as Jesus got out of the boat, he was met by a man who came out of the burial caves there. This man had an evil spirit in him ³and lived among the tombs. Nobody could keep him tied with chains any more; ⁴many times his feet and hands had been tied, but every time he broke the chains and smashed the irons on his feet. He was too strong for anyone to control him. ⁵Day and night he wandered among the tombs and through the hills, screaming and cutting himself with stones.

⁶He was some distance away when he saw Jesus; so he ran, fell on his knees before him, ⁷and screamed in a loud voice, "Jesus, Son of the Most High God! What do you want with me? For God's sake, I beg you, don't punish me!" (⁸He said this because Jesus was saying, "Evil spirit, come out of this man!")

⁹So Jesus asked him, "What is your name?"

The man answered, "My name is 'Mob'—there are so many of us!" ¹⁰And he kept begging Jesus not to send the evil spirits out of that region.

¹¹There was a large herd of pigs near by, feeding on a hillside. ¹²So the spirits begged Jesus, "Send us to the pigs, and let us go into them." ¹³He let them go, and the evil spirits went out of the man and entered the pigs. The whole herd—about two thousand pigs in all—rushed down the side of the cliff into the lake and was drowned.

¹⁴The men who had been taking care of the pigs ran away and spread the news in the town and among the farms. People went out to see what had happened, ¹⁵and when they came to Jesus, they saw the man who used to have the mob of demons in him. He was sitting there, clothed and in his right mind; and they were all afraid. ¹⁶Those who had seen it told the people what had happened to the man with the demons, and about the pigs. ¹⁷So they asked Jesus to leave their

territory.
[18]As Jesus was getting into the boat, the man who had had the demons begged him, "Let me go with you!" [19]But Jesus would not let him. Instead, he told him, "Go back home to your family and tell them how much the Lord has done for you and how kind he has been to you." [20]So the man left and went all through the Ten Towns, telling what Jesus had done for him. And all who heard it were amazed.

4:35–41 / After the selection of parables comes this story of Jesus' power over the wind and waves. The change from relatively calm teaching discourse to a violent storm and the display of Jesus' awesome authority over the forces of nature is intended to jolt the reader with a reminder that Jesus is more than a religious teacher. The parables are veiled discourse, and Jesus has spoken of the presence of the Kingdom of God in him as still something of a "secret" (4:11), "hidden" and "covered" (4:22). In this story something of the true significance of Jesus flashes forth momentarily, foreshadowing briefly the full light to come.

This incident also illustrates that the disciples, though given "the secret of the Kingdom of God," have their own problems in perceiving Jesus clearly. Their astonished questioning (4:41), **Who is this man?** seems to echo the crowd's bewilderment in 1:27 and is to be seen alongside the places where Jesus' critics raise questions about him as well (e.g., 2:7, 3:22). This theme, "Who is he?" is perhaps Mark's major concern throughout his book. Only God and the demons know the truth until Jesus' crucifixion and resurrection. Even the disciples, who see his power firsthand, cannot arrive at the full truth till then.

Mark intends to tell the story so that his readers see what the disciples did not. Jesus' actions and the language used to describe them seem pretty clearly to be allusions to OT passages where God's power over the sea is portrayed (e.g., Pss. 65:7; 89:9; 106:9; 107:23–32). The point of these allusions is to say that Jesus acts in divine power and authority. Indeed, he acts as God himself is described! Most of these OT references describe God's deliverance of Israel at the Red Sea in poetic language, picturing God as commanding the sea (e.g., Ps. 106:9) as if it were alive. Jesus here does the same (4:39), and the point is to hint that Jesus' presence is an event so significant that it is to be understood as a new "Exodus," a new salvation and reconstitution of the people of God.

Looking ahead, we should note that this incident is the first of another string of miracle stories extending through 5:43 and followed by the rejection of Jesus at Nazareth (6:1–6). In these miracle stories, Jesus successively deals with the powers of nature (4:35–43), the demonic (5:1–20), illness (5:21–34), and death (5:35–43). Each story, like the present one, is intended to reveal something of Jesus to the readers, so that the rejection in 6:1–6 is seen as all the more tragic.

We should also note that this is one of two sea miracles in Mark, the second found in 6:45–52. It likewise ends with the disciples pictured as failing to see what it really means.

5:1-20 / Mark's stories of Jesus' works are intended not only to tell something of what Jesus did but also to dramatize or symbolize important points. That is, to read these stories the way Mark intended, we must look for what they suggest as symbols, and this involves reading the accounts carefully, with an eye for detail. The present story particularly seems intended to symbolize important truths, and it repays close attention.

The first thing to notice is where this event takes place. Though there is some variation in the Gospel accounts and in ancient manuscripts as to the name of the town (called Gerasa here in 5:1, but see note), it is clear that the story is set on the eastern shore of Lake Galilee in an area called **the Ten Towns** (5:20, and note). The significance of this location is that this area was inhabited and controlled mainly by Gentiles in Jesus' time. So, for one of a very few times in Mark, Jesus is shown leaving the borders of his own country and ministering to non-Jews (see also 7:24–30). In view of the fact that Jesus says later in Mark that the Gospel is to be preached to all nations (13:10; 14:9), Mark's point here is at least partly to show Jesus laying down a precedent in going out of Jewish areas to a gentile territory.

A number of other factors fit this observation and corroborate it. The references to herds of pigs (5:11–13) suggests gentile territory, for the pig is a forbidden food in the OT Law observed by ancient Jews (Lev. 11:1–8). Also, the name by which the demoniac refers to God (5:7), **the Most High God**, is used in OT accounts where non-Jews speak of God (e.g., Gen. 14:17–24; Num. 24:16), where the God of Israel is spoken of in a gentile context (as in Dan. 4:17; 7:18, 22, 25, 27), and where the God of Israel is contrasted with the gods of other nations (e.g., Ps. 97:9). (The GNB translation of these various passages uses a variety of English terms, but it is the same Hebrew term, the equivalent of the Greek term used here in Mark.)

Another item in the account is clearer when we assume a gentile setting. After being set free from the evil spirits, the former demoniac is told to go tell **how much the Lord has done for you** (5:19). This contrasts with the characteristic command to silence given by Jesus encountered at various points in Mark (e.g., 1:43–44; 5:43; 7:36). These commands to silence, however, are all to Jews. This man, a Gentile in a gentile area, is allowed to spread the word about Jesus, and Mark no doubt intended this to be seen as a foretaste of the mission of the church to the nations, proclaiming the gospel.

The story is told with a lot of detail, and this suggests that Mark intended his readers to ponder the account and to see what is symbolized in it. The man is so described as to make him both a full captive to the powers of evil and beyond any human help (5:2–4). Further, his dwelling among the tombs, the "dwelling" of the dead, almost makes him like a zombie, a living dead-man. Finally, he is self-destructive (5:5) and obviously in torment. All of this looks like a powerful picture of how the NT describes the condition of humans apart from Christ: Spiritually dead and in bondage to evil (e.g., Eph. 2:1–3)

Of course the helpless condition of the man and the powerful grip of the demons are also intended to show the extent of Jesus' power and authority. The eerie conversation between Jesus and the demons, who say that they are many (5:9; see note), and the strange account of the destruction of the herd of pigs are intended only to show what a powerful force Jesus was up against. We simply have to set aside the questions these features of the story provoke, particularly for modern readers, and take them as intended by Mark, as features that demonstrate all the more the magnitude of Jesus' authority.

The cry of the demons at Jesus' approach, hailing him as Son of God, is intended to answer the frightened question of the disciples in 4:41, "Who is this man?" It is an example of a point Mark makes several times—though the human characters do not know what to make of Jesus, both God's voice and the demons tell the reader the answer (cf. 1:11, 24, 34; 3:11; 9:7). Notice also how 5:19–20 links Jesus with **the Lord** giving divine significance to him.

The remaining feature of the story that must be treated is the response of the crowd in 5:14–17. In 5:14, the people come **to see what had happened**. First, Mark describes the man in some detail. Clothed, in his right mind, the man is a powerful testimony of a momentous event (5:15). Then Mark mentions how the witnesses described the deliverance, and almost off the cuff, Mark writes, **and about the pigs** (5:16). Clearly, in view of the wonderful deliverance of the man, the destruction of the pigs is intended by Mark as insignificant except as an indication of the destructive power overcome by Jesus. But (and here Mark's penchant for irony emerges again) the people seem to be more bothered by the loss of the pigs than happy over the reclaiming of the man, and they ask Jesus to go (5:17). So, the crowd, which went out **to see what had happened**, saw only the loss of some property—only dead pigs, not the living miracle before them—and not the significance of Jesus shown in the miracle. This lack of perception on the part of the crowd is reflected also in the way Mark describes the response of people to the former demoniac's proclamation of Jesus' deed (5:20). As noted already (see comments on 1:22–27 and 2:12), Mark characteristically describes the response of people to Jesus' ministry as amazement. But, though this term connotes the powerful impression made by Jesus' ministry, it is Mark's way of describing a response that is considerably short of genuine faith and insight into Jesus' person (see note).

Finally, we should note that this story may be linked with the two that immediately follow (5:21–43), in that in all three Jesus ministers to people who are in varying ways religiously "unclean." The man here is likely a Gentile and lived among the tombs, both things making him unclean. In the next story, Jesus is touched by a woman suffering from some sort of disorder of her female organs involving a bloody discharge, an unclean condition according to Jewish religious teaching. Finally, Jesus raises, and touches, a dead girl. Dead bodies also were unclean and rendered whomever touched them unclean. In all these cases of the "unclean," Jesus is shown in triumph, liberating the people from their conditions.

Additional Notes

4:35 / **Evening**: This sort of detail, such as the references to **other boats** (4:36) and the **pillow** (4:38), are possibly simply the remnants of the firsthand version of the story. Otherwise it is hard to see why they are mentioned. They do not seem to have any symbolical significance.

4:37 / **Suddenly a strong wind**: Lake Galilee is known for the sudden storms that swirl its waters. These arise because it lies in a deep basin with hills all around it, causing severe wind patterns on its surface.

4:39 / **Be Still!**: Literally, this verb means "Be muzzled!" portraying the sea as a kind of animal or perhaps demonic force that is here subdued, recognizing its master.

4:40 / **Do you still have no faith?**: This is another instance in which Mark's emphasis upon faith appears (cf. 2:5; 5:34; 10:52; 11:22; also 5:36; 9:23). Compare Luke 8:25 ("Where is your faith?") and Matt. 8:26 ("What little faith you have!").

5:1 / **Gerasa**: The ancient manuscripts of the Gospels show variations on the place named, not only here, but also in the parallel accounts in Matt. 8:28 and Luke 8:26. The name given here refers to one of the towns of the area, and the variations involve other sites in the same area. The other sites mentioned in the manuscripts as variants are Gadara and Gergesa. The area was called Decapolis, meaning "Ten Cities" or "Ten Towns" (see 5:20).

5:2 / **This man**: Cf. Matt. 8:28, which mentions two demoniacs. Similarly, Matt. 20:30 has two blind men, though Mark 10:46 mentions only Bartimaeus.

5:9 / **Mob**: Literally, the name is "Legion," a term referring to a unit of Roman soldiers about six thousand strong. The term *Legion* also has the effect of making the scene like a battle between the powers of evil and Jesus, who comes in the name of the Kingdom of God. This imagery is likely intentional, for already Jesus has described his exorcisms as assaults upon Satan's strongholds (see 3:23–27).

5:20 / **The Ten Towns**: a large area to the south and east of Lake Galilee featuring ten cities that formed a league for trade and defense about A.D. 1. This area was mainly Gentile in population. (See "Decapolis," *IDB*, vol. 1, pp. 810–12.)

All who heard it were amazed: Mark characteristically describes the response of people as amazement or surprise (1:22–27; 2:12; 5:42; 7:37; 9:15; 12:17), but this does not connote full understanding or acceptance of Jesus. Even those who reject Jesus are described as amazed at him (Nazareth, 6:2–4; Pilate, 15:5, 44). The fact that the disciples too are amazed says little in their favor (6:51), likening their failure to perceive Jesus properly to the failure of the crowds!

9

Jesus Sought and Rejected

MARK 5:21–6:6a

Jesus went back across to the other side of the lake. There at the lakeside a large crowd gathered round him. [22]Jairus, an official of the local synagogue, arrived, and when he saw Jesus, he threw himself down at his feet [23]and begged him earnestly, "My little daughter is very ill. Please come and place your hands on her, so that she will get well and live!"

[24]Then Jesus started off with him. So many people were going along with Jesus that they were crowding him from every side.

[25]There was a woman who had suffered terribly from severe bleeding for twelve years, [26]even though she had been treated by many doctors. She had spent all her money, but instead of getting better she got worse all the time. [27]She had heard about Jesus, so she came in the crowd behind him, [28]saying to herself, "If I just touch his clothes, I will get well."

[29]She touched his cloak, and her bleeding stopped at once; and she had the feeling inside herself that she was healed of her trouble. [30]At once Jesus knew that power had gone out of him, so he turned around in the crowd and asked, "Who touched my clothes?"

[31]His disciples answered, "You see how the people are crowding you; why do you ask who touched you?"

[32]But Jesus kept looking around to see who had done it. [33]The woman realized what had happened to her, so she came, trembling with fear, knelt at his feet, and told him the whole truth. [34]Jesus said to her, "My daughter, your faith has made you well. Go in peace, and be healed of your trouble."

[35]While Jesus was saying this, some messengers came from Jairus' house and told him, "Your daughter has died. Why bother the Teacher any longer?"

[36]Jesus paid no attention to what they said, but told him, "Don't be afraid, only believe." [37]Then he did not let anyone else go on with him except Peter and James and his brother John. [38]They arrived at Jairus' house, where Jesus saw the confusion and heard all the loud crying and wailing. [39]He went in and said to them, "Why all this confusion? Why are you crying? The child is not dead—she is only sleeping!"

[40]They started making fun of him, so he put them all out, took the child's father and mother and his three disciples, and went into the room where the child was lying. [41]He took her by the hand and said to her, "Talitha, koum," which means, "Little girl, I tell you to get up!"

[42]She got up at once and started walking around. (She was twelve years old.) When this happened, they were completely amazed. [43]But Jesus gave them strict orders not to tell anyone, and he said, "Give her something to eat."

[1]Jesus left that place and went back to his home town, followed by his disciples. [2]On the Sabbath he began to teach in the synagogue. Many people were there; and when they heard him,

they were all amazed. "Where did he get all this?" they asked. "What wisdom is this that has been given him? How does he perform miracles? [3]Isn't he the carpenter, the son of Mary, and the brother of James, Joseph, Judas, and Simon? Aren't his sisters living here?" And so they rejected him.

[4]Jesus said to them, "A prophet is respected everywhere except in his own home town and by his relatives and his family."

[5]He was not able to perform any miracles there, except that he placed his hands on a few sick people and healed them. [6]He was greatly surprised, because the people did not have faith.

g. paid no attention to; or overheard.

5:21–43 / This passage presents us with the second clear instance in which Mark sandwiches together two incidents into one composite story (see earlier 3:20–35). Mark seems to do this because in each case he intends the two parts of the composite account to be understood in connection with each other, and this seems to be the case here. That these two incidents may have happened in connection with each other as described here in Mark is not necessarily challenged. But, since it is evident that Mark does not tell us everything Jesus did, it is always important to inquire why he recorded what he did in the way he did.

Some of the connections between the two incidents in the present account are obvious ones. For one thing, both incidents involve Jesus ministering to females: one, a grown woman, the other, a young girl. Also, both are in desperate, helpless states. The one is apparently incurably ill, and the other is first terminally ill and then dead. Another device that links the two incidents is the number twelve. The woman has a twelve-year ailment (v. 25) and the girl is twelve years old (v. 42).

The point of linking these two stories includes the "double-barreled" impact they make together in showing the compassionate power of Jesus. Perhaps especially in ancient settings, where women were regarded as less important than men, Jesus' interest in the welfare of these two needy females must be seen as very significant. Like the (probably gentile) demoniac in the previous passage, the women in this account represent social groups regarded as second-class by many in ancient times.

In addition, both events here emphasize faith, and this seems to be one of Mark's concerns in narrating them. Note that the woman thinks, somewhat superstitiously, that merely touching the clothes of such a holy man and healer as Jesus will bring the cure to her illness. Though the story first seems to confirm this idea, in that she is healed upon touching Jesus, the point of Jesus stopping and conversing with her (5:30–34) is to emphasize that it was her **faith** that made her whole. That is, the woman was healed because she put faith in *Jesus* and his power, *not* because the touch of a holy man automatically cures. Similarly, the father of the girl begs Jesus to *touch* her (v. 23), but Jesus emphasizes faith (v. 36) as the key to her rescue. This emphasis on faith is in fact found elsewhere in Mark (e.g., 4:40; 6:6; 10:52; 11:22–25), making it a prominent Markan theme. Mark presents Jesus' exercise of miraculous powers in the strongest way (cf. 6:53–56), but not for the purpose of encouraging crude, magical interpretations of Jesus. Rather, his maximal descriptions of Jesus' power are designed to indicate that Jesus is not just a teacher or a prophet. His presentation of Jesus' wondrous power is tied to his emphasis on the *person* of Jesus and does not reflect an intention to promote an interest in magical powers and practices.

As a matter of fact, his description of the raising of the dead girl seems designed to reject any idea of magical technique. He seems to create a note of mystery by saying that only the parents and three of the disciples were allowed into the room where the miracle was performed. He appears to compound this impression by giving the actual Aramaic words Jesus used, such foreign words sounding a bit like a magic formula; but then he dissolves this magical atmosphere by translating the "formula," (something not to be done in magic circles!). The translation makes it clear that this is no incantation or solemn formula but a simple order tinged with affection, **Little girl, I tell you to get up!** (see note). The command to silence (v. 43) is of course not an indication of secret, magical practices but is only another example of the secrecy theme in Mark that is connected with the larger Markan emphasis that only after his crucifixion and resurrection is it possible to make people see both who Jesus really is and the significance of what he did.

Both of these incidents happen in Jewish territory. The little girl is the daughter of a leader of a synagogue, and 5:21 tells us that Jesus has returned from the eastern shore of Lake Galilee, the gentile area where the demoniac was cured. These two incidents are followed by the rejection of Jesus in Nazareth, his home town, and they seem to prepare the reader to view that rejection as all the more unwarranted. But these miracles, together with the rejection, also seem to be symbolic prefigurations of the final rejection of Jesus, culminating in the trial and crucifixion. Is it insignificant that the woman had a *twelve*-year ailment, and that this number has a long biblical significance as symbolizing Israel? And the girl, the *twelve*-year-old daughter of a synagogue leader, is doubly linked with Israel. In other words, the sequence of miracles among those identified with Israel, followed by rejection by his own village, is probably intended to strike the informed reader as a glimpse of the overall outcome of Jesus' ministry to Israel.

Even the nature of the miracles is significant. The woman, who according to Israelite religious law was regarded as unclean and socially unacceptable in her medical condition (see note), is delivered from her helpless estate under the Law. And, though Jewish ritual requirements forbade her to touch any holy thing, she is delivered precisely by touching Jesus, the Son of God! Could this be intended by Mark as a dramatization of the emphasis that Jesus' ministry involved a transcending of the ritual definitions of clean and holy (e.g., 2:13–28; 7:1–23)? It is probably significant also that the other miracle is the raising of a dead person, for it no doubt is intended as an anticipation of Jesus' own resurrection. The sequence from 5:21–6:6, then, is another example of Markan irony. Although Jesus performs works that intimate his real nature and power, they result in rejection.

6:1–6a / Although it is not explicitly stated here that this episode took place in Nazareth, the description of the setting as **his home town** (6:1, or "his home area"), plus the mention of his family as living there (6:3), make it virtually certain that Nazareth is the intended location. But this story is not just the account of the rejection of Jesus in his home town, it is also intended as a symbol and portent of his rejection in Jerusalem by the leaders of the Jewish people. As noted earlier, this episode can be seen as concluding a section that may include everything from 3:7 to 6:6. In 3:1–6 we encountered the first clear rejection of Jesus, with a hint of a coming clash (3:6). Here again, there is a rejection of him on the Sabbath in a synagogue (cf. 3:1–2; 6:1–2). In the former case the issue was healing on the Sabbath. Here it is a matter of an inability to believe that this "home town boy" is anything special. But both incidents are really, from Mark's viewpoint, examples of an unwillingness to recognize Jesus as the heaven-sent envoy of salvation.

The material between 3:1–6 and the present episode in 6:1–6 describes various aspects of Jesus' ministry: a general account (3:7–12), the selection of the Twelve (3:13–19), the conflict with critics and family (3:20–35), parables (4:1–34), and a series of miracles that also serve as revelations of his significance (4:35–5:43). In the face of this narrative the present rejection is to be seen as indefensible and tragic.

This scene contains several themes already discovered in Mark. Jesus is shown as causing astonishment by his teaching and other deeds (6:2). Nevertheless, this astonishment does not mean insight or faith but something considerably less (6:3–6). Jesus does not respond to criticism by a direct disclosure of his person but rather in an indirect manner, by means of a proverblike statement (6:4). There is the emphasis on the importance of faith (6:6). There is also a second reference to Jesus' family, which appears to describe them again as opposing Jesus (see also 3:20–21, 31–35).

The reference to Jesus' family by the townspeople (6:3) could imply that his relatives were contributing to the reluctance to recognize him as divinely sent. This seems confirmed by the fact that **relatives** and **family** are included in the proverbial statement of Jesus in 6:4. This description of Jesus' family in negative terms is probably intended to show that the proper recognition of Jesus was no easier for his own countrymen, or even his own relatives, than for others, because the recognition evidenced in true faith is not based on proximity to Jesus in time or on kinship but upon a moral willingness to consent to God's revelation, a consent to some degree made possible by God's action upon the individual.

The two features of Jesus' ministry that cause amazement are his **wisdom** and **miracles** (6:2), and these require further comment. The term **wisdom** has a rich heritage in ancient civilizations and does not just mean "horse sense," as it tends to mean in common English usage. Rather, in the Jewish background of Jesus, **wisdom** connoted knowledge of God and his purposes, and so had to do specifically with religious teaching, though this religious teaching might address almost any question of human life. To portray Jesus as a teacher of **wisdom** in 6:2 is to describe him as one perceived as giving revelation of God. The response of the crowd implies clearly that they are unwilling to take Jesus' impressive teaching as evidence of his momentous significance. They are unable to get past his humble and familiar origins among them.

Furthermore, even the miracles that Jesus does do not produce faith. The crowd acknowledges that he performs such deeds but seems unable to fathom what his miracles signify about him. Mark's phrasing is difficult to follow, for in 6:2 the crowd refers to Jesus' miracles, and yet in 6:5–6 we are told that Jesus was unable **to perform any miracles there, except that he placed his hands on a few sick people and healed them.** The questions come tumbling forth. If Jesus did no miracle in Nazareth, to what miracles does the crowd refer in 6:2? Is not the healing of **a few sick people** by his touch precisely the sort of thing that seems to be regarded as a miracle elsewhere in Mark (cf. 5:23, 28)? What then does Mark mean by saying that Jesus could do no miracle here? However awkward Mark's phrasing seems to us, his intent was probably to say that just as faith has positive effects when present (e.g. 5:34, 36), so the absence of faith hinders the manifestation of God's saving power. That is, Mark wanted to portray the lack of faith in Nazareth in very negative terms, to contrast with the commendation of faith in 5:32. It is not really his purpose to say that a lack of faith completely ties God's hands but rather to indicate that receptivity to God, faith, is rewarded by God's miraculous power, and that there are opposite consequences in the absence of such receptivity. (See comments on 5:21–43.)

It is interesting that Jesus likens himself to a prophet in 6:4, for this is one of the labels given by observers, according to Mark (cf. 6:14–16; 8:27–30). There is no good reason to doubt that Jesus did liken himself to a prophet, though Mark wishes to emphasize that this label, though not entirely wrong, is inadequate.

As mentioned in discussing 5:21–43, the rejection here seems intended as a foreshadowing of the rejection of Jesus by the Jewish leaders that culminates in his crucifixion. In other words, this rejection by his own town and family prefigures the rejection by the larger circle of his own people, his nation.

Additional Notes

5:22 / **An official of the local synagogue**: In Jesus' time synagogues were led by a small group of laymen responsible for the conduct of services and the observance of Jewish religious law in their synagogue. The officials were chosen locally by the members of the synagogue.

5:25 / **Severe bleeding**: Though it is not stated explicitly, it is very likely that her problem was a hemorrhage from her womb. Such a problem, according to OT law, renders a woman unclean, and anyone or anything she touches is likewise religiously contaminated (Lev. 15:25–30). There is elaborate discussion of this sort of condition and possible treatment in the Jewish Talmud, the collection of ancient rabbinic teaching.

5:26 / **Treated by many doctors**: The translation frankly obscures what Mark says. The statement actually reads "she *suffered* much from many doctors," and records of the treatments prescribed for such conditions illustrate that this is a fair statement. The treatments prescribed often involved drinking vile-tasting mixtures and doing other such things, many of them even more strange and none of them likely to do any good, judged by modern medical knowledge. (See Lane, pp. 191–92.)

5:28 / **If I just touch his clothes** reflects what may have been a common kind of desperate hope, for there are other references in the NT and in non-Christian sources to such ideas and customs (e.g., 6:56; Acts 5:15; 19:11–12). These NT accounts do not deny that cures sometimes happened, but they also emphasize that such cures must be interpreted in the context of personal faith in Jesus, not merely magical superstition. The parallel accounts in Matt. 9:20 and Luke 8:44 refer to the "edge" of Jesus' clothes, meaning probably the fringe or tassels worn at the corner of clothes by ancient Jews as symbols of their dedication to God.

5:37 / **Peter and James and his brother John** seem to be presented as a kind of inner circle among Jesus' disciples (see also 9:2; 13:3; 14:33).

5:39 / **The child is not dead**: Jesus' words are probably intended figuratively, implying that all is not lost and that this dead child can be "awakened" again to life. There is a similar figurative expression attributed to Jesus concerning Lazarus in John 11:11–15.

5:41 / **Talitha koum** is an Aramaic phrase (the everyday language of Jewish Palestine in Jesus' time) and literally means "Arise, lamb," reflecting affection and tenderness.

6:1 / **His home town** is literally "his own area/country," but in the context probably refers to Nazareth. In 1:9, we were informed that Nazareth was his home town, and in 1:24; 10:47, 67; 16:6 he is called "Jesus of Nazareth."

6:3 / **The carpenter**: The Greek word used here can mean a worker in wood or in stone, according to ancient sources. In Matt. 13:55, Jesus is called the carpenter's son, suggesting that Jesus took up his trade from Joseph, his father. Jesus did not begin his ministry, of course, until young adulthood, and so must have supported himself (and his relatives?) by his trade for some years before taking up his ministry.

The son of Mary: It was very unusual to refer to someone as the son of their *mother* in ancient Jewish times. It has been suggested many times that this expression may have been a slur upon the legitimacy of his birth used by people of his home town. It is possible that this slur might have resulted if, as Matt. 1:18–25 indicates, it became known that Mary had become pregnant before her marriage to Joseph. Though Christian tradition attributes this to a miraculous act of God, in ancient Jewish tradition Jesus is apparently referred to as an illegitimate child. Both traditions agree that there was something irregular about his conception. In the Matt. 13:55 parallel, this phrase **son of Mary** does not appear, and instead we read the less offensive phrase, "isn't Mary his mother?"

James, Joseph, Judas, and Simon . . . his sisters: This passage and its parallel in Matt. 13:55–56 give us the most detailed information on the identity of Jesus' family. According to Roman Catholic and Eastern Orthodox traditions, Mary had no other children and so the individuals mentioned here are explained other than as full brothers and sisters (see note on 3:31). James, Jesus' brother, is mentioned as a leader in the early church elsewhere in the NT (1 Cor. 15:7; Gal. 1:19; 2:9–12; Acts 12:17; 15:13; 21:18), and a letter in the NT bears his name (James 1:1). In Christian tradition of the second century and later, this James acquired a legendary significance as a very devout man of strict religious self-discipline. The other brothers and sisters of Jesus are not referred to elsewhere in the NT. (On James, the brother of Jesus, see *IDB*, vol. 2, pp. 791–94.)

6:5 / **Not able to perform any miracles**: This phrase, which seems in conflict with the rest of the sentence, appears somewhat differently in the Matt. 13:58 parallel—"he did not perform many miracles there." This phrasing smooths out the difficulty in the Markan phrase and is one of several places where Matthew seems "tidier" in phrasing the same incident as found in Mark. This is the sort of evidence that prompts most scholars to believe that the writer of Matthew wrote after Mark and used Mark's Gospel as a source, making numerous editorial changes like this one.

10

The Mission and Herod

MARK 6:6b–29

Then Jesus went to the villages around there, teaching the people. [6b]He called the twelve disciples together and sent them out two by two. He gave them authority over the evil spirits [8]and ordered them, "Don't take anything with you on your journey except a stick—no bread, no beggar's bag, no money in your pockets. [9]Wear sandals, but don't carry an extra shirt." [10]He also told them, "Wherever you are welcomed, stay in the same house until you leave that place. [11]If you come to a town where people do not welcome you or will not listen to you, leave it and shake the dust off your feet. That will be a warning to them!"

[12]So they went out and preached that people should turn away from their sins. [13]They drove out many demons, and rubbed olive oil on many sick people and healed them.

[14]Now King Herod[h] heard about all this, because Jesus' reputation had spread everywhere. Some people were saying, "John the Baptist has come back to life! That is why he has this power to perform miracles."

[15]Others, however, said, "He is Elijah."

Others said, "He is a prophet, like one of the prophets of long ago."

[16]When Herod heard it, he said, "He is John the Baptist! I had his head cut off, but he has come back to life!" [17]Herod himself had ordered John's arrest, and he had him tied up and put in prison. Herod did this because of Herodias, whom he had married, even though she was the wife of his brother Philip. [18]John the Baptist kept telling Herod, "It isn't right for you to be married to your brother's wife!"

[19]So Herodias held a grudge against John and wanted to kill him, but she could not because of Herod. [20]Herod was afraid of John because he knew that John was a good and holy man, and so he kept him safe. He liked to listen to him, even though he became greatly disturbed every time he heard him.

[21]Finally Herodias got her chance. It was on Herod's birthday, when he gave a feast for all the chief government officials, the military commanders, and the leading citizens of Galilee. [22]The daughter of Herodias[i] came in and danced, and pleased Herod and his guests. So the king said to the girl, "What would you like to have? I will give you anything you want." [23]With many vows he said to her, "I swear that I wil give you anything you ask for, even as much as half my kingdom!"

[24]So the girl went out and asked her mother, "What shall I ask for?"

"The head of John the Baptist," she answered.

[25]The girl hurried back at once to the king and demanded, "I want you to give me here and now the head of John the Baptist on a plate!"

[26]This made the king very sad, but he could not refuse her because of the vows he had made in front of all his guests. [27]So he sent off a guard at once with orders to bring John's head. The

guard left, went to the prison, and cut John's head off; ²⁸then he brought it on a plate and gave it to the girl, who gave it to her mother. ²⁹When John's disciples heard about this, they came and took away his body, and buried it.

h. KING HEROD: *Herod Antipas, ruler of Galilee.*
i. The daughter of Herodias; *some manuscripts have* His daughter Herodias.

6:6b–13 / Just as the first rejection in the synagogue (3:1–6) is followed by ministry to a wide assortment of people (3:7–12) and by the empowering of the Twelve (3:13–19), so here, after the second rejection, Mark gives us an account of the empowering of the Twelve, who conduct an itinerant ministry in extension of Jesus' own work. Here again (6:7) as before (3:15), the disciples are given **authority** over evil spirits; and by this term, so important in Mark's description of Jesus (1:22, 27; 2:10; 11:27–33), we are to understand that the Twelve are actually given an extension of Jesus' own power and ministry. This is another instance of the way that the disciples, so plainly described as failing in other places in the narrative, are also described in very positive terms as intimately associated with Jesus in his work. Any reading of Mark must do justice to *both* aspects of the way the disciples are treated (a rule not always observed in some recent studies), for only then do the disciples serve their intended narrative role for the readers as example and warning.

In the instructions given to the Twelve the intent is basically to make them dependent upon the hospitality of those to whom they preach. They were to carry no provisions (**no bread, no beggar's bag, no money**), and the prohibition against two garments (**an extra shirt**) probably refers to the outer garment, a cloak, commonly used as a bedroll in ancient times by poor people, shepherds, and those who had no lodging for the night (see note). For both food and shelter, they were utterly dependent on others. When provided with accommodation (6:10), they were to accept it and were not to move to better quarters if offered them by more prosperous members of the village, this to show that the disciples were not to be lured by what people could provide. If rejected in a village, they were to perform a symbolic act of warning, ridding their sandals of the dust of the town to prefigure God's rejection of the town for its disobedience.

The attire of the disciples in Mark is a little different from the directions given in the parallel in Matt. 10:9, in which even the staff and sandals are forbidden. This difference between the two passages has generated much discussion but no agreed-upon solution (see Lane, pp. 207–8). It is interesting to note that the description of the disciples in 6:8–9, mentioning sandals and staff, may be intended to allude to the accounts of the Israelite flight from Egypt (Exod. 12:11), thus perhaps likening the disciples' ministry to the Exodus. If we are to see in the story of Herod that follows (6:14–29) a wicked king like Pharaoh in the Exodus story, it may be all the more likely that Mark here has used Exodus imagery in describing the mission of the Twelve.

This brings us to the observation that this story of the Twelve is interrupted by the account of the death of John the Baptist in 6:14–29 and ends only in 6:30, providing us with one of the examples of Mark's narrative technique of sandwiching two stories together. In such cases, the two stories are to be seen as each casting light on the meaning of the other. This account of the ministry of the Twelve helps to explain how Jesus' reputation came to the ear of Herod and describes the self-denial and dedication of the Twelve, engaged in a holy mission, in powerful contrast with the opulence and indulgent wickedness that appears in the following account of Herod's court. Conversely, the Herod story seems intended to hint that the ministry of the Twelve and Jesus is to involve conflict and ultimately the death of Jesus, prefigured in John's death.

6:14–29 / It is striking that so much space is devoted to the death of John the Baptist in Mark, more space than in any of the other Gospels (cf. Matt. 14:1–12; Luke 3:19–20; 9:7–9). This suggests that this episode had a special significance for Mark, as we shall see, prefiguring the death of Jesus. We must remember that at several points in Mark, Jesus and John are closely connected. Jesus begins his ministry after John's arrest (1:14), and Jesus links the message of John with his own ministry in 11:27–33. Further, it appears likely that the Elijah figure Jesus speaks of in 9:10–13 is in fact John the Baptist, and in this last passage the fate of this "Elijah" is linked with the fate of the "Son of Man," Jesus. Indeed, 9:10–13 is to be taken as the commentary on 6:14–29.

The likening of John the Baptist to Elijah helps to explain the way John's death is narrated in Mark. Herod, who both fears John and resents him, is made to resemble Ahab, the king of Israel, in his attitude toward Elijah; Herodias, who schemes to kill John, resembles Jezebel, Ahab's wife, who had a special hatred for Eijah (see 1 Kings 16:29–19:3; 21:1–29, and the historical notes on the figures in the present story). Thus, several characteristics of Mark's account are intended to help the reader see that John is the prophet like Elijah predicted in Malachi 4:5.

But Mark not only holds that John is the "Elijah" who heralds the appearance of the Messiah (Jesus), he also makes the death of John the foreshadowing of Jesus' death. Like Jesus, John is executed by the civil power. Like Pilate, Herod hesitates to harm his prisoner but finally does so for fear of the consequences if he does not. Like the chief priests who demand and engineer Jesus' death, Herodias finally gets her will with John. Like Joseph of Arimathea, the followers of John bury their leader. This connection of John's execution to Jesus' is no doubt the reason Mark has placed this story here in the midst of the account of the disciples' mission, for he intends his readers to remember that the ministry of Jesus and his disciples has to be seen in connection with Jesus' execution; and by this account he again casts the shadow of Jesus' cross over his narrative. For Mark, it is not finally the power of the miracles but the sacrifice of the cross that most clearly discloses Jesus' significance.

The account of John's death opens with a reference to various popular opinions about Jesus (6:14–15), and these are the same ones mentioned in the dialogue between Jesus and the Twelve (in 8:27–28) about who he really is. Now of course all three opinions are wrong in Mark's view; yet he cites them to show, not only that people were blind to Jesus' true significance, but also that the people did recognize in Jesus some sort of special significance like that of the OT prophets. The notion that Jesus was John the Baptist risen from the dead (v. 14) may have been meant literally or figuratively, but in either case what is indicated is that Jesus seemed to be proclaiming the same message of the coming Kingdom of God as John did, with prophetic urgency, only with additional power, as exhibited in the miracles. Mark, with his taste for irony, may have intended his readers to note how ironic this view of Jesus as the resurrected John the Baptist is in the light of the resurrection of Jesus himself later in the narrative.

The significance of calling Jesus Elijah is to be found in the light of ancient Jewish expectations about the "last days," when God would send the Messiah and would establish a kingdom of righteousness upon the earth. These expectations included the appearance of a final, great prophet to prepare Israel for the coming salvation, and this final prophet was sometimes described as one like Elijah or perhaps as Elijah himself returned to earth (see note). So Jesus was apparently regarded by some as this great prophet, though Mark shows that it was really John who should wear this honor (9:10–13).

Mark 6:14–16 shows that the real object in telling the story of John's death is not to entertain the reader with a juicy tale but to help the reader to understand Jesus better. John, not Jesus, is "Elijah," the great prophet who announces the Messiah, and his ministry was to prepare the way for Jesus, who is then to be seen as Messiah. But more than simply announcing the Messiah and his work, John prefigured it in his death, indicating that the Messiah's work too is to suffer death, and this to accomplish God's will.

This account, with its description of the opulent and morally bank-rupt court life of Herod, contrasts powerfully with the demands placed upon the disciples in 6:7–13 and with the next episode, in which Jesus and the Twelve are in the open country (6:31, 35). This contrast shows that the rightful "king" was not Herod (6:14), and that the places of earthly power and wealth with their customarily extravagant claims and style do not constitute the vehicle of God's salvation. Rather, as the next episode shows, it is in the humble ministry of Jesus that God manifests his provision for Israel and for the world.

Additional Notes

6:8 / **No beggar's bag**: In ancient Palestine, beggars were a familiar sight and were quite vocal in their requests for support. The disciples are forbidden to solicit like beggars and must depend upon what is offered to them in connection with the acceptance of their message.

6:9 / **An extra shirt**: Literally, the disciples are forbidden to wear "two gar-ments." In ancient Palestine, the standard attire was an inner garment and a cloaklike outer garment, used to ward off the cold and moisture in poor weather and at night as a bedroll, especially when sleeping in the open (Exod. 22:25–27; Deut. 24:10–13). The command here in Mark forbids the disciples to carry this outer garment. (For more information on clothing worn in ancient Palestine, see e.g., "Dress and Ornaments," *IDB*, vol. 1, pp. 869–71.)

6:13 / **Rubbed olive oil on many sick people**: Olive oil was widely used as a medicine in ancient Palestine, taken internally and applied to wounds and sores (e.g., Luke 10:34). It is also mentioned as applied to the sick in connection with prayer in the early church (James 5:14), probably as a symbolic act, and this is probably what is in view here. (See "Oil," *IDB*, vol. 3, pp. 592–93.)

6:14 / **King Herod** is Herod Antipas, one of the sons of Herod the Great (men-tioned in the nativity stories, Luke 1:5; Matt. 2:1–19). Antipas was named te-trarch of Galilee in 4 B.C. and ruled until he was banished by the Roman emperor Caligula in A.D. 39 upon the basis of charges from Herod Agrippa I, Antipas' nephew, who ruled Galilee after Antipas. Antipas always desired the title "king," and fancied himself as worthy of this royal status. Matt. 14:1 and Luke 9:7 both call him by his proper title, whereas Mark here refers to him as "king," very likely in mockery of his unfulfilled vanity. The whole Herodian family history is a complex tale of immorality and intrigues (see "Herod," *IDB*, vol. 2, pp. 585–94).

6:15 / **Elijah**: Immortalized in 1 Kings 17–19; 21; 2 Kings 1–2:12, Elijah is one of the great figures of the OT. On the basis of Mal. 4:5, some ancient Jews expected a prophet of the last days, like Elijah or perhaps Elijah himself, to prepare Israel for God's judgment and salvation. This expectation is alluded to in Mark 9:10–13 (parallel in Matt. 17:10–13), in Mark 15:35–36 (Matt. 27:47–49), and in John 1:21–25. (See "Elijah," *IDB*, vol. 2, pp. 88–90.).

6:17 / **John's arrest**: Josephus, the ancient Jewish historian, tells of John's arrest, attributing it to Antipas' fear of John inciting a revolt (*Antiquities*, book 18, par. 116–19; in Feldman, vol. 9, pp. 81–85). Certainly John's denunciation of Antipas' marriage to Herodias would have had political overtones, for in the ancient setting, to denounce the ruler's marriage was to denounce the ruler.

Herodias: The daughter of Aristobulus, she was the niece of Antipas, and was nearly forty at the time of her marriage to Antipas. Josephus also mentions the outrage caused by this marriage, because the Jewish religious law forbade a man to marry his brother's wife while the brother lived (Lev. 18:16; 20:21).

His brother Philip: There is disagreement as to who Herodias' first husband was, called Philip here, but only Herod in Josephus (cf. *IDB*, vol. 2, pp. 585–94; Lane, pp. 215–17).

6:22 / **The daughter of Herodias** is from Herodias' first marriage and is named Salome in Josephus (*Antiquities*, book 18, par. 136; Feldman, vol. 9, p.93). She is presented here as a young girl, probably in her early teens. A dance such as is referred to here at a banquet of drunken men would have been a suggestive and sensual event, and Herod's pleasure (6:22) may imply sexual excitement for his stepdaughter. This being so, Herodias and Salome are presented as cynically manipulating Herod by his own moral weakness. There is no historical basis for the legendary seven veils of Salome's dance. This dance is not mentioned by Josephus.

6:25 / **The head of John the Baptist on a plate**: The gruesome request presents the daughter as adding a touch of evil humor to her mother's suggestion. **On a plate** makes the head of John a kind of meal course at this wicked banquet.

Revealing Wonders

The apostles returned and met with Jesus, and told him all they had done and taught. [31]There were so many people coming and going that Jesus and his disciples didn't even have time to eat. So he said to them, "Let us go off by ourselves to some place where we will be alone and you can rest for a while." [32]So they started out in a boat by themselves to a lonely place.

[33]Many people, however, saw them leave and knew at once who they were; so they went from all towns and ran ahead by land and arrived at the place ahead of Jesus and his disciples. [34]When Jesus got out of the boat, he saw this large crowd, and his heart was filled with pity for them, because they were like sheep without a shepherd. So he began to teach them many things. [35]When it was getting late, his disciples came to him and said, "It is already very late, and this is a lonely place. [36]Send the people away, and let them go to the nearby farms and villages in order to buy themselves something to eat."

[37]"You yourselves give them something to eat," Jesus answered.

They asked, "Do you want us to go and spend two hundred silver coins[j] on bread in order to feed them?"

[38]So Jesus asked them, "How much bread have you got? Go and see."

When they found out, they told him, "Five loaves and also two fish."

[39]Jesus then told his disciples to make all the people divide into groups and sit down on the green grass. [40]So the people sat down in rows, in groups of a hundred and groups of fifty. [41]Then Jesus took the five loaves and the two fish, looked up to heaven and gave thanks to God. He broke the loaves and gave them to his disciples to distribute to the people. He also divided the two fish among them all. [42]Everyone ate and had enough. [43]Then the disciples took up twelve baskets full of what was left of the bread and the fish. [44]The number of men who were fed was five thousand.

[45]At once Jesus made his disciples get into the boat and go ahead of him to Bethsaida, on the other side of the lake, while he sent the crowd away. [46]After saying good-bye to the people, he went away to a hill to pray. [47]When evening came, the boat was in the middle of the lake, while Jesus was alone on land. [48]He saw that his disciples were straining at the oars, because they were rowing against the wind; so sometime between three and six o'clock in the morning he came to them, walking on the water. He was going to pass them by,[k] [49]but they saw him walking on the water. "It's a ghost!" they thought, and screamed. [50]They were all terrified when they saw him.

Jesus spoke to them at once, "Courage!" he said. "It is I. Don't be afraid!" [51]Then he got into the boat with them, and the wind died down. The disciples were completely amazed, [52]because they had not understood the real meaning of the feeding of the five thousand; their minds could not grasp it.

53 They crossed the lake and came to land at Gennesaret, where they tied up the boat. 54 As they left the boat, people recognized Jesus at once. 55 So they ran throughout the whole region; and wherever they heard he was, they brought to him the sick lying on their mats. 56 And everywhere Jesus went, to villages, towns, or farms, people would take their sick to the marketplaces and beg him to let them at least touch the edge of his cloak. And all who touched it were made well.

j. SILVER COINS: *A silver coin was the daily wage of a rural worker (see Mt 20.2).*
k. pass them by; *or* join them.

6:30–44 / From early times the feeding accounts have understandably attracted great attention, and continuing scholarly effort is made to try to understand them more fully. There are two feeding accounts in Mark— here, and at 8:1–10, where four thousand are fed—and also two accounts in Matthew (14:13–21; 15:32–39). Luke (9:10–17) and John (6:1–15) each report only the feeding of the five thousand. Much modern scholarly study has been devoted to the sources of the feeding accounts and other complex historical questions, but our interest here is mainly to try to understand the accounts as Mark intended his readers to understand them. (This will be work enough for us!)

We must begin our examination by noting that there are strong indications that the feeding accounts are very important events for Mark. For one thing, in the next episode (6:45–52) the disciples are said to have failed to perceive something crucial in the feeding of the five thousand, and for this reason they react wrongly during the sea miracle (cf. Matt. 14:22–33). Even more emphatically, 8:14–21, with all its mystery, at least indicates that both feedings disclose something terribly important, for the disciples are sternly rebuked when they fail to understand what it is. Further, even the fact that Mark has *two* feeding accounts is evidence that he considered the two miracles as important events, and that the accounts are intended to convey more than the simple point that Jesus could perform such a miracle; one feeding account would have been adequate to make that point. Also, it is worth noting that Mark devotes much more space to this, his first, feeding account than do Matthew or Luke (only John's account is about as long), perhaps indicating by his greater detail that the passage is a major event in his story of Jesus.

Essentially, all four accounts of the feeding of the five thousand present Jesus as miraculously supplying sufficient bread for the crowd though he starts with only five small loaves (see note). But the miracle was early seen as full of additional meaning. For example, in John 6:22–

59, after the feeding account, the discussion between Jesus and the crowd implies that the feeding miracle is likened to Moses supplying "manna" in the wilderness to the tribes of Israel. Let us look more closely at the account in Mark to see what point he was trying to make in telling his version of the story.

To discern what the feeding of the five thousand teaches in Mark it is helpful to take note of the elements in his account not found in the parallels and not present in the account of the feeding of the four thousand (8:1–10). First, it appears that the passage emphasizes that this feeding of the five thousand happens in a deserted area, this location being mentioned three times (6:31, 32, 35). If this is intentional, Mark may have meant to draw some parallel between this feeding and the supply of manna to the Israelites in the wilderness under the leadership of Moses (Exod. 16). This connection of Jesus' feeding miracle with Moses is further substantiated by the reference to the people as **like sheep without a shepherd** (6:34), which seems to be an allusion to Numbers 27:17, where Moses prays for God to supply a leader after him to take his role. This description of the people also brings to mind Ezekiel 34:1–31, where God promises to feed his "sheep" by sending a king like David to be their shepherd (esp. Ezek. 34:23). In other words, this allusion to these OT passages was probably intended by Mark to suggest to the reader that Jesus is here fulfilling the role of the longed-for king of Israel, the Messiah, who, like Moses, teaches (6:34) the people and feeds them. Even the little note that the people were organized into **groups of a hundred and groups of fifty** (6:40) seems to allude to Moses' organizing of the Israelites similarly during the wilderness march (Exod. 18:21, and see note). The effect of these characteristics, not found in the parallels or in the feeding of the four thousand (8:1–10), is to show that the event here is not to be seen simply as a great miracle but also as full of particular prophetic significance. The way the event is described is intended to show Jesus as Messiah, the divinely sent provision for Israel and the fulfillment of OT prophecies of a future salvation. Jesus' action is here "dressed" in OT imagery, so to speak, to make the point. Immediately following the episode about "king" Herod as it does, this account seems intended to show that Jesus is the rightful king and the true leader of Israel instead of the wicked Herod.

One feature found in all the Synoptic accounts of this feeding is the dialogue between Jesus and the Twelve about how to feed the crowds, in which the disciples are told by Jesus to take responsibility but they protest (6:35–38; Matt. 14:15–17; Luke 9:12–13). The disciples' protest in

Mark seems sharper, with their statement that it would take **two hundred silver coins** to supply the food needed. Thus, while in all Synoptic accounts the disciples fail to rise to the occasion, in Mark their failure is more sharply drawn. This fits the characteristic way Mark emphasizes that even the Twelve failed to perceive Jesus properly. In later Markan passages (6:52; 8:14-21), their particular failure to perceive the meaning of the feeding miracles is emphasized, something not done in the other Gospels. If the disciples' failure is presented as a warning to the reader, as seems likely, then Mark wants the reader to pay special attention to these feeding accounts and to take seriously the hints he has given (such as we have discussed) about what the feedings signify.

Another feature in all the feeding accounts is the numbers, and the question whether they are intended to represent something symbolically is often discussed. For example, is it significant that there are five thousand here and four thousand in the next feeding in 8:1-10? Do the five loaves represent anything beyond a small amount of bread? And what about the twelve baskets of fragments or even the two hundred silver coins? Certainly, some numbers did have a special significance in ancient times, as we noted when suggesting that the twelve apostles are intended to remind us of the twelve tribes of Israel. The possibility that the numbers portend something special is perhaps suggested by 8:17-21, where some of the numbers used in both feeding accounts are rehearsed. Although the danger of pressing such details too far is very real, some of the particular numbers used in the account here may be intended to suggest the larger significance of the feeding miracles.

Let us take the **five** loaves, for example. We have already noted that Mark's allusion to Numbers 27:17 (6:34) shows Jesus as fulfilling a role similar to Moses'. Further, 6:34 emphasizes that Jesus *taught* the crowds—further likening Jesus to Moses—whereas the parallels include references to healing (Matt. 14:14; Luke 9:11). With these things in mind, it is possible that the five loaves may be intended by Mark to remind the reader that the teaching of Moses was traditionally identified as a fivefold collection (the first five books of the OT). So, Jesus' feeding the crowd with five loaves may have been meant by Mark to assist the reader further in seeing the analogy between Jesus and Moses.

The **twelve** baskets of fragments (6:43) taken up after the feeding not only show that the feeding was a miraculous multiplication of provisions for the crowd but also may be intended to be symbolic. As indicated before, twelve is a number frequently associated with Israel in Jewish tradition and in the OT. Now in view of the accumulated evidence that this feeding account presents Jesus as fulfilling the role of Moses and David and that it uses OT phrasing to present the crowd as Israel in need of divine leadership (6:34, **sheep without a shepherd**), it seems likely that the **twelve** baskets of fragments are meant to assist the reader in seeing Jesus here as supplying the divine provision for Israel promised in the OT.

The other numbers (two hundred coins, five thousand people, two fish) are not so likely to have been intended to be symbolic, largely because they do not seem to have acquired the same sort of previous symbolic usage in Jewish life that the numers twelve and five bore. When we consider the next feeding account (8:1–10), we will examine the numbers there as well to see whether any of them may have been intended to disclose something about the meaning of that miracle. (See "Number," "Seven," and "Twelve," *IDB*, vol. 3, pp.561–67; vol. 4, pp. 294–95, 719.)

What we have noted about the feeding account here amounts to a clear indication that Mark intends his readers to see the event as disclosing not only Jesus' miraculous power but also the secret of his person and significance. That is, the feeding miracle is really more about Jesus than bread and like everything else in Mark, is meant to press the reader to consider who Jesus, the Son of Man, really is. When, later, the disciples are said to have failed to understand the feedings (6:52; 8:17–21), something peculiar to Mark's Gospel, he means that the disciples failed to see the divine sonship of Jesus disclosed in these miracles.

6:45–52 / Mark ties this incident closely to the preceding account of the feeding of the five thousand by noting in 6:52 that the disciples' fearful collapse here was caused by their failure to understand that the feeding miracle revealed Jesus' true significance and power. Since Mark thus ties together these two incidents, it is likely that he intends his reader to see them both as complementary revelations of Jesus. This means that this sea miracle is another manifestation of the divine significance of Jesus' person and not just a miracle story.

This is the second sea miracle in Mark (see also 4:35–41), and in our comments on the earlier one we noted that Jesus' command of the sea is so described as to make him seem to exhibit God's own power over nature. The same is true here, where Jesus not only calms the sea (6:51) but also walks upon it. Readers familiar with the OT would recognize the similarity to the way God is described there (see note) as the one who treads upon the sea, showing his mastery of it.

Now this suggests that the sea miracle is intended to show that the one who fed the multitude in the preceding account is more than a new Moses or a new shepherd-king like David; he possesses divine power. We have noted already that Mark's favorite title for Jesus is "the Son of God," and that for Mark this term signifies that Jesus has a relationship with God far more direct than is indicated by the previous use of the term for human beings in the OT or Jewish tradition. This sea miracle Mark intends as further evidence that Jesus is not just human but has a supernatural quality and divine significance. Even the way Jesus addresses the disciples, **It is I**, seems to imply this. The phrase appears in the OT as almost a title or formula of divine self-disclosure (e.g., Isa. 43:25; 48:12; 51:12, and see note), and it is likely that Mark's readers were intended to catch the allusion to these OT passages in Jesus' words and see the point that Jesus is speaking the way God does.

It seems strange to read that Jesus, seeing their danger, intended **to pass them by** (6:48), and it is very likely that this is an incorrect translation of the Greek phrase. The phrase can just as easily be translated "he intended to pass by them," meaning that he intended to make himself visible to the disciples to relieve their fear and to reveal his power to them. On this understanding of the phrase, Jesus' intent is frustrated, for when they see him they become even more frightened, supposing him to be a sea demon (6:49, **a ghost**; see note). Even when he shows them who he is, the disciples are **amazed** but do not comprehend the significance of this action (6:51-52); the reader is certainly not supposed to make the same mistake. Instead, the reader is expected to react with intelligent reverence and holy awe to this revelation of Jesus' person.

6:53-56 / This is another summary account of Jesus' ministry (like earlier examples in 1:39; 3:7-12), only this summary makes no reference to Jesus teaching or exorcising demons but concentrates on his healings. It is interesting to note that the passage emphasizes that people came to Jesus, indeed, thronged him, so that again we get the impression of Jesus and the Twelve as harried and beset with need wherever they went (cf. 1:37, 45; 2:1-4; 3:7-11; 3:20; 6:30-32). Here the attitude of the people is an almost superstitious reverence for Jesus as a wonder-worker, including the idea that even his clothing contained healing power (6:56; cf. 5:28). Mark records this information without comment, but he probably intended it simply to complement the preceding passage (6:30-52), in which he gives other examples of the mighty power at work in Jesus. The present summary passage is not another revelation scene like the feeding or the sea miracle, but it does further illustrate the point that Jesus bore the power of God. As we have noted already, Mark's attitude toward the popular notoriety of Jesus as a wonder-worker is that Jesus did indeed do such works but that the crowds' perception of Jesus was all too shallow and incomplete by the standards of the Christian gospel.

Additional Notes

6:30 / **The apostles returned**: The Twelve are called by their official name here, the name that indicates that they were authorized and sent out by Jesus. Their return here is from the mission described in 6:7–13, and this verse completes the mission story interrupted by the account of John's martyrdom in 6:14–29.

6:31 / **Didn't even have time to eat**:This is the second time Mark has referred to this (see also 3:20). It is all the more striking that Jesus and the Twelve feed the five thousand after the mention of this inability to satisfy their own needs.

6:32 / **A lonely place**: The terms used here and in 6:31 and 6:35 refer to uninhabited areas and are intended to recall the wilderness as the scene of God's protection and provision for ancient Israel in the time of Moses.

6:33 / **The place**: There is no clear indication in Mark of where the feeding incident is located. It is notoriously difficult to try to put together Jesus' travels and deeds in Mark into a clear itinerary. The many attempts only illustrate the disagreements among students of the text. Since Mark does not mention a location, he probably considered the matter unimportant. The Luke 9:10 parallel locates the event near Bethsaida (see note on 6:45).

6:37 / **Two hundred silver coins**: The coin in question (a denarius) amounted to a day's wage for a farm worker (e.g., Matt. 20:1–16), and two hundred would represent nearly a year's wage. Probably, the number simply signifies that a large amount of money would have been needed to supply the crowd with food. The reference to this amount appears also in John's account (6:7) but not in the other Synoptics.

6:38 / **Five loaves and also two fish**: The loaves were probably made of barley, the ingredient mostly used by the common people. They may have been quickly prepared flat loaves of circular shape, often taken along as a provision for a journey (see e.g., "Bread," *IDB*, vol. 1, pp. 46–64). The account emphasizes the bread (6:37 and 6:44, lit. "those who ate the loaves were five thousand men"), and the *two* fish do not seem to have a symbolic significance similar to that we suggest for the loaves and the bread fragments. The fish were probably dried, salted fish, which could be taken along for food on a trip. There was a large fishing industry on the shores of Lake Galilee (see e.g., "Fish," *IDB*, vol. 2, pp. 272–73).

6:39 / **The green grass**: In biblical language, a "wilderness" is not necessarily an arid desert but only an uninhabited area.

6:40 / **Groups of a hundred and groups of fifty**: In the OT, groups of these sizes were standard organizations of people, especially for military purposes (e.g., Exod. 18:21; Deut. 1:15; 1 Sam. 8:12). This may suggest that Mark is trying to describe the event as the ordering of a people by their king. The ancient documents from the Jewish religious sect at Qumran (the Dead Sea Scrolls) describe the organization of the elect for final salavation in similar terms (e.g., T. H. Gaster, *The Dead Sea Scriptures*, 3rd ed. [Garden City, N.Y.: Anchor, 1976], pp. 47, 86).

6:41 / **Jesus ... gave thanks ... broke the loaves ...**: Many interpreters draw attention to the similarity between the actions here and at the Last Supper in 14:22, suggesting that Mark intended his readers to see this miracle as a kind of Eucharist (or Holy Communion) meal. Certainly Mark's Christian readers would have seen the similarities, and early Christian art and liturgy show that Christians saw a connection. It should be pointed out, however, that the actions of praying, breaking the bread, and giving to others are simply the standard meal practices of religious Jews in ancient times. **Gave thanks** here is literally "he blessed (God)," which is what the Hebrew term for a grace before a meal means. In the other feeding account (8:1-10), however, Mark uses the word that does mean literally "to give thanks," the same word used in 14:22, *eucharisto*, from which our term *Eucharist* comes. The description of the feeding in 6:30-44 gives it more of an OT and Jewish dress, while the feeding in 8:1-10 lends itself more to Christian eucharistic connections.

6:45 / **Jesus made his disciples get into the boat**: There is no explanation of *why* Jesus sent away the disciples as well as the crowd (6:46) here. Some have pointed to the parallel account in John 6:14-15, where the crowd (and the disciples?) are about to make Jesus lead a messianic revolt, this being avoided by Jesus leaving the crowd suddenly. On this view, Jesus goes to pray (Mark 6:46) to obtain fortitude to resist the temptation of giving in to the excitement of the crowd and the disciples caused by the miraculous provision of food in the wilderness. (See, e.g., Lane, pp. 234-35.)

Bethsaida: The name means "house of the fisher." The town was located on the northern shore of Lake Galilee and possessed a natural harbor, widely used by fishermen. According to Luke 9:10, the feeding miracle took place near Bethsaida, and this makes the remark in 6:45, that the disciples were sent to **the other side of the lake** seem strange. (On the town, see, e.g., *IDB*, vol. 1, pp. 396-97 and *MBA*, 232.)

6:48 / **Between three and six o'clock in the morning**: Literally, Mark has "in the fourth watch of the night," referring to the military divisions of the night in Roman times.

Walking on the water: In the OT God is described as treading upon the waves of the sea, signifying divine control over nature, and especially over the sea as a symbol of chaos and unruliness (e.g., Ps. 77:19 and Job 9:8, where "the sea monster's back" in the GNB translation can be rendered "the waves of the sea"; cf. the RSV, NIV, NEB [margin]).

6:49 / **It's a ghost!**: The term **ghost** here in Greek can mean any kind of scary apparition, and since ancient Jews often regarded the unruly sea as inhabited by sea demons, this is probably what is intended here.

6:50 / **It is I**: The Greek phrase used here can mean ordinarily just what the translation makes of it, but it is used in the OT (e.g., Isa. 43:25; 48:12; 51:12; the GNB translation of these passages does not make this clear; cf. RSV or NIV) with special force as a formula for self-description by God, resembling the phrasing in Exod. 3:14 where God first reveals himself to Moses. Note especially how the whole passage in Isa. 51:9–16 is a most interesting background for the sea miracle account here. In Mark the phrase reappears on the lips of Jesus in the trial scene (14:62), and there, also, is probably intended as an allusion to these OT passages. Also, in 13:6, Jesus warns of imposters who would come making the same (divine?) claim for themselves. (See "I am," *NIDNTT*, vol. 2, pp. 278–83.)

6:52 / **The real meaning of the feeding of the five thousand** is literally "they did not understand about the loaves." It is the feeding miracle that Mark refers to here, but he may have wanted to call particular attention to the symbolic significance of the five loaves and the baskets of fragments.

Their minds could not grasp it: Literally, Mark says that their hearts were "hardened," a condition indicating lack of faith like the opponents in 3:5 (see note on that verse). In 8:17 the disciples are described similarly (see note on that verse). The idea of "hardened" hearts comes from the OT (Exod. 14:5; Ps. 95:8) and means a serious condition of unbelief or even disobedience. The disciples are thus described here in very negative terms.

6:53 / **Gennesaret** may refer to the small plain on the northwestern shore of Lake Galilee or to a town located on the plain (cf., e.g., Lane, p. 239, n. 127; "Galilee, Sea of," *IDB*, vol. 2, pp. 348–50; *MBA*, 231.) Mark does not explain why they wound up here if, as he says, they set out for Bethsaida (6:45), but it is often suggested that the wild storm of 6:48–51 blew the boat westward to this spot.

6:55 / **Sick lying on their mats**: This reminds us of the sick man of 2:1–12.

6:56 / **The edge of his cloak**: This reminds us of the woman of 5:25–28 (see comments and notes on these verses).

12

Clean and Unclean

Some Pharisees and teachers of the Law who had come from Jerusalem gathered around Jesus. ²They noticed that some of his disciples were eating their food with hands that were ritually unclean—that is, they had not washed them in the way the Pharisees said people should.

(³For the Pharisees, as well as the rest of the Jews, follow the teaching they received from their ancestors: they do not eat unless they wash their hands in the proper way; ⁴nor do they eat anything that comes from the market unless they wash it first.[l] And they follow many other rules which they have received, such as the proper way to wash cups, pots, copper bowls, and beds.[m])

⁵So the Pharisees and the teachers of the Law asked Jesus, "Why is it that your disciples do not follow the teaching handed down by our ancestors, but instead eat with ritually unclean hands?"

⁶Jesus answered them, "How right Isaiah was when he prophesied about you! You are hypocrites, just as he wrote:

'These people, says God, honor
    me with their words,
        but their heart is really far
        away from me.
⁷It is no use for them to worship me,
    because they teach man-made
        rules as though they were
        my laws!'

⁸"You put aside God's command and obey the teachings of men."

⁹And Jesus continued, "You have a clever way of rejecting God's law in order to uphold your own teaching. ¹⁰For Moses commanded, 'Respect your father and your mother,' and, 'Whoever curses his father or his mother is to be put to death.' ¹¹But you teach that if a person has something he could use to help his father or mother, but says, 'This is Corban' (which means, it belongs to God), ¹²he is excused from helping his father or mother. ¹³In this way the teaching you pass on to others cancels out the word of God. And there are many other things like this that you do."

¹⁴Then Jesus called the crowd to him once more and said to them, "Listen to me, all of you, and understand. ¹⁵There is nothing that goes into a person from the outside which can make him ritually unclean. Rather, it is what comes out of a person that makes him unclean."[n]

¹⁷When he left the crowd and went into the house, his disciples asked him to explain this saying. ¹⁸"You are no more intelligent than the others," Jesus said to them. "Don't you understand? Nothing that goes into a person from the outside can really make him unclean, ¹⁹because it does not go into his heart but into his stomach and then goes on out of the body." (In saying this, Jesus declared that all foods are fit to be eaten.)

²⁰And he went on to say, "It is what comes out of a person that makes him unclean. ²¹For from the inside, from a person's heart, come the evil ideas

which lead him to do immora hings, to rob, kill, ²²commit adultery, be greedy, and do all sorts of evil things; deceit, indecency, jealousy, sla der, pride, and folly—²³all these evil things come from inside a person and make him unclean."

l. anything that comes from the market unless they wash it first; or anything after they come from the market unless they wash themselves first.
m. *Some manuscripts do not have* and beds.
n. *Some manuscripts add verse 16:* Listen, then, if you have ears! *(see 4.23).*

7:1-13 / Although the GNB presents 7:1–13 as a separate unit, it is important to note that the discussion about Jewish traditional ideas of "clean" and "unclean," begun in 7:1–13, continues on in 7:14–23, and that this topic sets the stage for the episode in 7:24–30, where Jesus deals with a gentile woman's request for his ministry. The preceding summary passage (6:53–56) is thus a transitional point, and in chapter 7 we should recognize the beginning of a new section in Mark's narrative.

The **Pharisees** (last encountered in 3:6) and the **teachers of the Law** ("scribes," last mentioned in 3:22) reappear here as critics of the behavior of Jesus' disciples. This reminds us of 2:18–28, where Jesus' disciples were also criticized for their violation of religious practices of the Pharisees. The fact that the criticism is said to concern the disciples is designed to enable the Christian readers to identify themselves more closely with the narrative and its teaching. Early gentile Christians would have seen in this discussion of Jewish religious practices important teaching for their own life and beliefs, especially in the first-century church when the question of whether non-Jewish Christians were obligated to observe Jewish taboos was still very much alive (see the note on **unclean**). The fact that an explanation of Jewish customs is given (7:3–4) shows that Mark's readers were probably gentile Christians.

Though the complaint of the Pharisees and teachers of the Law is concerned with the observance of religious meal customs designed to maintain ritual purity, essentially the same question addressed in 7:14–23, Jesus' reply is a broad criticism of his opponents' basis for their customs, the tradition of their ancestors (7:3, 5). The matter raised by Jesus' critics here is the prescribed practice of a ritual washing of the hands before eating, a practice that formed part of the overall Pharisaic attempt to live in a perpetual state of priestly purity (see note). Keeping such customs showed that one was dedicated to God and wished to be distinct from the masses of sinners and less scrupulous Jews. Jesus' reply does not at first glance seem to speak directly to the question of ritual washing; instead he replies with a counteraccusation (7:6–8) and then an illustration of what he considers to be the perverse effect of the accumulated body of Jewish tradition (9–13). It is only in 7:14–23 that the original question of "clean/unclean," which lies at the base of the hand-washing practice, is taken up by Jesus. But Jesus' words in 7:6–13 really are relevant to the Pharisees' criticism of the disciples (7:1–5), because he attacks the basis of their view.

Indeed, 7:1–13 (and 7:14–23) is a good example of the nature of the conflict between Jesus and the Pharisees, a conflict we have already discussed in connection with 2:13–28 (see comments on these verses). Before we discuss this passage further, remember the context of the conflict. Jesus and his disciples were engaged in an itinerant ministry, proclaiming the imminent arrival of the Kingdom of God and taking food wherever it was offered, eating with those who offered it. For Jesus, the central concern was this ministry, which was based upon the fundamental conviction that the arrival of the Kingdom of God was not dependent upon ritual preparation (such as the Pharisaic lifestyle embodied) but upon God's will to bring it. Consequently, it was far more important to recognize the near arrival of the Kingdom and to demonstrate readiness for it by a radical re-ordering of one's life (e.g., 8:34–38; 9:33–37, 42–50; 10:1–12, 17–31; 12:28–34) than to conform to the practices of the Pharisees, which were so often concerned with ceremonial actions and tended to produce a religiously flavored elitism.

In the present passage, Jesus rejects the criticism of the Pharisees with its elitist overtones and answers with a charge that hits at the very heart of the Pharisaic intention. The supposed intent of the many rules of the Pharisees was both to make the Law of God applicable to every area of life and to ensure that the Law was observed by making it even more precise than it was in its OT form. All this might be commendable in intent, but in operation the result might be less so. Aside from the feelings of superiority just mentioned, in any program like that of the Pharisees there is the danger of making a particular application of God's Law a sacrosanct obligation that may eventually lose its original meaning and value with the passage of time and circumstances. Perhaps even worse, in a religious lifestyle that emphasizes the observance of a multitude of commandments as a means to religious and social respectability, there can arise the practice of enforcing particular commandments in such a way as to violate others (and plenty of examples in Christian circles are available too!). It is just this sort of error that Jesus attacks in 7:6–13.

Note the terms used in the passage that indicate Jesus' criticism of the Pharisees. In 7:3 and 5 the Pharisaic practice is said to be **teaching** from their **ancestors**, referring to sacred tradition derived from revered teachers of the past called the elders. In his reply, Jesus quotes an OT passage that refers to **man-made rules** (7:7), and he describes their sacred tradition as **teachings of men** (7:8), in contrast to **God's command**. In 7:9, he finally calls their tradition **your own teaching**, thus disowning it himself.

Jesus rejects the tradition of the Pharisees because he says it does not in fact represent the will of God but can be used to legitimize a breaking of God's command. The example chosen has to do with the procedure of dedicating one's possessions to God, thus placing a ban on their use by others. If a son made such a dedicatory vow, ancient scribal law of the Jews stated that the vow could not be canceled, even to support one's parents with one's possessions. (See note below on 7:12, **he is excused**.) So, Jesus accuses the Pharisees and scribes of playing off one law (about the keeping of vows to God) against another (the support of one's parents). In other words, beyond replying to the particular scribal custom of hand washing, Jesus rejects the whole basis of the criticism of his disciples, the scribal tradition, saying that it has no valid claim to represent God's will.

This fundamental point is crucial for the following passages, giving the basis for Jesus' rejection of the scribal attempt to define religious purity and preparing the reader for the incident with the gentile woman. Early gentile Christians would have seen in Jesus' words the basis for their own right to ignore many of the scruples of Judaism while claiming to be obedient to the will of God.

7:14–23 / In these verses Jesus returns to the question of ritual purity introduced in 7:1–5 and in effect sets aside the whole idea that certain objects or foods make the person religiously unclean or unfit to participate in worship and fellowship with others. Jesus plays on the contrast between what goes **into** a person and what comes **out** of a person while addressing the crowd (7:14–15); and in typical Markan fashion the disciples approach him for a private explanation of what he has said (7:17: cf. 4:10, 34; 9:9, 28, 30–31; 10:10, 23–31; 13:3–4), providing the opportunity for the teaching in 7:18–23. In the process of this inquiry by the disciples, they are again rebuked for failing to understand Jesus. Here again, as before, Mark intends the readers to learn from the failure of the Twelve and to absorb the lesson being taught.

As indicated above, the effect of Jesus' teaching here appears to be to set aside the whole idea of certain foods being "unclean." The Jewish practices and their abundant elaborations all are based on the OT Law, with its distinction between clean and unclean foods. In the OT, as a matter of fact, the idea is that one can contract ritual impurity by eating certain foods, and even by touching objects deemed to be impure; large portions of the OT Law are devoted to commandments about these matters (see note). This means that Jesus' teaching here not only seems to take issue with a major feature of traditional Jewish religious practice but also appears to rescind a major body of OT material dealing with such ritual laws. Certainly for Mark's early gentile readers the practical effect was to legitimate their ignoring of the ritual laws of Judaism. This is indicated in what seems to be a Markan editorial note at the end of 7:19 (see note). The more profound meaning of Jesus' words, however, was not simply to cancel Jewish practices but to point out that emphasis upon the observance of ritual practices runs the risk of ignoring the fact that the seat of sin and true impurity is the inner area of human intentions and thoughts. In the narrative context, Jesus' teaching means that the judgment against his disciples by the Pharisees ignored this more fundamental matter.

This criticism of reliance upon outward, ritual observance was not original with Jesus, being found in the OT prophets (e.g., Amos 5:21–27; Isa. 1:10–20); and the Jewish rabbinical tradition had voices making the same point. So, Jesus' teaching is not really an anti-Jewish blast or a full rejection of the OT. Rather, in his own situation it was a defense of him and his disciples against the criticisms of those who could not get past his failure to follow scrupulous observance of ritual laws, and in the situation of the early church, his teaching was a defense of Christian freedom from Jewish ritual obligations.

Elsewhere in the NT, there is evidence that the question of whether all Christians were bound by OT ritual laws was a major issue (Gal. 2:1–21; Rom. 14:1–23; Acts 15:1–29; and note the vision of Peter about "unclean" food, Acts 10:1–44). Indeed, down to the present time the question is raised by some Christian groups and is sometimes a matter of concern for scrupulous (and often young) Christians. In these words of Jesus, as well as in the teaching of the rest of the NT, Christians have found a basis for a life of holiness and devotion to the God of the OT revelation that does not involve the ritual practices of traditional Judaism.

In the immediate context of Mark 7, this teaching not only answers the problem raised in 7:1–5 but also prepares the reader for the next incident, where Jesus ministers to one regarded as unclean by standards of the ritual laws of Judaism.

Additional Notes

7:2 / **Ritually unclean**: The word here is *koinos*, in Greek meaning literally, "common"; but here it appears to represent the Hebrew word that describes one's hands as not certainly "clean," or religiously fit for eating (which in ancient Judaism was *always* a religious ritual), unless they were ceremonially dipped in water first. (For the technical terms of the Jewish laws, see, e.g., Lane, pp. 242–43, and the literature cited there.) The OT (Exod. 30:19; 40:12) required the Jewish priests to wash ritually before serving at the altar. Many Jewish laymen, such as the Pharisees, set themselves the aim of living by the more strict priestly standards, and so ritually washed their hands before daily morning prayer and before meals, as if the food eaten were priestly food. (See also comments and notes on 7:14–23.)

7:4 / **Many other rules** seems intended as a criticism of what Mark regarded as a complicated mass of regulations and procedures.

And beds: These words are absent in many important early manuscripts and scholars are divided over whether they were accidentally or deliberately omitted by some copyists (perhaps because washing beds seemed strange), or whether the words were added by some scribes who were familiar with Lev. 15, with its requirements about the ritual cleansing of beds.

7:6 / **Hypocrites**: This is the only occurrence of the word in Mark, though it appears several times in Matthew (e.g., 6:2, 5, 16; 23:13, 15, 25, 26, 27, 29) and in Luke (6:42; 12:56; 13:15). The term in Greek means a pretender or even a shyster and indicates that the critics here are accused of claiming to be diligent in following God's will while really being more concerned with appearances.

These people, says God begins a quotation from Isa. 29:13. Mark's version resembles more closely the ancient Greek translation of the OT known as the Septuagint and is not exactly the same as the Hebrew text of Isaiah, though the substance is the same.

7:10 / **Moses commanded** introduces quotations from Exod. 20:12 (parallel in Deut. 5:16) and from Exod. 21:17 (parallel in Lev. 20:9). Jesus takes the commands to include the idea that the grown child should be responsible for the needs of the parents.

7:11 / **Corban** is the Hebrew term that was used to describe objects or even people as dedicated to God exclusively. To make the statement **this is Corban** was to take a vow regarding the object(s) in question, a vow that could not easily be canceled (see next note). For the OT commands about vows, see, e.g., Deut. 23:21–32; Num. 30:1–16. The oath referred to here might have been a religious vow dedicating all one had to God rashly, without reckoning the needs of one's parents; or the statement might even refer to a rash vow taken in anger at one's parents to the effect that, as far as they were concerned, all one's goods were **Corban**, that is, withheld from their benefit. (Cf. Lane, pp. 249–52; Nineham, pp. 195–96.)

7:12 / **He is excused**: Actually, the Greek says "you do not permit him to do anything for his father or mother." There is evidence of ancient scribal rules that did not permit a son to renounce a vow once made, even if the effect of the vow was to cause a hardship for his parents. (See Lane, p. 251, for discussion and references to ancient literature.)

7:15 / **Unclean**: The Greek word here is a verb meaning "to render ritually unclean." The ritual practices of ancient Judaism were based on OT passages such as Lev. 11:1–47; Deut. 14:1–20 and were elaborated by scribal authorities in ancient times and on down to the present in more traditional forms of Judaism. "Kosher" foods are ritually "clean" foods fit for eating by scrupulous Jews. (For references to technical literature on the subject of clean/unclean in Judaism, see, e.g., Lane, pp. 249–58; also see "Clean and Unclean," *IDB*, vol. 1, p. 641–48.)

7:19 / **And then goes on out of the body** is literally "and then goes into the latrine."

In saying this, Jesus declared that all foods are fit to be eaten: Most modern translations and commentators understand the Greek phrase this way. In Greek, the phrase is a participial clause, reading literally after the preceding sentence "cleansing all foods." The phrase as translated here is taken as Mark's own comment and the participle is taken as dependent on "Jesus said" in v. 18. The phrase could also be understood as dependent on the immediately preceding clause thus: "and then goes on out of the body, cleansing all foods," meaning that all foods wind up in the same place! The KJV renders the phrase quite literally. If the popular opinion of the meaning of the phrase (as reflected in the GNB translation) is correct, Mark intended by this phrase to make the application of Jesus' teaching plain to his readers. There are other examples of such editorial comments in Mark (e.g., 3:30; 5:8; 7:3–4; 13:14).

13

Ministry in Gentile Territory

MARK 7:24–37

Then Jesus left and went away to the territory near the city of Tyre. He went into a house and did not want anyone to know he was there, but he could not stay hidden. ²⁵A woman, whose daughter had an evil spirit in her, heard about Jesus and came to him at once and fell at his feet. ²⁶The woman was a Gentile, born in the region of Phoenicia in Syria. She begged Jesus to drive the demon out of her daughter. ²⁷But Jesus answered, "Let us first feed the children. It isn't right to take the children's food and throw it to the dogs."

²⁸"Sir," she answered, "even the dogs under the table eat the children's leftovers!"

²⁹So Jesus said to her, "Because of that answer, go back home, where you will find that the demon has gone out of your daughter!"

³⁰She went home and found her child lying on the bed; the demon had indeed gone out of her.

³¹Jesus then left the neighborhood of Tyre and went on through Sidon to Lake Galilee, going by way of the territory of the Ten Towns. ³²Some people brought him a man who was deaf and could hardly speak, and they begged Jesus to place his hands on him. ³³So Jesus took him off alone, away from the crowd, put his fingers in the man's ears, spat, and touched the man's tongue. ³⁴Then Jesus looked up to heaven, gave a deep groan, and said to the man, "*Ephphatha*," which means, "Open up!"

³⁵At once the man was able to hear, his speech impediment was removed, and he began to talk without any trouble. ³⁶Then Jesus ordered the people not to speak of it to anyone; but the more he ordered them not to, the more they spoke. ³⁷And all who heard were completely amazed. "How well he does everything!" they exclaimed. "He even causes the deaf to hear and the dumb to speak!"

7:24-30 / The GNB heading for this story fails to note the real point of the passage, that it is a *gentile* woman whose faith succeeds. Although Jesus' criticism of scribal tradition in 7:1–13 and his rejection of the concern for ritual purity in 7:14–23 can be accounted for in the context of his own historical ministry, these teachings were also seen as relevant to the church after him, as we have noted in the comments on these passages. In the present passage, the relevance for the early church of all that has been stated by Jesus in Mark 7 becomes even more transparently clear. If the logical effect of Jesus' teaching is to legitimize those who do not follow Pharisaic ritual customs, such as the gentile believers, this incident gives an actual precedent for addressing Gentiles and for their inclusion in the circle of those to whom the benefits of the Kingdom of God can come. Early gentile Christians, conscious of not being of the chosen nation of Israel, would have seen themselves in the woman and would have found great encouragement in her story, and this is just what Mark intended.

This passage is an excellent illustration of how the Gospel writers tried to make Jesus' historical teachings and actions relevant for the readers of their own day, while also attempting to describe his ministry as the tradition portrayed it. Thus, in the present story, Jesus at first indicates that he is not simply a wandering wonder-worker and that his own calling is to Israel, the **children** (7:27) of the OT covenant with God, to whom the Kingdom of God must be proclaimed first (see note on **first feed the children**). This sounds very authentically like what the "historical" Jesus would have said. He is not remade by Mark into a cosmopolitan missionary who preaches to all nations. Nevertheless, two items in the story make it capable of being a justification for the church's later mission to all the world. First, there is the simple fact that Jesus does satisfy the woman's need, congratulating her determined and reverent appeal. The lesson intended by Mark is that Gentiles who show the same kind of readiness to recognize their need and to trust in Jesus can be saved. Secondly, and this is a Markan distinction not found in the Matt. 15:21–28 parallel, there is the little statement in 7:27 **Let us *first* feed the children**. This statement seems to anticipate the possibility of a later "feeding" of others like the woman and was no doubt intended by Mark to mean that the restriction of Jesus' own ministry to Israel both was proper and did not preclude a later mission to the Gentiles. In this phrase, we may see a reflection of the Apostle Paul's emphasis that it was God's will for salvation to be preached first to the Jews and then to all the world (e.g., Rom. 1:16; 2:9–11; cf. Acts 3:26; 13:26–48).

In seeing this passage properly in its Markan context, we should note how the subject of food appears at several points in the narrative near this incident. In 7:1–5, there is the question of eating in a state of ritual purity. In 7:14–23, Jesus discusses food, whether some foods make one "unclean." And here there is the reference to food (bread) as the symbol of the blessings of the Kingdom of God. Indeed, elsewhere in Mark there is the use of food as a symbol of these blessings. Particularly important are the two feeding miracles, the prior one in 6:30–44, which we have already described as intended to portray Jesus bringing the promised blessings of salvation to Israel, and the other feeding miracle in 8:1–10, which, we shall see, may be intended to complement the first feeding by hinting that Jesus' "bread" was to be given to Gentiles as well in the future. If this suggested relationship between the two feeding miracles in Mark is entertained for the moment, then all the material in Mark 7, and particularly the present incident in 7:24-30, may be understood as part of Mark's effort to get the reader to see that Jesus' ministry in Israel was a preparation and basis for a later, wider proclamation of the gospel.

In subsequent periods of the church, when the question of the basis of the mission to gentile peoples was no longer an issue, this story continued to be an inspiring example for the faith of Christians in the power and willingness of Christ to hear their petitions.

7:31-37 / This incident, unique to Mark, seems intended not only to give another example of Jesus' healing acts but also to disclose the larger significance of Jesus' ministry by allusion to OT prophetic hope. A couple of things in the passage indicate this. First, the description of the man's condition (7:32) involves a rare word (see note) that means "to speak with great difficulty, or with a speech impediment," a word found in the Greek translation of the OT in Isaiah 35:5-6, suggesting that Mark intended an allusion to this passage, which promises a time to come when God would bestow blessings such as miraculous healing upon the people. Secondly, the response of the crowd (7:37) also seems to allude to this passage, suggesting that the fulfillment of its promises has come in Jesus' ministry. Indeed, Isaiah 35 makes interesting background reading for Mark 7 (see notes), and Mark may have intended his readers to recall the whole passage by his allusions to it. Even though his first readers were likely gentile Christians, they would probably have been sufficiently familiar with the Greek OT to catch the allusion.

Also, this story, together with the preceding one, seems intended to support Jesus' rejection of the criticism of the Pharisees in 7:1-23 by contrasting their criticism of him with these incidents, exhibiting proof that Jesus is in fact the bearer of God's salvation. A connection with the preceding story may be in the location of the incident, apparently in gentile territory (the **Ten Towns**, see note). Thus, both these miracles happen in territory regarded as unholy or unclean by strict Jewish standards, particularly interesting in the light of the controversy about the legitimacy of clean/unclean distinctions in 7:1-23.

This healing story gives a very detailed description of Jesus' actions toward the needy person (7:33-34; cf. 8:22-25). Jesus' actions can be seen in at least two ways. First, they could be seen simply as a kind of sign language designed to show the man what Jesus intended to do for him, perhaps so as to encourage his faith. Thus, touching the man's ears and tongue might mean that Jesus intended to deal with these needs. Spittle (at least the spittle of certain men) was apparently regarded by many as having a healing force in both Jewish and pagan circles (see note), and so Jesus' spitting here may have been intended also to signify to the man an attempt to heal him (cf. 8:23; John 9:6). The looking up to heaven and sighing (**a deep groan**, 7:34) may have been intended as signs of prayer to God. However, it is also possible to see these actions, against the context of the stories of Jewish and pagan healers and wonder-workers of ancient times, as similar to the magical techniques they are reported to have employed (see note). It is not difficult to think that Jesus may have employed gestures in his healings and exorcisms that resembled the actions of others who attempted similar miracles, though there are important distinctions to be seen between Jesus' ministry and the professional exorcists and magical practices of the ancient world. Most importantly, Jesus' works formed part of his proclamation of the Kingdom of God and were intended as signs of its advance, and he seems to have been uninterested in taking advantage of the notoriety resulting from his ministry for personal gain, even showing an uneasiness with the notoriety itself when it was unaccompanied by any acceptance of his primary message.

Additional Notes

7:24 / **Territory near the city of Tyre**: Literally, the text reads, "he went into the boundaries of Tyre," meaning the area under Tyre's jurisdiction, an area from the city north and south along the coast for several miles and inland to the mountains. We don't know exactly where in this large territory this incident is placed. (See, e.g., *MBA*, 232.)

He could not stay hidden: Here again there is the Markan theme that Jesus tried to restrict the spread of his fame without success (cf. 1:44–45; 5:42–43).

7:25 / **An evil spirit**: The condition of people with the same affliction is described, e.g., in 5:1–5; 9:17–21.

7:26 / **A Gentile**: Literally, she is said to be a "Greek," but what is meant is a Greek-speaking native of the Phoenician area, an area converted to Greek language and culture after Alexander the Great in the fourth century B.C. Phoenicia is the area of modern-day Lebanon. (See, e.g., "Phoenicia," *IDB*, vol. 3, pp. 800–805.) The GNB translation properly renders what is meant: she is a non-Jew.

7:27 / **First feed the children**: The idea that in a special sense Israelites were the children of God can be found in the OT (e.g., Exod. 4:22; Deut. 32:6; Isa. 1. Hos. 11:1). It is not clear whether Jesus' images of **children/dogs** refers to this OT idea about Israel or whether it is simply an analogy based on common household life of the time—the family eats before the house pets.

Dogs: It is true that Jewish tradition sometimes refers to Gentiles derogatively as "dogs," but this may not be relevant here. The term Mark uses here seems to refer to household dogs, while the term *dog* as a slur can refer to wild dogs or to scavenger dogs of the street.

7:28 / **The dogs under the table eat the children's leftovers**: The woman's reply confirms that the **dogs** here are household pets **under the table**, and she cannily points out to Jesus that, although children are fed first, these dogs can get scraps that fall from the table without disturbing the meal. **Leftovers** here is not really what is meant. Rather, the term refers to the bits that fall from the table. In effect, the woman means, "You don't need to interrupt the 'meal' plans; I ask only for a scrap from the table." The tenacity and humility that assents to Jesus' mission, though she does not understand it, wins her Jesus' blessing. He could not become a mere itinerant wonder-worker, for his calling was to proclaim the fulfillment of Israel's prophetic hopes; but he could respond to this particular need, for the woman believed that Jesus could cure her daughter where he was by the mere command. (For scholarly treatments of Jesus' ministry to Israel and its relationship to Gentiles see, e.g., T. W. Manson, *Only to the House of Israel* [Philadelphia: Fortress, 1964]; J. Jeremias, *Jesus' Promise to the Nations* [Philadelphia: Fortress, 1982]).

7:31 / **The neighborhood of Tyre . . . Sidon . . . the territory of the Ten Towns**: On Tyre see the note on 7:24. **Sidon** here may mean the territory associated with the city (cf. Matt. 15:21), which lies north of Tyre in the area of modern Lebanon, ancient Phoenicia (see *MBA*, 232; "Sidon," *IDB*, vol. 4, pp. 343–45). On the **Ten Towns**, see note on 5:20. Though Jews lived in all these areas, they were mainly gentile in population, and it is their gentile character that links these areas in Mark's narrative, Jesus' travels in these districts prefiguring for Mark the gentile mission of the church after Jesus.

7:32 / **Could hardly speak** translates a word that appears in the NT only here, and in the Greek Bible of Mark's readers only in Isa. 35:6, making it likely a deliberate allusion here in Mark. The use of the term *deaf-mute* in the GNB heading for this story is not quite correct. What is probably described is a severe stammering or some other serious impediment. (See also note on 7:37).

7:33 / **Away from the crowd** is similiar to 8:23, where Jesus leads the blind man away from the village before healing him. It seems to be part of Mark's emphasis on Jesus' aversion to the excited throngs (also 7:36).

Fingers in the man's ears, spat, and touched the man's tongue . . . Ephphatha: As indicated in the discussion above, some scholars see similarities between these actions and the practices of other ancient healers and wonder-workers. For discussion and background material, see, e.g., "Miracle Workers," *IDB Sup*, pp. 598–99, and the other references cited there. Scholars disagree as to whether *Ephphatha* is evidence of Jesus speaking Aramaic or Hebrew here, though the most widely shared view is that it is Aramaic. (The two languages are closely related and both were used by Jews in ancient Palestine.) It was a common feature among ancient magicians and exorcists to use incantations composed of foreign words or even nonsense syllables, but as if to distinguish Jesus from such practices, Mark translated the term so that its meaning as a simple command is known (cf. also 5:41; 15:34). On the ancient use of spittle in connection with healing, see, e.g., "Spit," *IDB*, vol. 4, p. 437.

7:35 / **Able to hear, his speech impediment was removed**: Literally, the Greek is "His ears were opened and immediately the bond of his tongue was loosed." This is not only more vivid than the GNB translation, it also describes the man's previous condition as if he were held by some (evil) power. The healing is described in language like that of an exorcism; but Mark may have intended the similarity in language to signify that, like the exorcisms, this healing was a sign of the Kingdom of God making its advance in Jesus' power.

7:36 / **Jesus ordered the people not to speak of it**: Again we have a command to silence, a frequent note in Mark (cf. 1:44–45; 5:43; 8:26). It is significant that Mark says that silence was not observed, and that both here and in 1:45 he uses a word to describe the telling of the healings that is used elsewhere in the NT for the preaching of the gospel. This makes the naive report of Jesus' miracles a prefiguring of the later (and more intelligent) proclamation of the church.

7:37 / **He even causes the deaf to hear and the dumb to speak** seems to picture Jesus as bringing the blessings associated with the time of God's favor promised in OT prophecies such as Isaiah 35. It is interesting to think that Mark may have intended his readers to recall this very OT passage, with its reference to the area of Lebanon (Isa. 35:1–2; the same area as Tyre and Sidon), its promise of healing miracles (35:5–6), and the prospect of an ingathering of people by God to follow him in true holiness (35:8–10), all themes reflected in Mark's narrative in chapter 7.

14

Feeding the 4,000 and the Meaning of the Feedings

MARK 8:1–21

Not long afterward another large crowd came together. When the people had nothing left to eat, Jesus called the disciples to him and said, ²"I feel sorry for these people, because they have been with me for three days and now have nothing to eat. ³If I send them home without feeding them, they will faint as they go, because some of them have come a long way."

⁴His disciples asked him, "Where in this desert can anyone find enough food to feed all these people?"

⁵"How much bread do you have?" Jesus asked.

"Seven loaves," they answered.

⁶He ordered the crowd to sit down on the ground. Then he took the seven loaves, gave thanks to God, broke them, and gave them to his disciples to distribute to the crowd; and the disciples did so. ⁷They also had a few small fish. Jesus gave thanks for these and told the disciples to distribute them too. ⁸⁻⁹Everybody ate and had enough—there were about four thousand people. Then the disciples took up seven baskets full of pieces left over. Jesus sent the people away ¹⁰and at once got into a boat with his disciples and went to the district of Dalmanutha.

¹¹Some Pharisees came to Jesus and started to argue with him. They wanted to trap him, so they asked him to perform a miracle to show that God approved of him. ¹²But Jesus gave a deep groan and said, "Why do the people of this day ask for a miracle? No, I tell you! No such proof will be given to these people!"

¹³He left them, got back into the boat, and started across to the other side of the lake.

¹⁴The disciples had forgotten to bring enough bread and had only one loaf with them in the boat. ¹⁵"Take care," Jesus warned them, "and be on your guard against the yeast of the Pharisees and the yeast of Herod."

¹⁶They started discussing among themselves: "He says this because we don't have any bread."

¹⁷Jesus knew what they were saying, so he asked them, "Why are you discussing about not having any bread? Don't you know or understand yet? Are your minds so dull? ¹⁸You have eyes—can't you see? You have ears—can't you hear? Don't you remember ¹⁹when I broke the five loaves for the five thousand people? How many baskets full of leftover pieces did you take up?"

"Twelve," they answered.

²⁰"And when I broke the seven loaves for the four thousand people," asked Jesus, "how many baskets full of leftover pieces did you take up?"

"Seven," they answered.

²¹"And you still don't understand?" he asked them.

8:1-10 / This is the second feeding account in Mark (cf. 6:30–44), and the repetition of the same sort of miracle in so compressed a narrative as Mark plus the similarities of the two accounts have provoked a great deal of scholarly study. Since our objective here is to try to understand what Mark intended by including these two accounts in his Gospel, we shall not discuss the various suggestions about the oral or written sources that Mark may have used for these stories.

Mark 8:14–21 makes it evident that Mark saw both feeding miracles as important revelations of Jesus' significance. The fact that he devoted space to two accounts of the same sort of miracle suggests that each one had for him a special significance and that neither could be omitted without losing something important. With some attention to the earlier discussion of the first feeding account, we must try to see what the particular significance of the feeding of the four thousand is in Mark's narrative. To do so, it will be helpful to try to isolate the distinguishing features of this account.

The first thing we should notice is where this account appears in Mark. This feeding is mentioned right after the redefinition of clean/unclean in 7:1–23 and the two stories of miracles in gentile settings in 7:24–37, the later story alluding to Isaiah 35 with its prophetic hope of a time of divine salvation. Immediately following the feeding here in 8:1-10, there is the rejection of the Pharisees' demand for a sign to authenticate Jesus (8:11–13), a warning about the wrong attitudes of the Jewish leaders (8:14–17), another healing story (8:22–26), and very importantly, the discussion between Jesus and the Twelve showing how imperfectly all (including the Twelve!) understand him (8:27–30), leading up to the first prediction of Jesus' execution by the Jewish leaders and Jesus' warning that anyone who truly follows him must be prepared for a similar fate (8:31–38). That is, the larger narrative into which this feeding account is set is full of a growing tension between Jesus and the Jewish religious establishment, and teaching and events justifying a proclamation of the gospel beyond Jewish borders. By contrast, our study of the context of the first feeding account suggested that it presents Jesus as manifesting himself to Israel.

The second observation to be made concerns the details of the feeding account itself in comparison with the first feeding story. Here there is no allusion to the OT hope for a shepherd for Israel like Moses or David, as there is in 6:34, 40 (see comments and notes on these verses). Also, it is interesting to note that, though 6:34 emphasizes that Jesus' compassion leads him to *teach* the crowds, in 8:2 his concern for the crowd has to do with their *hunger* exclusively. That is, this account is much more concerned with Jesus providing a miraculous supply for the people. We note again, as in 6:32, 35, the description of the area as a **desert** or uninhabited area (8:4, see note). This is surely intended to allude to the OT passages that speak of God's future salvation as a new miracle in the "desert," like the miraculous preservation of Israel in the desert under Moses (e.g., Isa. 43:19–20), and that describe God's promised time of new blessing as involving a miraculous abundance in desert places (e.g., Isa. 35:1, 6; 51:3).

Another important detail is the little statement that some of the crowd have come **a long way**, better translated "from afar," which renders a term frequently used in the Greek OT to describe foreign (gentile) areas and in OT promises of a future ingathering of the people of God from such distant lands (e.g., Isa. 60:4, 9; Jer. 46:27; and passages found only in the Greek version of Jeremiah, 26:27; 38:10). It seems likely that Mark intended this word as an allusion to these passages, and by this allusion the readers are to perceive that this feeding is a sign that this promised ingathering is to be accomplished as a result of Jesus' ministry. Now, it is important to realize that, though the original prophetic oracles seem to have envisioned primarily a return of Jewish exiles from distant lands, early Christians took these passages as also predicting the ingathering of non-Jewish peoples into the church. Thus, Jesus' feeding of a crowd that includes some "from afar" is described as prefiguring the expansion of the people of God to include Gentiles.

These observations about the narrative context of this feeding account and its details allow us to see the purpose for two feeding accounts in Mark: The feeding of the five thousand shows Jesus bringing salvation to Israel. The feeding of the four thousand anticipates that his salvation will reach others (Gentiles) as well.

In further support of the idea that the distinguishing feature of the present feeding in Mark is that it anticipates more clearly the church and its worldwide mission, there is the previously noted detail of the wording used to describe Jesus' ceremonial actions over the bread. Whereas Jesus' prayer over the bread in 6:41 is described after the fashion of Jewish meal graces ("gave thanks," lit., "blessed [God]"), the term used in 8:6 expresses the traditional Christian (gentile) idea of meal grace ("to give thanks") and, more importantly, is the word associated with the church rite of Holy Communion or Eucharist (*eucharisto*). This variation in terms between the two accounts may be a further clue to help the reader realize what symbolic meaning Mark saw in the account. That is, the second feeding, because it includes those from afar, is therefore an anticipation of Christian Eucharist.

Two other matters demand comment. First, the impatience with Jesus shown by the disciples in 6:35–37 seems toned down in this passage, though they still do not seem to realize what Jesus intends to do in 8:4. The Markan theme of the dullness of the Twelve is reflected in both passages, but this is not the main point of the two stories.

Secondly, there is the variation in the numbers used. There have been various attempts to see every number in the two passages as symbolically significant, and some other scholars are skeptical of any particular significance for any of the numbers (e.g., Lane, p. 274). As suggested earlier, however, when treating 6:30–44, it seems difficult to avoid the symbolic association of twelve with Israel. Is there any significance to the seven loaves and seven baskets of fragments here? Two possibilities are worth consideration. There is, on the one hand, the use of seven to represent completeness and divine perfection. On the other hand, there is the association of seven (and seventy) with Gentiles (see note for references). It is even possible that Mark may have intended his readers to be reminded of both associations for the number. Nevertheless, in view of the evidence adduced above that the two feedings symbolize respectively a mission to Israel and to the world, it is perhaps more likely that the seven loaves and seven baskets of fragments, too, are hints that this feeding prefigures the proclamation of God's salvation to all the world.

8:11-13 / Having just led the reader through a list of miraculous events so described as to make it clear that they are signs of Jesus' significance as sent from God, Mark now has the Pharisees appear, demanding some proof of Jesus' significance! The intended effect is to make the hostility and spiritual blindness of the Pharisees seem all the greater. It is also interesting to note that, just as Mark has told the stories of the preceding miracles with allusions to OT passages so as to make the meaning of the events clearer, he tells this incident in a similar fashion.

The Pharisees ask for a **miracle to show that God approved of him**, literally, "a sign from heaven." The term "sign," not used frequently in Mark (see note), is familiar from the OT in reference to the miraculous works of God performed to rescue Israel and to demonstrate his love and power on their behalf (e.g., Exod. 7:3; 10:1; Deut. 6:22). "Signs" are also described as the sort of authenticating events that might attend the work of those who announce themselves as prophets (Deut. 13:1–5), though Israel is warned that they are not to follow such persons, even if signs accompany them, if they speak a message that would lead Israel astray from the Lord God. It is possible that the Pharisees may have asked for a sign from Jesus because they had real doubts about the validity of his ministry; after all, he did take positions at variance with what they regarded as the established ways for the righteous to live and believe. Mark, however, presents their request as an act of disobedience to the message of Jesus and to the miraculous indications of divine favor already given. Thus, the Pharisees' request is said to be done to **trap** Jesus.

Literally, the Greek says they sought to "test" or "tempt" him, and the word used here seems to allude to many OT passages that speak of Israel "tempting" God by doubting his previously demonstrated works and demanding new ones (e.g., Pss. 95:9–10; 78:17–20, 40–43, 56; 106:13–14; Num. 14:1–10, 20–25). Jesus' reply, a refusal of their demand for a sign, is also an allusion to OT pasages such as we have just mentioned. The term "generation" (translated here **the people of this day**) used here alludes to OT passages such as Deuteronomy 1:35; Psalm 95:10, where the rebellious Israelites who demanded further signs of God's powers are called an "evil generation," (translated "those people" in Ps. 95:10 in GNB).

In short, Mark's use of this vocabulary here is intended to make the Pharisees' request for further proof of Jesus' authority an act of disobedience like the disobedience of Israel in the wilderness, in the time of Moses. This disobedience by the Pharisees contrasts powerfully with the faith of the gentile woman of 7:24–30, or the acclamation of the crowd in 7:37, making the Pharisees' request all the more clearly a refusal to see what they do not want to acknowledge. This characterization of the Pharisees prepares the reader for the next passage (8:14–21), where the Pharisees are mentioned in a negative light as examples that the disciples are not to follow.

Jesus' refusal to give a sign to the Pharisees (8:12) must of course be read against the narrative of Mark, which is filled with miraculous indications of God's favor upon Jesus. The refusal is therefore filled with irony from Mark's standpoint. Jesus refuses to give them the very thing that God has been abundantly doing through him all along and that they are too blind to see.

8:14–21 / This is one of the more difficult passages in Mark, and yet it is also clearly an important one, given the fact that it seems to relate to other passages (the feeding miracles) and given the solemn statements of Jesus about understanding in verses 17–21. The parallels in Matthew 16:5–12 and Luke 12:1 show that the saying of Jesus was remembered in varying ways, which means that it must have been important and somewhat ambiguous in meaning (on the parallels, see the notes). Indeed, in order to see what Mark intended in this passage, it will be helpful to take note of the ways in which his account of this incident differs from these parallels.

The first thing to examine is the saying about the **yeast** of the Pharisees and Herod (8:14–15). This saying ties in immediately with the preceding incident in which Pharisees demand some outward proof from Jesus of his authority, a demand treated in Mark as a disobedient and rebellious act (8:11–13, and the comments and notes). The close placement of this saying after the incident with the Pharisees suggests the meaning of the **yeast** against which the disciples are warned. **Yeast** (often translated "leaven") was an ancient Jewish and Christian symbol for evil (see e.g., 1 Cor. 5:6–8), false teaching (Gal. 5:9; Matt. 16:12), and hypocrisy (the parallel in Luke 12:1). In Mark, the Pharisees (sometimes with the teachers of the Law) are presented not primarily as false teachers but as those who refuse to acknowledge that Jesus is sent from God and has the authority to speak and act for God (e.g, 2:1–3:6; 3:22–30), their rejection of Jesus reaching the point of outright hostility (3:6). Herod, too, is mentioned as having a hostile interest in Jesus (6:14–16), seeing in Jesus only another source of annoyance like John the Baptist. Thus, both the Pharisees and Herod (see notes on the variant readings) appear in Mark as representatives of a sprirritual blindness that goes beyond rejecting the light into hating it. It is no doubt this kind of attitude and action that Mark had in mind in writing these words about the **yeast** the disciples were to avoid. The parallel accounts in Matthew and Luke show these evangelists transmitting this saying of Jesus with their own emphases, but we must not allow the interpretations of the other evangelists to prevent us from seeing the particular meaning Mark saw in the saying.

Jesus' reference to yeast triggers the dialogue about bread in 8:16–21. Before studying this part of the passage, we must note that the GNB translation of verse 16 is unfortunately wrong. More correctly, the verse reads, "They discussed among themselves the fact that they had no loaves of bread," meaning that the disciples could not see why Jesus should be concerned about their having **yeast** when they had no bread, and the only way they could have had yeast with them was in bread (see note). This failure of the disciples to see that Jesus was not really talking about literal yeast shows that they themselves are dull in understanding, bringing on the stern rebuke of them in 8:17–18. This use of yeast as a symbol of something else, together with the rebuke of the disciples, alerts us that the readers too must take care to see with true perception what is being discussed.

This rebuke is the harshest comment on the dullness of the disciples thus far in Mark (cf. 4:13, 40; 6:52) and describes them in language borrowed from the OT where rebellious Israel is condemned for her disobedience to God and her unwillingness to hear his prophetic word to her (e.g., Ps. 95:8; Isa. 63:17, "hardness" of heart). Mark 8:18 is actually a quotation of Jeremiah 5:21, a prophetic condemnation of Israel that makes most interesting reading alongside the present passage, predicting the judgment of God upon Israel for failing to acknowledge the Lord God and referring to her wicked leaders (like the Pharisees in Mark?). (By his quotation of this passage, Mark may have intended his readers to refer to Jer. 5:20–31 to understand what he was trying to say about the significance of Jesus' ministry and the seriousness of rejecting it.) The stern nature of the rebuke must mean that what the disciples were supposed to see is not a small thing, or some general truth such as that Jesus always had the power to supply bread. Rather, Mark's language indicates that the disciples were in danger of missing the crucial point about Jesus, the secret of who he really is. With this in mind, let us follow the rest of the passage, verses 19–21.

Of the many attempts to deal with 8:19–21, there are three main approaches. First, there is the interpretation that sees the main point of the questioning by Jesus about the feeding miracles as simply the fact that the disciples should not be concerned about not having bread, for Jesus has already shown them that he can supply whatever is needed as he did in making the loaves sufficient for the two crowds. In this interpretation, there is no mystery about what the disciples should have perceived, only this point about Jesus' power. But in the interest of trying to clarify the passage, this interpretation seems to miss the indications that there is something more profound that the disciples were expected to perceive than simply Jesus' power to supply bread when it was needed. The parallel in Matt. 16:8–10 may more easily be taken in this way, but the Markan questioning about exactly **how many** baskets of fragments were collected after each feeding suggests that these details are important in a special way.

The second line of interpretation is to see the point of the questioning about the amounts of fragments of food as the demonstration that, though the disciples know these details, they do not know the larger meaning of the feeding miracles, this meaning being that Jesus is the Messiah and Lord (e.g., Lane, pp. 282–83). In other words, the numbers in the account are not really significant and do not have any mysterious meaning; they only show that the disciples can recall the outward facts of the events without a perception of the truth to which the miracles point.

The third line of interpretation is similar to the previous one in that the feeding accounts are seen as revealing the truth of Jesus' person, and the dullness of the disciples is seen as a failure to perceive this. Nevertheless, in this view the questioning about the numbers is understood as intended to indicate the meaning of the feeding miracles. That is, the numbers of the baskets of fragments at each feeding are seen as symbolic indications of who Jesus is. Our discussion of the two feeding accounts (at 6:30-44 and at 8:1-10) suggested that the numbers used in the accounts *do* include these symbolic meanings, and therefore this third interpretation of this account is the one favored here.

In the same way that the **yeast** of 8:14-15 is a symbol with an inner meaning, the feedings teach a hidden meaning that Jesus expects his disciples to catch, a meaning hinted at by the numbers twelve and seven respectively. It is not strange for Mark to have seen symbolic meaning in the feeding incidents and to have seen this meaning as essentially being the secret of Jesus' person, for it is a Markan characteristic to emphasize the secretive and mysterious nature of Jesus' message (cf. 4:10-13, 33-34; 6:52). The previously noted failure of the disciples to perceive the secret of the first feeding (6:52) makes them unable to recognize who Jesus really is in the sea miracle in 6:45-52. Mark intended to teach far more than the fact that Jesus could work miracles and could supply food from little. He meant his readers to come to a mature apprehension that Jesus was not just a prophet or wonder-worker but the Son of God, whose ministry not only brought the fulfillment of the prophetic hope of Israel but also was the basis for the preaching of salvation to the whole world. The Pharisees represent those who continually ask for more proof and are unable or unwilling to perceive what is shown them. The disciples, with whom the readers are to identify themselves, show a less hostile, but nevertheless seriously shallow, perception of Jesus. These two groups are intended to warn the readers that there is more than meets the eye in what Jesus did, and Mark's allusions to the OT and his use of symbolic numbers are supposed to help the readers see with more than outward eyesight. In the next incident (8:22-26), Mark gives a healing miracle that dramatizes this clearer perception he urges upon his readers.

Additional Notes

8:3 / **A long way**: As indicated in the comment section, this translates a word (*makrothen*) that seems to be an allusion to OT passages that speak of God gathering his people "from afar." Mark does not state where this feeding is located, though many scholars place the event near the Ten Towns location of the preceding miracle (7:31-37), that is, the southeastern shore of Lake Galilee. If it took place in this area, there might have been Gentiles as well as Jews in the crowd, but this is really irrelevant. Mark makes no point of the ethnic background of the crowd, using instead the biblical allusion cited above to hint at the significance of the gathering.

8:4 / **This desert** here means simply an uninhabited area and not necessarily something like the American desert. The term is also an allusion to OT passages (see comments) where God's future salvation is to make the desert abundant, and to the promise of a new salvation like the Exodus under Moses, when God supplied food to Israel in the desert. Mark uses the term to make the significance of the event clearer, not primarily to fix a specific location for the feeding.

8:5 / **How much bread do you have?**: Here again, as in 6:38, the emphasis is upon the bread, the fish apparently not so important as a vehicle of symbolic meaning. This is evident in the comment in 6:52, "they had not understood the real meaning of the feeding of the five thousand," lit. "the meaning of the loaves" (see note on 6:52). In the discussion of the feedings in 8:14–21 also, the questions concern the bread and its meaning.

Seven loaves: Note also that there are seven baskets of fragments gathered in 8:9 (see note). The number seven seems to have a symbolic meaning in the Bible having to do with perfection, or completeness, e.g., seven days of creation (Gen. 1), forgiveness seven times (Matt. 18:21). It also appears, however, that seven and seventy were associated with Gentiles. Thus, in Jewish tradition the gentile nations are said to number seventy (based on the list in Gen. 10:1–32). Or again in Jewish tradition, the Gentiles, who are not a party to the Israelite covenant with God, are sometimes said to be bound by the covenant with Noah (Gen. 9:1–17), which is said to have seven commandments (e.g., see G. F. Moore, *Judaism in the First Centuries of the Christian Era*, reprint [New York: Schocken, 1971], vol. 1, pp. 274–75). It has been noted also that there were seven leaders of the Greek-speaking Christians in Acts 6:1–7, and that these Christians are from gentile areas, the number seven being chosen to represent this in some way. Thus, in the present passage one must try to determine whether the number of loaves and baskets of fragments is intended as a symbol and if so, what the symbolic significance is. In the comment section, we note reasons for seeing the number seven here as hinting at a worldwide scope for Jesus' message. (For background references on numbers in the Bible and seven in particular, see, e.g., "Numbers," *IDB*, vol. 3, pp. 561–67; "Seven," *IDB*, vol. 4, pp. 294–95.)

8:6 / **Gave thanks**: In Greek this term is familiar in connection with the Christian rite of Eucharist, e.g., 1 Cor. 11:24. In 14:22–25, Mark uses the term meaning "to bless" to describe Jesus' prayer over the bread (14:22; cf. 6:41) and the term for "to give thanks" (*eucharisto*, 14:23) to describe his prayer over the cup (the same word used here). It is the latter term that had more Christian associations for Mark's readers in connection with their own sacred meal (Eucharist).

8:9 / **Seven baskets full of pieces left over**: Cf. 6:43 (twelve baskets). In early Christian times the gathering up of the fragments was seen as a prefiguring of the gathering of the people of God into the fellowship of the church (e.g., the prayer before Eucharist in the early Christian writing known as The Didache 9; accessible in popular editions such as J. B. Lightfoot, *The Apostolic Fathers*, reprint [Grand Rapids: Baker, 1965] and more scholarly editions such as K. Lake, *The Apostolic Fathers* [Loeb Classical Library, Cambridge: Harvard University Press, 1912]). The term **baskets** here is a different Greek word from that translated in 6:43, the latter being a small basket more associated with ancient Jewish life and the term here representing a larger basket more familiar in the general culture of the time.

8:10 / **Dalmanutha**: The parallel in Matt. 15:39 reads "Magadan," and ancient manuscripts of Mark include variant readings here, "Mageda," or "Magdala." There is no site identified as **Dalmanutha**, but some suggest that it is another name for Magdala (e.g., Lane, p. 275; *MBA*, 231), a town on the western shore of Lake Galilee associated with Mary Magdalene (Luke 8:2–3). (On the site, "Magdala," see *IDB Sup*, p. 561.)

8:11 / **Started to argue**: The term used here means that the Pharisees were disputing with Jesus, no doubt about the sort of issues that have already been mentioned as points of conflict between them (cf., e.g., 2:6–12, 16–17, 18–22, 23–28; 7:1–23). The demand for a sign therefore arises in the context of a strong disagreement about the will of God. In Jewish rabbinical tradition there are examples of rabbis appealing to God for a sign to authenticate their view in a dispute about the interpretation of religious laws.

A miracle: What is requested may have been something more spectacular than healings and exorcisms, the sort of thing others in the ancient world claimed to do. In 13:21–23, Jesus warns the disciples about later imposters who would come working "signs" to try to lead the church astray. It is possible that Mark's refusal to use the term "sign" to describe Jesus' works may have been motivated by a desire to avoid shallow comparisons between Jesus and wonder-workers of his time who tried to impress people with their powers. In another sense, however, it is clear that for Mark the miracles of Jesus were signs of God's favor and indications of the Kingdom of God breaking in upon human life through Jesus' ministry.

8:12 / **A deep groan**: The Greek term means a deep sigh, reflecting weariness and perhaps impatience with the disputations of the Pharisees. It is interesting to compare the various references to Jesus' emotion in Mark, e.g., 1:41 (but see note); 3:5; 6:6; 10:14; 14:34.

No such proof will be given: The Greek phrase used here is quite strong, amounting to a solemn oath. This surely must indicate both the heat of the argument going on here in the scene and the strength of Mark's condemnation of the Pharisees' request as well. The parallels in Matt. 16:4; 12:39; Luke 11:39, say that no sign will be given except "the miracle [lit. "sign"] of Jonah," explained in Matt. 12:40 as alluding to Jesus' death, burial, and resurrection.

8:13 / **The other side of the lake**: As mentioned before, it is very hard to keep track of the travels of Jesus in Mark's account, and this difficulty is especially great when trying to unravel Mark's references to the lake crossings. Since Mark makes no great point of the locations of some of these events, it is probably not important to his narrative.

8:14 / **One loaf**: Some have seen a confusion in the narrative in that this verse mentions a loaf of bread in the boat, whereas in 8:16 the disciples say that they have no bread. However clumsy his wording may seem, Mark probably meant that the disciples had forgotten to bring a supply of bread for the group, having only one small loaf in the boat, an amount sufficient for one person at best. Many have suggested that this detail of the one loaf has a symbolic meaning too, Jesus being the **one loaf** with them, sufficient for all their needs. Further, it is suggested that this **one loaf** is intended to bring out associations with the Christian Eucharist, which was celebrated by the partaking of a common loaf of bread symbolizing Christ as the source of their life and their unity. John 6:35–40 is an indication that early Christians portrayed Jesus as the "bread of life," and saw the feeding miracle as a dramatization of this fact. 1 Cor. 10:15–17 also shows the symbolic meaning of the one loaf of bread used in early Christian rites. (On the Eucharist in the NT, see, e.g., "Lord's Supper," *NIDNTT*, vol. 2, pp. 520–38.)

8:15 / **Yeast of the Pharisees and the yeast of Herod**: As indicated in the comments, yeast was frequently used in ancient times as a symbol for evil. The OT required the Jews to celebrate an annual period beginning with Passover during which no yeast was to be found in Jewish households and all bread eaten was to be unleavened bread (see Exod. 12:14–20). At other times, yeast was maintained by keeping a small portion of leavened dough on hand in the household that, when placed in a new batch of dough, would leaven the whole for baking (see, e.g., Matt. 13:33). The parallel in Matt. 16:12 refers to the yeast of the Pharisees and of the Sadducees and takes this as being their teaching. Luke 12:1 mentions only the Pharisees and refers to their hypocrisy. In some ancient manuscripts of Mark, in this place there is a variant reading mentioning the Pharisees and the Herodians, possibly because the reference in 3:6 to an agreement between Pharisees and Herodians made some copyists think that the mention of Herod must have been a mistake and that the hostile arrangement referred to in 3:6 was what Mark had in mind.

15

Physical and Spiritual Perception

They came to Bethsaida, where some people brought a blind man to Jesus and begged him to touch him. [23]Jesus took the blind man by the hand and led him out of the village. After spitting on the man's eyes, Jesus placed his hands on him and asked him, "Can you see anything?"

[24]The man looked up and said, "Yes, I can see people, but they look like trees walking around."

[25]Jesus again placed his hands on the man's eyes. This time the man looked intently, his eyesight returned, and he saw everything clearly. [26]Jesus then sent him home with the order, "Don't go back into the village."

[27]Then Jesus and his disciples went away to the villages near Caesarea Philippi. On the way he asked them, "Tell me, who do people say I am?"

[28]"Some say that you are John the Baptist," they answered; "others say that you are Elijah, while others say that you are one of the prophets."

[29]"What about you?" he asked them. "Who do you say I am?"

Peter answered, "You are the Messiah."

[30]Then Jesus ordered them, "Do not tell anyone about me."

[31]Then Jesus began to teach his disciples: "The Son of Man must suffer much and be rejected by the elders, the chief priests, and the teachers of the Law. He will be put to death, but three days later he will rise to life."

[32]He made this very clear to them. So Peter took him aside and began to rebuke him. [33]But Jesus turned around, looked at his disciples, and rebuked Peter. "Get away from me, Satan," he said. "Your thoughts don't come from God but from man!"

[34]Then Jesus called the crowd and his disciples to him. "If anyone wants to come with me," he told them, "he must forget self, carry his cross, and follow me. [35]For whoever wants to save his own life will lose it; but whoever loses his life for me and for the gospel will save it. [36]Does a person gain anything if he wins the whole world but loses his life? Of course not! [37]There is nothing he can give to regain his life. [38]If a person is ashamed of me and of my teaching in this godless and wicked day, then the Son of Man will be ashamed of him when he comes in the glory of his Father with the holy angels."

[1]And he went on to say, "I tell you, there are some here who will not die until they have seen the Kingdom of God come with power."

8:22-26 / Immediately following the discussion of 8:14–21 with its reference to the disciples' deaf ears and blind eyes (8:18), there is this healing of a blind man, and this is almost universally recognized by commentators as a story that also serves as a dramatization of the spiritual difficulty of the disciples. It is the unparalleled phenomenon of a healing occurring in two stages that particularly connects this story, not only with the preceding passage, but also with the following ones (8:27–38), in which the disciples show the need for a similar two-stage lifting of their spiritual dullness.

It is also clear that this story is to be connected with the account of the healing of the deaf man in 7:31–37, both because the two stories have several similarities in wording and because each story seems to allude to Isaiah 35:5–6. In both accounts people bring the needy person to Jesus, asking him to touch the person (7:31; 8:22). In both stories Jesus takes the person away from the people who brought him (7:33; 8:23). These two stories are the only ones in Mark that mention Jesus using spittle in the healings (7:33; 8:23). Of course, the healing of the deaf and blind are exactly two of the things mentioned in Isaiah 35:5–6 as the sort of miracles that will accompany God's final salvation. When we further note that these two stories are unique to Mark, this adds weight to the view that Mark used these events as important components in the narrative.

The leading of the person away from the crowd, common to both accounts, is not quite paralleled in any other miracle story in Mark, except in the story of Jairus' daughter (5:21–43), in which Jesus sends out the unbelieving and mocking crowd (5:40). But in 7:31–37 and 8:22–26 there is no mention of the crowd being hostile. Indeed, they bring the two men to Jesus for healing! It is possible that Mark mentions this removal of the person from the crowd as a part of his overall emphasis upon the secrecy in Jesus' ministry. But it is also possible that the narrative location of the two stories gives us the clue as to the significance Mark saw in this detail. As indicated in earlier comments, in Mark 7–8 there is the emphasis upon the tension between Jesus and the Jewish leadership and the foreshadowing of the spread of the gospel to Gentiles. With this in mind, it is possible to see that for Mark the removal of the two men from their village crowds in some sense signified the separation from one's past that Jesus' message demanded. In the contextually close account in which Jesus receives the acclamation as Messiah from his disciples, he predicts his own execution by the Jewish leaders and warns his followers that they must be prepared for the same fate (8:31–38).

As to the nature of the man's condition in 8:22–26, it would appear that the man once saw but had progressively gone blind, in that when partially healed he shows a recognition of what trees look like (v. 24). At the first stage of his healing, the man appears still to have a severe case of nearsightedness, with things at any distance looking quite blurry. Finally, the man is fully healed (8:25), and the wording Mark uses seems to indicate something of the actions of such a scene, with the man squinting intently (8:25) and then suddenly seeing everything clearly.

In the next two sections of this chapter we see how this story provides a fitting introduction to the account of the disciples' limited perception and their need for a fuller understanding of the meaning of Jesus' mission.

8:27-30 / This passage should really be read in connection with the following passage (8:31–9:1), which is given a separate heading in the GNB. Together, the two sections give us an open acclamation of Jesus as Messiah and the first of three predictions of Jesus' death, which triggers the rebuke of Peter, revealing the fact that his acclamation of Jesus was not based on a full understanding of Jesus' purpose and activity.

The answers given to Jesus' first question remind us of the list of the same opinions given in 6:14–15, and this repetition of these varying labels for Jesus intensifies the sense that the question about who Jesus really is must be seen as central for Mark. (On the significance of each of the labels mentioned in 8:28, see the discussion and notes on 6:14–15.) Already, Mark has given us examples of people wondering about how to label Jesus. There are the crowds of 1:27 and 2:12 who are amazed at his bold actions. There are the teachers of the law of 3:22 who say he is a sorcerer (a view not repeated in 6:14–15 or here in 8:28). There is the crowd at Nazareth who see in Jesus only a home-town boy (6:2–3). There are the disciples, also, who up to this point have shown wonder and bafflement at Jesus (4:41; 6:52). Only the voice from heaven (1:11) and the demons (1:24, 34; 3:12; 5:7) see the truth of Jesus' person!

In contrast to the varying labels of others, Peter, answering for the Twelve, acclaims Jesus as Messiah (8:29), the same title given to Jesus at the beginning of Mark (1:1, there translated "Christ," see notes). This indicates that for Mark the title is a correct one and that Peter's use of the title displays some recognition of Jesus' true significance. The subsequent use of the title in Mark shows that, although Jesus is the Messiah, he is not the Messiah of popular expectation. For example, in 9:41 Jesus speaks of his followers as those who "belong to Christ " (the GNB translation "belong to me" obscures this needlessly). In 13:21–22, Jesus predicts imposters who will claim to be Christ, calling them false prophets and "false Messiahs," and if they be false then he must be the true Messiah. At the trial scene in 14:61–62, Jesus is asked whether he is the Messiah and he answers affirmatively. But this scene also indicates that this judgment is not shared by the leaders of the Jewish people, the priests and the Council, for they respond that his confession amounts to blasphemy (14:63–64). Further, in the crucifixion scene, the onlookers mockingly hail Jesus as "Messiah, the King of Israel," and their demand that he come down from the cross illustrates the fact that their definition of Messiah (Christ) does not involve one who suffers and dies in shame. (There is the difficult passage 12:35–37 where the term Messiah appears, this passage also intended to show the reader that popular notions about the Messiah were inadequate. On this passage, see the comment.)

At first glance, it would appear that at last Peter and the Twelve have broken through their dullness of mind and are able to perceive who Jesus really is, but the reader is quickly shown that this is not so. In the next passage, this same Peter is rebuked for still being under the infuence of incorrect, human thinking. Thus, the confession in 8:29 must be read in its context, where it reflects an insight into Jesus that is only partially correct, resembling the eyesight of the blind man in the preceding story at the first stage of his healing.

Most students of Mark agree that this passage is a major turning point, introducing a new, large section that reaches to 10:52, largely devoted to Jesus teaching his disciples about his impending death and about the true nature of the discipleship to which they (and the readers) are called. This section is further characterized by references to Jesus teaching his disciples in private (e.g., 9:9–10, 30–31; 10:32), and when we remember that Mark intended his readers to identify especially with the disciples, it becomes clear that this section is not just a record of Jesus and the Twelve but also a body of teaching material for the readers.

Thus, the present passage brings into the open the use of the term **Messiah** (Christ) as a proper confessional term to apply to Jesus. But the following material will show that the term can be used properly only when it is informed by a genuine understanding of what it means for Jesus to be God's Messiah. That is why in 8:30 Jesus tells the Twelve not to circulate their confession of him as Messiah among anyone else. It is not just that others would not understand its proper meaning; even the disciples do not yet know what they are saying!

8:31–9:1 / This passage completes the scene begun in 8:27–30, gives us the first of three predictions by Jesus of his impending suffering and death (cf. 9:30–32; 10:32–34), and clearly sets the terms for discipleship as a following of him even to death. We must understand that in ancient Judaism there was no idea that the Messiah would suffer the sort of horrible fate that Jesus describes in 8:31, and that Peter's response in 8:32 is in one sense fully understandable. Nevertheless, Mark's point is that all definitions of what the Messiah is and does must be submitted to the fact that God's Messiah, Jesus, was led to bitter suffering and death in the service of God. To fail to do justice to this fact is to be on the side of erroneous human thought and against God's will. Indeed, it is to be under the sway of Satan, without even knowing it (8:33).

Mark 10:35–37 gives us some indication of the kind of glorious expectations that the disciples must have entertained in light of their belief that Jesus was chosen to be God's Messiah, the king of a new reign of divine righteousness and blessing. Perhaps in their own way Mark's first readers were in danger of failing to understand the central importance of Jesus' suffering and death as both basis and pattern for their own lives. If so, this would explain why Mark places such emphasis upon this point. As we have indicated in the discussion of the preceding passage, virtually the whole of 8:31–10:52 is devoted to emphasizing the necessity of Jesus' death (by repeating the prediction three times) and the theme that following Jesus means following his path of service and humiliation.

The suffering Jesus predicts is described as coming from a rejection of him by the Jewish leaders, the elders, the chief priests, and the teachers of the Law (see notes on these terms). We have already encountered the hostility of the teachers of the Law; the others are not mentioned outside of these predictions until Jesus arrives in Jerusalem (chaps. 11–15). The mention of these people means that the rejection is described as a formal decision about Jesus, for they made up the Jewish Council, the highest religious court of the Jews in Jesus' time. In 3:6 Mark told of a scheme to kill Jesus involving Pharisees and Herodians, but they are not mentioned in Mark's account of the trial and execution of Jesus.

This formal rejection of Jesus would have meant for Peter and the Twelve that Jesus' mission was a failure, and this is why Peter takes Jesus in hand to rebuke him, for Peter's conviction that Jesus is the Messiah means that God is with him and that he cannot fail. This is the irony of Peter's rebuke of Jesus; Peter thinks that the fact that Jesus is the chosen one is in contradiction to the dark prediction Jesus gives, not realizing that God's choice of Jesus means that he **must** (8:31) undergo the fate he describes. Peter rebukes Jesus in the name of God but is found to be taking a position Jesus regards as devilish (8:33)!

After his rebuke (same word) of Peter (8:33), Jesus issues what amounts to a call to discipleship and a warning of its cost (8:34–9:1). Because of the passage of time and the frequent spiritualizing of this passage, it is necessary to emphasize that the words must be taken literally if we are to read them as Mark intended. When Mark's first readers read these words, they could have understood them only as a warning that discipleship might mean execution, for in their time the cross was a well-known instrument of Roman execution used on runaway slaves, rebels, and other criminals of lower classes (see note). To be more precise, in Mark's time the cross was not just an indication of possible death for disciples, it was a warning of execution by the state authorities. Thus, in the same way that Jesus' ministry led him to a collision with both Jewish and Roman authorities, the disciples (and readers) are warned to be prepared for the same sort of trouble. This is made all the clearer by Jesus' warning about trying to save one's life by denying him. The situation envisioned in 8:35 is that of a trial in which one is commanded to renounce Jesus and live. It is interesting to note that Mark alone has the phrase **and for the gospel**, which shows that the saying is intended to be applied to the situation of the early church and its mission of preaching the gospel in spite of hostility and persecution (see note on **gospel**).

In Jesus' prediction of his sufferings, he uses the term **the Son of Man** (8:31), a term already encountered in Mark (2:10, 28; see comments and notes on these verses), and which appears several times later as well (in the two other predictions of Jesus' death, 9:31; 10:33, and in other passages, 8:38; 9:9, 12; 10:45; 13:26; 14:21, 41, 62). As indicated earlier in connection with the examination of 2:10, it is impossible (and of questionable profit) to try to review all the many suggestions about the meaning and origin of the term. The position taken in this commentary is that Jesus did use the term as a self-description (meaning something like "this mere man"). It is important to note that there are two uses of the term in the present passage, here in 8:31, and again 8:38. In the first, the **Son of Man** undergoes rejection, but in the second he will come again in glory and will either speak for or against one, depending upon how one has responded to him (Jesus). Thus, for Mark, the term **the Son of Man** seems to be an ironic way of referring to Jesus as the one who appears as a mere man now in the eyes of many but will one day reappear vindicated by God as the Messiah and the Son of God. It is possible too that the term **the Son of Man** alludes to Daniel 7:13–14, which mentions a figure described as "one like a son of man" (translated quite properly in the GNB as "what looked like a human being," which is what the Aramaic phrase means). If an allusion to this passage is intended by Jesus (and/or Mark on his own), the meaning of the term **Son of Man** would be a figure who undergoes trial and humiliation now but will be exalted later.

It is clear that Mark intends us to realize that we have come into a new section of the narrative, for he signals this by the phrase in 8:32, **He made this very clear to them**, which is better translated, "He was speaking to them openly." That is, there is no more use of parable and coded speech; now Jesus declares himself clearly. But Jesus not only speaks here clearly of his coming rejection and death, he also promises vindication for himself and for his followers (8:38-9:1). For the first time in Mark, there is reference to the glory that Jesus is to receive; but it is a glory won by obedience to the will of God (see note on **must** in 8:31).

The last verse of this passage (9:1) is one of the most difficult in Mark and has attracted a number of suggestions. The key to the verse is what is meant by the Kingdom of God coming with power, the last few words of the verse. The statement could be taken to mean that the new reign of God's righteousness over all the earth would be set up before Jesus' generation was over, and if taken this way it would mean that Jesus incorrectly predicted something that did not in fact happen (e.g., Nineham, pp. 231–32). One problem with this interpretation of 9:1 is that is appears unlikely that Mark saw it this way, for he probably wrote his Gospel some forty years or more after Jesus' crucifixion, almost at the end of the time frame described (see note on **some here who will not die**), and would have realized that no such complete transformation of the world had happened yet. The statement in slightly varying forms is found also in Matthew (16:28) and Luke (9:27), though they are thought to have written their works even later than Mark. It seems unlikely that the Gospel writers would have recorded a saying of Jesus that they and their readers understood to be a flat error. This means that the Gospel writers must have understood the saying differently than the interpretation mentioned above.

An important clue to how they understood the saying is the fact that each of the Gospel writers follows it with the account of the transfiguration of Jesus before a small group of disciples (Mark 9:2–13; Matthew 17:1–13; Luke 9:28–36). This suggests that each of the gospel writers understood the prediction to be fulfilled in the transfiguration and what it in turn signified and prefigured (see comments on 9:2–13), the resurrection of Jesus as Lord and Christ. That is, Mark and the other Gospel writers must have seen Jesus' prediction, such as we find in 9:1, as a promise of the resurrection and exaltation of Jesus to God's "right hand" (e.g., 14:62), which they understood as the mighty appearance of the Kingdom of God and the inauguration of the rule of Christ as King (e.g., 1 Cor. 15:20–28). For Mark, then, 9:1 meant that Jesus' own contemporaries, those who either doubted him (enemies) or imperfectly understood him (disciples), would not die before the validity of his message and ministry was shown in a powerful confirmation, that being the resurrection of Jesus, which the transfiguration episode (9:2–13) prefigures.

After this passage (8:31–9:1), which emphasizes the necessity of Jesus' suffering and summons disciples to a commitment like Jesus' own in the hope of ultimate vindication before the Son of Man, Mark gives a story that is designed to demonstrate the validity of all stated here, the transfiguration episode that follows (9:2–13). There is thus an intended connection between these two accounts, balancing a foreshadowing of Christ's glory to come with the emphasis upon humiliation and obedience.

Additional Notes

8:22 / **Bethsaida**: On the location of this town, see the note on 6:45. In a few ancient manuscripts we read "Bethany" instead, but this is to be disregarded in view of the strong support for the reading **Bethsaida**. Mark calls the place a **village** (vv. 23, 26), but we should think of a town of a few thousand people in the time of Jesus.

8:23 / **After spitting on the man's eyes**: On the ancient significance of spittle in healing, see the note on 7:33.

8:26 / **Don't go back into the village**: In several ancient witnesses right after this phrase, there is the inclusion of a command not to speak to anyone, but this is possibly taken by copyists from the healing of the deaf man in 7:36 and is to be omitted here.

8:27 / **Caesarea Philippi** was located near the northern shore of Lake Galilee in a beautiful setting. Herod Philip ruled the city in Jesus' time as part of his territory and had enlarged and beautified the structures of the town. It was named both after Caesar (Tiberius) and after Philip. The population was largely non-Jewish, and this fits Mark's locating of other revelations of Jesus in gentile territory (e.g., 7:24–37). (See *IDB*, vol. 1, p. 480.)

8:29 / **You are the Messiah**: The term "Messiah" is a translation of the Greek term *Christos* from which our title "Christ" comes. "Messiah" is derived from the Hebrew equivalent of *Christos*, *Mashiach*, both words meaning literally "Anointed One." The term is used many times in the OT as an adjective describing persons chosen by God for special office, such as king of Israel (e.g., Ps. 2:2, GNB translating it here, "the king he chose"; 1 Sam. 2:10, 35; 2 Sam. 1:14, 16), but in Jewish life in the time of Jesus the term had come to acquire a special meaning as the title of the expected one whom God would send to deliver Israel and to establish God's righteous rule upon the earth. (On the term, see further *NIDNTT*, vol. 2, pp. 334–43.)

The parallels to this passage make interesting study. In Luke 9:20 Peter says,

"You are God's Messiah," essentially the same as the statement here in Mark. It is the Matt. 16:13–20 parallel that is particularly worth noting. Two essential differences appear. First, Peter's confession is fuller, "You are the Messiah, the Son of the living God." Secondly, there is the famous congratulatory statement of Jesus to Peter (16:17–19) in which Peter is said to have been given an illumination by God. On the whole, even though Peter is later rebuked in Matthew's account (16:21–23), he seems to give Peter higher marks here than does Mark, illustrative of the generally softer way the disciples are presented in Matthew.

8:31 / **The Son of Man**: See the comments and notes on 2:10 on the meaning of the term as a title in Mark. For background and discussion of the wider use of the term, see, e.g., "Son of Man," *NIDNTT*, vol. 3, pp. 613–34.

Must: The word here in Greek suggests a necessity based on the divine will. It is a term that alludes to the conception that God has planned the whole program of redemption, a conception attested in the OT prophetic books and in later Jewish apocalyptic writings. (See "Apocalypticism," *IDB*, vol. 1, pp. 157–61; *IBDSup*, pp. 28–34.)

Elders, the chief priests, and the teachers of the Law: We have already encountered **the teachers of the Law**, "scribes" (see comments and notes on 2:6). The **elders** were respected leaders of the Jewish community charged with deciding issues of religious and civil law. There were such leaders in each local community, and also a group of such men sat on the Jewish high court, the Council ("Sanhedrin," see comments and notes on 14:55), which met in Jerusalem. The term **chief priests** here probably means not only the ruling chief priest but also those who had formerly held the position and members of the families of these men. The term in plural is used similarly by Josephus, the Jewish historian. These three groups (**elders, chief priests, teachers**) collectively made up the Jewish high council mentioned in 14:55 as taking action against Jesus.

Three days later: Literally the Greek phrase here means "after three days" and can mean simply "after a short time." The parallels in Matt. 16:21 and Luke 9:22 use the phrase "on the third day," reflecting the Christian tradition that Jesus' resurrection took place on the third day after his crucifixion (e.g., 1 Cor. 15:4).

He will rise to life: What is meant is that God will raise Jesus from death, and the parallels in Matt. 16:21; Luke 9:22 use a Greek word that makes this more obvious.

8:33 / **Get away from me, Satan**: strong language that reflects the way Peter's rebuke of Jesus was taken. It is possible that Jesus' words indicate that Peter's attempt to persuade him not to follow a path of humiliation was a genuine temptation that had to be rejected forcefully.

8:34 / **Forget himself**: Literally the Greek word is "deny himself," meaning that the disciple must be willing to lose all for the sake of following Jesus.

Carry his cross refers to the practice of making the condemned person carry the crossbeam upon which he was to be tied or nailed at the place of his execution. Death by crucifixion was a Roman execution by state authorities, familiar in ancient Jewish life on account of the Jewish rebels caught and executed. (On the practice of crucifixion and its implications in ancient Roman times, see Martin Hengel, *Crucifixion* [Philadelphia: Fortress, 1977]; "Crucifixion," *IDB*, vol. 1, pp. 746–47).

8:35 / **For me and for the gospel**: What is implied here is a trial before religious or state authorities in which one's profession of Christ is the issue. To lose one's life **for me** (Christ) would mean to refuse to renounce Christ in such a situation, even if the punishment were death. **And for the gospel** implies that the person charged has come to the attention of authorities on account of preaching the Christian message. **The gospel** in this absolute sense is with one exception used only in Mark and in Paul (see, e.g., 1:15; 10:29; 13:10; Acts 15:7; Rom. 10:16; 11:28; 1 Cor. 4:15; 9:14, 18, 23; 2 Cor. 8:18). The term means not only the message but also the activity of circulating it, and this little phrase (unique in Mark, cf. Matt. 16:25; Luke 9:24) must indicate that Mark wished his readers to know of the importance of the mission of the church. (On the term "Gospel," see *NIDNTT*, vol. 2, pp. 107–15).

8:38 / **When he comes** probably refers to the appearance of Christ in glory that was expected by early Christians and continues to be the hope of all traditional believers. Angels were expected to accompany him. See, e.g., 1 Thess. 4:13–5:11; 2 Thess. 1:6–10.

9:1 / **I tell you** is literally "truly [*amen*] I tell you," a solemn assurance. See note on 3:28.

Some here who will not die is literally "some standing here who will not taste death." This phrase could mean that some *may* die before the event occurs, but it is difficult to know whether this is the intention. If it is taken to mean this, the approximate time period would be about one generation, perhaps forty years or so. But as we indicated in the comments, Mark intends the statement to refer to the resurrection of Jesus, it appears, and so the phrase should be taken to mean that the event mentioned will surely take place and that those then alive would live to see it.

Until they have seen the Kingdom of God come is similar to the solemn assurance given by Jesus at his trial (14:62) that those who condemned him would see the Son of Man glorified. On the meaning of this statement, see the comments and notes on this passage. In both cases Jesus' words give the strongest assurance about what is promised.

16

Mountaintop Glory and the Descent

MARK 9:2–29

Six days later Jesus took with him Peter, James, and John, and led them up a high mountain, where they were alone. As they looked on, a change came over Jesus, ³and his clothes became shining white—whiter than anyone in the world could wash them. ⁴Then the three disciples saw Elijah and Moses talking with Jesus. ⁵Peter spoke up and said to Jesus, "Teacher, how good it is that we are here! We will make three tents, one for you, one for Moses, and one for Elijah." ⁶He and the others were so frightened that he did not know what to say.

⁷Then a cloud appeared and covered them with its shadow, and a voice came from the cloud, "This is my own dear Son—listen to him!" ⁸They took a quick look around but did not see anyone else; only Jesus was with them.

⁹As they came down the mountain, Jesus ordered them, "Don't tell anyone what you have seen, until the Son of Man has risen from death."

¹⁰They obeyed his order, but among themselves they started discussing the matter, "What does this 'rising from death' mean?" ¹¹And they asked Jesus, "Why do the teachers of the Law say that Elijah has to come first?"

¹²His answer was, "Elijah is indeed coming first in order to get everything ready. Yet why do the Scriptures say that the Son of Man will suffer much and be rejected? ¹³I tell you, however, that Elijah has already come and that people treated him just as they pleased, as the Scriptures say about him."

¹⁴When they joined the rest of the disciples, they saw a large crowd around them and some teachers of the Law arguing with them. ¹⁵When the people saw Jesus, they were greatly surprised, and ran to him and greeted him. ¹⁶Jesus asked his disciples, "What are you arguing with them about?"

¹⁷A man in the crowd answered, "Teacher, I brought my son to you, because he has an evil spirit in him and cannot talk. ¹⁸Whenever the spirit attacks him, it throws him to the ground, and he foams at the mouth, grits his teeth, and becomes stiff all over. I asked your disciples to drive the spirit out, but they could not."

¹⁹Jesus said to them, "How unbelieving you people are! How long must I stay with you? How long do I have to put up with you? Bring the boy to me!" ²⁰They brought him to Jesus.

As soon as the spirit saw Jesus, it threw the boy into a fit, so that he fell on the ground and rolled around, foaming at the mouth. ²¹"How long has he been like this?" Jesus asked the father.

"Ever since he was a child," he replied. ²²"Many times the evil spirit has tried to kill him by throwing him in the fire and into water. Have pity on us and help us, if you possibly can!"

²³"Yes," said Jesus, "if you yourself can! Everything is possible for the person who has faith."

²⁴The father at once cried out, "I do have faith, but not enough. Help me have more!"

²⁵Jesus noticed that the crowd was closing in on them, so he gave a command to the evil spirit. "Deaf and dumb spirit," he said, "I order you to come out of the boy and never go into him again!"

²⁶The spirit screamed, threw the boy into a bad fit, and came out. The boy looked like a corpse, and everyone said, "He is dead!" ²⁷But Jesus took the boy by the hand and helped him rise, and he stood up.

²⁸After Jesus had gone indoors, his disciples asked him privately, "Why couldn't we drive the spirit out?"

²⁹"Only prayer can drive this kind out," answered Jesus; "nothing else can."

9:2-13 / The open and forthright nature of Jesus' teaching about his coming death in 8:31–32 is matched here by a powerful disclosure of his true significance as the Son of God. The description of the event is studded with allusions to OT passages and themes, and it is necessary to see these to appreciate what Mark intended this story to convey to his readers.

The placement of this account right after Jesus' promise of his future, glorious vindication (8:38–9:1) is intended to show the reader a glimpse of that glory. The direct connection of this event with the sayings in 8:38–9:1 is made clear by the note **six days later** in 9:2, meaning six days after the sayings in 8:38–9:1 (cf. Luke 9:28 "about a week, " lit., "about eight days"). The mention of six days is, however, also very likely an allusion to Exodus 24:15, where after six days, Moses is summoned to a mountaintop and is given a revelation of God. We have already seen how Mark alludes to the OT to make clear the significance of the events he recounts. Here the point of the allusion is to alert the reader that what is about to take place is a manifestation of God (a theophany) like that mentioned in Exodus 24:15–18 and that a new revelation is here given that therefore surpasses the former one to Moses.

There is another, even more obvious, allusion to the OT in the mention of Moses and Elijah (9:4). In Moses we have the great founder of Israel's religion, the one to whom God gave the Law, and the greatest of all the great figures of the OT. Very importantly, Moses' promise of a prophet whom God would send when he was gone (Deut. 18:15) was understood by some ancient Jews and by early Christians to mean that God would send a great prophet of Moses-like stature in the final period before the appearance of the Kingdom of God. Among early Christians, Moses' statement was understood to be a prophetic promise of Jesus (e.g., Acts

3:22–26; 7:35–37). Moses' appearance in the vision of the disciples meant that he was endorsing Jesus as the one he had promised, the one who now bore all the authority of Moses in speaking for God. In support of this, there is the direct allusion to Deuteronomy 18:15 in 9:7, **listen to him**, being a quote of the final part of Moses' statement (translated in the GNB "You are to obey him").

As for the mention of Elijah (9:4), this too is an indication that the promised time of salvation has come. As indicated earlier (see comments and notes on 6:14–15), Mark's readers knew of the ancient Jewish expectation of an Elijah figure who would appear just before the end of the present world order to announce God's Kingdom and to prepare the people for it. Indeed, it is the expectation that is discussed in 9:11–13. Elijah's appearance with Jesus in the vision meant that Elijah was endorsing Jesus as Messiah, the bringer of the Kingdom of God. The disciples sense that this is what the vision means but are confused because the Elijah figure was supposed to appear on earth to announce the Kingdom before the Messiah appeared (9:11). Jesus' response (9:12–13) indicates that this Elijah figure has in fact already come, and from the way Mark describes John the Baptist (see comments on 1:1–8; 6:14–29), it seems that the reader is intended to realize that Jesus meant John (in the Matt. 17:10-13 parallel this identification is made explicit).

Thus, several features in the account make it clear that Jesus is the Messiah and that his presence is the fulfillment of hopes for God's salvation. But the passage shows that Jesus is even more than this. There are additional items in the narrative that show what this "more" is. First, there is the description of Jesus' transfigured appearance in 9:2–3. The reference to the **shining white** clothes (v. 3) is an allusion to Daniel 7:9, which is a description of a vision of God, and this allusion suggests that the experience of the disciples here in 9:2–13 is to be seen as a divine manifestation like the visions of OT prophets (in addition to Dan. 7:9-14, see also Isa. 6:1–13; Ezek. 1:4–28; 8:1–4). But this means that the "transfiguration" of Jesus shows him in a form like God, meaning that he is not just the Messiah, an especially godly human chosen to rule in God's name, he is himself "clothed" in divine glory.

Secondly, the voice from heaven in 9:7 confirms this transcendent significance of Jesus in acclaiming him **my own dear Son**. The phrase is exactly the same as the first part of the voice from heaven at Jesus' baptism (1:11) and, like that statement, bestows upon Jesus an unequaled status, "beloved Son" meaning that, of all those who have been called sons of God (in the OT, Israel, the king of Israel; in later literature, a righteous man), Jesus is to be regarded as above them all. Together with the transfigured appearance of Jesus, this statement shows that there rests upon him unparalleled glory and divine favor. The **cloud** (9:7) is an allusion to OT accounts in which the presence and glory of God are indicated by a cloud covering the spot where God manifests himself to someone (cf., e.g., Exod. 16:10; 19:9; 24:15–18; 34:5; 40:34–38), and this means that the unnamed voice from the cloud is the very voice of God.

But although this is a manifestation of the glory of Christ, Peter, as spokesman for the others, responds both in awe and confusion (9:5–6), suggesting that they erect tents for Jesus and the heavenly visitors, no doubt with the intention of prolonging the glorious experience. It is also possible that Peter's suggestion means that he thought that the experience meant that the Kingdom had fully arrived, that the end had come, and that God was about to bring fully to pass all the hopes for a new reign of righteousness upon the earth. In this he was wrong, still not realizing the necessity for the suffering of Christ described in 8:31, without which the Kingdom could not fully come, and also not realizing the necessity for the world mission of the church (about which Mark will tell us later, see, e.g., note on 13:10). Rather, this glorious experience was intended as only a foretaste and assurance of Jesus' true glory, and the dissolving of the vision in 9:8, which leaves them back in earthly conditions with **only Jesus**, shows this. The voice from heaven is intended not only to recognize Jesus as the Son of God but also to command the disciples to pay attention to what he is telling them about the task and suffering that lie ahead, both for Jesus and for them.

The command in 9:9 not to speak of the glory of Jesus until after the resurrection means that it is only in the light of the crucifixion and resurrection that Jesus' true person can be understood, for he is not just a wonderful visitor from heaven or an especially favored man given mystic glory but the one called to "give his life to redeem many people" (10:45). He can be worshiped intelligently only when he is seen as the divinely sent redeemer. Only then will it become clear who this **Son of Man** really is, and it is significant that Jesus continues to use this title of his earthly mission even after this experience, for his divine sonship cannot be understood yet. The disciples' continued confusion, mentioned in 9:10, shows that there could be no grasp of Jesus' true purpose until the events that came to constitute the center of the gospel, the death and resurrection, happened. The lesson for the reader is that any intelligent talk of the glory of Jesus cannot be done apart from emphasis upon his death and resurrection, and that any Christian preaching and devotion that is not centered on the meaning of these events is shallow and confused.

9:14:29 / Perhaps the first thing to ask about this story is why it is placed here in Mark's narrative. The answer to this question lies in the observation made earlier that virtually the whole of 8:27–10:52 is concerned with the two themes of the coming suffering of Jesus and the nature of discipleship. This is why the disciples are so prominent in the story; they are arguing with scribes in 9:14–15, are pictured as unable to cope with the demon-possessed boy in 9:18, and are instructed as to the cause of their failure in 9:28–29. This is not just another miracle story or another example of Jesus' power over demons; it is also intended to instruct Mark's readers (the church) about their task of continuing the work of Jesus.

More specifically, this story immediately follows the mountaintop transfiguration in all three Synoptic accounts, probably because the writers intended an analogy between this incident and the incident in Exodus 32 in which Moses returns from his mountaintop encounter with God to find faithlessness on the part of Israel. That is, the reader is presented with the examples, on the one hand of the unbelieving and bickering teachers of the Law (representing the Jewish establishment's rejection of Jesus) and the powerless disciples (who also show a lack of faith) and on the other hand, Jesus, who both meets the need before him and calls his followers to more faithful obedience to him. The opposition of the teachers of the Law (unique to Mark) is likened to the rebellion of the Israelites in Moses' time, but the disciples (again, with whom the readers are expected to identify themselves) are shown to be in danger of the same sort of spiritual blindness, which appears in their inability to deal with the problem at hand. The language used in Jesus' rebuke in 9:19, **How unbelieving you people are**, is intentionally similar to the terms used to describe the unbelieving Pharisees in 8:12 and the persecutors of Jesus' followers in 8:38 (see note), showing that this episode urges the readers to follow Jesus completely and to avoid the unbelief typified by the teachers of the Law.

Following as it does the story that prefigures the resurrection of Christ (the Transfiguration), this account is also intended to prefigure the postresurrection situation of the early church, when Christians would be called upon to minister in the name and power of Jesus as did the Twelve. This is confirmed by the words of Jesus in 9:19 (**How long must I stay with you?**), which anticipate the time when Jesus would no longer in fact be with his followers and they would have to carry on in faith. Implicit in the account is the idea that Jesus' followers are expected to have full faith in his power, even when he is not with them as he was with the Twelve, and that they must continue his ministry in the same power as he manifested. The point of the dialogue between Jesus and the father of the demoniac boy in 9:23–24 is to give an object lesson for Mark's readers on the importance of strong faith in Jesus. The fact that the story is such an object lesson is made transparent by the final and climactic word in 9:29 that prayer is the means for Jesus' followers to acquire the faith and resources to conduct the required mission.

Mark's account is much longer than the parallels in Matthew 17:14–21 and Luke 9:37–43 because of the space devoted to the dialogue between Jesus and the father. This dialogue includes both the exhortation to faith and details about the boy's condition, which serve to make it clear that this was a desperate need and that the power of evil was truly present. But the point of giving these details is to say that in just such a difficult situation Jesus' followers are expected to trust in Christ and to deal with the need as he did.

One final detail, unique to Mark's version of the story, is worth mentioning here. In 9:26 Mark says that the boy's convulsions left him in a condition looking like death but that Jesus **helped him rise**. Jesus' action is intended as a foreshadowing of his own victory over death in his resurrection, and as a symbolic indication that the power of Jesus is this life-giving power. (See note on 9:27.)

This incident brings us back down from the glorious height of the transfiguration experience and into the earthly world where the power of evil is confronted and where unbelief is a constant danger. In the same way that the disciples are brought back again into Jesus' earthly mission here after the transfiguration that prefigures and symbolizes Jesus' resurrection, so Mark's readers were to realize that they, after the resurrection of Chirst, were called still to an earthly mission of faith and of proclamation of Christ against the forces of evil. This exorcism, the last one mentioned in Mark, shows the power of Jesus (portrayed in the transfiguration) in action in practical terms and means that it is in such ministry (and not in visionary experiences) that Christ's power and glory are properly to be seen in the life of his followers.

Additional Notes

9:2 / **A high mountain**: Mark gives no location for this mountain, nor do the other evangelists. Early tradition placed the event at Mount Tabor, a prominent point in Galilee southwest of Lake Galilee, but this is impossible to verify. (See, e.g., *MBA*, 233.)

Peter, James, and John: These same three are taken with Jesus to the raising of Jairus' daughter (5:37) and to the place of final prayer in Gethsemane

(14:33). Peter figures prominently at many points in Mark (as in the other Gospels) and is singled out in the announcement of the resurrection (16:7). All early Christian tradition indicates that Peter was regarded as a leader even among the apostles and, with James and John, counted as a chief figure in the Jerusalem church, the "mother church" of the Christian movement in the first century (e.g., Gal. 1:18–19; 2:9). (On the particular place of Peter in earliest Christianity, see *Peter in the New Testament*, ed. R. E. Brown, K. P. Donfried, and J. Reumann [Minneapolis: Augsburg, 1973.])

9:3 / **His clothes became shining white**: In addition to the references given in the discussion above, note Rev. 1:9–18, where the risen and glorified Jesus is described in similar terms. On the OT and NT experiences called theophanies, see, e.g., *IDB*, vol. 4, pp. 619–20; *IDBSup*, pp. 869–900.

9:4 / **Elijah and Moses**: On the Jewish expectation of an Elijah figure near the end of the age, see the discussion and notes on 6:14–16, and "Elijah," in *IDB*, vol. 2, pp. 88–90; Lane, pp. 324–25.

9:8 / **They took a quick look around** is a poor translation of the Greek phrase, which means, rather, "Suddenly, looking around, they saw no one except Jesus with them."

9:12 / **The Scriptures say**: Literally, the phrase says "it is written," referring no doubt to OT predictions of the death of the Son of Man. No particular OT passages are cited, and so it is difficult to be sure which ones might have been meant, though Isa. 53:3 is is a good guess. This reference to OT prophecies confirms that the "must" of 8:31 refers to prophecies making the death of the Son of Man necessary as a part of God's plan of redemption.

9:13 / **Elijah has already come**: As indicated above in the discussion, this is a veiled reference to John the Baptist and is a commentary on his execution narrated in 6:14–29. To call John "Elijah" meant that he was seen by Jesus and Mark as the promised forerunner of the Messiah, and that his ministry and death were not in vain.

9:14 / **Teachers of the Law arguing with them**: We are not told by Mark the nature of the argument because this is implicit. As elsewhere, the teachers of the Law oppose Jesus and deny the validity of his ministry (cf. 2:6–7, 16; 3:22; 7:1–2).

9:15 / **When the people saw Jesus, they were greatly surprised**: The exact reason for their surprise is not given. The term used here means to marvel, and it and similar terms are used several times in Mark to indicate the uncomprehending awe of people at Jesus' power and teaching. (Cf., e.g., 1:27; 10:24, 32; 5:20.)

9:19 / **How unbelieving you people are**: Literally, the Greek is "O faithless [unbelieving] generation." The term for "generation" is used in 8:12 and 8:38 with reference to those who deny and oppose Jesus.

9:24 / **I do have faith, but not enough. Help me have more!** is literally: "I do believe. Help my unbelief!" This cry, so meaningful down the centuries to Christians in great distress, was no doubt intended by Mark to catch concisely the need of his readers to trust in Christ more fully and more intelligently. The **everything** that **is possible** in 9:23 is not meant to convey the idea that believing will magically produce anything one might desire but rather means that Jesus' power is available to faith to meet any need that arises *in the course of ministering in his name*.

9:27 / **Helped him rise** is literally "raised him," the same term used to describe the action of God in raising Jesus from the dead, e.g., Mark 14:28; Acts 3:15; 4:10; 5:30.

9:28 / **His disciples asked him privately**: Here again, there is the Markan theme of the special instructions given to the Twelve. Cf., e.g., 4:10–12, 33–34; 7:17.

9:29 / **Only prayer**: In some manuscripts there is the addition of "and fasting" after these words, but this reading appears to be the result of some copyists inserting a reference to the practice of fasting at a time when it had become a widespread Christian discipline.

17

Jesus' Death and Discipleship

MARK 9:30–50

Jesus and his disciples left that place and went on through Galilee. Jesus did not want anyone to know where he was, [31]because he was teaching his disciples: "The Son of Man will be handed over to men who will kill him. Three days later, however, he will rise to life."

[32]But they did not understand what this teaching meant, and they were afraid to ask him.

[33]They came to Capernaum, and after going indoors Jesus asked his disciples, "What were you arguing about on the road?"

[34]But they would not answer him, because on the road they had been arguing among themselves about who was the greatest. [35]Jesus sat down, called the twelve disciples, and said to them, "Whoever wants to be first must place himself last of all and be the servant of all." [36]Then he took a child and had him stand in front of them. He put his arms around him and said to them, [37]"Whoever welcomes in my name one of these children, welcomes me; and whoever welcomes me, welcomes not only me but also the one who sent me."

[38]John said to him, "Teacher, we saw a man who was driving out demons in your name, and we told him to stop, because he doesn't belong to our group."

[39]"Do not try to stop him," Jesus told them, "because no one who performs a miracle in my name will be able soon afterward to say evil things about me. [40]For whoever is not against us is for us. [41]I assure you that anyone who gives you a drink of water because you belong to me will certainly receive his reward.

[42]"If anyone should cause one of these little ones to lose his faith in me, it would be better for that person to have a large millstone tied around his neck and be thrown into the sea. [43]So if your hand makes you lose your faith, cut it off! It is better for you to enter life without a hand than to keep both hands and go off to hell, to the fire that never goes out.º [45]And if your foot makes you lose your faith, cut it off! It is better for you to enter life without a foot than to keep both feet and be thrown into hell.ᵖ [47]And if your eye makes you lose your faith, take it out! It is better for you to enter the Kingdom of God with only one eye than to keep both eyes and be thrown into hell. [48]There 'the worms that eat them never die, and the fire that burns them is never put out.'

[49]"Everyone will be purified by fire as a sacrifice is purified by salt.

[50]"Salt is good; but if it loses its saltiness, how can you make it salty again?

"Have the salt of friendship among yourselves, and live in peace with one another."

o. *Some manuscripts add verse 44:* There 'the worms that eat them never die, and the fire that burns them is never put out' *(see verse 48)*.
p. *Some manuscripts add verse 46:* There 'the worms that eat them never die, and the fire that burns them is never put out' *(see verse 48)*.

9:30–32 / This passage gives us the second of three predictions by Jesus of his death (cf. 8:31; 10:32–34). The new element in the prediction is the mention that the Son of Man will be **handed over to men**. The verb used here in Greek has a most interesting significance in the NT. It can mean to betray someone, and it is used in this sense to describe Judas' treachery in 14:41–42. But the term is also used to describe God's action where it carries the note of being handed over or given up for judgment or punishment (e.g., Rom 1:24, 26, 28), and very significantly, this includes the idea that God "handed over" Jesus to suffering on behalf of those to be redeemed (e.g., Rom. 8:32). Here in 9:30, the term probably refers to the betrayal of Jesus committed by Judas, but the fact that Jesus predicts this event as part of the divine plan means that in a more profound sense it is really God who will give up his Son to the judgment of hostile human courts (lit., "into the hands of men," see note).

This teaching is mentioned as reserved exclusively for his disciples (9:30), but we are also told that the disciples did not grasp what he was saying and were fearful to press the matter (9:32). Here the dullness of the disciples that Mark emphasizes at several points in the book and that caused a rift between Jesus and Peter in 8:32–33 continues to manifest itself, and the rift has not closed. We are to picture the disciples as perhaps worried that Jesus was seeming far too pessimistic for one whom they regarded as God's Messiah-designate. Both in 9:33–34 and 10:35–37, we are shown the disciples still assuming that in a short time they will be in chief positions with Jesus over the Kingdom about which he spoke. But based on the experience of Peter's attempt to correct Jesus in 8:32–33, the disciples are fearful to pursue the dark predictions Jesus makes. They cannot understand what seems to be a morbid preoccupation of Jesus, not realizing that it is they who are really wrongly preoccupied.

The message Mark wanted to communicate with these details of the reactions of the disciples was not that Jesus chose especially stupid disciples but, rather, that the gulf between Jesus and the Twelve shown here is the gulf that separates mere human ideas about what the Kingdom of God is and how it might come (of which ancient Jewish messianic expectation is only one example) from the divinely chosen way. The gulf between Jesus and the Twelve, Mark wants us to learn, was not and could not have been closed until the actual events of the crucifixion and resurrection brought to the disciples the realization of the fact and meaning of God's chosen way to establish his Kingdom in this world.

The repetition of the prediction of Jesus' death has the effect of making more prominent its place in Mark's narrative and also introduces us to the next passage, where again, as he did after his first prediction of his death, Jesus corrects the disciples as to what is involved for them to follow him.

9:33–37 / These verses must be seen as part of a collection of Jesus' words that includes the whole of 9:33–50, all concerning discipleship. Careful study of the parallels to these sayings in the other Synoptic Gospels will show that they appear in various contexts and in varying forms, which indicates that Mark has gathered the sayings here into a block of material of his own arrangement. In its Markan form, this material all seems to be intended to deal with relationships among Jesus' followers, as we shall see in our examination of the sayings. Some of the sayings later in this chapter (9:42–50) were associated with one another because they contained words that fostered an association (see comments and notes on these verses). Mark's grouping of all the material in 9:33–50 around the theme of proper attitudes and relationships among the followers of Jesus is indicated by the use of a literary device called *inclusio*, which involves a return to the opening topic of a section at its conclusion. Thus, 9:33 opens the section showing the disciples arguing with one another, and 9:50 concludes this section by urging the disciples to "live in peace with one another." This means that all the material in between is intended to be understood as giving teaching on "life together."

We should also observe the fact that after each of the three predictions of Jesus' death there is a correction of the disciples and teaching on what is involved in following Jesus. In each case the teaching is a call to sacrifice of one's self-interest and an apparent reversal of typical worldly values. Thus, in 8:34–38, Jesus says that the attempt to preserve one's life will be its loss. In 10:35–45, Jesus corrects the ambitions of James and John, indicating that among his followers the greatest person is the servant of the others. Here in 9:33–37, there is a similar point made (esp. 9:35), setting the disciples' ambition to be chief on its head.

Some might think it strange for grown men to be arguing as to who was the greatest among them (e.g., Nineham, p. 252), but in the context of such groups as the religious sect at Qumran (whose writings are popularly known as the Dead Sea Scrolls), where the whole community was ranked annually according to the worthiness of each individual, it does not appear strange for members of Jesus' band to have thought along similar lines. Indeed, seen against the example of such contemporary groups as the Qumran community, Jesus' words possess particularly timely force, and are a powerful contrast. But, of course, Jesus' words were not only relevant in the ancient Jewish setting; they challenge all human desires to make religion an opportunity for personal aggrandizement. One would have to say that the church has yet to learn the meaning of Jesus' words.

The relevance Mark saw between the exhortation to take the role of servant (v. 35, and see note on 10:44) and the saying in verse 37 is that the child functions as a symbol for one's fellow disciple; and the use of the child here is a kind of dramatized parable. Thus, to welcome **one of these children** means, in context, to treat honorably other disciples, taking the role of servant toward them. The child is not used here as an example of humility (as is the case in 10:13–16), for the issue in verse 37 is not imitation of the child but the treatment of **these children**. The logic of using the child as a symbol of one's fellow disciple is found in the fact that in Aramaic (probably the language Jesus used in teaching his disciples) and in Greek (the language in which Mark wrote) the term "child" can also mean "servant." Thus, the saying urging all disciples to be **servant** in verse 35 is followed by what amounts to a pun on the word **child**, urging all Jesus' followers to treat the "children/servants" well (v. 37). The words **in my name** in verse 37 mean something like "because they belong to me" or "for my sake," and they make it clear that the **children** about which Jesus speaks are his followers. They are to be "welcomed," not because they seem to be "great" by worldly standards, but because they are Christ's.

The strong identification between Jesus and his followers expressed in 9:37 is intended in this context to make the point that even the most insignificant follower of Jesus is to be treated with the greatest of respect. This thought prepares us for the next passage, 9:38–41, which seems to be devoted to dealing with the question of recognizing a follower of Jesus to whom such respect is due.

9:38–41 / The preceding passage (9:33–37) urges a willingness to serve others instead of a concern for greatness and makes the strongest kind of identification between Jesus and his followers. In this passage, which concerns the treatment of a person who is using Jesus' name in exorcisms but is not a member of the Twelve, the question seems to be how to recognize a follower of Jesus. This question follows naturally from the preceding discussion, for if one is to serve other followers of Jesus and is to count the treatment of them the same as treatment given to Jesus himself (9:37), one needs to know who the followers of Jesus are.

Since the material in the Gospels was preserved because it was deemed useful to the Church in dealing with doctrinal and practical questions of Christian life, the presence of this incident in the recorded tradition of Jesus' ministry may indicate that in Mark's own time there were questions about the full legitimacy of some Christians and/or their leaders. Paul's Letter to the Galatians shows one example of such a question about Paul's apostleship and the legitimacy of his message, and there may have been still other such controversies for which this incident was thought relevant.

We do not know whether this unnamed person was simply a wandering exorcist who picked up Jesus' name for use in his trade, the way exorcists and magicians seem to have used freely any name that might have power to compel demons to obey, or whether this person was a follower of Jesus, though not of the Twelve. There is an example of the magical use of Jesus' name in Acts 19:11-20, but the story there condemns the practice, implying that only those who are genuine followers of Jesus can use his name effectually. It seems to be a good guess that the person mentioned here in Mark is to be taken as a follower of Jesus and not simply someone trying to use Jesus' name in a magical spell, for elsewhere Mark seems to reject a magical view of Jesus' power (see notes and comments on 5:25-33; 6:5-6; 7:34). Further, the point under discussion is not the practice of exorcism but whether a person who is not identified with the Twelve can still be a true follower of Jesus with the right to minister in his name.

The thrust of Jesus' answer in verses 39-41 is to say that anyone who claims to be a follower of Jesus must be received unless he or she gives reason to think otherwise. Mark 9:40 in particular gives the benefit of the doubt to the unknown follower. It is interesting to note that this saying appears in the Luke 9:50 parallel and also in a different form and context in Matt. 21:30 and Luke 11:23. It appears that this saying was not coined by Jesus but was apparently a well-known maxim (see note), used here to give a principle for Christian fellowship. Mark 9:41 reinforces the point by assuring all that hospitality given to anyone who claims Jesus' name will be rewarded (see note on 9:41).

9:42-50 / In these verses we seem to have a collection of sayings somewhat artificially held together by the fact that particular words that appear in two or more of them serve to associate the sayings with one another. Once brought together, however, the sayings are all to be understood in their present context, which has to do with discipleship, particularly the obligations of disciples for one another.

The **little ones** of 9:42 is intended here as reference to Jesus' followers and takes us back to verse 37, where Jesus refers to his followers under the symbol of "these children." The Greek makes it clearer that it is not children but believers who are referred to here; literally the phrase is "these little ones who believe in me." The word translated here "to cause to lose faith in me" is literally "to cause to fall," and it refers to someone causing another to fall into unbelief, serious sin, or false teaching. The warning given here balances off the positive assurance given in verse 37 that kindness toward Jesus' disciples would be rewarded.

The word referred to immediately above is the "catchword" that reappears in 9:43–47 and explains why these sayings follow. In these verses the focus shifts momentarily from causing others to fall to causing one's own fall, and the sayings are full of the vivid language of Semitic speech. The hyperbole in the sayings should not be pressed literally, but the point is not to be lost that participation in the Kingdom of God is worth any sacrifice. The organs mentioned here are really symbols for various types of activity, for example, the hand that grasps for things it should not, the foot that goes where it ought not, or the eye that desires what it ought not. Mark 9:48 is an allusion to Isaiah 66:24, which speaks of everlasting judgment upon those who rebel against God. It is introduced here as a comment on the word **hell** (v. 47), indicating that what is meant is the final judgment of God to be given at the end of time.

The reference to **fire** in verse 48 is the catchword that introduces verse 49; the fire of the latter verse is not eternal judgment but probably the fires of trial and testing in the life of the believer, for this fire purifies. This statement alludes to the ancient practice of sprinkling salt on sacrifices for the Jewish altar (commanded in Lev. 2:13), and the reference to salt introduces the next two sayings in which the word "salt" appears.

The **salt** referred to in verse 50 is probably the humility and dedication that is reinforced by trial and testing. If the believer loses this **salt** he or she is not easily renewed (v. 50a), but by maintaining this **salt**, Jesus' followers can more easily be at peace with one another (v. 50b). The simple purity of dedication to Jesus that does not seek its own advantage enables one to be a servant to fellow disciples, and thus promotes peace.

Although these sayings are difficult at first, and Mark's decision to include them all here on the basis of the use of catchwords may strike us as strange, his intent was to pile up words of Jesus that could be used to make the point that Jesus' followers must take extremely seriously their responsibility to avoid acts that would drive away other disciples from the circle of discipleship.

Additional Notes

9:30 / **That place**: Again note the vague geographical references when precise identification of the place is either impossible for Mark, or, more likely, irrelevant for his purpose.

9:31 / **Handed over to men** is literally "handed over into the hands of men," "hands of men" implying hostility against Jesus; cf. 2 Sam. 24:14; Jer. 26:24, where similar phrasing occurs in contexts that imply hostility against someone.

9:33 / **Capernaum**: On the location of this site, see the note on 1:21. This town is frequently mentioned as if it functioned as a home base for Jesus during his Galilean ministry.

Indoors: The term here in Greek means literally "in the house," and this could imply a house belonging to or regularly used by Jesus and his band of disciples. Peter lived in Capernaum, as did others of the Twelve; cf. 1:29–30.

9:37 / **Whoever welcomes** . . . : This saying is paralleled almost fully in Luke 9:48. There are several other places in the Gospels where sayings very similar to this one appear, but in varying contexts, e.g., Matt. 10:40; John 12:44–45; 13:20.

9:38 / **John** is John Zebedee (see notes on 1:14–20), one of the three "core" disciples who are given special attention in Mark (see also 5:37; 9:2; 13:3; 14:33). It is interesting that after each of the three predictions of Jesus' death members of this inner circle are corrected by Jesus (cf. 8:32–33; 10:35–40).

9:40 / **Whoever is not against us is for us**: This saying, combining both this more inclusive form and the more restrictive form, appears in Cicero's speech before Caesar in defense of the Pompeiani, and in an ancient manuscript known as Oxyrhynchus Papyri 1224 there is a variant that reads, "He who is not against you is for you. He who today is far from you may tomorrow be near to you." (For references, see Lane, p. 344.)

9:41 / **I assure you**: the oathlike formula peculiar to Jesus' speech in the Gospels. See note on 3:28.

A drink of water: Note the variant form of this saying in Matt. 10:42, appearing in the context of the sending out of the Twelve. **A drink of water** is probably a reference to giving hospitality, water symbolizing this effectively in the ancient Near East.

Because you belong to me: Actually, the Greek says "because you are Christ's," but, of course, it seems undeniable that for Mark "Christ" meant Jesus. This is another indication (along with 1:1; 8:29; 14:61; 15:32) that Jesus is the Messiah (in Greek, *Christos*, "Christ").

9:42 / **A large millstone**: The mills used to grind grain in ancient Palestine were composed of two circular stones mounted on a pivot. The upper stone turned on the other, and grain poured in between them was ground into meal and flour. The large stone referred to here was the upper stone of a community mill, which required several people or a donkey to turn it. (See *IDB*, vol. 3, pp. 380–81.)

9:43 ff. / **Hell**: The Greek word here is *gehenna*, which comes from the Hebrew term referring originally to a ravine south of Jerusalem (*gē-hinom*). By the time of Jesus, the term had acquired a metaphorical usage denoting the future fiery judgment to be inflicted upon the wicked at the last judgment. (See *IDB*, vol. 2, pp. 361–62; "Hell," *NIDNTT*, vol. 2, pp. 206–210.)

9:43 ff. / **Cut it off**: In addition to the parallel at Matt. 18:6–9, see also Matt. 5:29–30, where what seems to be the same saying appears in another context.

9:50 / **If it loses its saltiness**: What is referred to here is the fact (attested by other ancient writers) that the unrefined salt gathered from the Dead Sea, which is mixed with impurities, could acquire a stale and flat taste. Of course sodium does not become unsalty, but the unrefined salt known in ancient Palestine could. (Cf. Luke 14:34–35; Matt. 5:13; Col. 4:6 for other symbolic uses of salt in the NT; and *IDB*, vol. 4, p. 167.)

Marriage, Children, and Possessions

MARK 10:1–31

Then Jesus left that place, went to the province of Judea, and crossed the Jordan River. Crowds came flocking to him again, and he taught them, as he always did.

2Some Pharisees came to him and tried to trap him. "Tell us," they asked, "does our Law allow a man to divorce his wife?"

3Jesus answered with a question, "What law did Moses give you?"

4Their answer was, "Moses gave permission for a man to write a divorce notice and send his wife away."

5Jesus said to them, "Moses wrote this law for you because you are so hard to teach. 6But in the beginning, at the time of creation, 'God made them male and female,' as the scripture says. 7'And for this reason a man will leave his father and mother and unite with his wife,[q] 8and the two will become one.' So they are no longer two, but one. 9Man must not separate, then, what God has joined together."

10When they went back into the house, the disciples asked Jesus about this matter. 11He said to them, "A man who divorces his wife and marries another woman commits adultery against his wife. 12In the same way, a woman who divorces her husband and marries another man commits adultery."

13Some people brought children to Jesus for him to place his hands on them, but the disciples scolded the people. 14When Jesus noticed this, he was angry and said to his disciples, "Let the children come to me, and do not stop them, because the Kingdom of God belongs to such as these. 15I assure you that whoever does not receive the Kingdom of God like a child will never enter it." 16Then he took the children in his arms, placed his hands on each of them, and blessed them.

17As Jesus was starting on his way again, a man ran up, knelt before him, and asked him, "Good Teacher, what must I do to receive eternal life?"

18"Why do you call me good?" Jesus asked him. "No one is good except God alone. 19You know the commandments: 'Do not commit murder; do not commit adultery; do not steal; do not accuse anyone falsely; do not cheat; respect your father and your mother.' "

20Teacher," the man said, "ever since I was young, I have obeyed all these commandments."

21Jesus looked straight at him with love and said, "You need only one thing. Go and sell all you have and give the money to the poor, and you will have riches in heaven; then come and follow me." 22When the man heard this, gloom spread over his face, and he went away sad, because he was very rich. [23]Jesus looked around at his disciples and said to them, "How hard it will be for rich people to enter the Kingdom of God!" [24]The disciples were shocked at these words, but Jesus went on to say, "My children, how hard it is to enter the Kingdom of God! [25]It is much harder for a rich person to enter the Kingdom of God than for a camel to go through the eye of a needle." [26]At this the disciples were completely amazed and asked one another, "Who, then, can be saved?" [27]Jesus looked straight at them and answered, "This is impossible for man but not for God; everything is possible for God." [28]Then Peter spoke up, "Look, we have left everything and followed you." [29]"Yes," Jesus said to them, "and I tell you that anyone who leaves home or brothers or sisters or mother or father or children or fields for me and for the gospel, [30]will receive much more in this present age. He will receive a hundred times more houses, brothers, sisters, mothers, children, and fields—and persecutions as well; and in the age to come he will receive eternal life. [31]But many who are now first will be last, and many who are now last will be first."

q. *Some manuscripts do not have* and unite with his wife.

10:1-12 / This passage containing Jesus' teaching on the subject of divorce is placed in the block of material devoted to teaching on discipleship (8:27–10:52) because it concerns one of the most important areas of responsibility (marriage) for disciples, or for anyone for that matter. It is possible that this passage is placed immediately after the preceding material that urges peace among disciples (9:50) because marriage provides one of the most common areas of strife, though it should be noted that 10:1 is a transitional statement, indicating that a new unit of material is being presented. From another perspective, it is possible that 10:1–31 may have been associated in Mark's purpose because the material deals successively with marriage (vv. 1–12), children (13–16), and possessions (17–31), all these things being earthly ties for disciples.

The question put to Jesus in the passage before us must be set in its ancient context to be appreciated fully. In ancient Judaism, divorce was a right only for husbands; women were legally the property of their husbands and had no power to end the marriage. Further, there was never any question about whether a man might be free to end his marriage by divorce, the only concern reflected in the ancient rabbinic tradition being that a man give proper official certification of the divorce to his wife. There was a difference of opinion between two major schools of ancient rabbinic thought about what were the legitimate causes for divorcing a woman, one school insisting that the only valid reason was sexual impurity in the wife, and the other arguing that the wife could be sent away simply if the husband grew tired of her. The latter view was dominant, no doubt because it was more covenient for a husband. The parallel account in Matthew 19:12 reflects in more detail the Jewish setting (see notes), and the version in Mark seems to be adapted to a gentile setting in which both men and women had legal right to divorce (cf. 10:11-12; Matt. 19:9).

One detail common to both the Markan and the Matthean versions of the incident that deserves mention is that people are said to have approached Jesus with the purpose of "testing" him (in the GNB, they **tried to trap him**, 10:2). The most likely explanation of this is furnished by the description of the conflict between John the Baptist and Herod over Herodias' divorce of her former husband in order to marry Herod Antipas (6:14-29). That is, the intent of Jesus' opponents here may have been to try to trap Jesus into saying something on the subject of divorce that would reflect upon Herod and Herodias' marriage unfavorably, enabling Jesus' critics to denounce him to Herod. Herod took John the Baptist's criticism of his marriage as possible incitement to revolt, and it is likely that the political situation in Galilee best explains the original reason for which Jesus was questioned about his views on divorce.

In the discussion of the question put to Jesus, there is reference to Moses' commandment concerning divorce found in Deuteronomy 24:1-4, a passage that actually only presupposes the fact of divorce and is mainly concerned with prohibiting a divorced and remarried woman from remarrying her first husband. The passage was taken by ancient rabbis, however, as giving sanction for divorce, and this text is at the basis of a great body of ancient Jewish discussion on all aspects of the matter. In the light of this background, Jesus' statement that this passage from Moses is not a reflection of the will of God but instead reflects the stubbornness of the Israelites (v. 5) appears to be unique and striking. To many ancient Jews this statement would have seemed to be an attack upon the sanctity and perfection of the OT Law; it is certainly an attack upon the use of this passage of the OT Law to justify the shedding of wives whenever husbands wished to do so.

The passages of the OT Jesus cites are from the creation account (v. 6 from Gen. 1:27; vv. 7-8 from Gen. 2:24), and his use of this material has two effects. First, it challenges the view mentioned above that the Law of Moses was the perfect and final reflection of the will of God, asserting that it was adapted to fallen and stubborn human nature. By his citation of the creation accounts, Jesus implies that the original Edenic will of God concerning marriage is both superior to the Law of Moses and continues to be the proper guideline by which marriage should be conducted. This point about the Law of Moses being used to justify conduct contrary to the will of God is similar to Jesus' argument that the tradition of the elders sometimes justified the use of OT laws to disobey the will of God (7:1–13).

Secondly, both of the particular passages Jesus cites assert the importance of the woman in marriage. In the first statement, from Genesis 1:27, both male and female are emphasized as the creation of God, implying that both must be respected, indeed, that they are equal partners. Further, the second passage (Gen. 2:24) re-affirms this with its emphasis upon the man's forsaking of others for the sake of his wife and its reference to the union formed by their marriage (one in v. 8 being literally "one flesh"). In the social and economic context of ancient Palestine, the absolute right of the husband to divorce often meant great hardship for divorced wives, who might be given at most a single lump-sum economic settlement if they were not accused of unchastity, though this sum would be no more than the woman's dowry given at marriage (see notes), and that might be very small in the case of a woman from poor parents. The effect of Jesus' position forbidding divorce was to reject the notion that the wife was the man's property and to insist upon recognition of the woman's right in marriage based upon the original creation pattern. This emphasis upon the woman's rights in marriage is further evidenced in the word of Jesus to his disciples in verses 10–12, where he says that a man who divorces his wife for another woman **commits adultery against his wife**. This idea is apparently totally unparalleled in ancient Judaism, where adultery was understood only as an offense committed against another man, either by seducing a man's daughter and depriving him of a marriageable girl, or by violating a husband's exclusive sexual rights with his wife.

The emphasis that it is God who joins together husband and wife (v. 9) refers to the creation plan of God that every marriage is obligated to follow, and it means that, like OT prophets (e.g., Mal. 2:10–16), Jesus defines marriage as a relationship in which both husband and wife are responsible both to each other and to God for maintaining its sanctity. For Mark's readers, this means that once again, as with the question of food practices (7:1–23) or fasting (2:18–22) or Sabbath observance (2:23–3:6), their conduct is not to be regulated by Jewish customs but by the specific demands placed upon his followers by Jesus himself.

10:13–16 / The appearance of this passage dealing with children right after the passage on marriage may have been prompted by the fact that the two subjects naturally are linked in life. There were some in the ancient church who felt that marriage was evil because they saw sexual intercourse as a fleshly pollution (this point of view seems to be what Paul corrects in 1 Cor. 7:1–40 and was certainly held by some later heretics among those called Gnostics). These same people also believed that the procreation of children was evil, and it is possible that this incident of Jesus welcoming children was intended by Mark partly to correct this attitude (see note). Whether this is correct or not, in its present context the saying certainly ties in with the general theme of discipleship in Mark 8–10.

The intention of those who brought the children to Jesus was that he would perhaps impart some blessing to them, for Jesus' touch is described elsewhere in Mark as regarded by people as conveying such blessings as health (e.g., 1:41; 3:10; 5:28, 41; 6:56; 7:32; 8:22). The impatience of the disciples (v. 13) is perhaps more understandable given the apparently ceaseless demands made upon Jesus and the Twelve by people, and given the general attitude of the time that children, while important and loved by parents, were nevertheless very definitely "to be seen and not heard." (Note Paul's contrast between a mere child, who is "just like a slave while he is young," and an adult in Gal. 4:1–3.) On the other hand, Jesus' welcoming of the children (v. 16) is another example of his positive attitude toward those who did not have important social status, such as tax gatherers (2:13–17) or women (10:1–12).

It is the objective social status of small children that is the background for Jesus' statement in verse 15 that one must **receive the Kingdom of God like a child**. This statement does not refer to any supposed innocence or humility or any other imagined qualities of children (romantic notions after all), but instead refers to the fact that in Jesus' cultural situation children were totally dependent upon the will of others and had no legal or social weight to make claims for particular treatment. It is this objectively humble position in society that Jesus has in mind, and he means that one must take the position of a **child**, unable to make demands and dependent upon the good pleasure of God. The person who imagines that he or she is somehow worthy of God's favor and that participation in the Kingdom of God depends upon social or religious rank will never really enter the Kingdom that Jesus announces.

Thus, this passage accords with the emphasis in 9:33–37 that disciples must be willing to place themselves in the rank of servant (the term "child" in Aramaic and Greek can also mean "servant," reflecting the fact that children were expected to be servants of their parents), taking the role that the world might regard as demeaning. This emphasis is the background for the next episode in which a wealthy man aspires to be a disciple but finds the demand too great.

10:17-31 / This is perhaps one of the most famous incidents in the ministry of Jesus and is found in all three Synoptics. Each of the three versions of the story contains interesting variations. For example, only Luke (18:18) describes the man as a "Jewish leader," and only Matthew (19:20) describes him as young. There are other individual features of the three accounts (see notes), and Mark has his share, but all versions of the story make the same point, that riches make it more difficult to be a disciple and that total sacrifice of one's goods and position in society may be demanded. The teaching material following the meeting with the rich man (10:23–31) amplifies this and gives assurance that God will honor the sacrifice.

The passage is positioned in Mark 8–10 because it contributes to the overall emphasis of this section upon the nature of discipleship. The rich man with so much at stake is a fitting contrast with the small children of the preceding passage whose social position Jesus makes an example for his followers (v. 15). The fact that the man refuses the call of Jesus and fails to become a follower makes the emphasis upon the dangers of riches all the more effective. There is no happy ending to this story, and the stark reality of the warning is the greater for it.

There is something of a contrast too between the man and the Twelve, who say that they have left all to follow Jesus (v. 28). Jesus does not dispute this, but his statement in verses 29–31 contains both the assurance of God's favor for those who make such a sacrifice and warnings that there is more testing ahead to be faced before a final judgment is given by God. In addition to the provisions God will supply for the needs of disciples in the present age (v. 30), there will be **persecutions as well**. In the age to come there will be eternal life, but there will be a great reversal of earthly status in the coming judgment of God (v. 31). The story of the rich man opens out into the teaching material in verses 23–31 and, together with that material, is intended by Mark to be read soberly by those who regard themselves as Jesus' followers.

This passage presumes a familiarity with the ancient Jewish conception that there is an end to this age and a new age coming in which only those acceptable to God will participate. Those who enter the age to come will be given eternal life, and this is the background of the man's question in verse 17. The man appears at first to be greatly devoted to obtaining life in the world to come, both by his question and by the obedience to God's commandments that he professes (v. 20). But the irony of the incident is that, when told by Jesus what he must do, the man refuses. He is told to part with the goods of this age since he is so interested in the next one, but he will not do so. His interest in the next world is not sincere enough to enable him to give up his preoccupation with this world (vv. 21–22).

The brief discussion with the man about his form of address to Jesus (vv. 17–18) is not just a quibble about religious propriety. The greeting, **Good Teacher**, Jesus takes as implying that the man is thinking with the traditional conceptions of much of ancient Judaism (and Christian groups too), that there are the "good" and the "bad," the deserving and the undeserving. This attitude is contrary to Jesus' whole standpoint that humans can only be in the position of the undeserving who are dependent upon the good pleasure of a good God. Jesus' correction of the man in verse 18 (**No one is good except God alone**) is not intended by Mark to cast any reflection upon the question of whether Jesus is divine. Instead, it is intended as a rejection of the idea implied in the man's address and question that one can acquire eternal life much as one might acquire some other desired possession.

The dialogue about the commandments in verses 19–20 seems intended to say that this was in fact a decent and proper man, not guilty of breaking the Law of God. His claim to full obedience is not disputed; and indeed, Mark alone has the little note that Jesus felt affection for the man (v. 21), further implying that the man was sincere. All this means that the only thing that stood between him and Jesus was the man's love for his possessions (v. 22). That is, the description of the man's otherwise commendable life is intended to make all the clearer the fact that it was riches that was the problem. In ancient times and on into the present, the opinion has been popular that riches in themselves are no problem, and that only when the wealthy man engages in evil practices is he in spiritual danger. But the force of this passage is precisely to the effect that riches in themselves *are* a hindrance to a person's participation in the Kingdom of God and that the mere accumulation of wealth and consequent attachment to it can prevent a person from following Christ.

This is made clear in the strongest terms in verses 23–25, where Jesus uses a variation on what appears to have been a common way of describing something as nearly impossible, a camel going through the eye of a needle (see note). One occasionally still hears the misinformed suggestion that this statement of Jesus referred to a small hole or gate in the wall of Jerusalem known as the needle's eye, but this is completely fanciful, and the widespread use of similar expressions in ancient Jewish tradition demonstrates that the terms are to be taken in their normal sense, a camel and an eye of a needle. The full force of this figure of speech is reflected in the reaction of the disciples (v. 26), who are surprised to be told that such wealthy and good people as the man in the story will not enter the Kingdom of God. Jesus' reply that only God can give people the ability to part with their possessions for the sake of the Kingdom of God (v. 27) reinforces what he has said about how difficult it is for the rich to answer his call.

The man is called, however, not to poverty for its own sake, but to discipleship to Jesus (v. 21, **come and follow me**). That is, the story is not just a criticism of wealth; it is also intended to teach that not even obedience to the OT Law and great social and economic standing will substitute for answering the call of Jesus. The question put to the man is whether he will follow Jesus if it means that he must give up his possessions. His possessions are a snare and hindrance, making it hard to **enter the Kingdom of God** (v. 23) precisely because they distract him from answering Jesus' invitation to follow him. Thus, though the story of the man and the following dialogue between Jesus and the Twelve give dire warning about riches, this is no mere advocacy of a social program involving redistribution of wealth or romantic praising of the idea of poverty. The issue is Jesus, the one who assures participation in the Kingdom of God, and the point is that following him and joining his mission are to be put ahead of all other interests.

The final exchange between Peter and Jesus (vv. 28–31) confirms that the central issue is following Jesus, and that not only possessions but also even relationships might have to be sacrificed. Also, Mark's wording in verse 29, **for me and for the gospel**, makes it clearer that the reason for the abandonment of one's possessions is actual participation with Jesus in the activity of proclaiming his message. Here again, we note evidence that for Mark participation in the mission of the church is a vital part of following Jesus (see note).

Jesus' words in verse 30 about receiving **a hundred times** what one has sacrificed seem tinged with irony and even humor. They do not really mean that discipleship to Jesus is a handy get-rich scheme, of course. Instead, the abundance described probably refers to the fact that those who give up their settled existence to follow Jesus in mission will have to be entertained by many **brothers, sisters, mothers, children** in many **houses** and supported from many **fields**, none of them really their own. The peculiarly Markan phrase, **and persecutions as well**, makes plain the reality behind the language—that in this age no comfort is promised. The follower is, however, promised eternal life in **the age to come**, and the teaching that the rich and mighty will be less likely to enter the Kingdom illustrates what is meant by the reversal described in verse 31.

Additional Notes

10:1 / **Judea** was the southern Roman province in Palestine, in which the chief city was Jerusalem. Judea was administered directly by a Roman governor during the time of Jesus' ministry, whereas Galilee was administered by Herod Antipas, a Roman-appointed client ruler. **The Jordan River**, which runs south from Lake Galilee to the Dead Sea, formed the eastern border of Galilee and Judea as well, and in order to avoid going through Samaria (which lay between Galilee and Judea), Jews in Jesus' time would cross over to the eastern shore of the Jordan and travel southward to cross back into Judea near Jericho, only a few miles north of the Dead Sea. By moving the narrative location to Judea, Mark alerts his readers that Jesus is going toward Jerusalem and that we are nearing the final stage of Jesus' ministry, in that city. (For more information, see "Judea," *IDB*, vol. 2, pp. 1011–1012; "Jordan," *IDB*, vol. 2, pp. 973–78; *MBA*, 235.)

10:2 / **Some Pharisees**: It is not absolutely certain that the original text of Mark contained this reference to Pharisees, for the words are missing in some ancient witnesses, in which the critics are unnamed.

To trap him means literally "to test" or "tempt" and appears also in 8:11 and 12:13, where other hostile questions are directed at Jesus.

Does our law allow a man to divorce his wife is literally "is it lawful for a man to divorce his wife." There is no question of this, given Deut. 24:1–4, and the Matt. 19:3 parallel seems to reflect more precisely the nature of the Jewish controversy between the schools of Hillel and Shammai about the proper *cause* for divorce. Mark seems to reflect an adaptation of the question for gentile readers, in which there is a greater contrast drawn between what the OT Law allows and what is commanded by Jesus. In ancient Jewish marriage custom, when a woman married she was given a dowry by her father that might consist of money, slaves, or other property, depending on her father's wealth. This dowry remained her property (and her only true property) in the marriage, and if she were divorced it had to be given to her by her husband, unless she were found guilty of sexual misconduct. A divorce document had to be written by the husband and given properly to the wife, in which the husband stated that the wife was fully free from him and could remarry if she chose. There was no court action and the whole process resembles more the modern-day practice of disposing of a piece of property such as a car or a house, in which a proper bill of sale or equivalent is the major requirement. (See further, "Marriage," *IDB*, vol. 3, pp. 278–87; "Divorce," *IDB*, vol. 1, p. 859.)

10:5 / **Because you are so hard to teach**: Literally, the term is because of your "hard-heartedness," which refers to a stubborn, willful attitude (see, e.g., Deut. 10:16). This is not the same wording in Greek as the description of the spiritual dullness of the disciples in 8:17.

10:7-8 / **And unite with his wife** is absent in some important ancient manuscripts, and scholars are unsure whether they were in the original text of Mark or were inserted by some copyists to harmonize this passage with the Matt. 19:5 parallel and the Gen 2:24 passage quoted. These words, together with the term "one flesh" (v. 8; translated in GNB as **one**), refer to the sexual union of intercourse, which makes of the two marriage partners a physical union that is not to be dissolved.

10:10 / **The disciples asked Jesus about this matter**: As elsewhere in Mark, here the disciples approach Jesus privately for explanation of his public pronouncements. Cf., e.g., 4:10–12, 33–34; 7:17–23; 9:28–29.

10:11 / **A man who divorces his wife**: The situation in view here is a man divorcing his wife in order to be free to marry another, or a wife (v. 12) doing the same to her husband, and as indicated in the discussion above, the case of Herod and Herodias, who both shed their spouses to marry each other, is the example given in Mark of what is condemned here. The Matt. 19:9 parallel to 10:11–12 differs in three ways. It has the little clause (translated in the GNB "even though she has not been unfaithful") that appears to give an exception to the rule against divorce in cases of sexual misconduct (though some scholars interpret the clause to refer to the dissolving of improperly contracted marriages). Secondly, in Matt. 19:9 there is no reference to a woman divorcing her husband (something not permitted according to Jewish law of the time). The form of the saying in 10:11–12 seems intended to refer more clearly to the Herod/Herodias case (where both divorced their spouses) and was capable of being applied more readily to the legal practices of the gentile world of the time, which allowed both men and women to initiate divorce.

Thirdly, the little phrase in 10:11 **against his wife** does not appear in Matt. 19:9, and the Markan form of Jesus' saying makes the divorce of one's wife to acquire another more sharply an offense against one's wife. For other parallels to the divorce saying, see also Matt 5:32 and Luke 16:18. It is interesting to note how this saying of Jesus is used by the Apostle Paul in 1 Cor. 7:10–11 to answer certain inquiries from the church about Christians ending their marriages.

10:13 / **The disciples scolded the people**: The verb here is the same one used in 3:39, where Jesus rebukes the wind, and in 8:32–33, where Peter and Jesus engage in heated conflict. It implies a strong action and again pictures Jesus and the Twelve in a major difference. This is indicated also in v. 14, where Jesus becomes "angry."

10:14 / **Let the children come to me**: As indicated in the discussion above, the positive attitude of Jesus toward the children may have been intended by Mark partly to give assurance of the legitimate place of children in the Christian fellowship. Cf. 1 Cor. 7:14, where Paul assures his readers that the children of a marriage of Christian with non-Christian are "acceptable to God" (lit., "holy").

Among at least some Gnostics both marriage and procreation were regarded as evil, though it must be pointed out that the evidence for Christian Gnostics is later than the time of Mark. Cf. Matt. 19:13–15; Luke 18:15–17; Matt. 18:3. See also "Family," *IDB*, vol. 2, pp. 238–41.

10:15 / **I assure you**: the oathlike formula peculiar to Jesus in the Gospels. See note on 3:28.

10:16 / **He took the children in his arms**: Cf. 9:36 for a similar gesture of affection.

10:17 / **A man**: Mark tells us no more about the man than that he was wealthy and had a good record of religious observance. Only Matt. 19:20 says that he was young, and only Luke 18:18 describes him as a leader in the Jewish community.

Knelt before him: This gesture of reverence is mentioned only in Mark and is perhaps intended to contrast with the man's ultimate unwillingness to obey Jesus.

Good Teacher: The greeting implies great respect and is difficult to parallel in Jewish materials of the time, though there are examples from the gentile literature of similar addresses for respected people. (See examples in Lane, p. 365.)

10:18 / **No one is good except God alone**: This saying reflects the typically Jewish idea that God is uniquely holy. It is intended as a mild rebuke of the man's flowery greeting. Cf. Matt. 19:16–17, which has a different form of rebuke. Jesus' words have no relevance to the Christian doctrinal view about the divinity of Christ, and perhaps the form of the saying in Matthew is intended to make this clearer.

10:19 / **You know the commandments**: The commandments referred to here are of course from the OT Law; all are from the Ten Commandments found in Exod. 20:12–16 and Deut 5:16–20, except **do not cheat**, which may be a reference to Sir. 4:1 (also known as Ecclesiasticus, a book listed in the Apocrypha). The Matt. 19:19 and Luke 18:19 parallels do not have this commandment, but Matthew includes the command to love one's neighbor from Lev. 19:18.

10:21 / **Jesus looked straight at him with love**: This detail is peculiar to the Markan form of the story and may be intended to make the man's refusal all the more tragic.

10:22 / **Gloom spread over his face**: literally, "shocked" at the word of Jesus. This detail is also peculiar to Mark.

10:25 / **A camel to go through the eye of a needle**: There are similar expressions of something being extremely difficult in the rabbinic materials of ancient Judaism, which refer to an elephant going through the eye of a needle. (For references, see Lane, pp. 369–70.)

10:29 / **Home or brothers**, *etc.*: Some ancient Markan manuscripts add "or wife" after **or father**, but this may be borrowed from the parallel in Luke 18:29, which clearly includes "wife" in the list of relationships that might be lost.

For me and for the gospel: Cf. Matt. 19:29, "for my sake," and Luke 18:29, "for the sake of the Kingdom of God." The Markan form of the saying is like the saying in 8:35 (cf. the note on this verse). Here, as there, the addition of **and for the gospel** means that the sacrifice is made for the sake of participation in the mission of Jesus and (in Mark's setting) the church.

10:31 / **Many who are now first will be last**, . . . : This saying in slightly varying forms appears at several points in the Gospels. Cf. the parallel to this passage in Matt. 19:30 and in addition Matt. 20:16; Luke 13:30. It is a good example of a saying of Jesus "floating" in the body of incidents and teaching material attributed to him and being attached to various contexts, probably because it so concisely expressed the revolutionary character of his message. It is also possible, of course, that Jesus in fact used such a pithy saying frequently as a kind of slogan. In the setting of Jesus, the saying expressed the view that those who thought themselves especially worthy of God's favor would in fact not find it, and that those deemed by many **last** (sinners, tax gatherers, etc.) would find God's favor.

19

Jerusalem Looms Ahead

Jesus and his disciples were now on the road going up to Jerusalem. Jesus was going ahead of the disciples, who were filled with alarm; the people who followed behind were afraid. Once again Jesus took the twelve disciples aside and spoke of the things that were going to happen to him. ³³"Listen," he told them, "we are going up to Jerusalem where the Son of Man will be handed over to the chief priests and the teachers of the Law. They will condemn him to death and then hand him over to the Gentiles, ³⁴who will make fun of him, spit on him, whip him, and kill him; but three days later he will rise to life."

³⁵Then James and John, the sons of Zebedee, came to Jesus. "Teacher," they said, "there is something we want you to do for us."

³⁶"What is it?" Jesus asked them.

³⁷They answered, "When you sit on your throne in your glorious Kingdom, we want you to let us sit with you, one at your right and one at your left."

³⁸Jesus said to them, "You don't know what you are asking for. Can you drink the cup of suffering that I must drink? Can you be baptized in the way I must be baptized?"

³⁹"We can," they answered.

Jesus said to them, "You will indeed drink the cup I must drink and be baptized in the way I must be baptized. ⁴⁰But I do not have the right to choose who will sit at my right and my left. It is God who will give these places to those for whom he has prepared them."

⁴¹When the other ten disciples heard about it, they became angry with James and John. ⁴²So Jesus called them all together to him and said, "You know that the men who are considered rulers of the heathen have power over them, and the leaders have complete authority. ⁴³This, however, is not the way it is among you. If one of you wants to be great, he must be the servant of the rest; ⁴⁴and if one of you wants to be first, he must be the slave of all. ⁴⁵For even the Son of Man did not come to be served; he came to serve and to give his life to redeem many people."

⁴⁶They came to Jericho, and as Jesus was leaving with his disciples and a large crowd, a blind beggar named Bartimaeus son of Timaeus was sitting by the road. ⁴⁷When he heard that it was Jesus of Nazareth, he began to shout, "Jesus! Son of David! Have mercy on me!" ⁴⁸Many of the people scolded him and told him to be quiet. But he shouted even more loudly, "Son of David, have mercy on me!"

⁴⁹Jesus stopped and said, "Call him."

So they called the blind man. "Cheer up!" they said. "Get up, he is calling you."

⁵⁰So he threw off his cloak, jumped up, and came to Jesus.

⁵¹"What do you want me to do for you?" Jesus asked him.

"Teacher," the blind man answered,

| "I want to see again." 52"Go," Jesus told him, "your faith has made you well." | At once he was able to see and followed Jesus on the road. |

10:32–34 / This third prediction of Jesus' death is written in such a way as to form the climactic prediction in the series. Every item in the passage serves this purpose. The geographical note, **going up to Jerusalem** (v. 32), indicates that Jesus' ministry is taking him to the city of his destiny. The description of the disciples' attitude, **filled with alarm** . . . **afraid** (v. 32), heightens the tension. In the actual prediction itself, there is the most specific description yet given of the events of Jesus' arrest and execution. For the first time there is the mention of gentile involvement (v. 33), and there follows a list of indignities that (v. 34) make a crescendo of cruelty.

With this prediction of Jesus' execution, we are nearing the end of this large teaching section (8:27–10:52) and the beginning of the final events of Jesus' ministry. The effect of this third, detailed prediction is to make emphatic the central significance of Jesus' death. The following passage (10:35–45) is the third correction of the disciples' wrongheaded notions of Jesus' ministry and of their own path of discipleship, and this last prediction sets up an effective contrast between what is to happen to the Son of Man and what the disciples are expecting for him and for themselves.

10:35–45 / After each of the three predictions of Jesus' death, there is a discussion between Jesus and his disciples in which he corrects their view of his work and of their role as disciples (cf. 8:32–9:1; 9:33–50); and this passage is the final example. Having just predicted in some detail the ignominious fate that awaits him in Jerusalem, Jesus is here approached by two of the inner ring of disciples (see note), who have their eyes only on the glory they imagine for him and for themselves (vv. 35–37). The thrust of Jesus' reply in verses 41–45 is very similar to his teaching in 9:33–37, emphasizing the image of **servant**, but there are other features that make this passage somewhat distinctive.

The question put by James and John (vv. 35–37) gives us the first clear indication of the kind of messianic expectation that the disciples held. What emerges is, on the one hand, both an understandable human ambition and a hope that is consonant with what we know of ancient Jewish expectation about the rule of the Messiah, and on the other hand, a dream that is seriously out of keeping with what the reader knows now to be Jesus' immediate fate and his teaching about the proper role of his followers. This is then another instance of Mark's portrayal of the Twelve as fumbling, failing disciples, who serve as a warning to the readers to be sure of their own understanding of and obedience to Jesus' teaching.

In a sense, the reader is prepared for this request for special places with Jesus from these individuals, for elsewhere in Mark, James, John, and Peter have been pictured as forming an inner circle among the Twelve (cf. 1:14–20; 5:37; 9:2; 13:3; 14:33–34). Jesus' reply, however, implies that their leadership among the Twelve means that they are called to join him in his trials and sufferings without guarantee of special places in the future Kingdom (vv. 38–40). The images in this dialogue are worth noting. They ask for chief "thrones," in effect, positions of prominence second only to Jesus himself. He speaks of a **cup** (**cup of suffering** is an amplified translation) and of a **baptism**, the ordeal that he is about to undergo. The disciples think perhaps that the cup and the baptism simply refer to fellowship with him and to being his follower, not realizing that Jesus uses the images here in a sense borrowed from the OT, where the terms "cup" and "deluge" are frequently used as images for divine judgment (see notes). That is, Jesus refers to his coming ordeal in terms that describe it as a divinely ordained fate for him, just as his predictions imply (cf. esp. the note on 8:31). The confident reply of the two brothers (**We can**, v. 39) is full of irony. They imagine that they know what they are promising, when in fact they do not.

In one way, Jesus' question in verse 38 is rhetorical, for the disciples are in fact incapable of fully sharing his ordained sufferings, which amount to a redemption provided for the world (v. 45). In another sense, however, Jesus' question and his further comment in verse 39 imply that they will participate in his own ordeal and will undergo sufferings of their own for his sake (as his predictions in 13:9–13 make explicit). But the fact that they will indeed share his sufferings does not settle the question of their position in the Kingdom of God. This, Jesus insists, is a matter for God alone (v. 40) to decide; and we get the impression from Jesus' statement that in fact this may already have been decided in God's sovereign plan.

The discussion between Jesus and the two brothers precipitates a wider controversy involving all the Twelve (v. 41), indicating that the attitude behind the request of James and John was shared by the whole lot. This sets the scene for the final words of the passage (vv. 42–45), in which Jesus reiterates basically the teaching given in 9:33–37, contrasting the patterns of life among **the heathen** (lit., "the nations," the same word translated "Gentiles" in v. 33) with the pattern that is to be followed among his disciples. In addition, however, there is a new statement (v. 45), which adds considerably to the previous emphasis upon the central importance of Jesus' own sufferings. The first prediction of Jesus' death in 8:31 described it as a "must," implying divine necessity. Mark 10:45 now explains the reason for this divine "must." Jesus' humble path of service and his sufferings, which will involve his death, are both example to his followers (vv. 43–45a) and redemption for them (v. 45b).

The metaphorical language used in verse 45, **to redeem many people** (lit., "a ransom/redemption for many"), is drawn from ancient economic life (see note) in which a slave, a prisoner, or a forfeited parcel of land or other possession might be freed by a purchase price paid. The metaphor presents Jesus' death as the price of the liberation of the **many**. The statement is paralleled in Matthew 20:28, and similar language is used elsewhere in the NT, for example, 1 Peter 1:18; Hebrews 9:12; Titus 2:14. In still other places the language varies, but the thought remains that Jesus' death was a redemptive event, indeed, *the* redemptive event that is the basis for the salvation offered in the Gospel (e.g., Rom 3:21–26; 4:25; 5:6; Heb. 1:3). All this is to say that in the description of Jesus' death given in 10:45, Mark reflects the basic teaching of early Christianity.

The appearance of this explanation of the death of Jesus here after the third prediction of his sufferings and death enhances the climactic sense of this portion of the central section of Mark (8:27–10:52); it prepares us for the narrative of the final events in Jesus' ministry, which lead up to his rejection by the Jewish leaders and his execution. Mark 10:45 shows us how Jesus' death is service on behalf of others, and it gives a powerful contrast to the misguided request of the two disciples that opens this passage.

10:46–52 / If we omit the story of the cursing of the fig tree (11:12–14, 20–25), which is not really a miracle story like the others in Mark, this incident in 10:46–52 is the last miracle story in Mark's account. This makes it something of a climactic miracle story and therefore worth careful attention. It also forms the conclusion to the long section (8:27–10:52) in which Jesus teaches about his coming sufferings and about the path of discipleship, and it seems to have been intended by Mark as an important vehicle for telling us about Jesus.

It is also worth noting that the section that this incident concludes (8:27–10:52) is introduced by another account of Jesus healing a blind man (8:22–26), these two miracles of sight acting like bookends to bind this material together. How appropriate also these miracles are as symbols, because this central section of Mark is devoted to the disclosure of Jesus' destiny in Jerusalem, the true significance of his mission, and the attempt to illumine the disciples (and the readers) about Jesus' person and their own role as his followers.

All three versions of the story (cf. Matt. 20:29–34; Luke 18:35–43) link the incident with Jericho, which alerts the reader to the fact that Jesus is now coming closer to Jerusalem, Jericho being the point at which pilgrims coming from Galilee crossed the Jordan River into Judea. One wonders also whether this location was intended to be taken as symbolic in import. Jericho was the first town captured by another "Jesus," Joshua (whose name in Hebrew and Greek is the same as Jesus'), on his way to doing the divinely ordained task of obtaining the land of Palestine for Israel (cf. Josh. 1:1–9; 6:1–27). So here, also, this "Joshua" is on his way to Jerusalem to obtain redemption for the people whom God will save.

Perhaps the feature of the story that has received the most attention in recent years in scholarly discussion is the title by which the blind beggar addresses Jesus, **Son of David**; and indeed the title demands our examination (see note). This is the only place in Mark where someone calls Jesus **Son of David**, one of only a few places where the figure of David is mentioned at all (cf. 2:25; 11:10; 12:35–37). Mark's favorite titles for Jesus are "Christ" (e.g., 1:1; 8:29; 9:41, see the note on this verse; 14:61; 15:32) and "Son of God" (e.g. 1:1, 11; 3:11; 5:7; 9:7; 14:61; 15:39). (The term "Son of Man" is of course frequently used by Jesus of himself but does not seem to have been regarded by Mark as a title expressive of Christian faith, since he never uses it as he does the preceding two titles.) The questions are basically two: First, did Mark approve of the title, thinking that it did express something true about Jesus, or did he reject it, thinking it hopelessly inadequate? Secondly, what did Mark understand the term to mean?

Taking them in reverse order may facilitate our effort to answer these two questions. In the attempt to determine how the title should be understood, scholars have studied the usage of this and similar terms in ancient Jewish literature, and the investigation goes on. Two things are reasonably clear, however. First, there is evidence that the title **Son of David** was a designation for the Messiah (e.g., in the Jewish writing known as the Psalms of Solomon, 17; and Mark 12:35) in the time of Jesus. Secondly, elsewhere in the NT, Davidic descent is claimed for Jesus, and this descent is presented as part of the claim that Jesus is the Messiah (e.g., Rom. 1:1–4; Matt. 1:1; 12:23; 2 Tim. 2:8; Rev. 3:7; 22:16). Although there is some evidence that the term **Son** (or descendant) **of David** might have connoted other things (such as exorcistic or healing powers), the clear weight of evidence is that Mark understood the term as a designation for the Messiah of Israel.

If this is correct, then we must ask whether Mark approved of the term being applied to Jesus. The answer to this question is perhaps a bit more complex. There is no doubt that Mark regarded Jesus as the Messiah (Christ), as 1:1; 8:29; 14:61–62 reveal. But it is also clear that Mark was aware that the term "Messiah" in itself did not communicate sufficiently clearly Jesus' true significance, if it were taken in its usual Jewish sense to mean simply a great leader endowed with righteousness to be sent by God to rule over Israel and restore the nation to spiritual and physical prominence (see discussion of 12:35–37 and 15:32). Similarly, Mark seems to have found the term **Son of David** inadequate by itself to describe Jesus' true person, as 12:35–37 indicates (though the discussion of this passage shows that some other scholars interpret the passage in other ways). That is, the term **Son of David**, in Mark's view, was both proper to apply to Jesus and also incomplete in describing his full significance.

In the present passage, therefore, it is probably correct to understand the cry of the blind man similarly. His acclamation of Jesus as **Son of David** reflects the fact that Jesus is the Messiah, coming to David's city as its rightful king; but it also reflects a perception of Jesus not yet informed by the cross and the resurrection, and not aware that he is in fact also the Son of God whose messianic work to establish a Kingdom of righteousness is to be done by giving his life as a redemption price. That is to say that the title **Son of David** is a messianic acclamation reflecting still a Jewish background and not yet the fuller Christian understanding of Jesus' messiahship. Like the acclamation of Peter in 8:29, the cry of the blind man is correctly understood only in light of the events to come in Jerusalem. Mark's readers then are to nod their heads knowingly as they read this passage, aware that the title **Son of David** only begins to hint at Jesus' true glory.

Of course, the fact that Jesus does not rebuke the man, but welcomes him for healing and commendation (v. 52), is clinching evidence that the man's cry is proper, and that he is a positive example of a response to Jesus' ministry—as is the fact that Mark says that the man began to follow Jesus like a disciple. Others try to hush the man (v. 48), but Jesus calls the man to blessing, and with a touch peculiar to the Markan version of the story, we are told that the man is cheered (v. 49) by the people and dramatically throws off his old cloak (v. 50) to answer Jesus' invitation. Whenever Mark furnishes his stories with these vivid details, it indicates that he wished to make the accounts prominent and effective in impressing upon the reader his portrait of Jesus. This account, so simple and yet so dramatic, seems to be intended as a demonstration of Jesus' merciful power, and the readers are no doubt to see their own illumination and salvation prefigured in the curing of the man.

Additional Notes

10:32 / Jesus was going ahead of the disciples: This detail, peculiar to the Markan account (cf. Matt. 20:17 and Luke 18:31), paints a verbal picture of the disciples' incomprehension of the events for which Jesus was preparing them and of the consequent gulf growing between them and him. The references to the **alarm** and fear of the disciples (v. 32) are also peculiar to the Markan form of the incident.

The people who followed: The GNB translation makes more precise (perhaps incorrectly) what is ambiguous in the Greek, which says literally "and those who were following him were afraid." It is perhaps more likely that Mark means the Twelve, and not some additional group.

10:33 / The Gentiles: This is the first indication in Mark's account that others besides the Jewish leaders will be involved in Jesus' death. The reference here is of course to Pilate, the Roman governor, who represented the Roman state and its domination of Jewish life in this time. The Greek term used here (lit., "the nations") is a translation of the common Hebrew term for all non-Jewish peoples (*ha goim*), reflecting the Jewish viewpoint (which Jesus of course knew and shared) that the world was composed of Israel and other nations. (See, e.g., "Nations," *IDB*, vol. 3, pp. 515–23.)

10:34 / Make fun of him, spit on him, whip him, and kill him: These details are an anticipation of the actual narrative of Jesus' interrogation and death; cf. 14:65; 15:15. There is also here very likely an allusion to Isa. 50:6, which together with other passages was seen as a prophecy of the sufferings and resurrection/vindication of Jesus.

10:35 / James and John: It is interesting that the Matt. 20:20 parallel says that the inquiry came from their mother, perhaps a version of the story intended to spare the disciples full responsibility for the request.

10:37 / Your glorious Kingdom: Jesus spoke of the Kingdom of God, but ancient Jewish expectations often involved the idea that the Messiah, who is characteristically pictured as a king like the great David of old, would execute God's rule upon the earth as his chosen representative (see "Messiah, Jewish," *IDB*, vol. 3, pp. 360–65). The request implies that the disciples expect Jesus to be given this status. Perhaps, in the actual situation of Jesus' ministry, the disciples' hopes grew more fervent as Jesus went toward Jerusalem on what became his last journey.

One at your right and one at your left: In ancient royal courts, the persons chosen to sit in these positions near the king were those who were the most powerful people in his kingdom. The two disciples ask for equivalent chief positions in Jesus' court.

10:38 / **The cup of suffering** ... **baptized**: The Greek is literally "the cup which I drink ... the baptism with which I am baptized." The GNB translation accurately indicates that the **cup** here represents the sufferings Jesus will undergo. In the OT the cup of wine is a frequent image for the wrath and judgment of God upon sinful people, e.g., Ps. 75:8; Isa. 51:17-22; Jer. 25:15-28; 49:12; 51:7; Lam. 4:21; Ezek. 23:31-34. The image of a cup (in the Hebrew) is also used to symbolize one's lot in life (Pss. 1:6; 16:5) or God's salvation (Ps. 116:13), but it is probably Jesus' way of referring to his coming sufferings (cf. 14:36), perhaps implying that he sees them as coming from God, though on behalf of others.

The imagery of a deluge or flood immersing one is used in the OT to describe being overwhelmed by disaster or trouble, e.g., Pss. 42:7; 69:2, 15; Job 22:11; Isa. 43:2, and this language may lie behind Jesus' use of the image of baptism in v. 38 (cf. Luke 12:49-50). The Matt. 20:23 parallel does not mention this image, having only the reference to Jesus' "cup." It is likely that Jesus' image of a baptism is influenced by John the Baptist's use of this rite in his ministry.

Further, it should be noted that in the two images of cup and baptism we have what were for Mark's Christian readers items familiar in the rites of the church, Eucharist and Baptism. That is to say that Mark must have known and intended that his readers would make associations with their own Christian rites, even more because he includes references *both* to the cup and to baptism. It is possible that Mark's purpose in this was to clarify for his readers that to drink Jesus' cup and to be baptized with his baptism—truly—meant more than partaking in the rites; it meant partaking in his mission and the attendant sufferings. The two disciples in the story think they understand Jesus' question and answer glibly (v. 39). Mark may have been concerned that his readers might have thought they knew what being a Christian meant, when in fact they too were shallow in understanding.

10:43 / **The servant of the rest** is very similar to the saying in 9:35 and was undoubtedly an emphasis in Jesus' teaching. In addition to the parallels in Matt. 20:26-27 and Luke 22:24-27, cf. also Matt. 23:11-12; Luke 14:11; 18:14, for similar thoughts. The term **servant** here (*diakonos* in Greek) is the same word used elsewhere in the NT to refer to various types of church ministries and indeed is the most common word to refer to church leaders and workers in the NT. We derive our word *deacon* from it. In v. 44, the term **slave** (*doulos*) is used as a synonym, though it refers to one who is in slavery, whereas **servant** can mean anyone who performs tasks for others.

10:45 / **To give his life to redeem many people**: As indicated in the discussion above, the idea of Christ's death as a redemption for others is common NT teaching. (On the concept, see, e.g., *NIDNTT*, vol. 3, pp. 189-205.) **Many people** translates the Greek term "many," the equivalent to a Hebrew word used in the rabbinic literature and in the Qumran writings from the Dead Sea caves as a technical term referring to the chosen community of salvation, those who will inherit the future Kingdom of God (for references, see, e.g., Lane, p. 384).

10:46 / **Jericho**: Herod the Great had rebuilt and beautified the town, making it his winter capital. In Jesus' time it was still a well-built, attractive town in a pleasant part of Palestine. (On the site and its history, see, e.g., *IDB*, vol. 2, pp. 835-39; *IDBSup*, pp. 472-73.) Both Matt. 20:29 and Mark 10:46 agree in describing the healing as taking place on Jesus' way out of Jericho, though Luke 18:35 says that it happened as Jesus was approaching the city. The NT Jericho was located a bit south of the OT site and only a few miles north of the northern end of the Dead Sea.

A blind beggar named Bartimaeus: Luke 18:35 does not give him a name and Matt. 20:30 mentions two blind men (cf. the two demoniacs in Matt. 8:28 with the one in Mark 5:1-2). Bartimaeus means "son of Timaeus" in Aramaic, and Mark gives this explanation in the words that follow these.

10:47 / **Jesus! Son of David!**: This is the only use of the title in Mark, though Davidic descent of the Messiah is mentioned in 12:35-37, and Jesus' entrance into Jerusalem is hailed by the crowds with reference to David (11:10). In addition, there is the reference to David's actions in Jesus' defense of his disciples in 2:25 (see comments and notes). By contrast, Matthew (1:1) and Luke (2:4) both claim Davidic descent for Jesus, and Matthew in particular uses "Son of David" frequently, indicating that he saw it as an important title for Jesus (9:27; 12:23; 15:22; 20:30; 21:9, 15; 22:42-45). There is some evidence that Solomon, the OT king and son of David, was revered in the time of Jesus as a great exorcist and healer and that the term "David's son" was applied to him as a kind of title. Thus, the cry **Son of David** here may have carried overtones of a healing power in the original situation of Jesus' ministry. In Mark, however, the term clearly seems to carry a messianic significance. (See also *NIDNTT*, vol. 3, pp. 648-53.)

10:50 / **He threw off his cloak**, etc.: This gesture and the other details of the action in the Markan narrative all help us to picture the scene and make it more powerful in the telling. The cloak here was the bedroll of such a helpless beggar and his throwing it away suggests that he believed that he would need it no more, that he would be healed.

10:51 / **Teacher**: The Aramaic term here, "*Rabbouni*," is a reverential address appropriate for respected rabbis in the time of Jesus.

10:52 / **Your faith has made you well**: This commendation is given to the woman in 5:34, and the faith of the companions of the paralytic is mentioned in 2:5. These are the only ones whose faith is commended in Mark, but cf. 7:29.

20

Jesus Enters Jerusalem and the Temple

MARK 11:1–25

As they approached Jerusalem, near the towns of Bethphage and Bethany, they came to the Mount of Olives. Jesus sent two of his disciples on ahead ²with these instructions: "Go to the village there ahead of you. As soon as you get there, you will find a colt tied up that has never been ridden. Untie it and bring it here. ³And if someone asks you why you are doing that, tell him that the Master' needs it and will send it back at once."

⁴So they went and found a colt out in the street, tied to the door of a house. As they were untying it, ⁵some of the bystanders asked them, "What are you doing, untying that colt?" ⁶They answered just as Jesus had told them, and the men let them go. ⁷They brought the colt to Jesus, threw their cloaks over the animal, and Jesus got on. ⁸Many people spread their cloaks on the road, while others cut branches in the field and spread them on the road. ⁹The people who were in front and those who followed behind began to shout, "Praise God! God bless him who comes in the name of the Lord! ¹⁰God bless the coming kingdom of King David, our father! Praise be to God!"

¹¹Jesus entered Jerusalem, went into the Temple and looked around at everything. But since it was already late in the day, he went out to Bethany with the twelve disciples.

¹²The next day, as they were coming back from Bethany, Jesus was hungry. ¹³He saw in the distance a fig tree covered with leaves, so he went to see if he could find any figs on it. But when he came to it, he found only leaves, because it was not the right time for figs. ¹⁴Jesus said to the fig tree, "No one shall ever eat figs from you again!"

And his disciples heard him.

¹⁵When they arrived in Jerusalem, Jesus went to the Temple and began to drive out all those who were buying and selling. He overturned the tables of the moneychangers and the stools of those who sold pigeons, ¹⁶and he would not let anyone carry anything through the Temple courtyards. ¹⁷He then taught the people: "It is written in the Scriptures that God said, 'My Temple will be called a house of prayer for the people of all nations.' But you have turned it into a hideout for thieves!"

¹⁸The chief priests and the teachers of the Law heard of this, so they began looking for some way to kill Jesus. They were afraid of him, because the whole crowd was amazed at his teaching.

¹⁹When evening came, Jesus and his disciples left the city.

²⁰Early next morning, as they walked along the road, they saw the

fig tree. It was dead all the way down to its roots. ²¹Peter remembered what had happened and said to Jesus, "Look, Teacher, the fig tree you cursed has died!"

²²Jesus answered them, "Have faith in God. ²³I assure you that whoever tells this hill to get up and throw itself in the sea and does not doubt in his heart, but believes that what he says will happen, it will be done for him. ²⁴For this reason I tell you: When you pray and ask for something, believe that you have received it, and you will be given whatever you ask for. ²⁵And when you stand and pray, forgive anything you may have against anyone, so that your Father in heaven will forgive the wrongs you have done."

r. the master; or its owner.
s. *Some manuscripts add verse 26:* If you do not forgive others, your Father in heaven will not forgive the wrongs you have done (*see Mt 6:15*).

11:1–11 / From here to the end of chapter 16 the action takes place in or very near to Jerusalem, much of it centering on the Temple area. In the passage before us, Jesus enters Jerusalem from the east (having come from Jericho, about eighteen miles away) in the company of a crowd of pilgrims who are going to the holy city for a religious celebration, perhaps Passover. The scene of the entry is full of jubilation and is intended by Mark as the appearance of the Messiah, Jesus, coming for his final overture to Jerusalem and to the sacred Temple.

The procuring of the animal for Jesus to ride is intended to remind the readers of OT passages that were understood as predictions of the Messiah. The clearest allusion is to Zechariah 9:9, with its prophecy of a future king of Israel coming to Jerusalem on a donkey. In the Matthew 21:4–5 parallel, this prophecy is quoted. In addition, there is a possible allusion to Genesis 49:11 in the detail about the **colt** being found tied (v. 4). Genesis 49:8–12 was taken by many ancient Jews and Christians as a prophecy of the Messiah, and an allusion to this passage as well as to Zechariah 9:9 would be a hint to the reader as to how to understand what was going on in 11:1–11.

It appears to have been customary for pilgrims coming to Jerusalem for such occasions as Passover to enter the city on foot, and Jesus' entrance mounted on the donkey signals a special dignity for him. This is indicated also by the description of the crowd spreading garments on the road before him (v. 8), a gesture of great respect appropriate for such people as kings (cf. 2 Kings 9:12–13), or for one like Jesus regarded by many as a prophet. The waving of green branches and the shouting of the religious slogans in verses 9–10 were actions typical of the joy of pilgrims coming to the holy city, but Mark intends his readers to see these details as further hints that Jesus' entrance is the fulfillment of all the hopes of ancient Judaism. The cry about the coming **kingdom of King David, our father**, is no doubt a reference to the ancient Jewish prayer that God would send the Messiah, the Son of David, who would restore the kingship to Israel as in David's time (see note).

It is important to note that the entrance is not just to Jerusalem but to the Temple itself, the seat of the religious significance of the city. This reference to the Temple prepares the reader for the incidents following in chapter 11, but it also is intended to show Jesus as the master who has come to the house that is rightfully his to inspect (perhaps an allusion to Mal. 3:1–2).

In the original situation of Jesus' ministry, it is unlikely that Jesus' entrance was understood as the appearance of the Messiah by any more than a few of his disciples at best. The enthusiasm of the crowd was both the reverence for a respected prophet figure such as they regarded Jesus to be and the joy of the religious festival they had come to celebrate. But, of course, Mark here as elsewhere intends his readers to see the true significance in the event, perceiving more deeply than the human figures in the story.

11:12-14 / With this passage we have the beginning of another example of Mark's sandwiching of two stories together in order to relate them to each other. In this case, Mark begins the story of the barren fig tree here in 11:12–14, interrupting it to relate Jesus' cleansing of the Temple in 11:15–19, and completing the fig tree story in 11:20–26. This means that the incident of the fig tree both interprets the cleansing of the Temple and is interpreted by the latter incident. Jesus' disappointment with the fig tree is like his disappointment with Israel and the Temple, her chief shrine. His judgment pronounced upon the tree is like the threat of God's judgment soon to fall upon the city of Jerusalem, which Jesus' words and actions in verses 15–19 prefigure.

The cursing of the tree (v. 14) is what is known as a prophetic sign-act, familiar to readers of the OT, an action in which a prophet demonstrates symbolically his message (e.g., Isa. 20:1–6; Jer. 13:1–11; 19:1–13; Ezek. 4:1–15). Thus, the act is not to be taken simply as a rash act of anger but as a solemn prophetic word pronounced for the benefit of the disciples (and for the readers). The green figs appear early in the spring before the leaves on the kind of tree in the story, and the fact that the tree has leaves but no figs means that it will produce no fruit. The note in verse 13 that **it was not the right time for figs** means that Jesus cannot have expected really to find any ripe figs with which to satisfy his hunger, and that his word in verse 14 is not an implusive act of pique. Rather, the tree's leaves promise fruit, but the absence of green fruit means that the tree's appearance is deceptive. It is this that Jesus uses as a symbol for the Temple: it has the appearance of dedication to God, but in substance falls short of doing his will (11:15–17). Some scholars find in the story an allusion to such passages as Jeremiah 8:8–17 or Micah 7:1–6, which predict the destruction of Jerusalem and judgment upon Israel for the failure of her leaders to demonstrate faithfulness to God.

Mark's note that the disciples heard what Jesus said (v. 14) is designed to prepare for the discussion in 11:20–26 in which the sudden withering of the tree is noticed and forms the basis for Jesus's exhortation about faith.

11:15-19 / This is surely one of the most famous incidents from the ministry of Jesus and is reported in all the Gospels (cf. Matt. 21:12–13; Luke 19:45–48; John 2:13–17). It is the only account in the Gospels in which Jesus engages in any kind of violent action against others, though there is no hint that he attempted to harm anyone; he intended only to force a halt to the objectionable trading operations going on in the sacred precincts of the Temple. It should be noted that this act brings on the plan of the priests to kill Jesus (v. 18), and that in the trial account (14:53–63) there are accusations (perhaps deriving from this incident) against Jesus that he spoke against the Temple (14:57–59). The discussion in 11:27–33 has to do with Jesus' action here and indicates that it was not taken lightly by those in charge of the Temple.

In order to understand the meaning of Jesus' action, one must appreciate the importance of the Temple in ancient Jewish life and know something of the layout of the Temple area. Essentially, the Temple area included the sanctuary, into which only the priests could go, the Court of Israel, into which all male Israelites could go to offer sacrifice to God, and the Court of the Gentiles, beyond which no Gentile could go unless he were a full convert to Judaism. Jesus' action took place in this gentile area in which the high priest had recently allowed stalls to be set up for the selling of ritually acceptable animals for sacrificial use (see note). These merchants and their stock of pigeons (the widely used sacrifice of the poor people) and perhaps other animals, plus the money changers who exchanged various currencies for the kind of coinage accepted for paying the annual Temple tax (Exod. 30:13–16), would have turned the Court of the Gentiles into an oriental bazaar, making it impossible for any Gentile to use the area for prayer or serious devotion to God. In the original situation, Jesus' action was probably supported by many others who found it offensive for the priests to have authorized the transacting of such business within the sacred precincts of the Temple.

The Temple was frequently the site for disturbances having to do with religious issues. In the mind of the average ancient Jew, the Temple was the most sacred spot on earth, and anything that seemed to do dishonor to the Temple produced intense and sometimes violent reactions from people. Ancient accounts tell us of disturbances over the way priests celebrated the rituals connected with the public Temple ceremonies, and so Jesus' action is not without parallel as an example of abrupt protest against the Temple authorities. Jesus must have felt that the presence of the commercial activities in the Temple areas was a final straw, indicating, to his mind, the utterly unspiritual bent of the priestly leadership in Jerusalem, and so he took this dramatic action. His quotation of Jeremiah 7:11 in verse 17, accusing the priests of having turned the Temple into a **hideout for thieves**, was not only the use of sharp language to describe his complaint, it was also an allusion to the prediction of the prophet Jeremiah that the sinfulness of the priestly leadership in his own day would bring on the judgment of God (see Jer. 7:1–15). This suggests that Jesus was hinting that a similar destruction of the Temple and the nation might result. The sympathy for Jesus' action on the part of the people is reflected in verse 18. The **teaching** at which the crowd was **amazed** was probably the action of Jesus in forcing out the merchants and condemning the priests for sacrilege.

The setting up of the traders' booths was, however, not only a general sacrilege, but also a particular hardship for those Gentiles who came to the Temple to inquire after and to worship the God of Israel. Mark's account of the incident seems to emphasize this in the way he quotes (v. 17) more fully than the other evangelists the statement from Isaiah 56:7, including the words **for the people of all nations**, not included by the others. This, of course, would have been noticed by Mark's readers, and they would have seen in Jesus' action and statement a portent of their own welcome to worship Israel's God, which was conferred in the Christian gospel.

Mark's sandwiching of this incident with the story of the barren fig tree was intended to help the reader to see that the Temple was like the fig tree. Outwardly, the Temple was an impressive institution, suggesting great devotion to God. In fact, Jesus' inspection of the Temple indicated that it was a hollow show, and that the priestly leadership was far more interested in revenue from the merchants than in reverence for God. For Mark's readers, the spiritual bankruptcy of the Jewish high priestly leadership was most fully revealed in their response to Jesus' action, their plan to execute him that portends the actual events of later chapters.

There is, however, perhaps more meaning to this incident, and Mark's readers may have been prepared by Christian teaching to see it. Specifically, there is evidence that from the early years of Christianity the church was seen as the new Temple of God (the people, not any building; cf., e.g., 1 Cor. 3:16-17). This notion may have been connected with the idea that Jesus' resurrection body, the glorified vehicle of the Spirit of God, was the new Temple (John 2:13-33) and that the church, which was his "body" in a spiritual sense (e.g., 1 Cor. 12:27), became in a sense the new Temple by union with the risen Christ. In short, Mark's readers may have seen Jesus' attack on the Jerusalem Temple as a prefiguring of the Christian belief that the sanctity and significance of that Temple has passed to Jesus and the church.

It should be noted that the trial account in 14:53-64 includes the charge that Jesus threatened to destroy the Temple and raise up a new one "not made by men" in three days (14:57-59), perhaps alluding to Jesus' resurrection. Mark describes the witnesses as false witnesses, but he may mean only that they were accusing Jesus of actual physical threats against the Temple, when in fact the meaning of Jesus' words was far more profound. It is deeply significant that Mark says that at the moment of Jesus' death the great curtain that separated the inner sanctuary from the outer courts was torn in two (15:38), dramatizing the loss of the Temple's significance as the place where God could be approached in a special sense, and hinting that Jesus had become the new access to God. In other words, to be understood as Mark intended, the story of Jesus' actions in 11:15-19 has to be read through the "lens" of early Christian understanding of Jesus and the church.

11:20-25 / This passage completes the story of the barren fig tree begun in 11:12-14 and includes sayings on faith and prayer that appear at various points in the Synoptic Gospels but are grouped together here by Mark. In the Matthew 21:18-22 parallel to the fig tree story, the withering occurs at once, but Mark has spliced into the fig tree incident the condemnation of the Temple in 11:15-19, so as to make it clear that the two events should be considered together. In 11:12-14 the fig tree is "cursed" for its barren condition, and here in verses 20-21 we have the result, the withering of the tree, which becomes the occasion for Jesus' comments on the power of faith.

The first saying in verse 23 speaks of faith that could move a mountain (**this hill**), and seems to be a version of a saying found elsewhere, in Matthew 17:20 (cf. also Luke 17:6). It seems to speak simply of great faith, but some scholars suggest that the saying may be an allusion to Zechariah 14:4, which mentions a removal of the Mount of Olives on the day of God's promised future salvation of Israel. That is, the saying may originally have been an encouragement for faith in God's coming salvation and not just a general statement about faith in God's power to work miracles. In its present context, however, Mark seems clearly to present the saying in the latter sense. This then introduces the next saying, in verse 24, which is a further exhortation to pray with faith in God. The final saying, in verse 25, is echoed in Matthew 6:14 and seems to be attached here to verse 24 because they both deal with prayer. (What appears as v. 26 in some older translations is probably an insertion in some manuscripts made by copyists who were familiar with the parallel saying in Matt. 6:14-15 and is not regarded as part of the original text of Mark.) Elsewhere in Mark there is a strong emphasis upon the importance of faith (cf. 2:5; 4:40; 5:34; 9:23-24; 10:52), making this one of his favorite themes. Here Mark presents Jesus as an example of faith, and he intends for his readers not only to admire Jesus' faith but also to imitate it.

This theme must not be separated, however, from the context. Overall, Mark teaches that Christians are to follow in Jesus' ministry, as we have noted already, and this means that the faith described here is to be seen as faith demanded in the course of mission, not faith that tries to obtain things for one's own benefit or faith that seeks to do stunts for the sheer excitement of it. Mark means the reader to see that, just as Jesus in conducting his ministry put full faith in God to honor his work with divine power, so the Christian is to trust in God in the conduct of his or her own ministry in Jesus' name. This emphasis upon Jesus' ministry as the setting for the miracle and faith described here is further evidenced in the passage that follows (11:27-33, where Jesus' opponents question him about the authority for his work.

Additional Notes

11:1 / **Jerusalem** was of course the chief city of Palestine, the religious center of ancient Judaism, where the Temple was located (see "Jerusalem," *IDB*, vol. 2, pp. 843-66). It is unclear exactly where **Bethphage** was located, but it is traditionally believed to have been slightly west of Bethany on the eastern slope of the Mount of Olives, about a mile from the eastern wall of Jerusalem. Its name means "house of unripe figs," referring to a species of figs that appears late in the season and never seems ripe, even when ready to eat (see "Bethphage," *IDB*, vol.

1, p. 396). **Bethany** (meaning uncertain) was within two miles of Jerusalem, on the eastern slope of the Mount of Olives. It seems to have been the place Jesus stayed when visiting Jerusalem, perhaps because he was offered hospitality there. It is described as the home of Mary, Martha, and Lazarus in John 11:1-44 and was the location for the supper at Simon's house (14:3-9). (See "Bethany," *IDB*, vol. 1, pp. 387-88.) The **Mount of Olives** is a ridge about two and a half miles long lying east of Jerusalem across a small valley. From the top of this ridge (about 2,900 feet) one can see the whole city, and in 13:1-4 Jesus discusses the destruction of the Temple and the city from there (see "Olives, Mount of," *IDB*, vol. 3, pp. 596-99). See also *MBA*, 235-36.

11:2 / **The village**: We are not told which village. It could have been either Bethphage or Bethany.

A colt tied up that has never been ridden: The term **colt** here can mean simply a young animal of any of several species, such as elephant, camel, donkey, gazelle, or horse. Here it is probably a young donkey that is meant. The parallel in Matt. 21:2 refers to a donkey and a young colt also, perhaps because of the mention of both in the Greek of Zech. 9:9. The description of the animal as one that had never been ridden is significant in light of the ancient rule that only animals that had not been put to ordinary use were appropriate for sacred purposes (cf. Num. 19:2; Deut. 21:3; 1 Sam. 6:7).

11:3 / **The Master**: Commentators differ as to what is meant here. For some, this term is a reference to Jesus himself. If this is correct, then it must be decided whether the word used here in Greek (*kyrios*) carries its more mundane meaning, "master," "sir," or its religious meaning, "Lord." Mark's readers would certainly have read the term in the latter sense. In Jesus' own ministry the term when applied to him probably designated him simply as the leader of the group. Lane (pp. 391-92) suggests that the reference is to the owner of the colt, who may have been with Jesus and his party.

11:8 / **Branches in the field**: The term used here denotes leaves, leafy branches, or rushes. John 12:13 mentions palm branches, but palms do not grow in Jerusalem and would have had to be brought from Jericho. The reference to these branches of greenery is taken by some as an indication that the actual entry into Jerusalem happened during the Feast of Tabernacles in the fall of the year, when the pilgrim ceremonies involved the waving of such branches. In this view, Jesus came to Jerusalem in the fall and ministered in and near the city until his arrest and execution in the spring during Passover (see, e.g., Lane, pp. 390-91).

11:9 / **Praise God! God bless him who comes in the name of the Lord!**: The word translated here **Praise God!** is the term "Hosanna," from the Hebrew expression meaning "Save now," but it had become a cry of acclamation used by pilgrims coming to the holy city for festivals. It and the rest of the words above are from Ps. 118:25, a portion of the Hallel (Pss. 113-118), which was chanted liturgically during the festivals of Tabernacles and Passover. (See "Hosanna,"

IDB, vol. 2, p. 648.) For information on these festivals, see "Booths, Feast of," *IDB*, vol. 1, pp. 455–58; "Passover," *IBD*, vol. 3, pp. 663–68.

11:10 / **The coming kingdom of King David**: In ancient times, Ps. 118:21–27 was interpreted with reference to David and the Messiah, who would restore the kingdom of David. The ancient Jewish prayer known as the Eighteen Benedictions contains a petition to God to restore David's kingdom to Israel, reflecting the hope mentioned here.

11:12 / **From Bethany**: It appears that Jesus spent the nights in Bethany and went into Jerusalem during the day. The distance is about two miles, making Bethany a suburb of the city.

11:13 / **A fig tree** is the *Ficus caricus*, a tree common in Palestine. Green figs ordinarily appear in early spring, followed by leaves on the branches. The fruit ripens in June. Jesus' visit to Jerusalem is commonly understood as occurring in Passover season, sometime in April. This is what Mark refers to in the note that it was not the time for figs. (See "Fig Tree," *IDB*, vol. 2, p. 267.)

11:15 / **The Temple**: In the period covered by the Bible, there were three successive temples located in Jerusalem on the same site. First, there was the Temple of Solomon, built in the tenth century B.C. and destroyed in the capture of Jerusalem in 586 B.C. by the Babylonians. Next, there was the Temple of Zerubbabel, a structure much smaller than the previous one, built in the sixth century B.C. when the Jewish exiles were allowed to return from Babylon. Finally, in Jesus' time, there was the Temple of Herod the Great, a magnificent structure that was begun in 20 B.C. and may not have been finished fully until near the time when it was destroyed by the Roman army in the Jewish revolt (A.D. 70). The Temple was the only legitimate place at which sacrifices to God could be offered, and it was administered by the high priest and his associates. All adult male Jews were supposed to attend the Temple for three annual chief religious celebrations: Passover (late spring), Tabernacles or Booths (fall), and Weeks (early summer). (See "Temple, Jerusalem," *IDB*, vol. 4, pp. 534–60.) For information on the use of temple imagery in the NT, see *NIDNTT*, vol. 3, pp. 781–94.

All those who were buying and selling: Ancient Jewish evidence indicates that there had been markets for the purchase of sacrificial animals on the Mount of Olives overlooking the Temple for some time, under the jurisdiction of the Jewish Council (Sanhedrin). In about A.D. 30 or so, the high priest seems to have authorized the setting up of similar businesses in the Temple precincts, and this is very likely what Jesus was protesting. (See Lane, pp. 403–4, for references.)

The moneychangers: The OT prescribed the payment of an annual Temple tax by every adult male Jew (Exod. 30:13–16) and required that it be paid in the proper coinage. In Jesus' time there were moneychangers to exchange regular coinage for the Tyrian shekel, the closest equivalent to the OT shekel. These moneychangers were only allowed to set up their tables in the Temple five days before the tax was due, and so this might mean that Jesus' action can be placed in these five days, about two weeks before Passover. (See Lane, p. 405, and "Money-changer," *IDB*, vol. 3, pp. 435–36.) There was nothing new in these money-changers being in the Temple during this period, and so Jesus' protest against them may have been based on their charging of high rates in the exchange of coins.

Those who sold pigeons: The pigeon or dove was a permitted animal sacrifice for the poor who could not afford larger animals, such as sheep, and was offered as sacrifice for a variety of purposes, such as the ritual purification of women after childbirth (Lev. 12:6), the ritual cleansing of lepers (Lev. 14:22), and others (Lev. 15:14, 29).

11:16 / **He would not let anyone carry anything through the temple court-yards**: This seems to reflect Jesus' high regard for the sanctity of the temple area, and agrees with the Pharisaic injunction (in the Talmud) against anyone using the temple area as a shortcut for other business.

11:19 / **When evening came, Jesus and his disciples left the city**: It is possible that Jesus did not stay in Jerusalem at night because it was not safe, and that he went to Bethany where he could not be surprised and arrested by the temple priesthood.

11:20 / **Early next morning**: Mark presents this discussion as happening on the way back to Jerusalem from Bethany, where Jesus spent the night with his disciples (v. 19).

11:21 / **The fig tree you cursed**: Peter takes Jesus' words, given in 11:14, as a curse. Some have pointed out that Jesus' saying may have been only a prophecy that the fruitless tree would die, and the remarkable thing is that it happened so soon.

11:23 / **I assure you**: the oathlike formula found only on Jesus' lips. See the note on 3:28.

Whoever tells this hill to get up: **This hill** may be a reference to the Mount of Olives, which they were crossing at this point. From the top one can actually see the Dead Sea in the east and this is probably the **sea** mentioned here. There may be an allusion to this saying in 1 Cor. 13:2, where Paul describes great faith.

11:25 / **When you stand and pray, forgive**: The standard posture for prayer among ancient Jews was to stand. Jesus' words about forgiveness of others in one's prayer echoes the Lord's Prayer (cf. Matt. 6:12 and Luke 11:4).

21

Debate in the Temple

They arrived once again in Jerusalem. As Jesus was walking in the Temple, the chief priests, the teachers of the Law, and the elders came to him [28]and asked him, "What right do you have to do these things? Who gave you such right?"

[29]Jesus answered them, "I will ask you just one question, and if you give me an answer, I will tell you what right I have to do these things. [30]Tell me, where did John's right to baptize come from: was it from God or from man?"

[31]They started to argue among themselves: "What shall we say? If we answer, 'From God,' he will say, 'Why, then, did you not believe John?' [32]But if we say, 'From man. . . .' " (They were afraid of the people, because everyone was convinced that John had been a prophet.) [33]So their answer to Jesus was, "We don't know."

Jesus said to them, "Neither will I tell you, then, by what right I do these things."

[1]Then Jesus spoke to them in parables: "Once there was a man who planted a vineyard, put a fence around it, dug a hole for the wine press, and built a watchtower. Then he rented the vineyard to tenants and left home on a trip. [2]When the time came to gather the grapes, he sent a slave to the tenants to receive from them his share of the harvest. [3]The tenants grabbed the slave, beat him, and sent him back without a thing. [4]Then the owner sent another slave; the tenants beat him over the head

and treated him shamefully. [5]The owner sent another slave, and they killed him; and they treated many others the same way, beating some and killing others. [6]The only one left to send was the man's own dear son. Last of all, then, he sent his son to the tenants. 'I am sure they will respect my son,' he said. [7]But those tenants said to one another, 'This is the owner's son. Come on, let's kill him, and his property will be ours!' [8]So they grabbed the son and killed him and threw his body out of the vineyard.

[9]"What, then, will the owner of the vineyard do?" asked Jesus. "He will come and kill those men and turn the vineyard over to other tenants. [10]Surely you have read this scripture?

'The stone which the builders rejected as worthless turned out to be the most important of all. [11]This was done by the Lord; what a wonderful sight it is!' "

[12]The Jewish leaders tried to arrest Jesus, because they knew that he had told this parable against them. But they were afraid of the crowd, so they left him and went away.

[13]Some Pharisees and some members of Herod's party were sent to Jesus to trap him with questions. [14]They came to him and said, "Teacher, we know that you tell the truth, without worrying about what people think. You pay no attention to a man's status, but teach the truth about God's will for man. Tell us, is it against our Law to pay taxes to the

Roman Emperor? Should we pay them or not?"

15But Jesus saw through their trick and answered, "Why are you trying to trap me? Bring a silver coin, and let me see it."

16They brought him one, and he asked, "Whose face and name are these?"

"The Emperor's," they answered.

17So Jesus said, "Well, then, pay to the Emperor what belongs to the Emperor, and pay to God what belongs to God."

And they were amazed at Jesus.

18Then some Sadducees, who say that people will not rise from death, came to Jesus and said, 19"Teacher, Moses wrote this law for us: 'If a man dies and leaves a wife but no children, that man's brother must marry the widow so that they can have children who will be considered the dead man's children.' 20Once there were seven brothers; the oldest got married and died without having

children. 21Then the second one married the woman, and he also died without having children. The same thing happened to the third brother, 22and then to the rest: all seven brothers married the woman and died without having children. Last of all, the woman died. 23Now, when all the dead rise to life on the day of resurrection, whose wife will she be? All seven of them had married her."

24Jesus answered them, "How wrong you are! And do you know why? It is because you don't know the Scriptures or God's power. 25For when the dead rise to life, they will be like the angels in heaven and will not marry. 26Now, as for the dead being raised: haven't you ever read in the Book of Moses the passage about the burning bush? There it is written that God said to Moses, 'I am the God of Abraham, the God of Isaac, and the God of Jacob.' 27He is the God of the living, not of the dead. You are completely wrong!"

11:27–33 / With this incident we are introduced to a longer passage concerned with Jesus' conflict with the authorities in Jerusalem (11:27–12:44). Here the Jewish leaders demand from Jesus the nature of the authority by which he does his works (vv. 27–28). The **these things** (v. 28) about which Jesus is questioned are no doubt his attack on the Temple business and his condemnation of the priestly leaders described in 11:15–19. From the standpoint of the Jewish leaders, it is a matter of reproaching this arrogant Galilean for his daring to criticize the august position of the high priest. From the standpoint of Mark, it is another example of people confronted with Jesus' authority being unable (and unwilling) to perceive the true nature of his mission.

The authority (**right**) of Jesus is a major theme in Mark (cf. 1:22, 27; 2:10; 3:15; 6:7); indeed, it is another way of referring to who Jesus really is. The demand of the Jewish leaders in 11:28 is, however, not sincere, being only an attempt to intimidate Jesus. This is why Jesus refuses to deal with their demand. They have shown by their failure to recognize God's prophetic call to repentance in the ministry of John the Baptist (v. 31) that they do not really want to be confronted with God's revelation.

In Jesus' demand that the Jewish leaders take a stand about John the Baptist, we have an explanation of why Mark's Gospel begins with John's ministry (1:1–8). John was seen by Jesus and by Mark as the prophetic herald of the coming salvation and judgment that Jesus' ministry brought for Israel and for the whole world. This linking of John and Jesus is reflected also in the saying about Elijah in 9:10–13, which identifies John as the herald of the time of redemption and connects his execution with Jesus' own death.

In the immediately following parable, Jesus likens Israel to a vineyard under the care of tenants and refers to servants sent to them who are mistreated and rejected. As we will see in the discussion of this parable, these servants are to be understood as the prophets of the OT, among whom John is grouped (11:32). This confrontation between Jesus and the Jewish leaders is, in other words, a vivid example of their characteristic rejection of God's prophets that Jesus condemns in 12:1–12. From this point in the narrative, there is only growing tension between Jesus and the Jewish authorities, leading to his arrest, trial, and execution. For Mark's readers, this incident demonstrates that the reason for Jesus' rejection was a spiritual blindness, not just to Jesus, but to John and all the other servants sent by God to prepare Israel for Jesus.

12:1-12 / Jesus' parable of the Tenants in the Vineyard is transparently a description of the leaders of Israel as unwilling to receive God's word sent to them by the prophets, as verse 12 demonstrates. In the preceding passage (11:27–33), these leaders showed their rejection of John the Baptist and their opposition to Jesus. The parable is intended to say that in these actions they are guilty of rejecting those sent to them by God and are like their ancestors who had rejected the ministry of earlier prophets (see notes). But the parable not only interprets the preceding encounter between Jesus and the Jewish leaders, it also provides the background for the incidents that follow. There, representatives of the Jewish leadership debate with Jesus in the attempt to trap him in an incriminating statement (12:13–34), and Jesus condemns them (12:35–44).

The imagery and theme of the parable draws upon a rich tradition found in the OT. The opening description of the vineyard in verse 1 seems to be an allusion to Isaiah 5:1–7, where Isaiah describes Israel as a vineyard that is unresponsive to the owner's (God's) wishes. Further, the OT frequently describes the prophets as God's servants (e.g., Jer. 7:25–26; 25:3–7; Amos 3:7; Zech. 1:6) and portrays Israel as disobedient to them (e.g., Jer. 25:3–7; 2 Kings 17:7–23). The reference to the **stone** (vv. 10–

11) that, though initially rejected, becomes the chief stone of the building is a quotation of Psalm 118:22–23, and Jesus' words in verse 9, threatening destruction for the wicked tenants, seem to be an allusion to Isaiah 5:5, except that in Jesus' parable it is the tenants and not the vineyard who are at fault and upon whom the owner's judgment falls.

Indeed, the subtle but important difference between Jesus' parable and the similar parable in Isaiah 5:1–7 is that here the emphasis falls upon the **tenants**, who are clearly the leaders of Israel to whom God entrusted the nation. Thus, what we have is an indictment of the religious leadership of Israel and not of the nation as a whole, except as it is led into disobedience by those attacked here. This is perhaps all the more important in the light of the sorry history of anti-Jewish feeling that has characterized too many periods of Christianity. Mark goes so far as to portray the crowd as favorable to Jesus, making it more difficult for the religious establishment to take action against him (v. 12). Though Mark clearly approved of the gospel being preached to Gentiles (e.g., 13:10) and was critical of the religious practices of Judaism (e.g., 7:1–4), he was not anti-Jewish and must have intended his readers to attribute the rejection of Jesus by Israel to the stubborn blindness of the Jewish leaders (the **tenants**) rather than to the people as a whole.

In the shift from the **slave** to the **man's own dear son** (v. 6) we see a hint of the Markan emphasis upon Jesus' true status (cf. 1:1, 11; 9:7) as the Son of God. Further, the sending of the **son** is described as the final overture of the owner (v. 6, **the only one left to send**, **last of all**), and this reflects the Christian belief that Jesus is the last and most important messenger from God (see note). In the original situation of Jesus' ministry, the full significance of the image of the **son** would not have been felt, but Mark's readers could not have avoided reading the term in the context of the Christian veneration of Jesus.

12:13–17 / This passage deals with the first of three questions put to Jesus by his critics in 12:13–34. Here, the purpose of the question is to **trap** him (lit., "to snare"). The attempt does not succeed, however, and Jesus impresses his opponents in this discussion tinged with hostility.

In order to understand the significance of the question and how it was intended as a snare for Jesus, it is necessary to take notice of the political situation of the time. The land of Palestine was under the rule of the Romans, and the Jews were in effect captives in their own country. Some Jews went along with this quite willingly and, as a consequence, were able to profit considerably. These people included the tax gatherers who worked for the Romans and their client rulers (the Herods), as well as other Jews, particularly from the upper economic classes, who (as do most wealthy people) benefited from a stable and strong government. The **members of Herod's party** (v. 13) probably represent this sort of Jew who had a stake in the ability of the Romans to govern Palestine successfully. Other Jews rankled under the Roman yoke, not only because of the common feelings of national pride or because of the heavy taxation required to operate the Roman imperial system, but also because of deeply held religious beliefs. These Jews regarded the Romans as idolatrous and wicked and their rule as an offense against God, the only rightful ruler of Israel. For these Jews there was perhaps no aspect of Roman rule more objectionable than the annual tribute or tax that had to be paid in the emperor's (Tiberius) silver coins, on which there was his likeness and an inscription that described him as Tiberius Caesar Augustus, Son of the Divine Augustus, that is, as a semidivine being. In other words, the tribute was not only an economic burden; more importantly, for many Jews, to pay the tribute (for some, even to handle the money) was to consent to the blasphemous claims of the Roman emperor. From the time the tribute was initiated in Palestine in A.D. 6, there had been serious trouble (see notes), and the issue continued to simmer, combining with other complaints to lead to the full revolt of the Jews against Rome in A.D. 66. The Jews who were violently opposed to the tax included a group known as Zealots, a group not mentioned by name in the NT (but see the note on 3:16) that became more visible after Jesus' time. But many other Jews were quietly resentful, and the Pharisees probably represent this latter point of view. The description of Pharisees and Herodians working together against Jesus (similar to 3:6) gives us therefore an extraordinary example of conspiracy.

The opening words of the questioners (v. 14) are clearly insincere, as verses 13, 15 indicate (see note on v. 13). The purpose of these people is to face Jesus with a dilemma. If he supports the paying of tribute, the Pharisees can accuse him of being a religious compromiser who, for all his talk about the Kingdom of God, supports the blasphemous Roman system. If he challenges the tribute, the Herodians can accuse him of sedition against the state, an offense punishable by death. There seems to be little room for Jesus to maneuver!

Jesus' answer, however, demonstrates both cleverness and profundity. His asking for a coin (v. 15) shows that he personally does not carry the offensive items; his questioners must supply the coin, indicating that they are clearly not so troubled by their question as they might pretend. The question (v. 16) about the **face** (lit., "image") and the **name** ("inscription") reflects the concern of the devout about the blasphemous claim of the emperor that the coin bore, and the point may be, "If you are not sufficiently bothered by the coin and what it represents to avoid carrying and using it, then you can surely have no objection to paying the tax yourselves." More profoundly, however, Jesus' final word in verse 17 seems clearly to mean two important things. First, Jesus seems to grant a measure of legitimacy to the government and not to side with those willing to take violent action to bring about a theocracy in Israel. Secondly, and even more importantly in the ancient Roman world, Jesus' words set a limit on the legitimacy of the state, putting God above the state and distinct from it. In short, Jesus seems to allow the paying of the tax, but by his distinction between God and Caesar he implicitly denies the claim to divine supremacy for the emperor that the coin bears. Jesus eludes the trick of his opponents and shows up their insincerity; but he also faces them with the serious responsibility to grant the state only a limited legitimacy and to place loyalty to God above all. It is this more profound implication to Jesus' reply that accounts for the amazement of the listeners in verse 17.

As a word directed to Mark's first readers, the passage must be seen from two standpoints. First, in the context, the passage is another example of the bitter opposition that Jesus aroused from the Jewish establishment, and the collusion of the Pharisees and the Herodians (normally at odds with each other on many matters) emphasizes this. It should be noted that in 11:27–33 a group led by the high priests opposes Jesus, and that later in the narrative, Sadducees (12:18–27) and "teachers of the Law" (12:28–40) come into conflict with him. Thus, one by one, Mark shows each of the major Jewish groups in Jesus' time opposing him, as the narrative builds toward the climactic scene of his trial and execution in chapters 14–15.

Secondly, the particular matter dealt with here, taxes to Rome, was still very much a concern for Christians in Mark's time (see notes), and Jesus' reply must have been received as guidance in working out their own relationship to a pagan government while they were trying to be loyal above all to God. Indeed, whenever Christians have been conscious of their obligation to God, it appears that they have become sensitive about any unwarranted demand of the state, and that Jesus' word in verse 17 has been the watchword for a critical loyalty that grants a measured place for the state—but not absolute primacy.

12:18–27 / Here Mark presents the second in the series of questions directed to Jesus, this question coming from a group not mentioned earlier, the Sadducees. The purpose of their question about the resurrection of the dead seems to be simply to try to show Jesus to be foolish and the doctrine of the resurrection, silly. As in the previous discussion (12:13–17), these critics are insincere in their question (v. 23), for they really do not believe that a resurrection will happen (v. 18). Again, however, Jesus is presented as outwitting them, his answer concluding with a concise pronouncement (v. 27) as in the previous incident (v. 17).

The Sadducees are mentioned in Mark only here, and though there are other references to them elsewhere in the NT and in other ancient historical sources (see note), our understanding of exactly what kind of group they were is far from complete. They may have been a priestly group, from the leading families of the priesthood, well-off economically, and very conservative in religious outlook. Part of this conservatism manifested itself in an unwillingness to accept the development of the "oral Law," the body of religious interpretation developed by the Pharisees. Both the NT and the ancient Jewish historian Josephus say that the Sadducees rejected the doctrine of the resurrection of the dead, which was a major point of controversy between them and the Pharisees (e.g., Acts 23:6–8). It appears that Pharisees and many other Jews not in their circle shared the belief that at the end of this world God would bring the dead (or at least the righteous dead) back to life, and it seems clear that Jesus shared this common belief. The motive of the Sadducees in the present account is to try to show that this belief is ridiculous. The problem they offer to Jesus does not reflect a serious desire to know the solution but is intended purely to mock the idea of the resurrection.

The question posed by the Sadducees here presupposes the OT law that a man whose brother died childless must marry the widow and beget children in the name of the dead brother (v. 19; cf. Deut. 25:5–10). The particular case described by the Sadducees (vv. 20–23) seems to be based on a story found in the book of Tobit (in the collection known as the Apocrypha, see Tobit 3:8, 15; 6:13; 7:11). In his response, Jesus accuses the Sadducees of knowing neither the Scriptures nor God's power (v. 24) and proceeds to illustrate his point by describing the resurrection of the body as a transformation to a new kind of existence like **the angels in heaven**, and by citing a well-known passage of the OT (Exod. 3:6) from the account where Moses first was encountered by God. In order to understand the logic of Jesus' response, it will be necessary to examine it more carefully.

Jesus' definition of the resurrection as bestowing a life like that of the angels (v. 25) is significant for two reasons. First, it appears that there was a difference of opinion among ancient Jews as to the nature of resurrection life, with some holding a view like Jesus' here and some expecting that the resurrected dead would have their earthly relationships restored to them. Jesus' saying in verse 25 apparently does not mean that the resurrected dead will be spirits without some sort of body, but that in their resurrected body they will not renew earthly relationships like marriage and begetting of children. Secondly, in likening the resurrected to the angels, Jesus may have deliberately chosen an analogy designed both to gall the Sadducees, who apparently did not believe in angels (so Acts 23:8), and to point out to them that their inability to understand the resurrection was related to their unwillingness to accept such beliefs as the existence of angels.

The text from the OT cited by Jesus as proof of the resurrection (v. 26) does not at first seem to support his conclusion very clearly, but more careful reflection reveals his reasoning. In the passage cited (Exod. 3:6) God declares to Moses that he has appeared to him to bring about the deliverance of Israel from the grasp of the King of Egypt, and the phrase quoted in verse 26 appears not only in this first encounter between God and Moses but also in other passages (Exod. 3:15, 16; 4:5) where God assures the people of his power to deliver them. Jesus' point is that, if Abraham, Isaac, and Jacob have passed into oblivion (as the Sadducees seem to have believed happened to all the dead), then God's description of himself as the God of these patriarchs of old conveys nothing about his power to save his people, and indeed this title is a mockery of any hope that God deserves the trust of his followers. Abraham, Isaac, and Jacob were given God's promise in a "covenant" (an agreement like a treaty or a contract) that he would bless them and be their savior and provider (see, e.g., Gen. 12:1-3; 15:1-18; 17:1-8). It is this covenant promise to which Jesus seems to allude in his argument, and his point seems to be that God's covenant is meaningless if it is canceled by death.

The final word in verse 27 seems to mean that, if death permanently ends the covenant relationship between God and his people, then the announcement to Moses quoted in verse 26 is nothing more than a chilling epitaph for the patriarchs and an admission of God's powerlessness in the face of this enemy. This cannot be so, however, and thus the word to Moses must be taken as God's proclamation that he has not forgotten his relationship with these patriarchs and that they and the rest of the righteous dead will yet enjoy his favor. (The parallel in Luke 20:38, "for to him all are alive," seems to be an attempt to draw out this point more clearly.)

Thus, Mark shows Jesus besting his opponents on another matter, demonstrating that the insincere flattery of the Pharisees in 12:14 ("you tell the truth") is in fact a proper description of him. But there is a special significance to this question about the resurrection, for the Christian gospel rests upon the claim that God raised Jesus to life as the pioneer and Lord of the resurrection (e.g., 1 Cor. 15:1–8, 20–23). Jesus' victorious reply, coming as it does shortly before Jesus' own execution and resurrection in chapters 15–16, was probably intended by Mark to show his readers that their faith in Jesus' resurrection (and their own future hope) was based upon the Scriptures and upon the very character of God.

Additional Notes

11:27 / **Chief priests, the teachers of the Law, and the elders**: These are the same figures mentioned in Jesus' prediction of his execution in 8:31 (cf. 9:31; 10:33). These people were the main groups represented on the high council of the Jews (the Sanhedrin).

11:28 / **What right**: The term **right** here and in vv. 29–33 is the same word translated "authority" in 1:22, 27; 2:10; 3:15; 6:7 (see also 13:34). Its frequent usage in Mark makes it an important theological term.

11:32 / **But if we say, "From man . . .":** Mark does not complete the sentence. Instead he gives a comment (the last part of v. 32) that indicates their reason for saying nothing.

11:33 / **We don't know** is presented as a lie. Jesus' response makes this plain. It is not that they do not know; they do not wish to acknowledge the possibility that God really authorized John to summon the nation and its leaders to repentance.

12:1 / **Planted a vineyard [and] rented [it] to tenants**: Jesus' parable reflects the familiar Galilean experience of the tenant farm, owned by a wealthy land-owner and rented out to others who worked the land for a share in its produce. (On the farming background, see "Agriculture," *IDB*, vol. 1, pp. 56–60).

12:5 / **They treated many others the same way**: In addition to the OT tradition that emphasizes Israel's disobedience to the prophets (e.g., Jer. 25:3–7; Amos 2:11–12), the Gospels give us other sayings of Jesus that lament the same thing (Matt. 23:37; Luke 13:34).

12:6 / **The man's own dear son**: The description of the son (lit., "beloved son") is the same as the way Jesus is hailed by God at the baptism (1:11) and at the transfiguration (9:7). The wording appears in the Luke 20:13 parallel but not in Matt. 21:37.

12:7 / **His property will be ours!**: The ancient law stated that land could be claimed by the tenants if there were no other claimant. By killing the owner's heir, they hope to have the land for themselves. (See Lane, pp. 416–19, for references and discussion.)

12:9 / **What, then, will the owner of the vineyard do?**: In the Matt. 21:40–41 parallel, this question is answered by others, whereas here Jesus answers his own question (also in Luke 20:15–16). It should be noted that in Greek **owner** is *kyrios*, a term that can mean simply a "master" such as a landowner but was also used in Greek as the title for God (the Lord). So in this term there is a deliberate hint that th.
    is landowner is in fact God.

12:10 / **The stone which the builders rejected**: 12:10–11 contains a quotation of Ps. 118:22–23, which has to do with a stone regarded as worthless by builders but then made the capstone of the building. The original reference was probably to the king of Israel and/or to the nation itself. In rabbinic discussion, the passage was understood with reference to Abraham, David, or the Messiah; and here the **stone** is clearly Jesus, who, though not recognized by the **builders** (the Jewish leaders), will become in fact the King-Messiah over all.

12:12 / **The Jewish leaders**: Mark has simply "they" in Greek, but he clearly means the Jewish leaders introduced earlier in 11:27–33. Their fear was that the attempt to seize Jesus openly in the Temple area where this parable was given might result in a riot, and this would make them look bad in the eyes of the Roman governor to whom they were responsible for maintaining order in the Temple precincts.

12:13 / **To trap him with questions**: The word translated "to trap" is used in the NT only here and means to "snare" as in capturing an animal. The word is used in the Greek OT in Prov. 5:22; 6:25. **With questions** is literally "in a saying" and means that they hoped to use some word of his against him.

12:14 / **Taxes to the Roman Emperor**: The term **taxes** here refers to the tribute paid to the emperor, which was based on a census such as was carried out in Judea in A.D. 6. This census caused an uprising among some devout Jews led by Judas the Galilean, who saw the census and the taxation for which it prepared the way as an affront to the loyalty owed to God alone and a sign of Israel's slavery to Rome. Though Judas was killed, the issue lived on, finally erupting in the Jewish revolt of A.D. 66–70. (On the nature of Jewish unrest at this time over taxation and other matters, see, e.g., David M. Rhoads, *Israel in Revolution 6–74 C.E.* [Philadelphia: Fortress, 1976]. **Roman Emperor** here translates "Caesar" in the Greek. The emperor at this time was Tiberius (A.D. 14–37).

12:15 / **Jesus saw through their trick**: literally, "Jesus seeing their hypocrisy." The term "hypocrisy" is used in Mark only here and the term "hypocrites" only in 7:6. Both terms refer to play acting or pretending and in the Gospels mean insincerity and religious pretense.

A silver coin: The coin in question was minted by the emperor and was considered his property even when in circulation. It was the only currency in which the tax could be paid. (See "Money," *IDB*, vol. 3, pp. 423-35, which has a drawing of the coin in question on p. 433.)

12:16 / Whose face and name are these: Literally, "whose image and inscription." The term "image" is the same word used in Greek in Gen. 1:27 to describe humankind as made in God's image. Some have suggested that Jesus intended an allusion to this passage, meaning that if the coin bore Caesar's image it belonged to him, and since humans bear God's image they owe him their all. We know of pious Jews who refused to handle this type of coin that bore what they regarded as a blasphemous claim for the emperor. The fact that Jesus asked for a coin may indicate that he too avoided the handling of the money for the same reason.

12:17 / They were amazed: It is fairly clear that Mark means that Jesus' opponents were still hostile and that any amazement on their part did not minimize their desire to be rid of him. Cf. Luke 20:26.

12:18 / Sadducees: This group is also mentioned in the NT elsewhere (Matt. 3:7; 16:1, 6, 11–12; 22:23, 34; Luke 20:27; Acts 4:1; 5:17; 23:6–8) and in other ancient Jewish sources (Josephus and rabbinic literature; see references and discussion in *IDB*, vol. 4, pp. 160–63). There are various scholarly attempts to describe them and their background, but much is unclear. They appear to have supported the right of the descendants of the Maccabees to exercise both royal and priestly powers in Judea and may have originated sometime in the second century B.C. Their ranks seem to have been decimated during the Jewish revolt of A.D. 66–70, and in the period following this war they were treated as heretics by the rabbis who came to control Judaism. We have no writing from this group, and our only descriptions come from Christian or rabbinic sources in which they are portrayed in an unfavorable light.

12:19 / This law: The law is known as the law of levirate marriage (Deut. 25:5–10). The book of Ruth gives us an example of this law in operation (3:1–4:12; see also Gen. 38:1–26). (See also "Levirate Law," *IDB*, vol. 3, p. 116; "Marriage," *IDB*, vol. 3, p. 282.)

12:20 / Seven brothers: The illustration used here seems to be a variation on the woman in Tobit who was married to seven men successively who all died without having children, though in Tobit they are not brothers.

12:25 / When the dead rise: On the Jewish doctrine about the resurrection of the dead, see "Resurrection," *IDB*, vol. 4, pp. 39–43. On the significance of the idea in the NT, see "Resurrection in the NT," *IDB*, vol. 4, pp. 43–53.

12:26 / The Book of Moses: The reference is to Exod. 3:6. The first five books of the OT (Genesis, Exodus, Leviticus, Numbers, Deuteronomy) were traditionally regarded as written by Moses. It appears that the Sadducees regarded these writings as possessing scriptural authority beyond the other writings in the OT, and so Jesus' choice of a text from this body of material may have been motivated by a desire to refute them on the basis of writings whose authority they would not contest.

The God of Abraham, the God of Isaac, and the God of Jacob: In addition to the passages from the OT cited in the discussion above, this phrase and similar ones appear also in many other ancient Jewish writings (see Lane, p. 429, for references).

22

The Debate Ends

[28]A teacher of the Law was there who heard the discussion. He saw that Jesus had given the Sadducees a good answer, so he came to him with a question: "Which commandment is the most important of all?"

[29]Jesus replied, "The most important one is this: 'Listen, Israel! The Lord our God is the only Lord.'

[30]Love the Lord your God with all your heart, with all your soul, with all your mind, and with all your strength.' [31]The second most important commandment is this: 'Love your neighbor as you love yourself.' There is no other commandment more important than these two."

[32]The teacher of the Law said to Jesus, "Well done, Teacher! It is true, as you say, that only the Lord is God and that there is no other god but he. [33]And man must love God with all his heart and with all his mind and with all his strength; and he must love his neighbor as he loves himself. It is more important to obey these two commandments than to offer on the altar animals and other sacrifices to God."

[34]Jesus noticed how wise his answer was, and so he told him, "You are not far from the Kingdom of God."

After this nobody dared to ask Jesus any more questions.

[35]As Jesus was teaching in the Temple, he asked the question, "How can the teachers of the Law say that the Messiah will be the descendant of David? [36]The Holy Spirit inspired David to say:

'The Lord said to my Lord:
Sit here at my right side
until I put your enemies under
your feet.'

[37]David himself called him 'Lord' so how can the Messiah be David's descendant?"

A large crowd was listening to Jesus gladly. [38]As he taught them, he said, "Watch out for the teachers of the Law, who like to walk around in their long robes and be greeted with respect in the marketplace, [39]who choose the reserved seats in the synagogues and the best places at feasts. [40]They take advantage of widows and rob them of their homes, and then make a show of saying long prayers. Their punishment will be all the worse!"

[41]As Jesus sat near the temple treasury, he watched the people as they dropped in their money. Many rich men dropped in a lot of money; [42]then a poor widow came along and dropped in two little copper coins, worth about a penny. [43]He called his disciples together and said to them, "I tell you that this poor widow put more in the offering box than all the others. [44]For the others put in what they had to spare of their riches; but she, poor as she is, put in all she had—she gave all she had to live on."

12:28-34 / As the final words of verse 34 indicate, this is the last of a series of questions directed to Jesus by representatives of various major groups in ancient Judaism, this question coming from a member of the "scribes," a class of people trained to interpret the OT Law for the life of the people. The question asked here is reflected in ancient Jewish sources as a matter of discussion. Since it was commonly understood that the OT Law included 613 commandments, it is understandable that there was a desire to try to organize this body of material around a basic commandment so as to give a fundamental premise on which to hang all the individual commands. For example, the great Jewish teacher Hillel, whose career is dated in the decades just before Jesus' ministry, is quoted as having replied to a Gentile who asked for a concise summary of Jewish law, "What you yourself hate, do not do to your neighbor; this is the whole Law, the rest is commentary. Go and learn it." Hillel clearly did not mean that all other commandments were irrelevant and could be ignored but that his summary gave the overall drift and character of the Law; and the scribe in the story before us would certainly not have intended to imply by his question that he felt that some commandments could be ignored if other, more important ones were kept. Rather, he was probably asking Jesus for his view of what he understood to be the fundamental purpose and character of the OT Law. The GNB translation in verse 28, **the most important of all**, should be rendered more correctly as, "the chief commandment of all," meaning the commandment on which the others hang.

In comparing the Markan form of the incident with the parallels in Matthew 22:34–40 and Luke 10:25–28, it is very interesting to note that Mark's telling of the story is unique. In Matthew 22:34, the scribe's question seems to be simply another attempt to engage Jesus in debate, and in Luke 10:25, not only is the question itself very different, but the scribe's intent is clearly described as hostile. Here in Mark 12:28, however, the scribe is presented as favorably impressed with Jesus' previous answer, and Mark alone has Jesus commend the scribe, declaring him **not far from the Kingdom of God** (v. 34). Thus, Mark clearly presents the man in a good light—in contrast to the previous groups who question Jesus in 11:27–12:27—even though he has Jesus condemn the scribes as a group in 12:38–40.

This all makes the positive way the scribe is treated very striking, and it justifies asking why Mark so describes the man and his question. The answer is probably that Mark wanted to show that the conflict between Jesus and the Jewish establishment was not based on a rejection of the OT or a complete disavowal of the Law by Jesus but instead on the refusal of the Jewish authorities to accept Jesus as the final interpreter of the OT Law. Of course, as Mark describes it, Jesus' power to interpret the Law as Messianic Lord involved a considerable re-ordering of what the Law was taken to mean on such matters as Sabbath (e.g., 2:23–3:6) or the clean/unclean distinctions (7:1–23); but the point of this passage seems to be to show that Jesus' criticism of scribal tradition did not amount to a rejection of the validity of the OT Law as a revelation of God. Rather, Jesus' reply to the scribe in 12:29–31 is intended to show what Jesus saw the proper point of the Law to be.

Now, it must be admitted that Mark and his readers understood Jesus' words to mean that absolute devotion to God (v. 30) did not involve keeping all the many regulations enforced in scribal tradition, and it appears that Jesus' own practice was seen by at least some Jewish religious authorities (such as the Pharisees and the scribes) as insufficiently observant of what they regarded as clear requirements on such matters as Sabbath and certain ritual concerns. In other words, the difference between Jesus and scribal authorities was, from the standpoint of both parties, serious, but Mark meant this passage to show that Jesus should not properly be seen as a Jewish heretic, and that in fact his grasp of what the Law really represented was quite profound. To make this point here, Mark has the scribe respond favorably to Jesus' reply to his question (v. 32–33), and he shows Jesus commenting favorably on the scribe's response (v. 34). Differences remain between the scribe and Jesus at the end, for the scribe is not said to have become a follower, but he and Jesus recognize that they are not totally at odds. Thus, one is given the impression that the rejection of Jesus by the Jewish leaders was based more on ill will and spiritual blindness on their part than on a justifiable claim of heresy against Jesus.

It is perhaps also significant that in the scribe's comment on Jesus' answer (vv. 32–33) love of God and neighbor is placed above and contrasted somewhat with Temple ritual. This statement, peculiar to the Markan version, may be explained by the fact that in Mark 11–16 a point that surfaces again and again is the claim that Jesus in some way replaces the Temple as the central place where God manifests himself. At the beginning of chapter 11 Jesus enters the city and goes directly to the Temple, making it clear that the Temple is the object of attention. Then follows the spliced story of the fig tree and the Temple disturbance (11:12–26), in which Jesus states that the Temple has become desecrated by the priestly leadership (v. 17). There follows a series of encounters between Jesus and the Jewish leadership (11:27–12:27), with the implication that they all take place in the Temple area (11:27). The Temple location is also indicated in the passage that follows the present episode (12:35), and again in

12:41. Immediately following this, there is the prediction of the destruction of the Temple in 13:1–2. Finally, we may note again that at Jesus' crucifixion the curtain of the Temple is ripped in two (15:38), giving us the final indication that Jesus' ministry really did bring to an end the validity of the Temple and its ritual as the prescribed place and way of meeting with God. To come back to the present passage, the scribe's statement about love for God and neighbor being more important than the Temple rituals (v.33) seems clearly to fit Mark's overall theme about the Temple being superseded. Mark's readers would have seen the scribe as anticipating their belief that the Temple rituals were expendable and thoroughly secondary to the higher obligations reflected in the two commandments cited, and Jesus' commendation of him seems intended to underscore this position.

12:35–37 / After a series of questions directed to him, Jesus now asks one of his own concerning the popular understanding of the Messiah in the Jewish expectation of his time. It is interesting to note that in 8:27 Jesus asked his disciples how he was viewed by others, and then how they viewed him (8:29), receiving as a reply to the latter question that they believed him to be the Messiah (8:29b). The material that follows these questions shows that Jesus wished to correct what he regarded as wrong notions about the Messiah (8:31–33) by affirming the necessity of his suffering and rejection by the Jewish leaders; and the transfiguration account (9:2–13) shows that Jesus is not only the Messiah but also the Son of God (9:7), implying a transcendent status for Jesus far above popular understanding of the Messiah. Here in 12:35–37, the question Jesus asks is also intended to correct or supplement the notions about the Messiah in circulation at that time.

To catch the meaning of the question, we must recognize the significance of the identification of the Messiah as **the descendant** [son] **of David** (v. 35). David is pictured in the OT as the great heroic king of Israel, and several of the prophets promise another king who would not only be an actual descendant of David but would exhibit the devotion to God and the success as a ruler for which David was remembered (e.g., Isa. 9:6–7; 16:5; Jer. 23:5; 30:8–9; Ezek. 34:23–24; 37:24; Hos. 3:5; Amos 9:11). In Jesus' time this hope for a king like David was a well-known feature of Jewish religious life and involved the vision of Israel vindicated over her foes, free from the yoke of gentile occupation and basking in the favor of God. That is, although the Messiah was not conceived of purely as a military leader or national hero, nevertheless it is correct that his appearance was very much connected with the hope for a deliverance of the nation from the hands of oppressors and wicked men.

In the present passage, Jesus' question implies that the definition of Messiah as the **descendant of David** is inadequate; and the nature of the implied inadequacy if twofold. First, to describe the Messiah as the **descendant of David** means that the David of sacred memory is the model for the Messiah's work and person; but Jesus' quotation of Psalm 110:1 as a reference to the Messiah shows David addressing him as **my Lord**, implying that David is not a fully adequate model and that the Messiah is actually greater than David. In the light of Mark's view of Jesus as Messiah (Christ), the reader is intended to see that Jesus' question is a hint that the Messiah properly understood (Jesus) is actually the Son of God, bearing transcendent power and significance above any human figure. Secondly, if the Messiah is not properly to be understood as simply the great heir of David's throne, then the nature of the Messiah's rule is different from and greater than that of David. The popular expectation of the Jews connected the Messiah with national deliverance, or at least deliverance for the righteous Jews; but in the context of Mark's picture of Jesus, the question in verse 35–37 implies that the work of the Messiah is to be far greater than that of David, involving redemption for all peoples and not just for Israel. In other words, the point of the question about the Messiah being a descendant of David is not the literal question of the family line but the use of David as the model and image for what the Messiah is understood to be and to do. Though Mark does not address the question of whether Jesus was from the lineage of David, the widely found testimony of the NT about Jesus' family is that he was of that line of descent (cf. Rom. 1:1–3; Matt. 1:1; Luke 2:4; 2 Tim. 2:8). It is hardly likely, therefore, that Mark would have understood this passage as calling Jesus' descent into question. Rather, the passage suggests that the full significance of Jesus as Messiah cannot be measured by connecting him with David. The divinely inspired David is quoted as connecting the Messiah with the throne of God (**at my right side**, v. 36), suggesting that the true Messiah is to be understood as bearing not only Davidic, but also divine, significance. The clear meaning of the passage is that the Jewish conceptions of the day were inadequate vehicles for containing the full role and person of the Messiah, and the full sweep of God's plan of redemption. At best, they only hinted at the scope of the Messiah's significance. Though the question in verse 37 is not answered, Mark's readers would have been able to supply the answer, knowing that in the light of the resurrection of Jesus it is clear that Jesus the Messiah is properly

David's Lord, being exalted to the **right side** of God himself and ruling in divine power.

12:38–40 / Having just shown the inadequacy of the understanding of the Messiah popular among the teachers of the Law (scribes), Mark now shows Jesus giving a general criticism of the scribes as a group for abuse of their respected position in Jewish society. It should be noted that the next passage (12:41–44) concerning a poor widow is intended to be read with this passage, for it provides a contrast with the portrayal of the scribes as too concerned with their own advantages. The section in Mark where Jesus is teaching in the Temple (11:15–12:44) begins with Jesus condemning the priestly leadership for their desecration of the Temple, caused by their concern for profit from the animal vendors whom the high priest allowed to operate for a fee in the Temple area (11:17); and here, near the close of the section, there is this criticism of the scribes for their pride and concern for self-benefit from their trade.

In Jesus' time, the scribes appear to have been forbidden to ask for pay for their expertise in the Law and had to support themselves or be supported through the generosity of others. Their great learning obtained for them great respect among the Jews, and as all too often is the case when religious leaders are given such deference, some scribes were not above enjoying their place far too much. Scribes wore white linen robes reaching to their feet as a sign of their devotion to the Law and their special place in Jewish life, and upon their approach other Jews would stand to show their respect and greet the scribe with titles of honor like "master" or "father." At banquets a scribe would often be given a special place of honor and recognized publicly. In synagogues the scribe would be offered a seat at the front facing the congregation. It is possible for anyone to allow such treatment to become too important, and Jesus' words indicate that some ancient Jewish scribes were guilty of this. In their case, the devotion to the Law of God that they were supposed to represent was obscured by their pompous attitude, and the honor they received became more important than the honor due to God. The rabbinic material deriving from the scribal tradition also contains warnings about those scribes who were guilty of the sort of abuse Jesus speaks of here, indicating that Jesus' condemnation was well deservd by some (see note).

The reference to the scribe robbing a widow of her home (v. 40) probably has to do with a scribe sponging off devout people who felt an obligation to support a scribe as a representative of God's Law. Both then and now there are examples of Jewish and Christian religious leaders who unscrupulously solicit support from simple, vulnerable people who are led to believe that they are supporting the very work of God but can ill afford to give as heavily as they are solicited to do.

These criticisms of the scribes appear at various points in the Gospels (cf. Matt. 23:1–36; Luke 20:45–47; 11:42–52) and in varying forms, indicating that the present saying has been placed in its context by Mark and is to be seen as part of the larger conflict between Jesus and the Jewish authorities described with sustained emphasis in chapters 11–12. As 12:28–34 indicates, not every scribe was guilty of the things mentioned in verses 38-40, and Jesus' words should be understood as a criticism of the abuses in practice and motivation that were a temptation for the scribal class. Such a saying found its original setting in the opposition to Jesus by the scribes and in their attempt to make him out as a menace to their view of Jewish religion. The saying was remembered and appears here in the gospel tradition because the opposition of the scribes was seen as contributing to the rejection and execution of Jesus, which is of course viewed by Christians as a monumentally wrong deed. In other words, the effect of the saying is to show that among those who condemned Jesus were people who did not deserve the honor and deference they received, and that the rejection of Jesus was motivated at least partly by those with vested interest in the way things were, those who did not find it convenient to consent to Jesus' proclamation of a new Kingdom of God that, like new wine, could not be contained in old "wineskins" (cf. 2:18–21).

Mark surely intended his readers to see in Jesus' words not only a condemnation of the abuses of Jewish teachers but also a warning about the development of similar abuses in Christian circles. In the same way that the behavior required of disciples is distinguished from that of gentile leaders (10:41–45), so here Jewish religious leaders are held up to criticism as a negative example.

12:41-44 / This episode concludes the section in which Jesus teaches and debates in the Temple area (11:15–12:44) and is connected with the preceding paragraph (12:38–40) by the fact that both mention widows. In addition, the simple piety of the widow in the present passage is a powerful contrast to the self-seeking ambition for which scribes are condemned in the former. As previously the disciples are given the example of the child (9:35–36; 10:13–16) as a figure of humble circumstances, so here we have another type of person who has no social standing offered as an example. Further, the contrast between the poor widow and the rich who give impressive gifts to the Temple reminds us of Jesus' warning about riches being an obstacle to discipleship and obedience to God in 10:17–31.

The virtue of the widow's gift lies in the fact that she gave **all she had** (v. 44), illustrating for the disciples the wholesale commitment for which Jesus called (e.g., 8:34–9:1; 10:28–31). Her action seems to be an example of the complete devotion spoken about in 12:28–34, where it is hinted that commitment to God is not to be measured in the impressiveness of the sacrificial gift one is able to offer (v. 33). The elevation of this simple woman to such an exemplary place seems to indicate what is meant in Jesus' words that in God's judgment "many who are now last will be first" (10:31).

In short, it is easy to see that Mark intended this passage as an embodiment of several of the themes of Jesus' teaching and wished his readers to identify themselves with this "nobody" over against the various representatives of the Jewish establishment who appear in the preceding narrative (11:27–12:40). In the next passage, the disciples marvel at the splendor of the Temple complex (13:1–2), but Jesus is not impressed, predicting the judgment of God upon the whole institution. It is only this widow in all her simplicity and poverty that Jesus cites as worthy of the attention of his followers.

Additional Notes

12:28 / **Had given the Sadducees a good answer**: The Sadducees are not explicitly mentioned in the Greek text, and it is likely that Mark had in mind the **good answers** Jesus had given to the Pharisees and Herodians in 12:13–17 as well.

Which commandment is the most important of all: literally, "Which is the first commandment of all?" The scribe's question probably did not mean to rank the commandments, implying that some were not so important as others, but rather asked which commandment is the fundamental one that explains all the others. Matt. 22:36 has literally, "Which is the great commandment in the Law?" whereas Luke 10:25 has a scribe ask, "What must I do to receive eternal life?" The Lucan form of the story is very different and it is not absolutely clear that it is a parallel to the present story in Mark.

12:29 / **Listen, Israel! The Lord our God is the only Lord** is a quote of Deut. 6:4 and is the first part of what is known as the Shema among Jews (referring to the opening word of the sentence in Hebrew), Deut. 6:4–8; 11:13–22; Num. 15:37–42. It has been the central feature of Jewish religious devotion for many centuries, and the fact that Jesus refers to it here shows that it must have been commonly recited in his own time. The second sentence quoted above is literally "The Lord our God is one," and in reciting the Shema the emphasis is to fall upon the final word, "one," which propounds the faith that there is no other god but the God of Israel. The Shema is the closest thing to a creed in ancient Judaism, giving a concise expression of the fundamental teaching of the OT.

12:30 / Love the Lord your God with all your heart . . . **soul** . . . **mind-** . . . **strength**" is a quotation of Deut. 6:5, though the OT passage mentions only the heart, soul, and strength. **Mind** here is probably an addition by Mark or by an early copyist to make it clear that **heart** includes mental and emotional energies.

12:31 / Love your neighbor as you love yourself is a quotation of Lev. 19:18. In the original setting of the OT, the **neighbor** was mainly a fellow Israelite, and in Jesus' time there is evidence that some Jews practiced a distinction between the way they felt obligated to treat a fellow Jew and the way they felt free to treat a Gentile. The Luke 10:25–29 account has the scribe asking Jesus for a definition of the **neighbor**, and this introduces the famous account of the Good Samaritan. The ancient Jewish material shows that others besides Jesus brought together these two commandments about love for God and neighbor (see references in Lane, p. 432, n. 49).

12:33 / Animals and other sacrifices to God: In Greek, the reference is to "whole burnt-offerings and sacrifices," the two basic categories of sacrificial acts in the OT. The former term designates sacrifices in which the entire victim was burned upon the altar (after ritual slaughter). The second term ("sacrifices") refers to offerings in which part of the gift was burned upon the altar, part given to the priest, and part consumed by the worshiper. (On the OT sacrificial system, see "Sacrifices and Offering, OT," *IDB*, vol. 4, pp. 147–59.)

12:34 / Not far from the Kingdom of God: The meaning is that the scribe has demonstrated by his answer to Jesus that he is sincere and that he is not guilty of the kind of manipulation of religious tradition for which Jesus condemns scribes elsewhere (12:38–40; 7:1–13). That which separates him from the Kingdom of God is his failure to become a follower of Jesus, and Mark does not tell what happens to the man, making the incident all the more intriguing.

12:34 / Nobody dared to ask Jesus any more questions signals the reader that this series of debates between Jesus and various Jewish groups (11:27–12:34) has come to an end.

12:35 / In the Temple: Note again the emphasis upon the Temple location for the saying (cf. 11:11, 15, 27; 12:41; 13:1). In ancient Jewish expectation, the Messsiah was sometimes understood as rebuilding or refurbishing the Temple, making it the seat of his kingdom. From 11:1 on, Mark has Jesus in the Temple teaching and manifesting himself in the role of Messiah, the difference being that in Mark's view Jesus' arrival means the end of the validity of the Temple rather than its enhancement (cf. 11:17; 13:1–2; 15:38).

    The descendant of David: literally, "the son of David," which had become a title for the Messiah by Jesus' time (see note on 10:47).

12:36 / **The Holy Spirit inspired David**: Among religious Jews and early Christians, the OT was regarded as inspired by God, meaning that, though human personality was involved, the result was a body of writings bearing the authority of God for its teaching.

The Lord said to my Lord: The word **Lord** translates two different words in the Hebrew original of the psalm quoted here (110:1). The first **Lord** is the Hebrew name for God (usually pronounced Yahweh, though among pious Jews the name is not pronounced); the second **Lord** renders *Adonai*, roughly equivalent to the English "Sir" or "Lord," and the Greek *Kyrios*. (See "God, names of," *IDB*, vol. 2, pp. 407–417.) Ps. 110 is the most frequently used psalm in the NT, being cited or alluded to in Matt. 22:44; 26:64; Mark 12:36; 14:62; 16:19; Luke 20:42; 22:69; Acts 2:34; Rom. 2:5; 8:34; 11:29; 1 Cor. 15:25; Eph. 1:20; Col. 3:1; Heb. 1:3, 13; 5:6, 10; 6:20; 7:3, 11, 15, 17, 21; 8:1; 10:12. The available Jewish evidence does not treat Ps. 110 as a messianic prediction, but this evidence is all much later than the NT writings, and this passage in Mark could be seen as evidence that the Psalm was understood messianically in Jesus' time; or this interpretation of Ps. 110 may have been original.

Sit here at my right side: The invitation is to sit at the right side of God's throne. In ancient royal courts, the right side of the king's throne was reserved for the person chosen to act with executive power for the king. The invitation here thus conveys the right to rule in the name of God.

Your enemies under your feet: In ancient oriental warfare, the conquered ruler was obliged to put his neck under the foot of the triumphant king, signifying defeat and subjection to the rule of the conqueror.

12:37 / **How can the Messiah be David's descendant**: literally, "in what way is he [Messiah] his son?" The point of the question is not the parentage of the Messiah but his position and status in comparison to David. In ancient oriental times a son was obedient to his father and was to consider his father his superior. The point of the question is then that, since David called the Messiah "my Lord," the Messiah must be far greater than David, not just another like David.

12:38 / **Long robes . . . respect in the marketplace**: The white linen robe was a sign of a religious leader in ancient Judaism, worn by priests and scribes. They often had long fringes at the corners as a symbol of great learning and devotion to the Law of God (see "Fringe," *IDB*, vol. 2, pp. 325–26). In rabbinic teaching, all the Jews were to rise at the approach of a scribe, the only exception being the worker on the job (for background references, see, e.g., Lane, pp. 439–40). The abuses cited here were both real and yet also recognized by the virtuous among the rabbis; cf., e.g., G. F. Moore, *Judaism in the First Centuries of the Christian Era* (New York: Schocken, 1971), vol. 2, pp. 190–94, 245–46, 273–75.

12:41 / **Near the Temple treasury**: Ancient Jewish tradition (the Mishnah) indicates that there were thirteen trumpet-shaped receptacles for the gifts of the people located in the Temple area called the Court of the Women (the farthest point to which women could go in the Temple area).

12:42 / **Two little copper coins worth about a penny**: The two coins of the widow were the *leptons*, the smallest denomination in coinage in circulation at the time. The two coins together equaled a **penny** (Greek, a *kodrantes*), an almost equally insignificant coin. (See "Money," *IDB*, vol. 3, pp. 423–435, esp. p. 428). If this amount was the widow's whole economic means (**all she had to live on**, v. 44), she was indeed poor!

23

Destruction and Persecutions to Come

MARK 13:1-23

As Jesus was leaving the Temple, one of his disciples said, "Look, Teacher! What wonderful stones and buildings!"

²Jesus answered, "You see these great buildings? Not a single stone here will be left in its place; every one of them will be thrown down."

³Jesus was sitting on the Mount of Olives, across from the Temple, when Peter, James, John, and Andrew came to him in private. ⁴"Tell us when this will be," they said, "and tell us what will happen to show that the time has come for all these things to take place."

⁵Jesus said to them, "Watch out, and don't let anyone fool you. ⁶Many men, claiming to speak for me, will come and say, 'I am he!' and they will fool many people. ⁷And don't be troubled when you hear the noise of battles close by and news of battles far away. Such things must happen, but they do not mean that the end has come. ⁸Countries will fight each other; kingdoms will attack one another. There will be earthquakes everywhere, and there will be famines. These things are like the first pains of childbirth.

⁹"You yourselves must watch out. You will be arrested and taken to court. You will be beaten in the synagogues; you will stand before rulers and kings for my sake to tell them the Good News. ¹⁰But before the end comes, the gospel must be preached to all peoples. ¹¹And when you are arrested and taken to court, do not worry ahead of time about what you are going to say; when the time comes, say whatever is then given to you. For the words you speak will not be yours; they will come from the Holy Spirit. ¹²Men will hand over their own brothers to be put to death, and fathers will do the same to their children. Children will turn against their parents and have them put to death. ¹³Everyone will hate you because of me. But whoever holds out to the end will be saved.

¹⁴"You will see 'The Awful Horror' standing in the place where he should not be." (Note to the reader: understand what this means!) "Then those who are in Judea must run away to the hills. ¹⁵A man who is on the roof of his house must not lose time by going down into the house to get anything to take with him. ¹⁶A man who is in the field must not go back to the house for his cloak. ¹⁷How terrible it will be in those days for women who are pregnant and for mothers with little babies! ¹⁸Pray to God that these things will not happen in the winter! ¹⁹For the trouble of those days will be far worse than any the world has ever known from the very beginning when God created the

world until the present time. Nor will there ever be anything like it again. [20]But the Lord has reduced the number of those days; if he had not, nobody would survive. For the sake of his chosen people, however, he has reduced those days.

[21]"Then, if anyone says to you, 'Look, here is the Messiah!' or, 'Look, there he is!'—do not believe him. [22]For false Messiahs and false prophets will appear. They will perform miracles and wonders in order to deceive even God's chosen people, if possible. [23]Be on your guard! I have told you everything ahead of time.

13:1-2 / Chapter 13 of Mark is one of the two large sections of teaching material uninterrupted by other things, the other block of material being the parables discourse in chapter 4. The present discourse begins with a prediction by Jesus that the Temple of Jerusalem will be destroyed (13:1–2), leading to a typical Markan scene in which the disciples ask Jesus privately for the meaning of his statement (13:3–4) and Jesus gives an extensive answer to their question (13:5–37). The fact that some of the material in chapter 13 and the parallels (Matt. 24:1–51 and Luke 21:5–36) appears in other places as well (cf. Matt. 10:17–22; Luke 12:11–12; 17:20–21, 31) suggests that the present form of the discourse may be a composite of sayings of Jesus strung together by Mark and/or those upon whom he drew for his material. In addition, the variations among the three main parallel accounts show that each evangelist has shaped this body of teaching material with the needs of his own readers in mind. But, of course, all this means that this material was considered very important and instructive in the early church and was used and re-used in its teaching and preaching. We ought, therefore, to pay careful attention to the material ourselves, both because of the importance it obviously has in all the Synoptics and because of the long and sometimes sorry history of interest in things pertaining to the end of the world and the return of Christ.

At the outset of our examination of chapter 13, two things must be emphasized. First, as verses 1–4 indicate, Jesus' sayings are all connected with the prediction about the destruction of Jerusalem, which took place in A.D. 70, and was a traumatic experience for Jews—and, it appears, for Christians as well. Secondly, the sayings of Jesus recorded here were perceived as relevant to the life of the church in Mark's own time, and therefore we must ask in the first instance what meaning the early church found before we dash too quickly into the matter of the relevance of the sayings for today. That is, to do justice to the sayings of Jesus here we must have patience for a historical inquiry into them, and we are to be alerted that the best background for them is not the modern newsmagazine but ancient Jewish and Christian sources.

If we look at the chapter as a whole for a moment, it is possible to divide it roughly as follows: After the introduction, which concerns the destruction of Jerusalem (13:1-4), there is Jesus' answer to the disciples' question, devoted first to general and then to more specific troubles that they will experience (13:5-13). There follows an event called here the Awful Horror, which will involve great suffering and possible deceptions (13:14-23); the assurance about the appearance of the son of Man (13:24-27); a parable dealing with the nearness of the events predicted (13:28-31); and finally, a series of general exhortations to watchfulness (13:32-37). In the following pages we will examine the individual paragraphs in more detail, but it is helpful to note that the dominant theme of the whole passage is a warning against being deceived by false claims about the end being near and by individuals who will try to pass themselves off as prophets—or even something more (vv. 6, 21).

This last observation about the major theme of the material gives us the most important clue to Mark's purpose in conveying it to his readers. He must have been concerned that they might actually be overdisturbed about the events referred to in the passage and might be deceived by false teachers concerning the hope of Christ's return. Thus, Mark's primary purpose here was not to inflame speculation about the time of the end of the world but rather to urge caution and wisdom. He cared more about the welfare of his readers than about encouraging them to try to calculate the details of God's future plans.

Mark 13:1-2, with its concern over the Temple's destruction, not only introduces the discourse but also caps the preceding section (11:1-12:44), in which the Temple has been the location, and sometimes the object, of the material. At the beginning of this section (11:1-11), Jesus goes to the Temple for an inspection and then pronounces it desecrated by the priestly leadership (11:15-19). Here, Jesus announces the judgment of God that is to fall upon the Temple. It is the desecration of the Temple, condemned earlier, that explains this harsh prediction in 13:2.

Such a prediction had a precedent in the prophecies of Jeremiah (e.g., 7:1-15), but in Jeremiah's time and in Jesus', the great body of the people believed that such a thing could not happen, for God would not allow the tarnish upon his honor and the blow to his people that such an event would represent. It is this feeling about the sacred importance of the Temple that fueled the fervent questioning of Jesus by his disciples (13:3) about the meaning of his prediction. Scholars disagree as to whether Mark was written before or after the fulfillment of Jesus' prediction; but whether it was still to come at Mark's writing or had already happened, his readers would certainly have seen the event as proof of God's judgment upon the nation and its leaders for their rejection of his own "dear Son," a judgment hinted at in Jesus' parable in 12:1–12 (esp. v. 9).

13:3-13 / In response to Jesus' startling announcement that the great Temple of Jerusalem will be destroyed, several of his disciples come to him to inquire about the details, and this introduces Jesus' teaching, which continues to the end of chapter 13. It should be noted that, though the disciples ask specifically when the prediction about the destruction of the Temple will come to pass (v. 4), Jesus does not give either a date or a specific sign by which to calculate the date. It seems at first as if Jesus has not heard their question properly, for he appears to ignore it, giving instead numerous warnings about being taken in by events that will seem to be the end of the world (vv. 5–23). Indeed, the questions asked by the disciples in verses 3–4 do not receive any direct reply until verses 28–37, and to anticipate our discussion of these verses, even there the answer is far from specific, concentrating instead on warnings to be ready at all times.

It is quite clear, then, that Mark intended his readers (who would naturally identify themselves with the disciples) to see their own preoccupation with the time of Christ's coming corrected by Jesus' sayings. Note the refutations of the idea that the events mentioned in this passage and later are signs of the end: verse 7, **don't be troubled** by wars; verse 8, earthquakes and famines are but **the first pains of childbirth**; verse 10, the gospel must be preached to **all peoples** before the end; verse 13, endurance over the long haul is what is needed (cf. vv. 21–23, and comments on these verses). That is, the disciples' questions in verses 3–4 do not really tell us what the teaching of Jesus is about here; instead they illustrate the kind of excitement that Jesus (and Mark!) wishes to replace with a sober and disciplined life necessary for the trying times to come upon his disciples.

In verses 5–13 the repeated warnings (**watch out**, v. 5; **don't be troubled**, v. 7; **watch out**, v. 9; **do not worry**, v. 11) have to do first with general troubles such as wars, earthquakes, and famines (vv. 5–8), and then with persecutions of Jesus' followers (9–13). The events mentioned in verses 5—8 are very much the sort of troubles that seem to have been expected in the final stages of the world (cf., e.g., Rev. 6:1–8; 2 Tim. 3:1–5). Here these events are affirmed as things that **must happen**, but Jesus denies that they indicate a speedy end of the world (v. 7). Like the first pains of childbirth (v. 8), they signal that something important is coming, but do not indicate how long the painful wait will be. In short, Jesus confirms the idea that the sort of events described here are part of God's plan and do not indicate its interruption but its advance; at the same time he declares that they do not reveal when the divine plan for the world will be consummated.

In verses 9–13 the focus shifts from the standard events featured in what is known as apocalyptic expectation, as reflected in ancient Jewish and Christian writings, to the specific troubles that his followers must expect in the course of their mission in the world. It is interesting to note that the things described here are all formal legal proceedings against them; and we have the record of such persecutions given to us elsewhere in the NT (e.g., Acts 4:1–23; 5:17–42; 6:8–7:60; 12:1–5; 16:19–40; 18:12–17; 22:30–23:10; 24:1–27; 25:1–12). The persecutions mentioned in verses 9–10 involve both Jewish (**synagogues**) and gentile settings (**rulers and kings**). The opposition to Jesus' followers will come even from their own relatives (v. 12) and will seem to be supported by everyone (v. 13), a dire picture indeed. Nevertheless, in the midst of the persecution and apparent abandonment by all, the disciples are promised that they will be given power to speak courageously, the Holy Spirit giving them prophetic inspiration (v. 11).

Certainly, the NT writings indicate that the original twelve disciples did in fact experience the very sort of troubles described here; but in Mark's time the troubles were by no means over, and his readers would have found Jesus' words directly appropriate to their own situation. Jewish Christians (such as Paul the Apostle, 2 Cor. 11:22–25) sometimes found intense opposition from other Jews, and though there is no evidence of systematic persecutions of Christians throughout the Roman Empire in the first century, in local areas (including Rome under Nero in the 60s) trouble was sometimes severe (cf. Rev. 2:8–13; 1 Pet. 4:12–19).

In addition to toning down the idea that the end can be calculated by the occurrence of such events as are mentioned in verses 5–13, the passage also contains a strong emphasis upon the importance of the mission to which the disciples are to give themselves. Instead of describing certain events that will function as the indicators of the end, Jesus draws attention to the worldwide preaching of the gospel (v. 10). Just as the Twelve were given Jesus' authority and power to do his works (3:13–15; 6:7–13), so here his followers are promised divine aid in their mission so that they will speak, like Jesus and the prophets of the OT, in the power of the Holy Spirit. Just as the readers know that Jesus was persecuted, put to trial, and unjustly condemned (14:53–65; 15:1–37), so they are told that his followers must expect the same kind of trouble. Thus, this passage reflects the Markan concern about discipleship that we have noted already in various passages; and again, the pattern of discipleship is modeled after Jesus' own mission and its consequences (cf., e.g., 10:38–45).

13:14–23 / After describing various distresses that will come upon the disciples, Jesus now turns to one particular distress that is described in such a way as to make it the climactic trouble to be experienced by them. As our comments and notes will show, what is described here is the very event predicted in 13:1–2 that precipitated the disciples' questions about the future, the destruction of Jerusalem and its Temple, which in fact happened in the Jewish revolt of A.D. 66–70. Scholarly opinion is divided over whether Mark wrote a short time before, or after, the siege of Jerusalem, but whether the event was still expected or had already happened, Mark's first readers would have found this discussion of it intensely interesting.

The term Mark uses in 13:14, **the Awful Horror** (RSV, "the desolating sacrilege"; KJV, "the abomination of desolation"), is taken from the book of Daniel in the OT (see 9:27; 11:31; 12:11), which describes great hardship and troubles for Israel, including a final assault upon her religion as part of the end-time trials before God's ultimate deliverance. The term is a kind of code word and an allusion to these passages in Daniel, as the editorial aside in verse 14 indicates. Jesus' prediction of the destruction of the Temple would certainly have seemed to his disciples to be possible of fulfillment only as part of the events of the end, for they would not have been able to understand otherwise how God could possibly allow such a horrible thing to happen to his Temple. This seems to be reflected in the attitude of the disciples described in 13:1 and in their agitated questions in 13:3–4. The drift of Jesus' statements in verses 14–23, however, is that even the fall of Jerusalem (which the disciples would regard as "the Awful Horror") does not signal the end of the age. Instead of encouraging the attempt to calculate the end by the means of such events, Jesus continues to advise prudent actions (vv. 14b–20) and a skeptical attitude toward any who come along with extravagant claims for themselves (vv. 21–23).

As in the previous verses (5–13), the language here reflects life in Palestine of the first century. The words are directed toward those who live in Judea (v. 14b); and they are told to flee to the hill country, leaving Jerusalem instead of taking refuge in it. They are advised to flee quickly from the approaching army (vv. 15–16); and there is the touching note about the special hardships for women who are pregnant or nursing (v. 17) and about how difficult the refugees will find it if they must flee into the hills in winter (v. 18).

In addition to calling the coming destruction of Jerusalem by the prophetic term **the Awful Horror**, it is described as an unparalleled disaster (vv. 19–20) that will be mitigated only by the merciful hand of God (v. 20). Even so, it is not the time of the end, and the disciples must be on their guard against false hopes and deceptive claims (vv. 21–23). Jesus' purpose in predicting the disaster is not to reveal the time of the end but to prepare his disciples for the event so that they are not deceived by the excited appeals of the misguided (v. 23). In effect, Jesus revises the popular Jewish idea that the end would follow immediately **the Awful Horror**, making it instead simply the greatest trouble of many to be experienced by his followers, and locating it in an indefinite period of time during which they must carry out their mission, survive as best they can, and avoid being taken in by false teachers (vv. 13, 15–16, 21–23).

In fact, when the Jewish revolt broke out and it quickly became apparent that the Roman army would sweep away Jewish resistance from the main part of Palestine, many Jews fled into Jerusalem for safety, probably assuming that God would not allow the holy city to be sacked again by the heathen. Josephus, the ancient Jewish historian, tells us that during the siege of Jerusalem several rival groups with leaders claiming to be sent by God to deliver the people struggled with one another for control within the city, and it appears that many believed that God would do wonders to enable the inferior forces of the Jews to defeat the Romans. The revolt, when it came, was deeply motivated by religious feelings among the Jews; and in the light of the actual events of the war, Jesus' commands here take on clearer significance. Basically, they amount to directions to avoid becoming involved in the war, recognizing that God will not defend the city but will allow it to be destroyed, and that this destruction is not an immediate prelude to the end of the world and the beginning of the age to come.

Whether Mark's readers still awaited the fall of Jerusalem or looked back upon it in retrospect, they were intended to understand that it represented the judgment of God upon the Temple and upon the religious leadership of Judaism for their disobedience to his word—especially for their rejection of God's Son, Jesus. They were to see that it was no longer the Temple that should be regarded as the center of God's attention but rather the followers of Jesus, the **chosen people** mentioned in verses 20, 22. And they were to realize that the coming of the end was not tied to the

Jewish Temple and the religious observances it represented, but rather to the successful accomplishing of the worldwide preaching of the gospel mentioned in 13:10.

Additional Notes

13:1 / What wonderful stones and buildings: Though Herod the Great was not well liked among the Jews, the Temple he planned and began was the pride of religious Jews in the time before its destruction. Descriptions of the structure in Josephus and in the rabbinic materials do not fully agree, but by all accounts it was magnificent in size and appearance. (See "Temple, Jerusalem," *IDB*, vol. 4, pp. 550–60.) To mention just a few details, the stones used measured over 25 by 8 by 12 feet; the courts were surrounded by huge colonnades; and there were ornate decorations in bright colors made of precious materials.

13:3 / The Mount of Olives lies directly east of the Temple area and overlooks the city. See the note on 11:1.

Peter, James, John, and Andrew: Again, we note the inner circle mentioned by Mark elsewhere, but usually without Andrew (cf. 1:16–20; 5:37; 9:2; 10:35–37; 14:33). We also see here the Markan pattern of a pronouncement by Jesus followed by a private request for explanation (cf. 4:10; 7:17; 9:28).

13:4 / What will happen to show that the time has come: literally, "what is the sign when these things are about to be accomplished?" The question involves the idea that some event will be given by God as a portent of the end of the world.

13:5 / Don't let anyone fool you: The verb here means "to deceive." It appears also in v. 6, and in v. 22 in a more intensive form, showing that the concern about deception is a major theme of the passage.

13:6 / Claiming to speak for me: The Greek phrase is literally "in my name," and can describe someone who is a follower of Jesus (cf. the same or similar constructions in 9:37–41; 13:13); but the people referred to in the present verse are said to claim **I am he!**—perhaps implying that they claim to be the Christ. It is also possible that their claim is an allusion to the divine name for God (cf. discussion and notes on 6:50) and amounts to an assertion of their own divinity!

13:7 / The noise of battles close by and news of battles far away: literally, "wars/battles and reports of war."

Such things must happen: The word **must** here is the same word used in 8:31 and is usually understood as reflecting the idea that the events described must happen because they are part of the divinely foreseen plan of the age. This idea is at the core of the religious outlook known as "apocalypticism," which was quite widely shared in Jesus' time among Jews and later by Christians (see "Apocalypse, Genre," and "Apocalypticism," *IDBSup*, pp. 27—34).

The end of this world/age is what is meant. The disciples' question was probably motivated by the assumption that the destruction of the Temple could occur only at the end of the world and as part of the establishment of the world to come, in which the Kingdom of God would be fully consummated and evil would cease. Jesus' teaching in vv. 5–23 is to the effect that the calamitous events described do *not* signal the end and must be endured until in God's good time that end appears (cf. v. 13).

13:8 / The first pains of childbirth: The image of the world distresses before the appearance of the world to come being like birth-pains seems to have been familiar in ancient Jewish and Christian thinking; cf., e.g., Rom. 8:18–23.

13:9 / You will be arrested and taken to court. You will be beaten in the synagogues: **Court** here translates the Greek word *sunedria*, referring to Jewish councils in local cities where disciplinary action against Jews could be pursued. **Beaten in the synagogues** refers to the floggings that could be administered to Jews who were found guilty of serious breaches of conduct. The floggings were to consist of thirty-nine blows with a whip across the back, based on Deut. 25:1–3 (which calls for forty lashes, thirty-nine being given in practice so as to avoid exceeding the prescribed number); the Apostle Paul mentions receiving such floggings five times (2 Cor. 11:24). Such punishments could be given only to Jews who were willing to submit to them to maintain membership in the Jewish community.

To tell them the Good News: literally, "for a testimony to [or against?] them"; cf. 6:11, where the words "a warning to them" translate the same Greek phrase as appears here.

13:10 / Before the end comes: literally, "first," in Greek, but the meaning is that the gospel must be preached to all nations "first" before the end. **To all peoples** translates "to all nations" or "to all the Gentiles," reflecting the Jewish perspective upon the world, seen as consisting of Jews and the Nations/Gentiles.

13:11 / Say whatever is then given to you: What is meant here is explained in the next sentence about the Holy Spirit inspiring the disciples with an ability to speak. Obviously, this means that in the trial situation, the disciples are not to be concerned primarily with defending themselves but rather with proclaiming clearly their faith. This is the only reference in Mark to the Holy Spirit being given to disciples, but cf. John 14–15; 20:19–23; Luke 24:49; Acts 1:8.

13:12 / To be put to death: It appears that Jewish courts did not usually have the power to carry out death sentences but could bring a condemned person before Roman, civil powers for such punishment. There is the example of Stephen in Acts 7:54–60, though this appears to have been a kind of mob action in the absence of Roman approval. Acts 12:1–2 mentions the death of James Zebedee at the hands of Herod Agrippa (ruler of Judea, A.D. 41–44, who was the client ruler for the Romans).

13:14 / "The Awful Horror" standing in the place where he should not be:

The GNB gives the impression that it is a person, **he**, but in Greek the term is neuter, and it could be an event that is in view. The term **Awful Horror** (from Dan. 9:27; 11:31; 12:11) was used here to represent the Jewish attitude toward the idea of the destruction of the Temple, an attitude no doubt shared by the Twelve but perhaps not so familiar to the readers; hence the note to the reader to understand the term properly (cf. Rev. 13:18 for a similar aside about a coded expression). The Matt. 24:15 parallel has "standing in the holy place" for "where he should not be," and the Luke 21:20 parallel drops the code term altogether and openly refers to "Jerusalem surrounded by armies," describing the siege as "the Days of Punishment" prophesied in the OT. (For a full discussion of Jewish resistance to Roman rule in the first century, see David M. Rhoads, *Israel in Revolution 6–74 C.E.* [Philadelphia: Fortress, 1976.])

Those who are in Judea must run away to the hills: There is an early tradition reported by the ancient writer Eusebius (*Ecclesiastical History*, iii, 5.3; about A.D. 300) that Christians living in Jerusalem fled the city to a town called Pella, east of the Jordan River, and that this action was taken in response to an oracle of God given to them before the war. The full accuracy of the tradition is disputed, however, and in any case it is difficult to link the oracle with 13:14. (For discussion of the Jerusalem church in the first century, see, e.g., F. F. Bruce, *New Testament History* [Garden City: Anchor, 1972], chaps. 16, 28.)

13:19 / The trouble of those days: In light of modern events such as the Second World War, mass genocide of Jews, and the prospect of nuclear war, the description of the fall of Jerusalem seems somewhat exaggerated, but we must remember that these words were spoken to people who were expected to go through this trouble, and that for them it was the worst thing they would experience and could imagine. In the actual event, the war was quite costly. Josephus tells us that so many Jews were crucified that the hills were denuded of trees to provide the crosses!

13:20 / For the sake of his chosen people . . . he has reduced those days: The **chosen people** (Greek, "the elect ones") in the OT are Israel (e.g., 1 Chron. 16:13; Ps. 105:43; Isa. 65:9, 15), but in the NT are the church (e.g., 1 Pet. 1:1; 2 Tim. 2:10; Rom. 8:33; Col. 3:12; etc.). On the idea of God's choice of people, see "Elect," *NIDNTT*, vol. 1, pp. 536–43. "Reducing" the days means limiting their duration so that the destruction is not so great as to wipe out the people of God and thus destroy their mission. The idea behind Jesus' statement is the conviction that God is ultimately in charge of history and will not permit its evil turns to exceed the bounds he has set.

13:22 / They will perform miracles and wonders: The idea that false prophets as well as true ones can work miracles appears in Deut. 13:1–5, and an allusion to this passage may be intended here. (Cf. 1 John 4:1–3; 2 Thess. 2:1–12; Rev. 13:11–18).

24

The Coming of the Son of Man

"In the days after that time of trouble the sun will grow dark, the moon will no longer shine, [25]the stars will fall from heaven, and the powers in space will be driven from their courses. [26]Then the Son of Man will appear, coming in the clouds with great power and glory. [27]He will send the angels out to the four corners of the earth to gather God's chosen people from one end of the world to the other.

[28]"Let the fig tree teach you a lesson. When its branches become green and tender and it starts putting out leaves, you know that summer is near. [29]In the same way, when you see these things happening, you will know that the time is near, ready to begin.[u] [30]Remember that all these things will happen before the people now living have all died. [31]Heaven and earth will pass away, but my words will never pass away.

[32]"No one knows, however, when that day or hour will come—neither the angels in heaven, nor the Son; only the Father knows. [33]Be on watch, be alert, for you do not know when the time will come. [34]It will be like a man who goes away from home on a trip and leaves his servants in charge, after giving to each one his own work to do and after telling the doorkeeper to keep watch. [35]Watch, then, because you do not know when the master of the house is coming—it might be in the evening or at midnight or before dawn or at sunrise. [36]If he comes suddenly, he must not find you asleep. [37]What I say to you, then, I say to all: Watch!"

u. the time is near, ready to begin; *or* he is near, ready to come.

13:24–27 / Having described the coming trials that his disciples must face, including the destruction of Jerusalem, Jesus now deals with the appearance of the Son of Man in glory and what amounts to the consummation of the Kingdom of God. The preceding events (vv. 5–23) are all the result of the evil in the world and will involve suffering for God's people, but now we come to an event that is the direct manifestation of God and will mean vindication and salvation.

The Son of Man here is to be understood as Jesus, appearing openly in divine glory, and the description of him is similar to 8:38. As mentioned in considering that verse, the use of the title Son of Man indicates that the one who now seems to be a mere man will one day be exalted to an unparalleled position of glory, acting in the role of God. In Daniel 7:13–14, a figure described as "what looked like a human being" (Hebrew, "one like a son of man") is brought before the throne of God and is given great power and dominion, and this is the passage to which allusion is being made in 13:26. But here in Mark the victory of the Son of Man is far greater than what is described in Daniel 7. He is described as coming **in the clouds with great power and glory**, much the way God's appearance is described in the OT (e.g., Ps. 104:3; Isa. 19:1; Exod. 16:10; 19:9; 34:5). He sends out the angels (v. 27) and gathers the chosen people, acts of God in the OT (e.g., Deut. 30:3; Ps. 50:3–5; Isa. 43:6; 66:18–21; Jer. 32:37; Ezek. 34:11–16; 36:24; Zech. 2:6, 10). In the OT prophecies of God's manifestation of his glory in the last days, the scattered people of God are usually gathered to Jerusalem and to God himself; but here they are gathered to the Son of Man, who commands the angels of God as if they were his. In this prophecy we have a clear affirmation of the central place Jesus, the Son of Man, has in the expectations of Christians, a clear reflection of the divine role he is understood to exercise.

Verses 24–27 are constructed out of vocabulary heavily borrowed from a variety of OT passages, and the traditional nature of the language must be recognized, for the description of the events is not intended as a specific and literal indication of their appearance. Rather, these allusions to the OT (which the readers were expected to catch) are intended to indicate the *meaning* of the events. The cosmic disturbances described in verses 24–25 resemble OT descriptions of manifestations of God's judgment in Israel's history (cf. Joel 2:10; 3:15; Isa. 13:10; 34:4; Ezek. 32:7–8; Amos 8:9). The language originated in ancient Israelite times when the sun, moon, and stars were believed by many peoples to represent deities who exercised control over world affairs, and the original meaning of saying that when God acted these celestial bodies would be disturbed was that those powers believed by other nations to control history would be shown up as helpless creatures who would reel under God's power, just as would people upon the earth. Of course, in Mark's time belief in the power of the celestial bodies was still strong (and still seems to be strong, given the popularity of astrology columns in modern newspapers) and the meaning of the statements would not be lost on his readers.

It is important to note the loose chronological connection between the appearance of the Son of Man and the previous events of verses 5–23. We are told simply that **after that time of trouble** (v. 24) the final victory will come, with no indication of how long afterward. This means that the events of verses 5–23, events that Jesus' own followers actually experienced, are described as part of the plan of God and steps in the drama leading to the final manifestation of God's rule; but they are not said to be the immediate precursors of the end. Beyond the dark days ahead of them, the disciples are to see the shining appearance of the Son of Man in glory, triumphant with his followers, though they are not told how far beyond chronologically. So, Mark's readers are reminded of the sure hope described in verses 24-27; they too must work and wait with assurance, but with no knowledge of the chronological period involved.

13:28-31 / On the eastern slope of the Mount of Olives in ancient times, the fig trees were a prominent and well-known feature (cf. 11:12-14), and the reference to the characteristics of this tree in the context of teaching delivered on that mountain (13:3) is very natural. There, the tree begins to show leaves only late in the spring, and the observer knows that summer is surely to come. The leafing of the fig tree is a **lesson** (Greek, "parable"), signifying the way the events of verses 5-23 (**these things**, v. 29) are to be taken by Jesus' followers. Though the events are distresses, the disciples are to react in faith, taking them as signs indicating, not that God has lost control of history, but that he is sure to bring it to his predetermined end.

It is important to note carefully the wording of verses 29-30, or one might easily misinterpret Jesus' saying. The **these things** of verse 29 clearly refers to the "these things" of verse 4 and verse 8, and the "everything" (Greek, "all things") of verse 23, that is, the troubles that his disciples are to expect, including the destruction of Jerusalem. Logically, if verses 24-27 describe the end, then these verses cannot be the "these things" that assure one that an end will come! Thus, the **these things** of verse 30 must also refer, not to the end itself, but to the tribulations described in verses 5-23. **These things** will happen in the lifetime of the Twelve (v. 30), but that does not mean that the end will happen in so short a period of time.

Also, in verse 29, we are told that the events of verses 5-23 signal that **the time is near, ready to begin**. The Greek reads literally "it [or he] is near, at the doors," and what is referred to is probably the consummation described in verses 24-27. That is, the distresses of verses 5-23 are to be taken as evidence that the consummation is surely coming. But this does not mean that the troubles are to be taken as indications that the end will happen immediately, for the whole point of verses 5-23 has been to debunk any attempt to calculate the date of the end by the occurrence of these events (see comments on these verses). Further, verses 34-37 specifically deny that anyone but God can know when the end will come and urge that the disciples can only try to be prepared always. So, the words in verse 29, "near, at the doors," must be taken to mean that the end is sure—just as summer surely follows spring—not that the end can be plotted in time on the basis of the events referred to. Verse 31 supports the idea that the emphasis is upon the assurance, likening the surety of Jesus' words to the surety of God's word (cf. Ps. 102:25–27; Isa. 40:6–8; 51:6).

13:32-37 / Finally, in these verses, Jesus comes to the question concerning the time when the end will appear, but his answer is likely to be disappointing to anyone wishing to be able to calculate the end, as is the fashion of some ancient and modern so-called prophecy experts. In the preceding verses (28–31), Jesus has assured his disciples in the strongest terms that the prophecy of the fall of Jerusalem (which triggered the whole discussion) and the attendant distresses of verses 5–13 will be fulfilled within a generation (v. 30). Here, when speaking of the end, however, Jesus refuses to give a time (v. 32) and instead places emphasis upon constant watchfulness.

The striking reason given for not stating the time of the end is that Jesus does not know (v. 32), for this is a secret known only to **the Father himself! That day** (v. 32) is not defined but was intended to be familiar to the readers who would have recognized the term from many OT prophetic contexts where it is used as a kind of technical term for the future manifestation of God (e.g., Amos 8:3, 9, 13; 9:11; Mic. 4:6; 5:10; 7:11; Zeph. 1:9–10; 3:11, 16; Joel 3:18; Zech. 9:16). In those OT passages it is what is called the day of the Lord that is in view, a future time when God will work wonders to rescue his people and to bring righteousness upon the earth (e.g., Amos 5:18–20; Isa. 2:12–19; Zeph. 1:7, 14–16; 2:2–3; 3:8–11). Thus, the day of God's victory is pictured, as in the fashion of apocalyptic thought, as an appointed time kept in the secrets of God.

When the disciples are told to **watch** (vv. 33–37), what is meant is that they are to be on duty, doing their jobs, not that they are to watch for portents indicating when the end will come. The words translated **watch** (see notes), and the example of servants left with work to do while the master is gone (vv. 34–36) indicate that this is what is meant. The contrast is **sleep** (v. 36), signifying failing to do one's duty and not taking seriously the warning of the master's return. The work that the servants are to do is of course not primarily scanning the horizon for the master's return and then rushing about in a dither but rather the steady, regular performance of their tasks. Thus, Jesus' words in verses 32–37 mean that his followers are to go on with their mission, preaching and living for the gospel, ready for the return of their master at any time, so that he will find them "on the job."

The final word in verse 37 opens out the exhortation beyond the Twelve (**you**) and includes Mark's readers (**all**), again demonstrating how Jesus' words were transmitted by the evangelists with the intent that they be applied to their own readers. Whether the fall of Jerusalem had occurred or not, the readers were supposed to learn from Jesus' predictions that the distresses and persecutions that they might face were all a part of the playing out of the drama leading to the end; and they were to take inspiration from this and from Jesus' exhortation about staying alert at their task so that they might press on, undaunted in the necessary proclamation to all nations (13:10).

With this final exhortation, the long discourse on the future (chapter 13) ends. The doom of Jerusalem has been announced, and the disciples (and readers) forewarned about what lies before them after Jesus has been taken away. This done, Mark next returns to the account of the events that led to Jesus' death and resurrection (chapters 14–16). In 12:1–12, we were told clearly what the Jewish religious leaders would do to Jesus, the "Son," and the narrative in chapters 14–16 gives the actual happenings. The section connected with the Jerusalem Temple (11:1–13:37) is at an end. The Temple is described as desecrated (11:15–19), and the bankruptcy of the religious establishment has been shown (11:27–12:44). In chapter 13, the overthrow of the Temple is predicted (13:1–2, 14–23); and this event is set within the context of a new religious activity, the preaching of the gospel (13:9–13, 32–37), that replaces the Temple ritual as the center of God's activity. In the following chapters, Mark gives those events that are the final basis for the preaching of the gospel, the death and resurrection of Jesus.

Additional Notes

13:24 / **In the days after that time of trouble**: literally, "But 'in those days,' after that trouble." The word "but" in Greek connotes a strong contrast, suggesting that we are moving from one type of event (historical events such as the fall of Jerusalem) to another type (the end of history). "In those days" is a stereotyped phrase borrowed from various OT prophetic passages, although the GNB sometimes obscures this (e.g., Jer. 3:16, 18; 31:29; 33:15–16; Joel 3:1; Zech. 8:23), and is used with reference to events connected with the plan of God, but without any specific chronological connection. (See, e.g., Lane, p. 474.) The **trouble** is probably the whole period of mission and tribulation described in vv. 5–23.

13:24-25 / **The sun . . . the moon . . . the stars . . . the powers in space**: The last phrase in v. 25 should be translated "the powers in heaven shall be shaken," and it refers to the celestial bodies collectively as **powers** (or "gods"), as they were viewed by many peoples in the ancient world. These statements about the celestial world form a four-line construction resembling a Hebrew poetic form in which the last line (**the powers . . .**) summarizes the first three (**the sun . . . the**

moon . . . the stars). (On the nature of Hebrew poetry, see, e.g., "Poetry, Hebrew," *IDB*, vol. 3, pp. 829–38.)

13:26 / **And glory**: In the OT, "**glory**" is an attribute of God, and the description of the Son of Man by this term clothes him in divine attire. Cf. 8:38; "Glory," *IDB*, vol. 2, pp. 401–3; *NIDNTT*, vol. 2, pp. 44–48.

13:27 / **The four corners of the earth . . . from one end of the world to the other**: literally, "from the four winds, from the end of the earth." The term, "the four winds" is used in the OT to refer to worldwide dimension (e.g., Ezek. 37:9; Dan. 7:2; 8:8; 11:4), and in Zech. 2:6 describes the far-flung dispersal of Israel. "The end of the earth" is probably an allusion to Deut. 30:4, which promises that God will regather Israel when they have been scattered in his judgment. Here the promise of a regathering of Israel is revised to refer to an ingathering of various peoples in the church.

13:28 / **A lesson**: Greek, "a parable," the last parable mentioned in Mark's account (cf. 4:1–34; 12:1–12).

13:30 / **Remember that**: The translation hardly does justice to the Greek phrase here that connotes solemn assurance like an oath, literally, "Truly I say to you that" (see note on 3:28).

Before the people now living have all died: literally, "this generation shall not pass away before all 'these things' happen." The term "generation" is used elsewhere in Mark to refer to those who did not accept Jesus and to the period of time in which the disciples must remain true to him (cf. 8:12, 38; 9:19) but is probably used here to mean that the events of vv. 5–23 ("these things") will happen within the lifetime of Jesus' contemporaries (cf. 9:1)

13:32 / **That day or hour**: On the background to the term "day of the Lord," see *IDB*, vol. 1, pp. 784–85. In the NT the term is often used with reference to Christ (e.g., 1 Cor. 1:8; 5:5; 1 Thess. 5:2–3; 2 Thess. 2:1–2; 2 Pet. 3:10; 2 Cor. 1:14; Phil. 1:6, 10; 2:16); see further "Day of Christ," *IDB*, vol. 1, p. 783).

Nor the Son: This phrase evidently caused theological problems for some copyists, for the words are omitted in a few manuscripts. The same is true of the parallel in Matt. 24:36, where the same words are found. These words indicate that however much Mark saw Jesus as a figure who exercised divine prerogatives he (with all NT authors) did not confuse Jesus with God the Father.

13:33 / **Be on watch, be alert**: Here and in the following verses there are three Greek words used that indicate watchfulness associated with guards or servants whose duty must be done even at nighttime.

13:35 / **Evening . . . midnight . . . before dawn . . . sunrise**: These terms represent the four military watches of the night according to Roman reckoning. In Jewish reckoning, there were three night watches, and so Mark has probably adapted the saying to the terms familiar to his readers.

Devotion and Treachery

MARK 14:1–11

It was now two days before the Festival of Passover and Unleavened Bread. The chief priests and the teachers of the Law were looking for a way to arrest Jesus secretly and put him to death. [2]"We must not do it during the festival," they said, "or the people might riot."

[3]Jesus was in Bethany at the house of Simon, a man who had suffered from a dreaded skin disease. While Jesus was eating, a woman came in with an alabaster jar full of a very expensive perfume made of pure nard. She broke the jar and poured the perfume on Jesus' head. [4]Some of the people there became angry and said to one another, "What was the use of wasting the perfume? [5]It could have been sold for more than three hundred silver coins[v] and the money given to the poor!" And they criticized her harshly.

[6]But Jesus said, "Leave her alone! Why are you bothering her? She has done a fine and beautiful thing for me. [7]You will always have poor people with you, and any time you want to, you can help them. But you will not always have me. [8]She did what she could; she poured perfume on my body to prepare it ahead of time for burial. [9]Now, I assure you that wherever the gospel is preached all over the world, what she has done will be told in memory of her."

[10]Then Judas Iscariot, one of the twelve disciples, went off to the chief priests in order to betray Jesus to them. [11]They were pleased to hear what he had to say, and promised to give him money. So Judas started looking for a good chance to hand Jesus over to them.

v. SILVER COINS: *See 6.37.*

14:1-2 / These verses introduce the events of the arrest, trial, and execution of Jesus and resemble previous indications of hostile intentions against Jesus (cf. 3:6; 12:12). Although previously the Pharisees are frequently mentioned as criticizing and opposing Jesus (e.g., 2:16–3:6; 7:1–5; 8:11; 10:1–2; 12:13), they are not linked by name with the actual arrest and execution in Mark (cf. Matt. 27:62; John 18:3). Instead, it is the priests and scribes who are mentioned here. The material in 14:1–15:47 is called by scholars the passion account ("passion" coming from the Greek word for "suffering"). Mark has been described as a passion account with an extensive introduction, and though this is a bit of an exaggeration, it is correct to note the crucial place this part of the Gospel occupies in the whole plan and emphasis of the book. The three predictions of the execution (8:31; 9:30–32; 10:32–34) in the central section of Mark show that the event was both destined by God and essential for the completion of Jesus' mission. Elsewhere in the NT, the events of Jesus' death and resurrection are described as the outline of the gospel message of Christianity (1 Cor. 15:1–6); and the detailed description of the actual arrest, trial, and execution in all the Gospels confirms that this material was a most important part of the sacred tradition of Jesus.

The reason for mentioning that the authorities did not intend originally to make their move during the feast days (v. 2), even though they did arrest Jesus during that time, was probably to show that the timing was in God's hands and not finally in the hands of Jesus' enemies. This is in keeping with the biblical outlook on the execution of Jesus. It is seen as a wicked deed for which the human agents are fully responsible; nevertheless, all was foreseen by God and worked toward the accomplishing of his greater purpose.

14:3–9 / This account of the devotion of a woman to Jesus is not mentioned in the Lucan passion narrative, which tells of Judas' agreement to betray Jesus immediately after the description of the plot of the authorities (cf. Luke 22:1–6). The "interruption" of the plotting of Judas with the priests by this story in Mark and Matthew (26:6–13) seems designed to present a powerful contrast between this woman's loving generosity and the wicked treachery of Judas. Indeed, the woman is a contrast with all the Twelve, who are probably the **people** mentioned in verse 4 who criticize the woman for her extravagance. She is credited by Jesus with performing her act in recognition of his coming death (v. 8), whereas the Twelve have been described several times as unable to grasp this event even though Jesus had predicted it (cf. 8:31–33; 9:32; 10:35–38). Jesus' solemn vow (see notes) in verse 9, that the woman will be remembered wherever the gospel is proclaimed, is fulfilled by the inclusion of the story in the narrative here; and she presents another example of the complete dedication to Jesus that is demanded of all disciples (cf., e.g., 8:34–38; 10:29–31). It is striking that it is the woman's *deed* and not her name that is remembered, but her anonymity focuses attention all the more upon her undiluted devotion and generosity (but see notes).

The perfume the woman used is described as made from **nard**, an aromatic oil extracted from a root found in India. It was sealed in an **alabaster** flask to preserve it, and the flask would have had to be broken to use the perfume. The description of the value of the perfume (**three hundred silver coins**) suggests that the substance might have been a family heirloom, something that could be sold in times of financial need. If so, the woman's act was like parting with one's savings. It was customary to anoint the head of an honored guest at a meal, but the woman's act went far beyond normal courtesy, and it is little wonder that it aroused the surprised response mentioned in verse 4.

It should be understood that it is Jesus who makes her act an anticipation of his coming death; there is little reason to think that the woman may have actually meant her gift to be an anointing of Jesus' body for his coming burial. For her it was simply an act of great love and devotion; but Jesus, conscious of the coming violence against him, by prophetic anticipation interprets her gift in the context of what is to come.

It is not her foreknowledge of his coming death but her complete attention to him that provided the actual basis for Jesus' commendation of her. While the Twelve are concerned with the duties of the Festival, such as the required gift to the poor (v. 5), and have demonstrated a preoccupation with their own coming rewards (e.g., 10:35–45; 9:28), the woman concerns herself solely with giving honor to Jesus. It is this undivided devotion to Jesus that the readers are intended to emulate.

14:10-11 / This account of Judas' agreement with the authorities to betray Jesus is remarkably restrained, in view of the parallels that mention such things as the betrayal price (Matt. 26:15), Satanic influence (Luke 22:3; John 13:2, 27), and something of the information that Judas could supply (Luke 22:6) about Jesus' movements. Mark's sole purpose seems to have been to place this account of treachery alongside the preceding account of the complete devotion of the unnamed woman (vv. 3–9). In doing so, Mark gives the most striking example of how the gulf between Jesus and members of the Twelve had widened. Earlier, there are examples of the Twelve being insensitive to Jesus' teaching (e.g., 4:10–13; 6:36–37, 51–52; 8:14–21, 31–33; 9:32–37; 10:13–16), but with Judas' plan to betray Jesus we see the beginnings of their complete collapse described in 14:50, 66–72.

Many have speculated about the reason for Judas' betrayal of Jesus, but none of the Gospels says anything more than that the act was wicked and that Judas was influenced by Satan. It may be that Judas became disillusioned with Jesus and was swayed by the accusations that Jesus was a lawbreaker and blasphemer. The evangelists were uninterested in the reasons for Judas' action. Their narration of Judas' betrayal seems to be intended mainly to supply the readers with a warning example from which they are to distinguish themselves by unbroken devotion and loyalty to Jesus.

Additional Notes

14:1 / **The Festival of Passover and Unleavened Bread**: According to the OT, Passover (which commemorates the deliverance of Israel, under the leadership of Moses, from the land of Egypt) is to be observed on the fourteenth day of the month Nisan (in the spring), and the festival of Unleavened Bread is to begin the following day and last for seven days. From ancient times, the two festivals were linked, and either term could refer to the combined period of time. The OT descriptions and regulations about the two festivals are found in Exod. 12:1–20; Deut. 16:1–8 (see also "Passover and Feast of Unleavened Bread," *IDB*, vol. 3, pp. 663–68). Passover/Unleavened Bread was one of three pilgrim festivals during which every adult Jewish male was supposed to be in Jerusalem; but after the destruction of the Temple in A.D. 70 this rule was relaxed by the rabbis.

Chief priests and the teachers of the Law: The Gospel of John describes a meeting of the authorities before the feast to discuss how to arrest Jesus (11:47–53), and cf. also Matt. 26:1–5. Their desire to arrest Jesus secretly was motivated by fear of a riot, indicating that Jesus was well liked among the pilgrims to the city, many of whom were no doubt from Galilee, where Jesus had worked for some time. This desire was fulfilled with the assistance of Judas Iscariot, one of the Twelve, whose contribution consisted in disclosing to the authorities where Jesus might be found at night and almost alone (cf. vv. 10–11, 43–50).

14:3 / **At the house of Simon**: We do not otherwise know of this man, who is described as **a man who had suffered from a dreaded skin disease** (lit., simply "Simon the Leper," perhaps a nickname?). John 12:1–8 describes a strikingly similar incident, but the impression is that the supper was at the house of Lazarus, Mary, and Martha; and the woman who anoints Jesus in the account is Mary. John mentions the nard as worth three hundred silver coins (12:5), and there is the discussion about the poor (12:6–8), emphasizing the complaint as from Judas Iscariot. In Luke 7:36–50, there is a similar account of a sinful woman who enters the house of a Pharisee named Simon and, after washing Jesus' feet with her tears, anoints him with ointment from an alabaster flask. It seems likely that, in the course of the telling, perhaps two distinct stories influenced each other, with details from one being inserted into the other.

A woman came in with an alabaster jar . . . of pure nard: Women did not ordinarily enter a formal dinner where men were eating, except to serve them. This woman's entrance would have raised a few eyebrows about her failure to observe social customs. On the substance she used, see "Nard," *IDB*, vol. 3, p. 510. For examples of the anointing of the head of a guest at a meal see Pss. 23:5; 141:5; Luke 7:46.

14:4 / **Some of the people there**: Mark probably means Jesus' disciples. Cf. John 12:4–5; Matt. 26:8.

14:5 / **Three hundred silver coins**: The coin in question (a denarius) was the basic daily wage of the common worker (e.g., Matt. 20:2) and is the same coin mentioned in 6:37.

The money given to the poor: Jewish custom called for special remembrance of the poor at Passover time (cf. John 13:27–29). For references to Jewish tradition, see Lane, p. 493.

14:7 / **You will always have poor people with you**: The contrast is between the perpetual opportunity to help the poor and the immediate situation of Jesus' coming death. Although some have tried to make Jesus' statement here a justification for allowing some people to suffer poverty, this is obviously a severe twisting of its meaning. Indeed, v. 7 is an allusion to Deut. 15:11, which commands great generosity to the poor.

14:9 / **I assure you**: Here, again, is the solemn oathlike phrase peculiar to Jesus in the NT. See the note on 3:28.

14:10 / **Judas Iscariot**: On the meaning of the name Iscariot, see the note on 3:19.

14:11 / **A good chance to hand Jesus over to them**: The desire of the priests was information on where to find Jesus alone, or at least away from the pilgrim crowds among whom he was so popular and who might try to prevent his arrest. Judas was able to tell the priests where Jesus would meet (probably secretly) on Passover night with his disciples and was able to provide positive identification of him. John 11:57 suggests that the chief priest may have circulated an offer of a reward for information leading to Jesus' successful capture.

The Last Meal

On the first day of the Festival of Unleavened Bread, the day the lambs for the Passover meal were killed, Jesus' disciples asked him, "Where do you want us to go and get the Passover meal ready for you?"

[13]Then Jesus sent two of them with these instructions: "Go into the city, and a man carrying a jar of water will meet you. Follow him [14]to the house he enters, and say to the owner of the house: 'The Teacher says, Where is the room where my disciples and I will eat the Passover meal?' [15]Then he will show you a large upstairs room, fixed up and furnished, where you will get everything ready for us."

[16]The disciples left, went to the city, and found everything just as Jesus had told them; and they prepared the Passover meal.

[17]When it was evening, Jesus came with the twelve disciples. [18]While they were at the table eating, Jesus said, "I tell you that one of you will betray me—one who is eating with me."

[19]The disciples were upset and began to ask him, one after the other, "Surely you don't mean me, do you?"

[20]Jesus answered, "It will be one of you twelve, one who dips his bread in the dish with me. [21]The Son of Man will die as the Scriptures say he will; but how terrible for that man who will betray the Son of Man! It would have been better for that man if he had never been born!"

[22]While they were eating, Jesus took a piece of bread, gave a prayer of thanks, broke it, and gave it to his disciples. "Take it," he said, "this is my body."

[23]Then he took a cup, gave thanks to God, and handed it to them; and they all drank from it. [24]Jesus said, "This is my blood which is poured out for many, my blood which seals God's covenant. [25]I tell you, I will never again drink this wine until the day I drink the new wine in the Kingdom of God."

[26]Then they sang a hymn and went out to the Mount of Olives.

14:12–21 / In these verses, we have the description of Jesus' entrance into Jerusalem to celebrate Passover with his disciples, and the mention of Judas' treachery as foreknown to Jesus. The overall purpose of the narrative is to show dramatically that the one who betrayed Jesus was actually one who shared Jesus' company and ate with him, Mark probably intending by this description an allusion to Psalm 41:9–10 (which is cited specifically in John 13:18).

The fact that the disciples were not given a name or an address but were sent to look for a man fitting a particular description (vv. 12–16, and see note) suggests that previous secret arrangements had been made. Such secrecy was required, probably, because Jesus knew that the authorities were looking for an opportunity to arrest him away from the large public gatherings. On other nights Jesus went to Bethany, but on Passover night Jewish men were required to eat the evening meal within the city of Jerusalem; and this meant that Jesus would have had to remain within the jurisdiction of the priestly authorities late into the night (Passover usually lasted until nearly midnight).

The note of intrigue finds further emphasis in Jesus' warning about betrayal from within his own circle (vv. 18–20), and the effect of this announcement for the reader is to isolate Jesus, not only from the Jewish authorities, but even from his own followers, making him seem totally alone though surrounded by others. The betrayal by Judas is not to be the only example of failure from within the Twelve, for later (vv. 27–31) Jesus predicts that all of them will abandon him. The dramatic irony is full. Here is Jesus eating with his circle of close followers, making secret arrangements to avoid detection, yet knowing that it is all in vain and that the very ones with whom he is sharing such intimate company include a traitor and deserters who will collapse when the test comes.

In the following passage (vv. 22–26) Jesus' words over the bread and the cup make the meal a prefiguring of the Christian rite of Communion or Eucharist, and Mark's readers were intended to read this account of the failure of the disciples and realize that Jesus' obedience to the divine demand that he lay down his life for the redemption of the "many" (10:45) was accomplished without the assistance and encouragement of anyone. Further, the failure of Judas and the rest of the Twelve was intended to provoke in the readers a solemn commitment that they, after likewise eating at their Lord's table, should not be found guilty of failing him in time of testing, as did the Twelve.

14:22-26 / Mark's account of the last supper is one of four in the NT, and each one has special features that indicate that the record of this meal of Jesus and the Twelve was affected in varying ways by the continuing celebration of the rite of Eucharist, or Lord's Supper, in the early church (see Matt. 26:26–29; Luke 22:15–20; 1 Cor. 11:23–25). Scholars differ over several matters in their attempt to reconstruct the original form of the sayings over the cup and the bread and also in their opinions about which of the four accounts gives us the earliest version of the event. We cannot discuss all these questions here; instead, our aim will be to understand the account before us in Mark, though we will make some reference to the other accounts in the notes.

The Passover meal was full of symbolism and involved using the elements on the table as object lessons in teaching the meaning of the occasion; so Jesus' use of the bread and the cup as symbols fits the atmosphere of the Passover celebration. The decisive difference, of course, is that Jesus' words do not look back to the Exodus from Egypt, as in the Passover teaching, but forward to his own death, portrayed as the foundation of a new covenant (v. 24). This too is appropriate, for the Passover meal commemorated the first covenant of God with Israel, which was based on his deliverance of the nation from slavery in Egypt and ratified on Mount Sinai.

In the course of Christian history, controversies about the proper way to celebrate Eucharist and the interpretation of the rite have torn the church and still divide large bodies of Christians from one another (e.g., Roman Catholics and Protestants). Each view of Eucharist claims to be based on the NT passages, and anyone who comments on these texts runs the risk of offending one group or another. Nevertheless, all types of Christian understanding of the Eucharist benefit from an examination of the NT passages strictly within their own historical context and apart from the later practices of the various Christian denominations. Though this is more difficult to do than it is to advocate, it is the aim in what follows.

In the original situation of Jesus with the Twelve, reference to the bread and the cup as **my body** . . . **my blood** (vv. 22–24) would have been recognized immediately as the use of symbols, as was already familiar in the Passover meal. That is, there was no question of the bread and cup actually being the body and blood of Jesus when the living Jesus stood before them. So, if the last supper is regarded as actually having happened, not (as some have suggested) as a totally fictitious event, the understanding of its meaning must take seriously the original situation. Certainly Mark and his readers believed that the last supper actually happened, and it is their understanding of the passage that we seek here.

We must begin by remembering the serious meaning, in the ancient world, of eating together, something already discussed earlier in connection with Jesus' eating with sinners (see comments on 2:13–17). To share a meal meant to establish or perpetuate a relationship, to become one company with the others at the table. Thus, almost any meal had a kind of sacred significance, and it is easy to see why meals were a common part of the rituals of many religious groups of the ancient world. Jesus' leadership in the meal, and his identification of the bread and wine with his own person and work, made this supper especially a fellowship with Jesus, a partaking with him. His distribution of the torn bread with the words **This is my body** (v. 22) meant "This is my person," and to partake of the bread meant to join oneself to Jesus and his fate. The disciples are to be understood as still unaware of what these words portend about Jesus' fate, but the readers are intended to understand more fully, and in their own continued celebration of the meal begun here, they are to recognize that their partaking of the bread means a willing sharing with one another of close fellowship with Jesus, not just ritually in the Eucharist setting, but in all of life and mission. The sharing of the bread dramatizes not a consuming of Jesus in some mystical sense, but the closest of unions with him and with one another (cf. 1 Cor. 10:16–17).

The reference to the cup of red wine as **my blood which is poured out for many** (v. 24) does not mean that the wine somehow becomes mystically the blood of Jesus, for the mention of blood poured out is a Semitic way of describing violent death (cf. Gen. 4:10–11; 9:6; Deut. 19:10; 2 Kings 21:16; Ps. 106:38; Jer. 7:6; Matt. 23:35). So, what is meant is that the cup represents the death of Jesus, which is interpreted as happening on behalf of others (**for many**) and as the sacrificial blood/ death that institutes a new covenant. To share this cup is to include oneself in the **many** (v. 24) for whom Jesus died.

Thus, we do not have two elements (bread and wine) each with a distinctive significance, but rather both elements are brought under one meaning, and sharing them represents the inclusion of oneself into the fellowship redeemed by Jesus' death and called to follow him. In the original situation of Jesus and the Twelve, the sharing of the bread and wine anticipated the death of Jesus, but Mark's readers partook of the Lord's Supper looking back at the death of Jesus. Nevertheless, for these readers, sharing the Lord's Supper signified their inclusion into the fellowship begun with the Twelve, and it was still the *Lord's* Supper; that is, Jesus was understood as spiritually present in the sharing of the bread and wine, making their fellowship not just a commemoration of his past presence but an experience of his continuing presence with them. The bread and the cup, by their association with this last supper recorded here, were tangible evidence to the readers of their participation in the salvation created by Jesus' sacrificial death.

In addition, the Markan account of the last supper reflects the connection of the meal with the hope for the consummation of the Kingdom of God (v. 25). That is, Jesus' vow in verse 25 that he will never again drink wine until the appearance of the Kingdom makes the last supper and every subsequent celebration of it in Christian Eucharist rites an anticipation of the future fellowship of the redeemed and their Lord in the Kingdom of God. The celebrations of the early church not only looked back to Jesus' sacrificial death but also looked forward to the coming joy of the future (cf. 1 Cor. 11:26, "You proclaim the Lord's death until he comes").

The earliest traditions of Christianity indicate that the Lord's Supper was a regular part of church meetings, and that the memory of a last supper of Jesus with the Twelve was a regular part of the story of Jesus. Mark's account here contains several detailed indications of its connection with the early stages of Christianity, and it plays an important role in the total passion narrative. The story shows that the Christian fellowship represented in the celebration of the Lord's Supper goes back to this event in the ministry of Jesus and, in effect, presents this "last supper" as the first Lord's Supper, in which the elements used (bread and wine) acquired specific association with the sacrificial death of Jesus. The words over the bread and cup (vv. 22–24) interpret the coming death of Jesus, by making it constitutive for the new covenant of God that is the basis of the church. Like the word in 10:45 (see comment), these sayings confirm that the death of Jesus had powerful significance and provide us with an example of the early theology of the church. Finally, the passage links the celebration of the supper with the hope for the Kingdom of God, showing us how the early church held together its view of the death of Christ, its own continuing Eucharistic fellowship, and the forward-looking expectation of the consummation of God's Kingdom.

Additional Notes

14:12 / **The first day of the Festival of Unleavened Bread**: Technically, the Festival of Unleavened Bread does not begin until the day after Passover night, but there are indications that sometimes the day the Passover lambs were sacrificed was loosely called the first day of Unleavened Bread (references in Lane, p. 497). The reference to the sacrificing of the lambs in v. 12 confirms that the setting is the day before Passover evening.

14:13 / **A man carrying a jar of water**: In ancient Palestine, women usually carried water in jars upon the head, while men carried water in skins held in their hands. Thus, this man would have been easy to spot in a crowd. The man's behavior was probably a pre-arranged signal for the disciples to recognize, and they were to follow him without saying a word. The man must have known that he was engaging in a dangerous business, and he was possibly a follower of Jesus. He had possibly obtained a lamb for the supper also, for the priests would have refused to allow Jesus (whom they regarded as a heretic) to participate in the ritual killing of the lambs, which had to take place in the Temple area and under their supervision. The fact that it is expected that he will know who **the Teacher** is (v. 14) confirms that he is part of a plan to keep Jesus' whereabouts secret.

14:16 / **The Passover meal**: It is a notoriously difficult problem that John's Gospel appears to describe Jesus' crucifixion as happening on the day of the killing of the Passover lambs (18:28; 19:14, 31, 42) and does not describe the last supper of Jesus and the Twelve as a Passover meal (13:1). The reasons for John's version of the meal and the timing of Jesus' death are perhaps not fully recoverable but appear to be based on his theological emphases and his use of symbolism, making the death of Christ the new Passover sacrifice, replacing the traditional lamb (in keeping with his use of the title "Lamb of God" to describe Jesus, 1:29, 36). The procedures for the Passover meal required the eating of a roasted lamb sacrificed in the Temple, bitter herbs, a fruit-paste dish, unleavened bread, and red wine. The participants had to recline at the dinner, demonstrating their freedom obtained at the Exodus from Egypt. One of the participants (Jesus in this case) acted as host of the meal and led the ceremonies, which included set questions from another member of the group about why this meal was different from all others. The host replied and pointed to the items on the table, explaining their symbolic significance (e.g., the bitter herbs symbolized the bitter bondage of Israel in Egypt). Because the meal was to be unhurried and involved much discussion, it lasted a long time, but it had to be finished before midnight. For a description of ancient Passover ceremonies see, e.g., Lane, pp. 500–2; *NIDNTT*, vol. 2, p. 522.

14:18 / **At the table eating**: The Greek describes them as "reclining and eating," in keeping with the Jewish practice that dates from Hellenistic times that one must recline (after the ancient Greek banquet custom) at the Passover meal to demonstrate one's freedom, either on couches or on rugs on the floor.

I tell you: Again, this is the solemn phrase indicating an oathlike force to the saying. See note on 3:28.

One who is eating with me: This emphasizes the nature of the treachery as coming from within Jesus' intimate circle of followers and is likely an allusion to Ps. 41:9. This idea is repeated in v. 20, where the betrayer is specifically described as **one of you twelve, one who dips his bread in the dish with me** (reflecting the ancient Palestinian meal custom of using pieces of the flat unleavened bread as the eating utensil).

14:21 / **The Son of Man will die as the Scriptures say**: Literally, the Son of Man "departs as it is written concerning him." No specific OT reference presents itself clearly to mind, and it is likely that no one passage was meant. Instead, the words probably mean simply that the sufferings of the Son of Man are a part of God's plan (see the note on 9:12) and are indicated in a variety of passages, such as Isa. 53:1–6; Ps. 41:9–13.

It would have been better for that man if he had never been born:

Though the death of the Son of Man is part of God's plan, still the betrayer is guilty of a great crime. No particular fate of Judas is mentioned in Mark (but cf. Matt. 27:3–5; Acts 1:18–19); instead, this statement simply emphasizes that he will be judged for his deed.

14:22 / **A piece of bread**: Better translated "a loaf of bread," this may refer to the Passover practice in which the leader of the group opens the meal by pronouncing a blessing over the bread and then distributes it to the other participants. It is likely that the bread mentioned here, and the cup of v. 23, were separated by the Passover meal, and that Mark has given us a condensed account that mentions only the actions and meal elements important for Christian tradition.

Gave a prayer of thanks, broke it: The phrase here, **a prayer of thanks**, translates "he blessed (God)," referring to the Jewish practice of giving thanks over the bread at a meal by saying, "Blessed are you, Lord, our God, who brings forth bread from the earth." In Jewish meal practice of ancient times, it was considered irreverent to cut bread with a knife, since bread was a gift from God, and so bread was "broken" or torn with the hands.

This is my body: The original significance of the phrase in Aramaic, the language Jesus customarily spoke with his disciples, would have been "this is my self," for the most likely Aramaic equivalent to the Greek word translated **body** here meant "person," "self," and the Greek word should therefore be understood with this in mind.

14:23 / **A cup**: At Passover, a lengthy meal, four cups of red wine were prescribed. The cup mentioned here may have been the final cup ending the meal. Thus, as suggested in the note on the bread above (v. 22), Mark has preserved Jesus' words over the bread that initiated the meal and the cup that closed it. (An alternate view is that this was the third cup of the Passover meal, and that verse 25 refers to the final [fourth] cup, from which Jesus abstains, vowing to complete his obedience to the will of God before he drinks again of wine. See the note on this verse.) Similarly, it is believed that the early Lord's Supper celebrations of the church began with a ceremonial sharing of bread that included a repetition of the words of Jesus (**this is my body**); then came a full meal, then a final cup of wine over which the words **this is my blood**, etc., were pronounced. What survived in later Christian celebration of the Lord's Supper were thus the initial and final parts of a full meal. (For information on the scholarly study of the Lord's Supper in the early church, see "Lord's Supper," *NIDNTT*, vol. 2, pp. 520–38; *IDB*, vol. 3, pp. 158–62.

Gave thanks: This is the Greek word from which the term Eucharist comes (*eucharisto*), and means "to give thanks," reflecting the joyous nature of early celebrations of the Lord's Supper (cf. note on v. 22, and discussion and notes on 6:41; 8:6–7).

14:24 / **This is my blood which is poured out for many**: To speak of poured-out blood in ancient Palestine meant to refer to violent death (see refs. in comments), and it is the *event*, not the substance of blood, that is referred to here. That is, Jesus was again teaching his disciples that he would face such a death shortly, and that his death would be on behalf of others. The **many** here are those who will become part of the **covenant** that his death will create (on **many** see the note on 10:45). For information on the various Lord's Supper accounts in the NT and the variations in the wording over the bread and cup, see *NIDNTT*, vol. 2, pp. 524–26.

My blood which seals God's covenant: A **covenant** was a treaty or agreement between two parties, two rulers or other individuals. In the OT, the relationship between Israel and God was called a covenant, and the Law was understood as part of this agreement, being the covenant obligations of Israel. In Jer. 31:31–34, the prophet promises a "new covenant," describing the former one (given under Moses at Mount Sinai after the Exodus from Egypt) as broken by Israel's disobedience. The records of covenant making in the OT show that the sacrifice of animals was a vital part of the "sealing" of the agreement, as in Exod. 24:1–8, and Jesus' words allude to this passage, making his death the sacrifice that brings into being a new covenant. The phrase is literally "this is my blood of the covenant which is shed for many," though some ancient manuscripts add "new" before "covenant," alluding to Jer. 31:31. Matt. 26:28 adds "for the forgiveness of sins" after "for many." The wording of the scene in the Luke 22:14–20 parallel is different still, and scholars differ about the original wording of the Lucan account, for the manuscripts have serious variations. (For background on the meaning of the term, see "Covenant," *IDB*, vol. 1, pp. 714–23; *IDBSup*, pp. 188–97, 623–25; *NIDNTT*, vol. 1, pp. 365–76.)

14:25 / **I tell you**: This is the same solemn formula used elsewhere on Jesus' lips with the force of an oath. See the note on 3:28.

I will never again drink this wine until. . . : Some ancient manuscripts read "I will not again drink." "**This wine**" is literally "the fruit of the vine," a Semitic expression meaning **wine** here. Jesus is taking a vow of abstinence, promising that he will not share in another festal cup until he has done the will of God and participates with his disciples in the joy of the consummated Kingdom of God. The translation **until the day I drink the new wine** is literally "until I drink new," the word **new** here referring to the joyous situation of the fully realized Kingdom of God of the future.

14:26 / **They sang a hymn and went out to the Mount of Olives**: The Passover was concluded usually by the singing of the second part of the Hallel (Pss. 113–118), and this is probably the **hymn** mentioned here. They went out to a quiet garden lying outside the city wall (14:32), where it would be cooler, for continued prayer. (See "Hallel," *IDB*, vol. 2, p. 314.)

27

Jesus' Arrest and Abandonment

Jesus said to them, "All of you will run away and leave me, for the scripture says, 'God will kill the shepherd, and the sheep will all be scattered.' [28]But after I am raised to life, I will go to Galilee ahead of you."

[29]Peter answered, "I will never leave you, even though all the rest do!"

[30]Jesus said to Peter, "I tell you that before the rooster crows two times tonight, you will say three times that you do not know me."

[31]Peter answered even more strongly, "I will never say that, even if I have to die with you!"

And all the other disciples said the same thing.

[32]They came to a place called Gethsemane, and Jesus said to his disciples, "Sit here while I pray." [33]He took Peter, James, and John with him. Distress and anguish came over him, [34]and he said to them, "The sorrow in my heart is so great that it almost crushes me. Stay here and keep watch."

[35]He went a little farther on, threw himself on the ground, and prayed that, if possible, he might not have to go through that time of suffering. [36]"Father," he prayed, "my Father! All things are possible for you. Take this cup of suffering away from me. Yet not what I want, but what you want."

[37]Then he returned and found the three disciples asleep. He said to Peter, "Simon, are you asleep?

Weren't you able to stay awake for even one hour?" [38]And he said to them, "Keep watch, and pray that you will not fall into temptation. The spirit is willing, but the flesh is weak."

[39]He went away once more and prayed, saying the same words. [40]Then he came back to the disciples and found them asleep; they could not keep their eyes open. And they did not know what to say to him.

[41]When he came back the third time, he said to them, "Are you still sleeping and resting? Enough! The hour has come! Look, the Son of Man is now being handed over to the power of sinful men. [42]Get up, let us go. Look, here is the man who is betraying me!"

[43]Jesus was still speaking when Judas, one of the twelve disciples, arrived. With him was a crowd armed with swords and clubs and sent by the chief priest, the teachers of the Law, and the elders. [44]The traitor had given the crowd a signal: "The man I kiss is the one you want. Arrest him and take him away under guard."

[45]As soon as Judas arrived, he went up to Jesus and said, "Teacher!" and kissed him. [46]So they arrested Jesus and held him tight. [47]But one of those standing there drew his sword and struck at the High Priest's slave, cutting off his ear. [48]Then Jesus spoke up and said to them, "Did you have to come with swords and clubs to capture me, as though I were an outlaw? [49]Day after day I was with

you teaching in the Temple, and you did not arrest me. But the Scriptures must come true."

⁵⁰Then all the disciples left him and ran away.

⁵¹A certain young man, dressed only in a linen cloth, was following Jesus. They tried to arrest him, ⁵²but he ran away naked, leaving the cloth behind.

14:27-31 / This discussion follows the account of the meal both in Mark and in the Matthew 26:31-35 parallel. Luke 22:31-34 is a variant tradition of the discussion. The present passage shows Jesus anticipating the collapse of his followers, which is described in 14:50 and 14:66-72. But it also looks beyond this collapse to Jesus' resurrection (v. 28) and to a reunion and re-affirmation of the disciples, referred to in 16:7. In other words, the effect and intent of the passage in its present setting seems to be to show that the failure of the disciples was foreseen by Jesus and was taken as prophesied (v. 27) in the OT. This means that their failure was not a failure in the plan of God, however it might seem so at first. Further, the passage anticipates the fact that the activity of the disciples as leaders of the Christians after Jesus' crucifixion was based not on some courage or virtue of their own, but solely upon the grace of the risen Jesus, who restored them to his fellowship and to places of leadership.

Peter, as the traditional leader of the Twelve, is singled out in the narrative for particular emphasis, both here and in the later part of the chapter where he fulfills the prediction that he will deny Christ (14:66-72). Peter's brave talk, set against his later cowardice, only makes more emphatic for Mark's readers the point that the life and mission of the church rests upon Christ alone, not upon human leadership.

14:32-42 / This is another of the most well known scenes from the Gospels, the subject of paintings and of countless sermons and meditations. The tradition that Jesus prayed fervently before his arrest is preserved in variant forms in John 17:1-18 and Hebrews 5:7, as well as in the parallels to the present account, Matthew 26:46 and Luke 22:40-46. As a final preparation before the rush of violent events to follow, Jesus resorts to a quiet area just outside the eastern wall of Jerusalem for prayer. The two motifs that seem to dominate the passage are Jesus' obedience to God in spite of his dread in the knowledge of what is to follow, and the disciples' continued failure to sense how important the moment at hand is.

The sentimental suggestion that Jesus sought from his disciples some comfort in the face of the coming storm has no basis in the text, for Jesus turns to God and not to them. Rather, his repeated urgings to them to stay awake and pray reflect a concern that they be prepared for the physical and spiritual dangers that lie ahead for them. Mark's readers have been prepared by repeated references to the dullness of the Twelve to understand that they were incapable of giving Jesus anything. Their late-night drowsiness is to be read as another example of their insensitivity to what Jesus has been telling them about his coming violent death. The threefold reference to their disobedience to his urgings to pray (vv. 37–41) makes their failure emphatic.

The description of Jesus' distress (vv. 32–33) and his fervent prayer that if possible he might be spared the coming ordeal (v. 35), followed by his obedient acceptance of what he knows to be God's plan (v. 36), gives us the most memorable glimpse of the humanity of Jesus. Mark's readers, who have been warned through Jesus' words to the Twelve (e.g., 8:34–38; 10:38–39; 13:9–13) that they too may have to face trial and even execution for his sake, were surely intended to see Jesus' prayer as a powerful example to them of the submission to the will of God they were to emulate in their time of testing. That is, Mark's account is not motivated by a desire to give a sentimental picture of Jesus, but it is intended to give his readers a role model to follow and is motivated by a practical concern for their ability to stand firm in their trials for their faith.

The prayer of Jesus, which describes what is about to happen as God's will (v. 36), teaches the readers that the handing over of the Son of Man to **sinful men** (v. 41) was, in its most profound sense, something done by God and not by Judas. Thus, what could otherwise be seen as apparent failure and chaos, Jesus' arrest and execution, is again affirmed to be part of the deliberate plan of God.

14:43-52 / Here, the act of betrayal begun in 14:10–11 is carried through. Led by Judas, a group from the chief priests comes to seize Jesus by force, and from this point on the ordeal of Jesus' sufferings begins in earnest. Although Mark describes the arresting group as a **crowd** (v. 43), we should probably think in terms of a small force of perhaps a dozen or a little more, for the object was to make the arrest without creating a great commotion, in a place where Jesus would be alone with only his closest followers—the Twelve. Judas' contribution to the priest's intent was precisely information as to Jesus' movements and when he would be easiest to capture. Without this kind of information, the arrest would have been much more difficult, for as indicated earlier (11:11), Jesus characteristically entered the city only with the pilgrim crowds and left it before nightfall to go to Bethany, outside the jurisdiction of the High Priest's police force.

Every detail in the narrative plays its role. Judas is specifically described as **one of the twelve disciples**, making his betrayal emphatic (v. 43). The well-armed group (v. 43) coming to seize Jesus presents a striking contrast to the humble submission of Jesus mentioned in the preceding passage (v. 36). The recognition sign agreed upon, a kiss from Judas (vv. 44–45), and the respectful greeting, **Teacher** (*rabbi*), combine to make Judas' treachery all the more villainous. The one blow struck in Jesus' defense (v. 47) is so futile as to be almost comical; and the rout of the disciples (v. 50) makes this token resistance even more pitifully useless.

The fascinating reference (peculiar to Mark) to the **young man** who flees naked (v. 51–52) from the scene of the arrest has occasioned various theories as to why it is given here. Some have suggested that the unnamed young man is to be identified as John Mark, the traditional author of this Gospel, and that what we have here is a personal memoir of the author, admitting to his own cowardice. But aside from the fact that it is not completely certain that the author is to be identified as John Mark (see Introduction), there is reason to think that the description of the young man's action here is not just a memoir.

First, it seems possible that the author intended an allusion to Amos 2:16, with its description of a time of crisis when even the "bravest" will run away "naked" (on this allusion, see note), the point of the allusion being to show that the action of Jesus' followers was all foreseen, just as Jesus' earlier citation of Zechariah 13:7 showed (in 14:27). Further, it is interesting to compare this scene of the young man's flight, coming at the beginning of the events leading up to Jesus' execution, with two other scenes later in the narrative. In 15:46, Jesus' naked corpse (his clothes having been taken from him by the soldiers, 15:24) is clothed before burial in a "linen sheet," the same term in Greek (*sindon*) used to describe the young man's garment here in 14:51–52. Thus, the young man in this scene unknowingly anticipates the burial of Jesus; the young man runs away, leaving his linen cloth, while Jesus goes to his death and to burial in another such cloth, perhaps a dramatic portrayal of the substitutionary nature of Jesus' death. Also, in 16:5, at the tomb on the first Easter morning, another "young man" (to be taken no doubt as an angel, see note) announces that Jesus is risen from death. Perhaps Mark intended his readers to see this connection as well (only Mark describes the angel as a "young man"); one young man runs away, leaving Jesus to his death, but another, splendid "young man" wearing a "white robe" (16:5) declares Jesus' triumph.

In any case, the possible allusion to Amos 2:16, coupled with Jesus' description of the arrest as a fulfillment of prophecy (14:49), combine to make the main point of the story, that Jesus' arrest, though its immediate cause was human treachery, was actually part of the divine plan for redemption.

Additional Notes

14:27 / **You will run away and leave me**: literally, "You will all be offended" or "you will all stumble." The same word is used in v. 29; 9:42–47 (see notes); 6:3 ("they rejected him") and 4:17 ("they give up at once").

The scripture says: The quotation is from Zech. 13:7, and the whole of Zech. 13:1–9 makes interesting background reading for the passion account, for it speaks of a time when God will provide a new cleansing from sin (13:1) and refers to a blow against the "shepherd who works for me" (lit., "who stands next to me") as part of a process that leads to the creation of a new people of God (13:7–9).

14:28 / **I will go to Galilee ahead of you**: This promise is mentioned by the angel in 16:7 and seems to be a prediction of an appearance of the risen Jesus in Galilee. The Gospels contain traditions of resurrection appearances both in Galilee (Matt. 28:16; John 21:1–23) and in Jerusalem and the surrounding area (Luke 24:13–52; John 20:11–29); cf. 1 Cor. 15:5–8.

14:30 / **I tell you**: This is the final example in Mark of the solemn formula that connotes an oathlike assurance. See the note on 3:28.

Before the rooster crows two times tonight . . . : This statement could also be translated "Today, this night, before the rooster crows two times, you will deny me three times."

14:31 / **I will never say that**: The Greek phrase here, "I will never," is a very strong negation, meaning "I will by no means," and it makes Peter's promise all the more ironic in the light of his later failure.

14:32 / **Gethsemane** means (in Hebrew) "olive press," and it was probably an orchard of olive trees with a press for extracting oil that gave the place its name. It lies in the Kidron Valley, just outside the eastern wall of Jerusalem and below the Mount of Olives.

14:33 / **Peter, James, and John**: here again, we see the inner circle among the Twelve, mentioned also in 5:37; 9:2; 13:3. They appear to have been taken by Jesus apart from the rest.

14:34 / **The sorrow in my heart is so great that it almost crushes me**: literally, "my soul is sorrowful unto death," an allusion to Ps. 42:6. This psalm provides interesting commentary on the scene of Jesus' anguish and prayer.

14:35 / **He might not have to go through the time of suffering**: literally, "the hour might pass from him." The GNB translation obscures the intended connection between "the hour" that Jesus here prays to avoid and "the hour" of v. 41, which comes after Jesus' acceptance of the will of God. In both places, "hour" is a figurative term for the occasion before Jesus, involving his coming sufferings.

14:36 / **Father . . . my Father**: In the Greek, the first **Father** is the Aramaic term *Abba*, which appears to have connoted familiarity or endearment, being the term used by children for their own father and not the more formal Aramaic term for father. The same Aramaic term appears also in Rom. 8:15 and Gal. 4:6, suggesting that early in the church the term was preserved, even in Greek-speaking churches, as an element of sacred tradition deriving from the prayer practice of Jesus, who seems to have used this term regularly in his address to God in prayer, even though it appears that the usual Jewish prayer practice involved the use of more formal titles for God (see *NIDNTT*, vol. 1, pp. 614–15).

This cup of suffering: literally, "this cup," but the meaning is certainly the ordeal to come. Cf. the use of the symbol "cup" in 10:38–39 and the discussion there.

14:37 / **Simon**: This was evidently Peter's given name, the name Peter having been bestowed by Jesus (cf. 1:16, 29–36; 3:16 and discussion).

14:38 / **Temptation**: The word here can mean "testing," "trial," and Jesus' concern is that they pray for strength to go through the coming ordeal without failing. The word **fall into** here can be translated "enter" and resembles the wording of the Lord's Prayer in Matt. 6:13; Luke 11:4, which includes the petition to be spared the sort of ordeal that might cause one's faith to collapse, probably referring to persecution.

The spirit is willing, but the flesh is weak: The allusion here is to Ps. 51:12, and the meaning has nothing to do with the human spirit versus human **flesh**. Rather, the contrast involves God's Spirit, who is willing to supply strength to support human (**flesh**) weakness. To make this clearer, the GNB translation should have capitalized **spirit**.

14:41 / **To the power of sinful men**: literally, "into the hands of sinners." "Sinners" was a term used with reference to Jews who did not live according to the will of God and with reference to the Gentiles, who were viewed collectively by Jews as sinful since they did not live by the OT Law. Here the term probably refers to the priestly authorities who are pictured thus as disobedient to God, and to the Roman ruler (Pilate) who will be responsible for Jesus' death.

14:43 / **A crowd armed with swords and clubs**: This was probably a small contingent of the Temple police, who worked under the High Priest and whose job it was to maintain order in the Temple area. Their arms were theirs by permission of the Roman governor, who delegated some responsibility for the Temple to the High Priest. John 18:3 describes the arresting force as including "Roman soldiers," suggesting that Pilate was cooperating in the arrest.

Chief priests, the teachers of the Law, and the elders: These are the same figures mentioned in the passion prediction in 8:31 (cf. 10:33).

14:44 / **The man I kiss**: A kiss was a normal greeting for disciples to give to their master in ancient Palestine (see references in Lane, p. 525; and "Kiss," *IDB*, vol. 3, pp. 39–40).

14:47 / **One of those standing there**: Mark meant one of Jesus' disciples. John 18:10 identifies the man as Peter. Cf. Luke 22:35–38, with its reference to some of the disciples being armed.

14:48 / **Did you have to come with swords and clubs**: Jesus' remark is intended as a complaint about being treated like a common criminal and about the covert nature of the arrest, and he demands to know why they had not the courage to make a public arrest if there were charges against him. V. 49 refers to a prolonged teaching ministry in the Temple area, described in summary fashion in 11:1–12:44.

14:50 / **All the disciples left him**: This fulfills Jesus' prediction in 14:27. Peter is described as following Jesus and the arresting party to the house of the High Priest in vv. 54, 66–72.

14:51 / **A certain young man**: As indicated in the discussion above, the young man's naked flight is probably an allusion to Amos 2:16, though the GNB translation obscures this allusion by translating the Hebrew "shall flee away naked" as "will drop their weapons and run." Some have pointed to Gen. 39:12, where Joseph runs away from the attempted seduction by Potiphar's wife, leaving his robe; but it is difficult to make sense of what such an allusion would signify, and it is probably to be rejected.

28

Trial and Denial

Then Jesus was taken to the High Priest's house, where all the chief priests, the elders, and the teachers of the Law were gathering. ⁵⁴Peter followed from a distance and went into the courtyard of the High Priest's house. There he sat down with the guards, keeping himself warm by the fire. ⁵⁵The chief priests and the whole Council tried to find some evidence against Jesus in order to put him to death, but they could not find any. ⁵⁶Many witnesses told lies against Jesus, but their stories did not agree.

⁵⁷Then some men stood up and told this lie against Jesus: ⁵⁸"We heard him say, 'I will tear down this Temple which men have made, and after three days I will build one that is not made by men.'" ⁵⁹Not even they, however, could make their stories agree.

⁶⁰The High Priest stood up in front of them all and questioned Jesus, "Have you no answer to the accusation they bring against you?"

⁶¹But Jesus kept quiet and would not say a word. Again the High Priest questioned him, "Are you the Messiah, the Son of the Blessed God?"

⁶²"I am," answered Jesus, "and you will all see the Son of Man seated at the right side of the Almighty and coming with the clouds of heaven!"

⁶³The High Priest tore his robes and said, "We don't need any more witnesses! ⁶⁴You heard his blasphemy. What is your decision?"

They all voted against him: he was guilty and should be put to death.

⁶⁵Some of them began to spit on Jesus, and they blindfolded him and hit him. "Guess who hit you!" they said. And the guards took him and slapped him.

⁶⁶Peter was still down in the courtyard when one of the High Priest's servant girls came by. ⁶⁷When she saw Peter warming himself, she looked straight at him and said, "You, too, were with Jesus of Nazareth."

⁶⁸But he denied it. "I don't know . . . I don't understand what you are talking about," he answered, and went out into the passageway. Just then a rooster crowed.ʷ

⁶⁹The servant girl saw him there and began to repeat to the bystanders, "He is one of them!" ⁷⁰But Peter denied it again.

A little while later the bystanders accused Peter again, "You can't deny that you are one of them, because you, too, are from Galilee."

⁷¹Then Peter said, "I swear that I am telling the truth! May God punish me if I am not! I do not know the man you are talking about!"

⁷²Just then a rooster crowed a second time, and Peter remembered how Jesus had said to him, "Before the rooster crows two times, you will say three times that you do not know me." And he broke down and cried.

w. *Some manuscripts do not have* Just then a rooster crowed.

14:53–65 / Each of the four Gospels gives an account of the trials of Jesus before Jewish and Roman authorities, but the variations in their accounts make it difficult to try to construct a complete picture of the events. In addition to the variations among the four Gospels, there are also questions about the nature of the sources of information available to early Christians in constructing their accounts of the trials, since obviously no Christians were present. We cannot tackle fully these questions here, both because it is the primary aim of this commentary to understand the text of Mark as it stands rather than to try to reconstruct in detail the historical sequence of the events lying behind the text, and because in any case there is not adequate space here to do justice to a discussion of the historical questions surrounding the trials, which have occupied numerous articles in scholarly journals and several books. We shall make some limited observations relevant to these questions in the notes, but our major interest here as elsewhere will be to try to follow what Mark intended his readers to perceive in his account (for a careful discussion of the historical questions in brief, see "Trial of Jesus," *IDBSup*, pp. 917–19, and the literature cited there).

As the Markan account stands, Jesus is taken to the High Priest's house (v. 53), with Peter following at a distance (v. 54). There is some sort of hearing before Jewish authorities (vv. 55–64) and a reference to indignities heaped upon Jesus (v. 65), with the interest clearly centered on the charge of the false witnesses (vv. 55–60) and on Jesus' **blasphemy** about being the Son of God (vv. 61–64). Further, it must be noted that the Markan account of the hearing before Jewish authorities is sandwiched in with the story of Peter's "trial" before the crowd in the courtyard (vv. 54, 66–72). This splicing of the two stories together suggests that here, as in other places where Mark uses this technique (e.g., 3:20–35; 5:21–43; 6:7–30; 11:12–21), his purpose was to use each story to interpret the other. His primary object was not a chronological description of the events after Jesus' arrest but rather the teaching of certain theological points to his readers about the significance of Jesus' trial.

Basically, the account of Jesus' trial in Mark seems designed, along with the rest of the Gospel, to show who Jesus really is and (more specifically here) to present him as a role model for the readers of the kind of courageous and faithful behavior they were to emulate in the face of such a trial themselves (having been warned earlier that such experiences are to be expected, 8:34–38; 13:9–13). The authorities try to find Jesus guilty of threatening to destroy the Temple (vv. 57–59), but Mark emphasizes that Jesus was guilty of no crime and that the attempt to find evidence against him was unsuccessful (v. 55–59, and notes). Yet, in the presentation of the claims of these false witnesses (**lies**, v. 56), there is another example of Markan irony, for the witnesses unknowingly hint at the truth of the gospel in their testimony. Although Jesus had not, it appears, actually threatened to destroy the Temple himself (cf. 13:1–2), he had predicted that the Temple would be destroyed in the future and had implied that the destruction would come by the will of God as judgment upon the Jewish authorities for their rejection of his message (cf. also 12:1–12). As we noted in our discussion of the material in 11:1–12:44, Mark presents Jesus as replacing the Temple as the access to God (see also 15:38 and comments there), and he sees Jesus' death as the new sacrifice that renders the Temple ritual useless. When, therefore, the witnesses describe Jesus as promising that he will raise up a new Temple, they do not recognize that on a more profound level this is precisely what he will do. They were wrong to accuse Jesus of threatening the Temple himself and wrong to think that he promised to build another Temple, but the readers are to see that Jesus' death *is* the end of the Jewish Temple, and his resurrection the raising up of a new "Temple."

This deeper significance of the false charges against Jesus is suggested by the reference to the new structure arising **after three days** (v. 58), which is an obvious allusion to the resurrection of Jesus (cf. 8:31; 9:31; 10:34). Further, the contrasting characterizations of the Jewish Temple and the new Temple as **this Temple which men have made** and **one that is not made by men** respectively are intended by Mark as a hint to the reader to see the resurrection of Jesus prefigured here. The description of the new Temple reflects the use of the same or similar terms elsewhere in the NT to contrast the superior quality of the redemption bestowed through Jesus Christ to the structures of the Jewish religion (see notes), and Mark appears to have worded the charge in such a way as to help his readers see the ironic truth in it.

But if the charge of the false witnesses only hints at the true significance of Jesus, the exchange between Jesus and the High Priest (vv. 60–64) makes it all clear. Here, finally, all secrecy is removed and Jesus answers openly to the priest's question, affirming that he is **the Messiah, the Son of the Blessed God**, and warning that he will be vindicated in divine glory (v. 62). The question of the priest (v. 61) uses the very titles that Mark has already presented as the clearest indications of who Jesus really is. From the opening line (1:1) on, the reader has been told that this "Son of Man" is really the Christ (Messiah) and the Son of God (cf. also 1:11, 24; 3:11; 5:7; 8:29–30; 9:7; 10:47; 12:6, 35–37; 13:32; 15:39). Although up to this point in the narrative Jesus has silenced those who used such titles, now he openly accepts them. His reply is received by the

Jewish authorities as **blasphemy**, but the reader knows that it is the truth and sees the scene as a veritable revelation event. Here again Mark employs irony, for the cry of the High Priest, **blasphemy**, is in fact so wrong as to make the cry itself blasphemous, for it amounts to a blatant rejection of the one the reader knows God has acknowledged (1:11; 9:7)!

As indicated earlier, Mark appears to have written this passage not only to show Jesus openly affirming who he is, but also to provide the readers with a shining example of how they were to react when put to trial on account of their faith in Jesus. The false witnesses show that this is really a trial based solely on the claim that Jesus is the Son of God and has nothing to do with any illegal behavior of Jesus. By this account, the readers are implicitly instructed to see to it that any trial they experience is based solely on their faith and not on any misdoings on their part (cf. 1 Pet. 3:13–16; 4:12–16). Jesus' forthright acknowledgment of his claim (**I am**, v. 62) is to be taken as an example of the unhesitating courage the readers are to show in confessing their faith in Jesus as the Son of God. It is, finally, this recognition that Jesus is being presented here as a role model that explains why Mark has spliced together the account of the trial and the account of Peter's denial of Jesus. The accounts are to be seen as two opposing examples of responses under fire. Jesus gives a good confession and courageously goes to his execution; Peter (vv. 66–72) collapses shamefully under "interrogation" by a mere servant girl (vv. 66–70) and by an anonymous bystander (vv. 70–71). The terrible failure of Peter (discussed more fully in our next section) only serves to make Jesus' behavior all the more admirable.

In the rest of the passion narrative Mark shows Jesus before Pilate, the Roman authority, and describes the execution (15:1–47). The trial before Pilate, however, is passed over quickly, because here Mark has taken the time to show Jesus affirming his rightful status and courageously handling his accusers. Some have thought that the emphasis upon the Jewish trial shows some anti-Semitic streak in Mark, but this is to miss the more profound reason for the emphasis. Jesus' claim is to be the Messiah, the Son of the God of Israel, the fulfillment of OT promises; and this is why Mark shows Jesus in a final confrontation with the Jewish authorities and the alternate reading of the OT and the different set of religious claims that they represent. It is precisely because Mark wishes to make the point that Jesus is the rightful Messiah of Israel that he emphasizes the wrongfulness of the rejection of him by the Jewish leaders. There is no denying the fact that this amounts to a criticism of Jewish rejection of Jesus, and it is sadly true that this kind of theological polemic was used in later centuries as a justification for reprehensible persecutions of Jews by political and ecclesiastical leaders under governments that claimed to be Christian. But to read this later, perverted idea of religious zeal into the Gospel of Mark is not only incorrect historically, it is also to accuse the author of something to which he never dreamed that Christians could stoop. Mark's account of the trial was meant to present in sharp terms the claim of Jesus' significance in the context of the revelation of God to which both the OT and the Jews bear witness, and to give his readers a model of how they should courageously give witness to that claim.

14:66-72 / As indicated earlier, Mark (and Matthew in his parallel account in 26:57-75) sandwiches together the account of Jesus' hearing before the Jewish leaders and the story of Peter's denial before a group of bystanders, for the purpose of making all the clearer the contrast between the courage and faithfulness of Jesus under fire and the cowardice of Peter. In 14:54, Mark says that Peter followed Jesus and the arresting party to the High Priest's house and joined a crowd in the courtyard to wait to see what would happen to Jesus. The detail about the servant girl (vv. 66, 69) is probably intended to make Peter's cowardice seem all the greater. While Jesus stands firm before the highest religious authorities in ancient Judaism, Peter collapses in the face of a mere serving girl (cf. Luke's version, which mentions first a girl and then a man questioning Peter, 22:56-58).

In all three Synoptic versions of the story, Peter denies Jesus three times, serving to make his failure emphatic and full. In the Markan and Matthean versions, Peter's final denial is described as involving strong oaths, and this makes the third denial climactic in the series (cf. 14:71; Matt. 26:74; Luke 22:60). In addition to this slight variation, there are other interesting peculiarities in each version of the story. Luke alone refers to Jesus' turning to look at Peter (22:61) at the moment of the third denial. Matthew (26:73) alone specifies that it was Peter's accent that indicated that he was a Galilean, whereas Mark (14:70) simply states without explanation that the others could tell where Peter was from. But another detail, this one peculiar to Mark, is of greater interest, because it seems to have caused ancient copyists some problems.

In 14:30, Jesus predicts that Peter will deny him before the rooster crows *twice*, this prediction being cited retrospectively in 14:72. Now in 14:72a, Mark indicates that a rooster crowed for the second time just after Peter's third denial of Jesus, but the ancient manuscripts are divided over whether a first crowing of a rooster is mentioned in 14:68, with some containing the statement and some omitting it. The evidence is so divided that it is difficult to be sure whether the reference to this first crowing of the rooster originally appeared in 14:68, but probably it did—and was omitted by some copyists who sought to reconcile Mark's account with the parallels in Matthew and Luke that mention only one crowing. Perhaps the meaning of describing Peter's denials as all taking place before the rooster's second crowing was to say that they happened in the space of a short period of time (see notes), showing that Peter's collapse of faithfulness did not take place over the course of a prolonged interrogation but in the context of a few embarrassing questions from people in the courtyard.

In this passage, Peter, the representative of the Twelve, falls to the lowest point of failure in discipleship, providing a negative example almost as bad as the betrayal of Jesus by Judas. Indeed, it is striking that the tradition of Peter's denial of Jesus forms a part of all four of the Gospels (see John 18:15–18, 25–27). One would think that there would have been embarrassment about reciting the failure of such a prominent leader in early Christianity, and perhaps this only shows how very much the Gospel accounts were not produced to promote the reputation of early Christian leaders but to emphasize the absolute significance of Jesus. The first readers of the Gospels certainly were acquainted with the fact that Peter became an important leader in the church, and there is no reason to believe that any of the Gospels was written to impugn his reputation. Rather, this story was probably intended to show that even the respected leaders of the church were totally dependent upon the merciful forgiveness of Jesus for their participation in the fellowship that bore his name. In this way Jesus is magnified, and all others, even such a famous leader as Peter, are placed on the level of mere human disciples. No doubt Mark's readers, for example, would have found much encouragement in realizing that this collapsed disciple pictured here was restored by the risen Jesus to full fellowship, a restoration that is anticipated in 16:7, where the "young man" in white clothing promises that the risen Jesus will appear to the disciples and again call them to follow him.

But Mark's readers were also intended to read this account as a lesson in how not to react when they might be interrogated for their faith. Having been warned already that they would face persecutions and trials (13:9–13), they are given in Peter's story a warning of the shame of denying their Lord. Peter's tears (14:72b) are mentioned to show this shame, and the tearful Peter is a dramatic example of what it means to deny one's faith in Christ.

Finally, with this incident, the reader is left with Jesus alone, the disciples having fled and their spokesman (Peter) having failed miserably. In the coming events of his sufferings, Jesus is alone to do the will of God, and the message is thereby presented that the salvation obtained through Jesus' work was obtained by him alone, unaided by any human instrument.

Additional Notes

14:53 / **The High Priest's house**: Matt. 26:57 and Luke 22:54 agree that this was the initial destination after Jesus' arrest. John 18:13–14, 19–24, 28 describes the movements a little differently, but we must recognize that no one account is a complete description of events. Also, it is not necessarily to be assumed that the interrogation of 14:55–64 took place at the High Priest's house, for there could have been a move elsewhere that is not mentioned in Mark (cf. Luke 22:66). Finally, it should not be presumed that the hearing described in vv. 55–64 took place at night (again, cf. Luke 22:66). Mark's linking of the trial of Jesus and the denial by Peter was done for purposes of contrasting them, and not to give a chronological description of the events. It is possible that there was some interrogation of Jesus at the house of the High Priest and that the actual trial or some sort of quasi-formal hearing took place early the next morning, as Luke's account suggests.

The chief priests, the elders and the teachers of the Law: Again, we note the same figures mentioned in the passion prediction in 8:31 (cf. 14:43). These groups made up the Jewish Sanhedrin, the highest court of ancient Judaism (see "Sanhedrin," *IDB*, vol. 4, pp. 214–18; *IDBSup*, pp. 784–86). See also 14:55 and note.

14:55 / **The whole Council**: **Council** here translates the term *sunedrion* (Sanhedrin), a group of seventy-one leaders of the Jews, composed of the leading priests and respected men, that operated by permission of the Romans in cases dealing with Jewish religious law. The claim in John 18:31 that this council did not at this time have the power to carry out capital punishment is disputed by some scholars, but there is reason to accept it as correct (see *IDBSup*, pp. 917–19).

14:56 / **Many witnesses told lies**: literally, "many gave false witness," alluding to Exod. 20:16, the commandment against bearing false witness. Here the witnesses are themselves shown to be breaking the OT Law. Jewish practice required that any charge be supported by at least two witnesses, and that their testimony had to agree perfectly. This is what is alluded to in the statement that **their stories did not agree**.

14:58 / **This Temple which men have made... one that is not made by men**: The phrase **which men have made** (lit., "made by hands") translates a word used in the Greek translation of the OT to describe the idols of the gentile nations (e.g., Lev. 26:1, 30; Isa. 2:18; 10:11; 19:1; 21:9; 31:7, translated in the GNB as "idols"). Thus the Temple is described as a human object that has no more validity than the images of the pagans. The same word appears in Acts 7:48; 17:24; Eph. 2:11; Heb. 9:11, 24 referring to temples and rituals regarded as not valid, or as greatly inferior to the redemption bestowed in Christ.

The term translated **not made by men** (lit., "not made by hands") is another word not found (so far) outside the NT (2 Cor. 5:1; Col. 2:11) and connotes the idea of validity and approval by God for whatever is described by the term. The Matt. 26:60–61 parallel does not use these terms in describing the charge against Jesus, showing that Mark has carefully worded the charge to bring out the kind of point described in the discussion above. Luke does not refer to the charge in his account. John 2:18–22 attributes to Jesus a similar saying but explicitly makes it refer to Jesus' resurrection. There may also be an allusion to Isa. 66:1–2, with its criticism of the Temple as a residence of God. In the crucifixion account, people mock Jesus with a similar charge (15:29–30), and in 15:38 Mark tells of a sign that the Jewish Temple has indeed been rendered invalid by the death of Jesus. (See also the discussion of 11:15–19.)

14:61 / The Messiah, the Son of the Blessed God: The last phrase is literally, "the son of the Blessed," such adjectives as **blessed** being used in ancient Judaism as substitutes for the direct reference to God, out of reverence for him. The placing of the two designations **Messiah** and **Son of the Blessed** (Son of God) together shows that Mark regarded them as somewhat synonymous (cf. 1:1).

14:62 / I am is probably to be taken as both a directly affirmative answer to the question of the High Priest and as an allusion to the self-designation of God familiar to readers of the Greek OT (see note on 6:50). Thus, Mark's readers are intended to see that Jesus' answer is in fact on a deeper level an affirmation of his divine status! Cf. the answers recorded in Matt. 26:64 and Luke 22:67–70; the differences suggest that Mark's version is deliberately intended to make the point suggested here.

The Son of Man seated at the right side of the Almighty and coming with the clouds of heaven: The term **Almighty** renders the Greek word "Power," another reverential synonym for God (Lane, p. 537). The whole description of the future exaltation of the Son of Man alludes to Dan. 7:13–14 (where "one like a son of man" is given rule by God) and Ps. 110:1 (where one described as "my lord" is given a seat of authority at the right hand of God). These same OT passages are alluded to in the earlier passages in Mark where the future glory of Jesus is hinted (8:38; 13:26; 12:35–37; and notes on these verses). It is doubtful that Mark took the assurance **you will all see** (v. 62) to mean that the glorious return of Christ would happen within the lifetime of the members of the Jewish Council. Rather, he probably intended the words as the firmest assurance that the event will happen, and that those who condemned Jesus will be shown wrong on the day of judgment.

14:63 / **Tore his robes**: It is unlikely that the High Priest was wearing the special priestly vestments used on high holy days, for these were kept by the Roman governor and lent to the High Priest only on those days—to show who was really in charge. Tearing one's clothes was a sign of great grief (e.g., 2 Kings 19:1) and indicates that the High Priest found Jesus' reply to be outrageous.

14:64 / **His blasphemy**: In later times rabbinic law restricted the definition of blasphemy to pronouncing the name of God (Yahweh) explicitly in an irreverent manner (based on Lev. 24:15-16), but it is not to be assumed that this narrow definition of the crime was in effect in Jesus' time.

It has been pointed out numerous times that there is no evidence that claiming to be the Messiah was a blasphemy, and so many scholars cannot see what the crime was in the scene as described here. The answer may lie in a combination of factors about Jesus' answer and his ministry. First, the description of the future exaltation of the Son of Man here (v. 62) attributes to this figure a position next to God himself, and it may be this clothing of the Son of Man with quasi-divine status that was at least part of the offense (cf. also comments on 13:26-27). Secondly, there is great reason to believe that Jesus' ministry involved both teachings and actions that were considered by scrupulous Jewish leaders as breaches of the Law of God and as incitement of others to do the same (e.g., 2:1-3:6; 11:15-19; and the discussion of these verses). If Jesus thus made the claim that he had been sent from God to do and to teach these things, it is not difficult to think that some Jewish leaders would have found him to be guilty of "leading astray" the people (Deut. 13:1-5) and of bringing reproach upon the name of God (Lev. 24:15-16). If Jesus affirmed that he was the Messiah (as in v. 62) or gave reason to think that he intended this, he could have been seen as claiming divine justification for actions considered outrageous and violations of the Law of God.

The term **blasphemy**, then, likely means here a mockery of God. (See "Blasphemy," *IDB*, vol. 1, p. 445; Lane, pp. 538-39.) The term is obviously an important one in Mark and its use reflects the Markan taste for irony. In 2:7, Jesus is accused of blasphemy in forgiving a man's sins, for that is a prerogative of God alone. The accusers, however, do not realize that Jesus does have such authority, and it is they who are really guilty of "blasphemy" in disparaging the Son of God. In 3:28, Jesus warns solemnly about blasphemy against the Holy Spirit (see discussion), in a passage in which his miracles are attributed to Satan. Here again, his critics accuse him of something they themselves have committed by refusing to acknowledge his claims! Finally, in 15:29, Mark describes the insults of the onlookers as blasphemy (the GNB translation obscures this; see the notes on this verse) and confirms that it is not Jesus but his opponents who are guilty of this crime.

14:65 / **Guess who hit you**: Literally, the word here is "prophesy," meaning that we have here a mockery by the Jewish authorities and guards of the idea that Jesus is sent from God and has any sort of prophetic power. This mockery should be seen along with the later account of the Roman mockery in 15:16-20 (see comments on this passage).

14:68 / I don't know ... I don't understand: literally, "I neither know nor understand. . . . " His words imply that he absolutely has no knowledge of the subject, of course an outright lie!

Just then a rooster crowed: This phrase is not found in some ancient manuscripts of Mark, and it is possible that it was inserted by some copyists to make sense of the reference in v. 72 to a second crowing. But it is perhaps more likely that the phrase was omitted by copyists in the desire to harmonize the account with the parallels in Matthew (26:69–75) and Luke (22:56–62), which mention only one crowing.

14:70 / Peter denied it again: The verb used here, "deny," is the word used by Jesus in the prophecy of Peter's failure in 14:30–31. The term is used here and in v. 68. In these verses, Peter denies the accusation made by the servant girl, but the point is that in doing so he is denying Jesus.

You, too, are from Galilee: Matt. 26:73 says that Peter's accent indicated that he was not from Judea but from the northern part of Palestine. This connection of Jesus and the Twelve with Galilee suggests that Jesus was known as a popular figure of that area and was less closely identified with Judea.

14:71 / Then Peter said, "I swear that I am telling the truth! May God punish me if I am not reads more literally "He began to invoke curses [upon himself] and to swear." The rather free GNB translation does, however, catch the spirit of Peter's action.

14:72 / Just then a rooster crowed a second time: Reports of the crowing habits of roosters in Palestine indicate that the first crowing occurs at about 12:30 a.m., the second at about 1:30 a.m., and the third about an hour after the second. The period of the night from midnight to about 3 a.m. was known as cockcrowing in the watches of the night observed by the ancient military in Palestine. Thus, the time involved between Peter's first and final denials is described as about an hour at most. (See Lane, p. 543, for references to the literature.)

29

Handed over to the Gentiles

Early in the morning the chief priests met hurriedly with the elders, the teachers of the Law, and the whole Council, and made their plans. They put Jesus in chains, led him away, and handed him over to Pilate. [2]Pilate questioned him, "Are you the king of the Jews?"

Jesus answered, "So you say."

[3]The chief priests were accusing Jesus of many things, [4]so Pilate questioned him again, "Aren't you going to answer? Listen to all their accusations!"

[5]Again Jesus refused to say a word, and Pilate was amazed.

[6]At every Passover Festival Pilate was in the habit of setting free any one prisoner the people asked for. [7]At that time a man named Barabbas was in prison with the rebels who had committed murder in the riot. [8]When the crowd gathered and began to ask Pilate for the usual favor, [9]he asked them, "Do you want me to set free for you the king of the Jews?" [10]He knew very well that the chief priests had handed Jesus over to him because they were jealous.

[11]But the chief priests stirred up the crowd to ask, instead, that Pilate set Barabbas free for them. [12]Pilate spoke again to the crowd, "What, then, do you want me to do with the one you call the king of the Jews?"

[13]They shouted back, "Crucify him!"

[14]"But what crime has he committed?" Pilate asked.

They shouted all the louder, "Crucify him!"

[15]Pilate wanted to please the crowd, so he set Barabbas free for them. Then he had Jesus whipped and handed him over to be crucified.

[16]The soldiers took Jesus inside to the courtyard of the governor's palace and called together the rest of the company. [17]They put a purple robe on Jesus, made a crown out of thorny branches, and put it on his head. [18]Then they began to salute him: "Long live the King of the Jews!" [19]They beat him over the head with a stick, spat on him, fell on their knees, and bowed down to him. [20]When they had finished making fun of him, they took off the purple robe and put his own clothes back on him. Then they led him out to crucify him.

15:1–5 / In this passage the Jewish leaders meet to make a formal decision about Jesus (v. 1) and they hand him over to Pilate, the Roman governor, whose interrogation of Jesus is then briefly described (vv. 2–5). All three Synoptic Gospels record a morning meeting of the Jewish Council to deal with Jesus (cf. Matt. 27:1; Luke 22:66), and this fact is further evidence that any hearing held during the night must have been either an interrogation or some sort of pretrial hearing, not a formal trial. Otherwise no additional morning meeting would have been necessary.

The reason for taking Jesus to Pilate is not given in the Synoptics, but in John 18:31 we are told that the Jewish Council did not then have the right to carry out executions. This has been disputed by some scholars, but there is sufficient reason to accept the tradition as correct (see "Trial of Jesus," *IDBSup*, pp. 917–19). It is interesting to note, however, that although the charges against Jesus in the trial before the Jewish authorities are religious in nature (threats against the Temple, 14:57–58; "blasphemy," 14:64), Pilate's question in 15:2 suggests that in bringing Jesus before the civil court the Jewish authorities accused him of sedition, for this is what claiming to be king meant. Mark 15:3–4 simply refers to **many things** without specifying the charges, but Luke 23:2 is more specific, listing charges that Jesus advocated the withholding of taxes due to Rome and that he claimed to be the Messiah, the king of the Jews. Certainly there is every reason to believe that at least the latter charge was made, for there is not only the tradition found in the Gospels but also the fact of Jesus' execution by crucifixion, a means of execution used especially on those deemed by the Romans to be rebellious (see now M. Hengel, *Crucifixion* [Philadelphia: Fortress, 1977]). Thus, whatever we may think about the nature of Jesus' own understanding of his mission and person, the evidence suggests that the authorities saw fit to regard him as a danger that had to be eliminated. This in turn suggests that, however indirect Jesus may have been in announcing a view of his own person, there must have been something about his ministry that gave the authorities reason to crucify him as a messianic claimant. Thus, the early church's claim that Jesus is the Messiah (Christ) does seem to be linked with the nature of the ministry of the historical Jesus; the crucifixion is clear evidence that the idea that Jesus was the Messiah was not invented by the church after his execution.

In Mark's account of the trial before the Jewish authorities, Jesus is silent in the face of all accusations (14:55–61) until he is asked directly whether he is the Messiah (14:61). Then, he openly makes the confession of who he is (14:62). Here, in the trial before Pilate, Jesus renews his silence, and this time it is not broken (15:3–5), except for the rather noncommittal reply in verse 2 (**so you say**). This theme of Jesus' silence seems to be intended to serve two purposes. First, it gives the readers a good example of refusing to defend oneself in a religious trial, in keeping with the directions given in 13:11 not to try to plan a defense but to rely on the Holy Spirit to give a good testimony to the gospel (cf. also 1 Tim. 6:13). Further, the silence of Jesus seems to be linked with the false charges of the witnesses in the Jewish trial and the accusations of the chief priests in 15:3, which must also be understood as "false" in some way. That is, Jesus' silence seems to be a hint to the reader that there is something wrong about the charges, that they do not fairly represent who Jesus really is in some serious sense. For example, the false witnesses in 14:55–60 accuse Jesus of threatening to destroy the Temple. As our discussion of this passage shows, this is regarded by Mark as a false charge, for in fact what Jesus is recorded as having done was to predict the destruction of the Temple. Here, the various charges referred to in 15:3 appear to involve the claim that Jesus proclaimed himself a new king, against the rule of the emperor, for Pilate's question in 15:2 suggests this. From Mark's standpoint, this too is an incorrect description of Jesus' claim and of his significance, and is thus also a false charge.

But here again there is more to be said than simply that the charges are false. Just as the false witnesses of the Jewish trial unknowingly hint at the true significance of Jesus as the replacement of the Temple (see discussion of 14:55–60), so here the charge that Jesus seeks to be king hints at something Mark regards as true about Jesus—here again Mark displays his love of irony. Although Jesus is not a mere pretender to the throne of the Jews, a revolutionary who seeks to unseat the Romans in Palestine like other Jewish revolutionaries of the time (such as Barabbas, 15:6–15), Mark *does* regard Jesus as the Christ, and therefore as the true king of Israel (1:1; 8:29; 14:61–62). Thus, the Jewish authorities, and Pilate too, in one sense actually speak the true significance of Jesus without realizing it, intending something different and showing thereby their blindness to the truth. This note of irony that reappears here in 15:1–5 seems to govern the rest of the account of Jesus' execution, as we shall show in our discussion of the following narrative. It is the ironic meaning of the term **king of the Jews**, and its alternate form, "king of Israel," that explains why they appear six times in this chapter (cf. four times in Matt. 27 and four times in Luke 23). Pilate and the Jewish authorities have in mind an earthly king, and hurl the term in Jesus' face in ridicule of his apparent helplessness in their hands. But Mark means his readers to see that, because Jesus is really the Son of God, the bearer of divine significance (1:1, 11; 9:7), he *is* really the king of Israel.

15:6–15 / All four Gospels connect the sentencing of Jesus to death with the release of one called Barabbas (cf. Matt. 27:15–26; Luke 23:18–25; John 18:38–40), and this tradition seems to have been intended to portray vividly two things. First, the cry of the people for Barabbas, the criminal, shows their utter blindness in asking for the guilty to be released and the innocent Jesus to be executed. Secondly, there seems to be a reflection of the deeper theological significance of the death of Jesus seen by the early Christians, who understood Jesus' death as a substitutionary "ransom" on behalf of sinners (cf. Mark 10:45). That is, the freeing of Barabbas probably dramatized for early Christians their own deliverance from the guilt of their sins by virtue of the death of Christ on their behalf.

In Mark, the release of Barabbas fits in with the overall ironic treatment of the execution of Jesus as well. Jesus is accused of being a revolutionary, a pretender to the kingship of the Jews (15:2–3), a false charge in Mark's view (see discussion of 15:1–5). Barabbas, who is described as a revolutionary (15:7) and a murderer, is released, whereas Jesus is executed on the basis of the false charge against him, a charge much more fitting for the man who gets away.

The custom mentioned in 15:6 of releasing a prisoner at Passover is not specifically referred to elsewhere in other historical accounts of the period (e.g., Josephus) and is regarded by some scholars as purely legendary invention. This, however, is an argument from silence, and the fact that the custom is referred to in all four Gospels shows that it must have been a part of ancient and commonly shared Christian tradition. Such a well-supported tradition should not be lightly disregarded. Further, there is some hint of the practice of releasing a prisoner at Passover in the ancient Jewish codification of rabbinic teaching called the Mishnah, and it is probably wise not to dismiss the gospel tradition on this matter (see Lane, pp. 552–53, for discussion and references to the literature).

In the passage before us Pilate senses that Jesus is probably harmless, as far as Rome is concerned, and that the priestly authorities are motivated by jealousy of Jesus (15:10) in trying to get him condemned. But this should not be taken to mean that Pilate was basically a fair man and that his desire to release Jesus was prompted by any noble motive. It is more likely that, having satisfied himself that Jesus was not actually a revolutionary, Pilate concluded that Jesus was simply a serious thorn in the side of the Jewish leaders, and that the issue between them was another of what Pilate regarded as the stupid religious controversies always afflicting the Jews. Since Pilate appears to have had little regard for Jewish sensitivities about religious matters and seems to have had trouble with the Jewish authorities on more than one occasion, he may very well have seen this as an excellent opportunity to bedevil them by releasing someone they wanted out of their hair. That is, his motive for trying to release Jesus was likely the desire to make life more difficult for the religious authorities so they would have less time to trouble him.

Whatever the nature of his motive, Pilate finally agrees to the demand of the crowd and hands Jesus over to be executed. Thus, although the gospel tradition portrays the Jewish leaders as heavily responsible for Jesus' execution, it is clear that the Roman authority actually condemned Jesus and conducted the execution. The utterly regrettable tendency among many Christians down through history to make the death of Jesus purely the responsibility of the Jewish authorities (and thereby the Jewish people as a whole) is a distortion of the gospel tradition and must be rejected for both historical and religious reasons. Though it is true that the Gospel writers all accuse the Jewish authorities of blindness and evil intent in bringing Jesus to Pilate, they had no desire to justify the anti-Semitic attitudes of later generations. Rather, they wished to stress that the rejection of Jesus by the Jewish authorities was the rejection of God's Christ, the true fulfillment of the ancient Jewish hope for messianic salvation. At the same time, the Gospels all agree that the execution of Jesus was conducted by the political authorities, the Gentiles (Romans), and thereby they place any blame for Jesus' death upon both Jewish and gentile representatives. This is indicated, here in Mark, for example, by the use of the same verb "to hand over" to describe both the action of the priests (v. 10) and the action of Pilate (v. 15), a verb with definite theological meaning in Mark (see notes).

15:16-20 / As indicated in the discussion of the preceding passage (15:6–15), the Roman practice of crucifixion involved more than simply hanging a person upon a cross to die; it involved the complete degradation of a person and unrestrained torture, so as to make the punishment the most feared of all in the ancient world. In these verses we have an abbreviated description of such cruelties heaped upon Jesus; however, Mark's purpose is not to emphasize the physical sufferings endured by Jesus but rather the indignities he endured in spite of who he really is. Thus, Mark says virtually nothing about Jesus' response to the things done to him, and the actions of the soldiers are all given as examples of mockeries of the idea of Jesus being the king of the Jews. Here, Pilate's mocking use of the title **King of the Jews** is repeated (v. 18), and the purple robe, the thorny crown, the bowing down to Jesus, accompanied by beatings and by spitting upon him, all involve the soldiers lampooning the idea of Jesus being a king. As previously, Mark's purpose here is mainly to bring out the ironic significance of these acts, for in fact, Jesus is the true king of Israel.

It is also interesting to compare this description of the mockery of Jesus by the Roman guards with the earlier description of a mockery of

Jesus by the Jewish authorities and guards (14:65). There are similarities; in both scenes Jesus is beaten, spat upon, and ridiculed. But there is an interesting difference. In the account of the Jewish mockery, it is the idea of Jesus being a prophet or one endowed with divine powers that is lampooned ("Guess who hit you," 14:65; see note on this verse). In the account before us here, it is the royal status of Jesus that is ridiculed. This difference reflects the evidence that the charges against Jesus in the Jewish hearing were religious in nature, whereas the charges against Jesus before Pilate were political. One must note also, in the light of the later tendency of some Christians to emphasize Jewish responsibility for the death of Jesus, that Mark presents a mockery of Jesus by Jews and Romans, showing thereby that the Romans by no means executed Jesus grudgingly, but with a cruel relish.

Additional Notes

15:1 / **Met hurriedly** does not translate anything in the text of Mark but is an editorial touch of the GNB translators. It is, on the other hand, likely that any morning meeting of the Jewish authorities was a quick affair.

They put Jesus in chains: The Greek text says simply "having bound Jesus," and the translation here is therefore needlessly overspecific.

Handed him over: The term here is used several times in Mark (cf. 1:14, John the Baptist's arrest; 3:19; 14:10, 11, 18, 21, 41–44, Judas' betrayal of Jesus; 9:31; 10:33, predictions of Jesus' death; 13:9–12, the arrest and betrayal of disciples; 15:10, 15, the actions of priests and Pilate in condemning Jesus) and nearly always has a sinister connotation, describing various betrayals and the arrests of John the Baptist, Jesus, or his disciples. It should be noted that both the Jewish leaders here and in 15:10, and Pilate in 15:15 **handed over** Jesus and are thus guilty together in committing the evil act of killing Jesus.

Pontius **Pilate** was the Roman governor of Judea A.D. 26–36 and is described by Josephus and Philo (ancient Jewish writers) as having had a tempestuous relationship with the Jewish people, caused by his own maliciousness and crudeness in ruling them. He was apparently finally removed from his post and sent to Rome on account of complaints by the Jews. In the Gospel accounts of Jesus' execution, the references to Pilate generally accord with this picture, but later Christian legend sometimes transforms him into a hero or even a Christian convert! These legendary developments must be regarded as totally misleading, however, and the reader should avoid romantic notions of Pilate as a noble figure forced against his better judgment to do something beneath him. The Matt. 27:19 reference to Pilate's wife and the Matt. 27:24–25 reference to Pilate's washing of his hands are not mentioned by Mark and may have contributed to the early stages of a legendary development that later reached the point of making Pilate a saint (as he is in the Coptic church of Egypt). Luke 23:6–16 refers to a hearing before Herod Antipas as well as a trial before Pilate, but this is unique to Luke. (Cf. "Pilate, Pontius," *IDB*, vol. 3, pp. 811–13; and *IDBSup*, p. 668.)

15:5 / **Pilate was amazed**: Here Pilate's response to Jesus is similar to the response of others in Mark, but amazement is consistently contrasted with full understanding and faith (cf. 1:27; 5:20; 10:24, 32; 15:44).

15:6 / **At every Passover Festival**: literally, "at the feast," but clearly Passover is the feast in mind here.

15:7 / **Barabbas** means "son of Abba [father]" and was borne by others, including rabbis (see Lane, p. 554). His name may indicate that he was the son of a prominent Jewish figure of the time. He is described here as having committed murder in **the riot**, a term often used to describe a rebellion, leading some to suggest that he may have been a revolutionary like the Zealots. In some manuscripts of Matthew, he is called Jesus Barabbas in Matt. 27:16–17, but the manuscripts in question are not the best witnesses to the original text of the Gospels. Nevertheless, it is possible that this was his full name, for Jesus was a common name among Jews of the time (being simply the name sometimes rendered Joshua, the great hero of the conquest of Palestine in the OT book that bears his name). See "Barabbas," *IDB*, vol. 1, p. 353; Lane, p. 554.

15:9 / **The king of the Jews**: This is the second use of the title by Pilate (cf. v. 2), and in both cases he probably intended it as a mockery of Jesus and of all things Jewish. In other words, he saw the helpless Jesus standing before him as a laughable example of the vain hopes of the Jews in the face of the might of Imperial Rome. Cf. also v. 12, where Pilate again uses the term. The same term is in fact used consistently by the Romans again in 15:18, where the soldiers mock Jesus, and in 15:26, quoting the mocking title placed above the head of the crucified Jesus. By contrast, when the Jewish figures speak, they use the term "king of Israel," v. 32.

15:10 / **Because they were jealous**: Mark probably means to describe the chief priests as resentful of the popular effect of Jesus' ministry in Jerusalem as in Galilee (see e.g., 12:12, 37b). Jesus' condemnation of the priestly leadership when he drove the merchants from the Temple (who had been licensed to operate their stalls by the high priest) was perhaps the final straw, requiring them to move against one who threatened their hold on the people.

15:15 / **He had Jesus whipped**: The Greek word used here designates the Roman scourging, which involved the use of use of a whip made of leather thongs connecting pieces of bone and metal like a chain. This instrument was capable of flaying the flesh so that the victim's bones and entrails were made bare, and some died under the ordeal. There was no regulation about how many blows a person might receive, and the object of this punishment, as even more so with crucifixion, was to cause the victim the maximum in pain and suffering. The Roman soldiers were encouraged to use their imagination in the arts of cruelty, and vv. 16–20 only hint at the terrifying things done in such cases. (See Lane, p. 557, for references to the punishment in ancient sources.)

15:16 / **Inside to the courtyard of the governor's palace**: literally, "inside the court(yard), which is [the] praetorium." The term translated **courtyard** could mean also the "court" or palace of a royal figure, and there is some disagreement among scholars as to whether "praetorium" refers to the Roman fortress (Antonia) located in the Temple area, or to the palace of Herod, which was used as the residence of the Roman governor when he visited Jerusalem. The GNB translation seems to opt for the latter location, and there is some weight of evidence in favor of that option. (See "Praetorium," *IDB*, vol. 3, p. 856; Lane, p. 548.)

The rest of the company: implies that Jesus was made the sport of the whole detachment of soldiers who accompanied the governor to Jerusalem. The actual crucifixion force usually involved four soldiers for a prisoner, under the command of an officer.

15:17 / **A purple robe**: The ancient purple dye was obtained from a kind of Mediterranean shellfish and was extremely valuable. It was associated with royalty, so clothing Jesus in this color signified a mockery of the claim that Jesus was a king. (See "Purple," *IDB*, vol. 3, pp. 969–70.)

A crown out of thorny branches: The main object of this device was not to inflict physical pain but to lampoon Jesus as a clown-king. Ancient images of royal crowns frequently show the kings wearing crowns with radiating points, symbolizing the glory flowing from the head of the monarch. The thorny or spiked branches used here mock this type of crown, using materials ready at hand from the acanthus shrub or from palms. (See "Crown," *IDB*, vol. 1, pp. 745–46; "Thistle, Thorn," *IDB*, vol. 4, pp. 630–31.)

15:18 / **Long live the King of the Jews**: literally, "Hail, King of the Jews!" This probably represents the Greek version of the Roman salute of the emperor, here offered to Jesus in derision.

15:20 / **Put his own clothes back on him**: Jesus would have been stripped for the flogging mentioned in v. 15, and then the naked prisoner was wrapped in the purple robe as part of the mockery. Here, before being led to the place of execution, his own clothes are wrapped about him. Later, in v. 24, he is stripped again and his clothes divided among the execution squad.

30

Crucified, Dead, and Buried

MARK 15:21–47

On the way they met a man named Simon, who was coming into the city from the country, and the soldiers forced him to carry Jesus' cross. (Simon was from Cyrene and was the father of Alexander and Rufus.) [22]They took Jesus to a place called Golgotha, which means "The Place of the Skull." [23]There they tried to give him wine mixed with a drug called myrrh, but Jesus would not drink it. [24]Then they crucified him and divided his clothes among themselves, throwing dice to see who would get which piece of clothing. [25]It was nine o'clock in the morning when they crucified him. [26]The notice of the accusation against him said: "The King of the Jews." [27]They also crucified two bandits with Jesus, one on his right and the other on his left.[x]

[29]People passing by shook their heads and hurled insults at Jesus: "Aha! You were going to tear down the Temple and build it back up in three days! [30]Now come down from the cross and save yourself!"

[31]In the same way the chief priests and the teachers of the Law made fun of Jesus, saying to one another, "He saved others, but he cannot save himself! [32]Let us see the Messiah, the king of Israel, come down from the cross now, and we will believe in him!"

And the two who were crucified with Jesus insulted him also.

[33]At noon the whole country was covered with darkness, which lasted for three hours. [34]At three o'clock Jesus cried out with a loud shout, "Eloi, Eloi, lema sabachthani?" which means, "My God, my God, why did you abandon me?"

[35]Some of the people there heard him and said, "Listen, he is calling for Elijah!" [36]One of them ran up with a sponge, soaked it in cheap wine, and put it on the end of a stick. Then he held it up to Jesus' lips and said, "Wait! Let us see if Elijah is coming to bring him down from the cross!"

[37]With a loud cry Jesus died.

[38]The curtain hanging in the Temple was torn in two, from top to bottom. [39]The army officer who was standing there in front of the cross saw how Jesus had died.[y] "This man was really the Son of God!" he said.

[40]Some women were there, looking on from a distance. Among them were Mary Magdalene, Mary the mother of the younger James and of Joseph, and Salome. [41]They had followed Jesus while he was in Galilee and had helped him. Many other women who had come to Jerusalem with him were there also.

[42] [43]It was toward evening when Joseph of Arimathea arrived. He was a respected member of the Council, who was waiting for the coming of the Kingdom of God. It was Preparation day (that is, the day before the Sabbath), so Joseph went boldly into the presence of Pilate and asked him for the body of Jesus. [44]Pilate was surprised to hear that Jesus was already dead. He called the army officer and asked him if Jesus

had been dead a long time. [45]After hearing the officer's report, Pilate told Joseph he could have the body. [46]Joseph bought a linen sheet, took the body down, wrapped it in the sheet, and placed it in a tomb which had been dug out of solid rock. Then he rolled a large stone across the

entrance to the tomb. [47]Mary Magdalene and Mary the mother of Joseph were watching and saw where the body of Jesus was placed.

x. *Some manuscripts add verse 28:* In this way the scripture came true which says, "He shared the fate of criminals" *(see Lk. 22.37).*
y. had died; *some manuscripts have* had cried out and died.

15:21–32 / It is striking that the event that was the central item in the story of Jesus' obedience to the will of God is narrated here with such stark simplicity and economy of words (compare the Lucan version, 23:26–43). The mention of Simon, the Cyrenian Jew (v. 21), a person included in all the Synoptic accounts of the crucifixion (cf. Matt. 27:32; Luke 23:26), looks like an echo of early tradition. In Mark, there is the distinctive reference to two sons of the man (Alexander and Rufus, v. 21), perhaps indicating that the men were known to the first readers. There are also the details of Jesus being offered drugged wine (v. 23) and of the gambling for Jesus' garments (v. 24). The emphasis of the passage, however, is clearly upon the merciless mockery from the bystanders (vv. 25–32), who continue a ridicule of Jesus begun in the account of the hearing before the Jewish authorities (14:65).

This mockery of Jesus completes the picture of his apparent total helplessness, which is reflected in the references to the flogging (15:15), the ridicule of the soldiers (15:16–20), the necessity of using someone else to help carry the cross beam (15:21), the parting of his clothes (15:24), and the mocking sign attached to his cross (15:26). Mark's intent in presenting Jesus' execution in such stark terms is to confront the reader with the brutal reality of Jesus' humiliation. But of course, in the context of Mark's theology, the reader is to see that precisely in this brutal humiliation of Jesus the redeeming purpose of God comes to expression. That is, the one humiliated here is really the obedient servant of God, the Son of God, whose suffering is in the will of God, and for the "many" (cf. 10:45).

It is likely that several details in the passage are intended to allude to OT passages that were seen as prefiguring the sufferings of Jesus. For example, the wine laced with myrrh (15:23) may allude to Psalm 69:21 (see notes). The parting of Jesus' garments among the soldiers (15:24) may allude to Psalm 22:18; and the reference to the criminals crucified alongside Jesus may be intended as an allusion to Isaiah 53:12, where the servant of God is rejected and counted among "evil men" and "sinners."

The taunt that Jesus threatened to destroy the Temple and build a new one in three days echoes the charge against him in the interrogation before the Jewish authorities in 14:57–59, and like that charge, the taunt is both misleading and yet an ironic foreshadowing of what Mark urges was the true significance of Jesus' death. As we noted in discussing the account of the Jewish interrogation, the charge about the Temple is not strictly what Jesus said, but Mark's reference, later on in the crucifixion narrative (15:37–38), to the tearing of the Temple curtain suggests that, in a deeper sense, by *his death* Jesus did bring an end to the validity of the Temple and, in his resurrection "in three days," did institute a new means of access to God, a new Temple, his resurrection body.

The final, ironic touch in the passage before us is the taunt of the bystanders and the Jewish authorities for Jesus to try to save himself (15:30, 31) and to come down from the cross (15:32) that they might believe that he is the Messiah. This taunt both reveals their distorted notion about what truly constitutes the work of God's servant, the Messiah, and points to the very heart of what Jesus' work is. The taunters say, **He saved others, but he cannot save himself!** and unknowingly state the very truth of the crucifixion. Jesus' death is a "ransom" for others (10:45), and precisely in order to save these **others** he must not and cannot save himself! We have noted already how very much Mark uses irony, but surely this is the high point of ironic narrative in his whole Gospel, with Jesus' enemies ignorantly speaking the core truth of the gospel. In their taunts, they mockingly address Jesus as **the Messiah, the king of Israel**, wording that both indicates that the two terms **Messiah** and **king of Israel** are synonyms here and reflects the Jewish equivalent of the Roman derision that hung on Jesus' cross, **The King of the Jews** (v. 26, and see notes). If we understand Mark's use of irony here, we can see that he intends his readers to grasp the fact that Jesus truly is the king of Israel, the Messiah from God, even though the crucifixion seems to contradict every known form of Jewish expectation about what the path of the Messiah would be when he appeared, and even though for non-Jewish readers as well the idea that the Son of God would undergo crucifixion was repugnant and difficult to accept (see Paul's discussion of the attitudes of Jews and non-Jews toward the message of the crucified Christ in 1 Cor. 1:18–25).

15:33–41 / This portion of the narrative of Jesus' execution is full of dramatic events, including the darkness from noon till three o'clock (v. 33), Jesus' cry to God (v. 34), his last cry (v. 37), the tearing of the Temple curtain (v. 38), and the statement of the Roman officer (v. 39). But at least some of these events are intended to hint at the significance of Jesus' death. For example, the darkness not only seems intended to suggest in general that something momentous was happening, but it also may be an allusion to Amos 8:9 ("I will make the sun go down at noon and the earth grow dark in daytime"), and perhaps to the plague of darkness (Exod. 10:21-22) put upon the land of Egypt during the time of Moses. If this latter allusion is intended here, it (like the Amos 8:9 passage) would mean that the darkness was a sign of divine judgment upon Israel for the rejection of Jesus.

Jesus' cry in verse 34, the only words from the cross recorded in Mark, also seems intended as an allusion, this time to Psalm 22:1, a psalm already alluded to in earlier verses of the narrative. Some scholars take this allusion to mean that Jesus is to be seen as serenely quoting perhaps the whole of Psalm 22, the prayer of the righteous man under assault from his enemies, and that the cry does not indicate a sense of abandonment and hopelessness on Jesus' part. Others think that the cry is to be taken literally, and that in his death Jesus experienced abandonment by God and the torment of the sinners for which he died (thus, Lane, pp. 572-73). But to take one view against the other would be to miss part of what Mark intends here. Mark surely means for his readers to understand that Jesus' death was genuine suffering and shame, and any notion of a serene Jesus on the cross does not do justice either to what we know about crucifixion or to Mark's narrative. However, the quotation of this cry of Jesus is intended to show that Jesus' death was the fulfillment of the suffering of the righteous man pictured in Psalm 22, meaning that Jesus was truly innocent and also that his death was according to God's plan as prefigured in the OT Scriptures. That is, the purpose of the allusion to Psalm 22:1 was not to give some insight into the psychology of Jesus but rather to reveal the significance of the event, and much of the discussion about Jesus' words here is wide of the point because it is motivated by psychological or doctrinal concerns that are not part of Mark's purpose. (On the problems concerning the Semitic words quoted here, see the notes.)

Jesus' address to God, *Eloi, Eloi*, is misunderstood by some standing near the cross to be an appeal to Elijah the prophet, who is mentioned in ancient Jewish tradition in connection with the final appearance of God's Kingdom (see notes). This misunderstanding seems to be mentioned to demonstrate again how far from the truth the bystanders are, for they not only misconstrue Jesus' words but also labor under the assumption that Jesus is appealing to be released from the cross (v. 36). Mark has already shown his readers, however, that "Elijah" has indeed come, in the person of John the Baptist, and that this Elijah did not come to usher in an immediate and outwardly victorious appearance of the Kingdom of God but to summon Israel to repentance (1:4-5), and to prepare the way for Jesus, the Messiah (1:1-3, 9-11). Also, Mark has shown his readers that this "Elijah" specifically prepared for Jesus' work by being rejected and violently put to death (6:14-29; 9:11-13). The irony of the present scene is, therefore, that these bystanders wait to see if Elijah will come to save Jesus from his crucifixion, when in fact "Elijah" has already come and has himself been executed, prefiguring Jesus' own death. The bystanders speak of Elijah, knowing nothing of him, just as they mock Jesus as a false Messiah (v. 32), when they completely misunderstand the term they are using.

In contrast to the misguided curiosity of the bystanders, Mark then gives another event that signifies that indeed Jesus is the Messiah and that his death does not signal defeat but victory. Jesus' loud death cry (v. 37) is accompanied by a tearing in two of the Temple curtain (v. 38, see notes), which seems to mean that Jesus' death provides the basis for a new access to God, a new "Temple," and that the Jewish Temple and what it represents have been superseded. Thus, the Temple, which is the chief institution of the Jewish tradition that rejected Jesus, is itself now invalidated. There seems to have been an ancient Jewish tradition that the Messiah would restore the Temple or rebuild it, and Mark appears to be modifying this tradition by saying that in the death of Jesus, the Messiah, the old Temple was rendered obsolete. This incident, together with the way Mark handles the charge against Jesus that he threatened to destroy the Temple and build another "in three days," also hints that this Messiah does indeed build a new Temple, but a new kind of Temple "not made with hands": his resurrection body (see comments on 14:58).

Perhaps as striking as anything else in the scene, however, is the statement on the lips of the Roman soldier at the foot of the cross, **This man was really the Son of God!** Although it is likely that any such statement uttered by a Roman soldier would have originally meant something like, "This man behaves like a divine hero," likening Jesus to the ideals of popular Hellenistic religious tradition, Mark seems to intend his readers to interpret the statement as an ironic confession of the true significance of Jesus. The statement is ironic because this Gentile who participated in the execution of Jesus is the only human character in Mark who uses the title **Son of God**. Elsewhere, the term is used by God at Jesus' baptism (1:11) and at the transfiguration (9:7), and by demons on several occasions (3:11; 5:7; cf. 1:24, 34), but never by a human character (the demoniacs are pictured as being used by the demons as mouthpieces). (Additionally, in 1:1 Mark gives the title "Son of God" along with "Christ" as the proper descriptions of Jesus' significance.)

A comparison of the parallels of the present scene in Matthew 27:54 and Luke 23:47 shows that, though Matthew has the soldier make the same statement, Luke phrases it somewhat differently ("Certainly he was a good man!"), suggesting that the form of the saying in Mark is probably deliberate and intended to be noticed. This statement on the lips of the Roman soldier both shows the soldier ironically proclaiming Jesus' true significance, in contrast to the misguided mockery of the other (Jewish) bystanders, and, probably, prefigures the fact that the proclamation of the gospel to all nations resulted in many Gentiles indeed confessing Jesus to be the Son of God and the Christ. Mark does not suggest that the soldier really knew the significance of his statement (see notes) but rather that the soldier's statement had a greater significance than he may have realized; by positioning this statement in this context Mark intends the reader to perceive that larger significance.

The final item in this passage is the reference to several women who were witnesses of the crucifixion (vv. 40-41). These same women are mentioned in 16:1 as going to the tomb where Jesus had been buried and being met there by a "young man" who announces to them that Jesus is risen from death (16:5-8). Mentioning the women here seems to be intended for two purposes. First, there is the obvious contrast between the disciples—the chosen apostles—who fled and denied Jesus, and these women who stayed with Jesus devotedly. These women exhibit the courage and devotion one would have expected from the apostles. It is in keeping with Mark's use of irony that he features women as the positive role models of discipleship, for among many in the ancient world (and, unfortunately, still!) women were regarded as symbols of weakness. In other words, Mark inverts the stereotype of women, making these women the only ones courageous enough to follow Jesus to the cross and the only ones in the passion account who do not either deny Jesus or ridicule him.

Secondly, the mention of these women here makes them the human links between Jesus' crucifixion and his resurrection. In 15:47, two of them are mentioned as seeing where Jesus had been buried, and in 16:1-8 they return later to the tomb to care for Jesus' body and become the first witnesses to the resurrection. Thus, at each crucial stage of the main Gospel events, the crucifixion, the burial, and the resurrection (cf. 1 Cor. 15:1-4), these women are mentioned, both giving them great prominence and pointing to them as guarantors of the events. It is the same women who saw Jesus crucified and buried who also first see the vacant tomb and first hear the news of the risen Lord. There may very well have been a desire to emphasize the reality of all the events by emphasizing the presence of these same women at them all.

15:42-47 / In Roman practice, a person executed for treason (the charge placed against Jesus) was not ordinarily given a burial but was left on the cross to be devoured by scavengers. Only by special permission of the Roman magistrate could such a criminal be given an ordinary burial, and even then public mourning was forbidden. By contrast, Jewish custom required that even criminals be given burials, on the day of their death if at all possible. To fail to observe this custom was to defile the land, and so pious Jews felt obligated to give a burial even to an enemy (note Deut. 21:22–23, the biblical basis for the Jewish custom). It is against this background that the actions of Joseph of Arimathea must be seen.

In the present passage, Joseph seeks to bury Jesus both because Jewish law forbade a dead body to be left exposed beyond the day of death and because at sundown of this day came the Sabbath (vv. 42–43). Thus, the shame of Jesus being left exposed would be all the greater, fouling the sacred day of the week. Because Jesus had been executed for treason against Rome, only Pilate could give permission for the burial (v. 43). Pilate may have complied with the request because he recognized that the case against Jesus was somewhat flimsy or because he simply did not want a disturbance that might have resulted from failing to honor Jewish sensibilities about burying the dead.

Joseph here makes his only appearance in Mark, and the description of him is very brief. He is said to have been a **respected member of the Council** (v. 43), though it is not absolutely clear whether the council in question was the Jerusalem Sanhedrin or some other local council (see notes). Matthew 27:57 says he was rich and a disciple of Jesus, though John 19:38 describes him as a secret disciple on account of his fear of the Jewish authorities. Luke 23:50–51 calls him "a good and honorable man," and supports Mark's description of him as **waiting for the coming of the Kingdom of God**, which is simply to say that he (with most pious Jews of the time) believed in the hope for the salvation of Israel and the appearance of the messianic age. Whatever his exact attitude toward Jesus, it is striking that the Gospel tradition agrees that he, and not a member of Jesus' family or of the Twelve, went to obtain Jesus' body. Ordinarily, a close relative would ask the special permission necessary to bury a convicted criminal. Thus, the picture of Jesus' abandonment is filled out still more, so that Joseph takes the place that should have been taken by others. In the actual situation, it was perhaps prudent for the Twelve to have remained in hiding, for there may have been some initial interest among the authorities in arresting them as well. But in the context of Mark's description of Jesus' disciples as abandoning him (14:50), we are probably to think of their failure to appear for Jesus' body as an example of cowardice as much as prudence.

Pilate's surprise about Jesus being already dead (vv. 44–45) is explained when one realizes that crucified criminals are said to have often taken a couple of days or so to die. The army officer of verses 44–45 is probably to be seen as the same one mentioned in verse 39 who observed Jesus' last moment and was in charge of the execution force.

The detail about the **linen sheet** (v. 46), found in all the Synoptic accounts (cf. Matt. 27:59; Luke 23:53; John 19:40 uses different wording), takes on special significance in Mark perhaps, on account of the uniquely Markan scene earlier (14:51), in which a young man flees the arrest of Jesus leaving "a linen cloth" (same term in Greek). As mentioned in our treatment of that scene, Mark may have intended his readers to notice that the dress of the young man anticipates the death attire of Jesus (see the discussion of 14:51). There, a "young man" dressed for death and burial escapes, leaving Jesus to face his death and burial alone and, in Mark's view, on behalf of that young man and the others whom he represents.

The description of Jesus' burial place seems intended to show that Jesus was buried with respect and by a man of some wealth (see notes) and may also be designed to indicate that Jesus' burial site was known, preparing the reader for the next scene, in which the women mentioned in verse 47 go to the same tomb and find it miraculously empty (16:1–8). Scholars have quite properly noted that the conviction of the earliest Christians that Jesus was risen from death was based primarily upon the appearances of the risen Jesus (cf. 1 Cor. 15:1–9; Acts 1:3), but it seems evident that Mark and the other Gospel accounts also emphasize the tradition of the empty tomb as evidence of Jesus' resurrection. The details about the burial site seem intended here to show that this tradition did not arise out of confusion about where Jesus had been buried. In all the Gospel accounts, certain women disciples are mentioned as the ones who were able to verify the burial spot (v. 47), making them important elements in the Christian tradition, even though Jewish legal practice did not recognize a woman's testimony as acceptable evidence in courts.

With this scene, the tragedy of Jesus' ministry seems complete. The hero is dead. His disciples have fled, and he is buried only through the piety and generosity of this Joseph, while a few women disciples look on helplessly. But Mark's readers knew, and the next scene proclaims clearly, that Jesus' ministry is not a story of tragedy and that this is not the end. Still, the reader should not pass too quickly to the resurrection scene but should linger for a while in this narrative of Jesus' death and burial, absorbing the full force of it all, so that the still greater force of the resurrection event is fully felt. It is the crucified and abandoned Jesus who is raised from this death, this shame, this apparent tragedy. Thus, God's raising of Jesus was the vindication of this one who was vilified as a false Messiah and a criminal. That is to say that the full meaning of the resurrection of Jesus can be seen only when the glory of the Easter event is placed alongside the darkness of the Friday afternoon described in the present passage.

Additional Notes

15:21 / **Simon, who was coming into the city from the country**: We are not told Simon's business, nor whether he was a pilgrim to Jerusalem for Passover or a resident of the city. The two sons of Simon mentioned here, Alexander and Rufus, may have been known to Mark's readers. In Rom. 16:13, a certain Rufus is mentioned, and this, together with the possibility that Mark's Gospel was prepared for the Roman church, has led some to speculate that this Rufus may be the one mentioned here; but this cannot be determined. Simon was constrained to carry for Jesus the crossbeam of the cross, upon which the victim was hung. Normally the condemned person carried his own crossbeam to the place of execution; but in this case, Jesus' prolonged interrogation, severe flogging, and beatings must have left him too weak for this last ordeal.

15:22 / **Golgotha, which means "The Place of the Skull"**: The term **golgotha** is a transliteration of the Aramaic word for **skull**. We do not know why the place was so named, but some have suggested that the site may have been a hill near the city shaped somewhat like a skull. There are two sites proposed for the crucifixion, one marked by the Church of the Holy Sepulcher and the other called Gordon's Calvary (named after Gen. Charles Gordon), near which is the site known as the Garden Tomb, one of the places proposed as Jesus' burial site. See "Golgotha," *IDB*, vol. 2, p. 439; "Holy Sepulcher, Church of," *IDBSup*, pp. 413–14.

15:23 / **Wine mixed with a drug called myrrh**: Ancient Jewish tradition refers to respected women of Jerusalem having the custom of giving a narcotic drink to people condemned to die and mentions Prov. 31:6–7 as the basis of the custom. Wine would, of course, dull the senses somewhat, if taken in a significant quantity, but also there is some evidence that myrrh was known to have narcotic properties and was mixed with wine to enhance its ability to dull intense pain (see Lane, p. 564, for references; and "Myrrh," *IDB*, vol. 3, pp. 478–79). Jesus' refusal of the drink pictures him as choosing to be fully alert during the execution. The reference to the drugged wine may very well be an allusion to Ps. 69:21, "when I was thirsty, they offered me vinegar," intended to show that Jesus' suffering was a fulfillment of OT passages taken by early Christians to be predictions of Jesus' ministry.

15:24 / **They crucified him**: Crucifixion was apparently the most feared of all forms of death in the ancient world and was considered so shameful and painful that Roman citizens were exempt from this punishment (the form of execution for them being beheading). M. Hengel, *Crucifixion* (Philadelphia: Fortress, 1977) is the fullest discussion of the practice and of the social attitudes toward this form of execution. There was no one form of crucifixion and no one shape of the instrument used; it was sometimes an upright stake, sometimes an X-shaped device, and often a T-shaped one, as appears to have been the case with Jesus, for the text refers to the carrying of the crossbeam to the place of death (15:20–21). The victim was attached to this crossbeam by ropes, or sometimes by large nails through the forearms, and then this beam was lifted up and mounted on an upright beam already planted in the ground. From the skeleton of a crucified man executed in the first century A.D., we know that the victim's ankles were placed together and one large spike was driven through them from the side. (See the more complete description and illustration in *IDBSup*, pp. 199–200.)

And divided his clothes among themselves, throwing dice: This detail both adds to the picture of Jesus' complete shame and the callous indifference of the executioners and also seems to allude to Ps. 22:18, "they gamble for my clothes and divide them among themselves." This psalm was seen as an especially full picture of the execution and sufferings of Jesus, being alluded to again in v. 29 (cf. Ps. 22:7) and in v. 34 (cf. Ps. 22:1).

15:25 / **It was nine o'clock in the morning**: This time reference (lit., "the third hour") is problematical both because John 19:14 gives the time of Pilate's decision to crucify Jesus as "almost noon" (lit., "about the sixth hour") and because it seems very early for so much to have happened. It is not impossible that it is correct, but the difficulties with this time reference should be recognized. It may be significant that Mark's narrative makes time references at three-hour intervals (cf. 15:33, "noon"; 15:34, "three o'clock"; 15:42, "toward evening," being about six o'clock). Mark may have divided up the day of crucifixion by means of this time scheme for teaching purposes (perhaps to aid in remembering the events of the narrative), or even to reflect liturgical practices of the early church (about which, however, we know very little!). Lane (pp. 566–67) argues that this time reference is an early scribal insertion and does not stem from Mark, but he admits that there is no manuscript basis for omitting the statement.

15:26 / **The notice of the accusation**: The condemned man carried to the place of death a wooden sign on which was written the crime for which he was to be executed. At his execution, this notice was placed on his cross, intended as a deterrent for others who might consider the same crime. The notice placed on Jesus' cross both expressed contempt for Jewish aspirations of freedom from Rome and gave the charge for which Jesus was condemned, political subversion against Roman rule.

15:27 / **Two bandits**: These criminals may very well have been others deemed subversives by the governor, for the term "bandit" is often used by Josephus, the ancient Jewish historian, to refer to Jewish rebels. Luke 23:39–43 alone has the conversation between the two criminals, in which one rebukes the other for insulting Jesus and is promised a place with Jesus in Paradise. Early Christians saw Jesus' execution alongside other criminals as a fulfillment of Isa. 53:12, "he willingly gave his life and shared the fate of evil men," and in some manuscripts there appears after v. 27 the statement, "In this way the scripture came true which says, 'He shared the fate of criminals,' " making this allusion explicit. The present numbering of verses in the NT was made long ago using manuscripts that contained this statement, and so in modern versions that use more ancient and superior manuscripts, there is no v. 28.

15:29 / **People passing by shook their heads and hurled insults**: This appears to allude to Ps. 22:7, "All who see me make fun of me; they stick out their tongues and shake their heads." The taunts of the bystanders are like the taunts of the enemies of Ps. 22:8, who ridicule the good man's hope for God's vindication.

15:32 / **We will believe in him**: The best manuscripts lack the Greek word translated by the last two words in the phrase. The bystanders offer to believe that Jesus is the Messiah if he demonstrates overtly the kind of victory they describe. Mark's point is that true faith in Jesus recognizes that precisely in his crucifixion did he do the work of the Messiah.

15:33 / **At noon** is literally "when the sixth hour had come," that is, the sixth hour after dawn, or about noon. See note on 15:25 for discussion of Mark's time scheme in the crucifixion narrative.

For three hours is literally, "until the ninth hour," or about 3 P.M. The same expression is used at the beginning of v. 34 (translated in the GNB "at three o'clock").

15:34 / *Eloi, Eloi, lema sabachthani* is an Aramaic translation of the Hebrew of Ps. 22:1. Matt. 27:46 and some manuscripts of Mark give the cry as "*Eli, Eli, lema sabachthani*," in which the first two words, "My God, my God," are in Hebrew and the last two in Aramaic. If Jesus indeed addressed God in the Hebrew words "*Eli, Eli*," this would better explain how bystanders misunderstood him to be appealing to Elijah, for the Hebrew words sound more like Elijah's name, but it is impossible to decide with certainty exactly what Jesus may have said and in what language, for each Gospel account seems primarily concerned with giving us the meaning of the crucifixion rather than a documentary and complete description.

My God, my God, why did you abandon me? This translates the Aramaic phrase and is an allusion to Ps. 22:1. As indicated in the discussion earlier, it is perilous to try to make this statement the basis of a view of what Jesus felt on the cross. Mark's purpose in giving this statement is to make the allusion to Ps. 22:1, so as to portray Jesus as the righteous sufferer who is beset unjustly by his enemies and appeals to God. This allusion reveals Jesus' true character in the face of the ridicule and false charges on the lips of the bystanders. Interestingly, the statement does not appear in the Lucan parallel in 23:44–46.

15:35 / **Elijah**: On ancient Jewish expectation about the appearance of Elijah, the OT prophet, or one like him, in the last days before the coming of the Kingdom of God, see the comments and notes on 6:15 and 9:11–13.

15:36 / **Cheap wine** was the wine of the common people and soldiers, who were unable to afford better. So, the bystanders offer to Jesus what they themselves were drinking, and their intent was to keep him alive and alert for a while longer. The wine was offered to Jesus by means of a sponge on the end of a stick probably because Jesus' cross held him up too high to be reached easily.

15:37 / The phrase **a loud cry** implies a strong cry, not the sort of faint gasp expected from a man who had endured such torture as Jesus; and the reader is probably intended to see the cry as a hint of the victory of the cross. Cf. Luke 23:46 and John 19:30, which give varying versions of this last cry.

15:38 / **The curtain hanging in the Temple** could mean the curtain hanging between the court, where the altar for burnt offerings was, and the actual sanctuary, or the curtain hanging between the two areas of the sanctuary, one called the holy place, and the other called the most holy place or holy of holies. It is interesting to note that ancient Jewish tradition also refers to remarkable happenings at the entrance to the sanctuary some forty years before the destruction of Jerusalem in A.D. 70, about the year that Jesus was executed! (See Lane, pp. 564–75, for references; for the layout of the Jerusalem Temple, see "Temple, Jerusalem," *IDB*, vol. 4, pp. 534–60.)

15:39 / **The army officer** is literally "the Centurion," a Roman officer who commanded one hundred foot soldiers. See "Centurion," *IDB*, vol. 1, pp. 547–48. The officer's comment is offered after he **saw how Jesus had died**, meaning that he admired the strength and courage exhibited by Jesus.

15:40 / **Some women** is Mark's first mention of these women, but there are references to women disciples in other Gospel accounts, e.g., Luke 8:1–3; Matt. 27:56. Mary Magdalene was from the town of Magdala and in Luke 8:2 is described as having been delivered by Jesus from demonic possession. We know nothing more about the second Mary than the names of her sons, James and Joseph, who were possibly known to Mark's church. Likewise, we know nothing more about Salome, unless she is the same one mentioned in Matt. 27:56 as the mother of the Zebedee brothers, James and John, members of the Twelve. A great deal of romantic speculation has developed about Mary Magdalene and her relationship to Jesus, but none of it is based on anything in the Gospels, where she appears simply as one of the many whom Jesus had helped, and who became devoted followers of him. See "Mary," *IDB*, vol 3., pp. 288–89, par. 2. Among the **many other women** (v. 41) who were disciples of Jesus, Luke 8:3 mentions a Joanna and a Susanna. In addition, there are the two sisters, Mary and Martha, mentioned in John 11:1–37; 12:1–8, and still others who remain unnamed.

15:42-43 / **Toward evening . . . Preparation day**: In Jewish reckoning the day begins at sunset, so the Sabbath begins on Friday evening. Pious Jews hurriedly prepare on Friday the food to be eaten on the Sabbath (since no food can be cooked on that day). Mark 15:34 describes Jesus' death as happening sometime in the late afternoon, and so Joseph had to move quickly to bury Jesus before nightfall, in keeping with the rule in Deut. 21:22–23.

Joseph of Arimathea: Arimathea is possibly the Greek name for a village known as Ramathaim in Hebrew, located about twenty miles east of Joppa (see "Arimathea," *IDB*, vol. 1, p. 219). It appears that Joseph had come from this village and at some point had established residence in Jerusalem. John 19:39 mentions Nicodemus as assisting in the burial, but he is not mentioned in the Synoptic accounts. If Joseph was a man of some means, he would probably have had servants to assist him, and so it is not impossible for the preparation of Jesus' body and the burial to have been accomplished in the few hours left before sundown. (See "Joseph of Arimathea," *IDB*, vol. 2, pp. 980–81.) **A respected member of the Council** translates a Greek phrase (lit., "a respected member of a council") that does not specify what council is meant, though it is traditional to assume that Mark means the chief council mentioned in 14:55, the Sanhedrin.

The Kingdom of God was the theme of Jesus' preaching but also the hope of pious Jews of the time, as is indicated in the Jewish prayers that date from this period (still part of Jewish liturgy) in which Jews prayed for God to establish his Kingdom, meaning the kingdom of righteousness often associated with the Messiah. (See comments on 1:14–15).

Boldly: Because Jesus had been executed for treason, anyone asking for his body could have been suspected of being sympathetic to his cause. Thus, Joseph ran some personal risk in requesting that he be allowed to bury Jesus. Still, Jewish attitudes about the necessity of burying the dead were very strong (see Lane, p. 578, for references to ancient sources), and it was taught that whoever performed this service for the dead did an act of great piety.

15:45 / **The body**: Here and in v. 43, the Greek manuscripts are divided over the terms used, but most scholars believe that the term "body" is the original reading in v. 43, and that the term for "corpse" is the original term used here. It is interesting that, though the Greek term for "corpse" used here is neuter in gen-der, Mark consistently uses the masculine pronoun in v. 46. Thus, the GNB translation "it" is literally "him" there.

15:46 / **A linen sheet**: In recent years there has been much attention given to a burial shroud, the Shroud of Turin, that some have suggested may have been the burial shroud of Jesus, but this item is still under study. Before placing Jesus in the burial sheet, the corpse would probably have been washed hurriedly. John 19:39–40 says that spices normally used in preparation of bodies for burial were used, but Mark 16:1 says that the women went to the tomb after the Sabbath with spices to complete the proper duties for the dead.

A tomb: The burial place was probably an abandoned quarry that had been converted into a burial site. The tombs of the wealthy were usually designed for the burial of a family and so could accommodate several bodies. This tomb had as yet not been occupied, according to Matt. 27:60 and John 19:41. (On the design of ancient Palestinian tombs, see "Tomb," *IDBSup*, pp. 905–8.) The stone placed across the entrance was designed to keep out animals and intruders and may have been a flat, rounded stone that sat in a channel dug in the base of the entrance. Such channels were cut on a slope so that the stone could be rolled into place easily but would require the effort of several people to remove. Hence, the concern of the women mentioned in 16:3–4. The description of the tomb here would have been seen as an indication of Joseph's wealth, and this perhaps would have reminded the readers of Isa. 53:9, where God's servant is said to be "buried with the rich." There is evidence that the servant figure of Isa. 53 was understood by early Christians as a foreshadowing of Jesus.

15:47 / **Mary Magdalene and Mary the mother of Joseph** are two of the women mentioned also in vv. 40–41 and in 16:1–8. See the notes on these verses.

31

On the Third Day, He Rose

MARK 16:1–8

After the Sabbath was over, Mary Magdalene, Mary the mother of James, and Salome bought spices to go and anoint the body of Jesus. [2]Very early on Sunday morning, at sunrise, they went to the tomb.[3-4]On the way they said to one another, "Who will roll away the stone for us from the entrance to the tomb?" (It was a very large stone.) Then they looked up and saw that the stone had already been rolled back. [5]So they entered the tomb, where they saw a young man sitting at the right, wearing a white robe—and they were alarmed.

[6]"Don't be alarmed," he said. "I know you are looking for Jesus of Nazareth, who was crucified. He is not here—he has been raised! Look, here is the place where he was placed. [7]Now go and give this message to his disciples, including Peter: 'He is going to Galilee ahead of you; there you will see him, just as he told you.' "

[8]So they went out and ran from the tomb, distressed and terrified. They said nothing to anyone, because they were afraid.

16:1–8 / The resurrection of Jesus was the single most important event in the formation of faith in Jesus in the early church. The resurrection not only overturned the effects of the crucifixion, giving life where there was death, but more importantly, signified that Jesus had been vindicated by God and made the prince and pioneer of salvation for all others who should believe in him. In 1 Corinthians 15:12–28, Paul gives a concise description of the meaning of Jesus' resurrection, portraying the risen Jesus as the basis of the hope of Christians for their own salvation, and as the enthroned Lord who is to cause all things to submit to him for the glory of God the Father. This passage is but one of the many in the NT that indicate how central the resurrection of Jesus was in the proclamation of the early church (cf., e.g., Acts 2:22–36; Rom. 1:3–4). Thus, for Mark the story given here was not an epilogue to his account of Jesus' ministry; rather, it was the climactic revelation that vindicated Christian belief and made plain the true significance of Jesus.

In studying Mark's account of the resurrection, we are presented with special difficulties not encountered in the other Gospels. Each of the Gospel accounts of Jesus' resurrection has features that distinguish it from the others: Matthew's story of the descent of the angel (28:2–4) or his account of the mountain scene in Galilee (28:16–20); Luke's account of the appearance of Jesus to the two disciples on the road to Emmaus (24:13–35); John's account of Jesus' appearance to the Magdalene (20:11–18), his story of Thomas (20:24–29), or his account of the appearance to the disciples on their fishing trip (21:1–24). These various accounts can be approached either as difficulties, to the person trying to make a single harmonized narrative of the happening after the first Easter, or as evidence of the richness of the early Christian tradition concerning the Easter events; but with Mark there is the special problem of having to try to determine how he actually ended his Gospel, in view of the variations in the manuscript tradition.

Readers of the King James Version (properly called the Authorized Version) of the Bible will be familiar with what is designated as verses 9–20 of Mark 16, but readers of more modern translations will find these verses set off from the rest of Mark with an editorial note that they are not found in some of the most highly regarded manuscripts of the Gospel. The GNB puts this material in square brackets under the label An Old Ending to the Gospel, for example. In addition, there is evidence in the ancient manuscripts of other material that may have formed two other endings of Mark in some editions of the Gospel. The GNB gives one body of this material under the heading Another Old Ending. We shall discuss all this material more fully in the next section of this commentary, and here we want to concentrate simply on 16:1–8, about which there is no question of authenticity. But we cannot discuss this material without considering later the suggestion of a number of scholars that in fact Mark originally ended his Gospel story at 16:8 and that this was thus the final scene in the book as it came from Mark's hand. Before we turn to this question, it may be best to examine the content of the passage.

Perhaps the first thing to note about the passage is that, properly speaking, it does not give us an account of the actual resurrection of Jesus but instead tells us of the arrival of women at Jesus' tomb after the resurrection, when they are met by a **young man** who announces to them that Jesus is risen (vv. 5–7). Indeed, it is interesting to observe that none of the Gospels tries to describe the actual resurrection event, although later in Christian tradition some tried to supply descriptions (see notes). In a sense, it speaks well of the Gospel writers that they restricted their reports basically to the traditions about the things actually experienced by the early disciples, such as the encounter with angels (as here in Mark) and with the risen Jesus (such as are described in the other Gospels and in the material described as Mark 16:9–20). It speaks well of them because all indications are that the earliest Christian tradition about Jesus' resurrection had to do only with the postresurrection appearance of angels announcing Jesus' resurrection and with appearances of Jesus himself; and so in the canonical Gospels we have a respect for the earliest (and therefore most reliable) form of the Easter tradition.

In the present passage, the women who are placed at the scene of Jesus' execution (15:41) and at the scene of Jesus' burial (15:47) go to the tomb to mourn and to offer their last gesture of love for the dead Jesus. The **spices** mentioned in 16:1 were not for embalming (not a Jewish burial custom at this time) but for perfuming the corpse, a gesture of love and respect. Excavations of ancient Jewish tombs have uncovered perfume flasks that contained aromatic substances. The women's intent to **anoint** the corpse (v. 1) means that they probably wished to pour the perfumed oils over the dead master. Such perfumes were costly, and this act therefore involved a sacrifice financially. The purchase of this sort of substance and the intent to perform this burial rite means that they had no expectation of a resurrection of Jesus. They waited until after Sabbath, going early on the Sunday morning (v. 2) because the strict rules of Sabbath observance made it improper to perform such rites on the holy day. In the Jerusalem climate during the late spring (when the execution and burial took place), dead bodies decompose quickly, and so the women would have been prepared for an uncomfortable experience in the tomb.

The reader, however, knows that earlier Jesus received the act of devotion of the woman at Bethany (14:3–9) as an anointing of his body for burial and is prepared, therefore, to see the women's sincere intention here as ironically futile. The reader knows what the women in the story cannot know that this Sunday morning will not be an occasion for mourning and for belated rites of burial, but for the startling news that the dead Jesus is powerfully alive. Mark intensifies the narrative suspense with his description of the women discussing among themselves the problem of how to remove the heavy stone so that they can minister to the dead master (vv. 3–4). Their concern about the stone is addressed (v. 4), for they find the stone removed, not to allow access to a dead Jesus, but to demonstrate the reality of his resurrection!

Mark's description of the figure they meet at the tomb prolongs the suspense to the very last moment. He does not describe the figure as an angel (what the reader knows the figure must be), as does Matthew 28:5, but as a **young man** (cf. Luke 24:4 and notes) attired in a **white robe**. The women's reaction is alarm (v. 5), indicating that they still do not suspect the glorious news. Only with the actual words of this "young man" do the women begin to take in the truth. The unambiguous announcement shows the reader that the conviction that Jesus is risen does not rest upon surmise or conjecture but upon a clear declaration.

There is more than an announcement, however, for the "young man" issues a command to the women to convey the news to the disciples and to remind them of Jesus' promise that he would meet them again in Galilee—alluding to Jesus' statement found in 14:28. In this command, we have the first of a chain of actions that involved the glad proclamation of the Easter message, first among the core of disciples, and then on to later Christians, including Mark's readers and Christians of subsequent generations. That is, the command signifies the divine mandate laid upon the early Christians to share the news of the risen Jesus and prefigures the subsequent mission of Christians to the whole world.

Mark's version of the angelic command includes the reference to Galilee as the place where **you will see him** (v. 7). Matthew 28:7 has a similar statement, but Luke 24:6–7 simply mentions Galilee as the place where the promise of the resurrection was first given. This is in keeping with the fact that Luke's accounts of the appearances of the risen Christ are all located in Judea. Matthew mentions a brief resurrection appearance to the women near the tomb (28:9–10) but clearly emphasizes a Galilean appearance (28:16–20). As for Mark, the question is what kind of resurrection appearance, if any, was a feature of his narrative. The material in verses 9–20 describes appearances of Jesus to the Magdalene (v. 9), to two disciples (vv. 12–13), and to the "eleven," probably in Jerusalem (vv. 14–20), but most scholars do not believe that these verses are the original ending of Mark. One of the reasons for this view is that these verses make no mention of an appearance in Galilee, although the announcement in verse 7 specifically mentions this area as the locale where the risen Jesus will be encountered. The command in verse 7 leads the reader to expect a description of a Galilean appearance, if any is to be given, but none of the alternate endings of Mark fulfills the expectation excited by the verse.

Some scholars have argued that **Galilee** in verse 7 is a symbol that refers to Christian discipleship and not to the geographical territory of that name. They note that in Mark Galilee is described as the place where Jesus led the Twelve in ministry and Judea as the place where he was rejected and executed. Thus, according to this view, in Mark's narrative Galilee comes to represent the discipleship connected with that area. So, in verse 7, Mark meant simply that the disciples would encounter Jesus as they returned to their mission; and Mark intended his readers to understand that they likewise would "see" Jesus spiritually in their "Galilee" of discipleship and service. This suggestion has not met with universal acceptance among scholars and must be treated as highly speculative. There seems to have been early Christian tradition describing appearances of the risen Jesus both in Galilee and in Judea, and in both locations the appearances include a commissioning of the disciples (cf. Matt. 28:16–20; Luke 24:36–49; John 20:19–22; 21:1–19). Thus, the statement in 16:7 seems to be simply a reflection of the early Christian tradition that the risen Jesus did appear to his followers in Galilee. Since none of the proposed endings to Mark mentions an appearance in Galilee, however, we are left to wonder whether the original form of Mark did contain such an account.

The final item in the passage before us is the response of the women to the command of the "young man" (16:8). The women are told to go to the disciples and tell them what they have been told (v. 7). Instead, we read that the women flee in great agitation and fear and say **nothing to anyone**. It is striking that the parallels in Mathew 28:8 and Luke 24:8–9 say the opposite, describing the women as obeying the command of the angel at the tomb and proclaiming to the disciples the news of Jesus' resurrection. This difference has led some to propose that the original ending of Mark contained an account in which the women overcame their fear and did speak to the disciples. Something like this is related in the material described as Another Old Ending, but nearly all scholars doubt that this material is part of the original text of Mark. The so-called long ending, labeled in the GNB An Old Ending to the Gospel, relates an appearance of Jesus to Mary Magdalene but does not solve the question of what the women mentioned in verse 8 did, this silence being further indication that the material was not an original part of Mark. Thus, we are left to wonder what maÿ have followed verse 8 in the original text of Mark. The suggestion that original material has been lost through damage to the final portion of the original manuscript remains only an interesting, but unproven, suggestion.

In recent years, some scholars have suggested that Mark originally ended his Gospel at verse 8, and that no further material followed (e.g., Lane, pp. 590–92). In this view, Mark did not intend to bring his Gospel to a close with an ending giving a resurrection appearance of Jesus and a commissioning of the Twelve but instead wanted his readers to be confronted with a story of Jesus' resurrection that was somewhat open ended and unconcluded. That is, in this view, Mark wanted his readers to be left with the command about going to Galilee (v. 7) to see Jesus, and he desired them to take the command to themselves in some way. Did he want his readers to go to Galilee themselves to wait for Jesus to appear in resurrection glory, as some suggest? Or did he use "Galilee" symbolically (as described earlier), intending his readers to understand that they were to follow Jesus and the Twelve in discipleship in their "Galilee," believing that in due time Jesus would appear in glory? If Mark did end his Gospel here, it would be an unusually clever and subtle device, so clever and subtle that perhaps no one detected his intent until modern scholarly research succeeded! (See the comments of Nineham, p. 442.) On the other hand, if Mark did end his Gospel at 16:8, such a strange ending would certainly explain the several other endings that appear in the manuscript tradition, for they would all be attempts to provide a more suitable conclusion. It must be pointed out, however, that the several attempts in the ancient manuscripts to provide an ending for Mark could also have been prompted if Mark's original ending were lost early after the writing of the book. The question of whether Mark ended his Gospel at 16:8 or whether his original ending was lost remains a matter of scholarly disagreement and research. In the absence of conclusive evidence or argument, the reader is advised to be aware of the question and to recognize that at 16:8 we leave the certain text of Mark and enter into uncertainty about what may have come next, if anything. (We shall discuss the various endings in the manuscript tradition in the next section.)

The difficulties about the nature of what might have followed 16:8 should not be allowed to obscure what is contained in the passage before us. In 16:1–8, the Jesus who was left abandoned by his followers to face execution alone, who suffered the callous and shameful ridicule of the Jewish and Roman authorities, and who had to be buried at the charity of Joseph of Arimathea is proclaimed to be powerfully alive and vindicated by God against all the slanders and charges. And, very importantly, the risen Jesus renews his summons to the very disciples who abandoned and denied him (Peter!) to renew their discipleship and to become again his followers. Thus, this earliest form of the proclamation of the Christian gospel in Mark, the news of the risen Jesus, not only heralds the victory of Jesus over death but also announces and embodies the forgiveness that is part of the gospel message. The cowardly disciples are implicitly forgiven their cowardice in the words of the "young man," and this forgiven core of disciples becomes the foundational group of the Christian community of those who likewise know themselves to be forgiven of their sins. Whatever Mark may have intended with reference to the women who, at least initially, flee from the tomb too frightened to comply with the command, the reader certainly has been given the news of Jesus' resurrection and is called to follow the risen Jesus, proclaiming the victory and forgiveness of the gospel.

Additional Notes

16:1 / **The body of Jesus**: The Greek says literally "him," but the meaning is clearly Jesus' corpse, which the women expected to find in the tomb.

16:3-4 / **The stone had already been rolled back**: Matt. 28:2-4 describes the descent of an angel who rolls back the stone, but no such thing is mentioned in Mark or the other Gospel accounts. An ancient Latin manuscript (Codex Bobiensis) has a statement following the women's question in v. 3 that describes angels descending from heaven and rising back to God together with Jesus "at the third hour of the day" (see the translation of the passage in Lane, p. 582).

In the apocryphal writing called the Gospel of Peter, which may perhaps have originated as early as the second century, there is a more elaborate attempt to describe the resurrection, which describes the heavens opening and two angels descending in great brightness to the tomb of Jesus. The stone rolls away by itself and the angels enter. The guards at the tomb (derived from Matt. 27:62-66; 28:4) are frightened by this, and while relating these events to their leader and to the Jewish elders (who are supposedly there also), they see three figures emerge from the tomb, two of them supporting the third and a cross following them. The two (angels) reach to the heavens in height, but the third (Jesus) is described as taller still, "overpassing the heavens." As they emerge from the tomb, a voice from heaven mentions Jesus as having preached to the dead, and the cross is heard to answer "yea" (the text can be read in translation in E. Hennecke, W. Schneemelcher, *New Testament Apocrypha*, trans. R. M. Wilson [Philadelphia: Westminster, 1963], vol. 1, pp. 185-86).

It is evident that, compared with these examples of the attempt to supply descriptions of the resurrection, the canonical Gospels are quite reserved and place emphasis upon the declaration that Jesus is risen, leaving the event itself without description.

16:5 / **A young man**: Mark seems here to use the language of appearances, giving the initial impression of the women. The gleaming attire of the figure, **a white robe**, indicates that this is a heavenly figure (cf. the description of Jesus' attire at the transfiguration scene in 9:2-3). Matt. 28:5 describes the figure as an angel, and Luke 24:4 refers to "two men in bright shining clothes."

16:6 / **He has been raised** translates exactly the force of the Greek word, which is a passive form of the verb "to raise." God is the one who raised Jesus, and the resurrection is, thus, not an act of Jesus' might, but a divine vindication of Jesus. (For a discussion of the place of Jesus' resurrection in the NT and its meaning for today, see G. G. Ladd, *I Believe in the Resurrection of Jesus* [Grand Rapids: Eerdamans, 1975]; and for a review of recent scholarly opinion of the subject, see, e.g., G. O'Collins, *The Resurrection of Jesus Christ* [Valley Forge, Penn.: Judson, 1973]; "The Resurrection in Contemporary Theology," *NIDNTT*, vol. 3. pp. 281-309).

16:7 / **His disciples, including Peter**: Here the power of this statement is los
unless one remembers that in Mark especially the Twelve are presented as un
comprehending followers who failed in the crunch. Thus, the ones summoned
here to follow Jesus anew are the very ones who have abandoned and denied
Jesus, and this can only mean that implicit in the summons is the word of renewa
and forgiveness of them. The special mention of Peter is intended to heighten thi
forgiveness, in the light of Mark's story of Peter's threefold denial of Jesus i
14:66–72. In 1 Cor. 15:3–8, Paul gives a list of early disciples to whom the rise
Christ appeared and singles out Peter for special mention (15:5), just as here i
the announcement of the "young man."

16:8 / **Distressed and terrified . . . afraid**: Similar language is used elsewher
in Mark to describe human reaction to a wondrous event, a miracle or revelatio
of divine power, e.g., 2:12; 5:42; 4:41; 5:15, 33; 9:6.

32

Two Old Endings to Mark

AN OLD ENDING TO THE GOSPEL
[After Jesus rose from death early on Sunday, he appeared first to Mary Magdalene, from whom he had driven out seven demons. [10]She went and told his companions. They were mourning and crying; [11]and when they heard her say that Jesus was alive and that she had seen him, they did not believe her.

[12]After this, Jesus appeared in a different manner to two of them while they were on their way to the country. [13]They returned and told the others, but these would not believe it.

[14]Last of all, Jesus appeared to the eleven disciples as they were eating. He scolded them, because they did not have faith and because they were too stubborn to believe those who had seen him alive. [15]He said to them, "Go throughout the whole world and preach the gospel to all mankind. [16]Whoever believes and is baptized will be saved; whoever does not believe will be condemned.

[17]Believers will be given the power to perform miracles: they will drive out demons in my name; they will speak in strange tongues; [18]if they pick up snakes or drink any poison, they will not be harmed; they will place their hands on sick people, and these will get well."

[19]After the Lord Jesus had talked with them, he was taken up to heaven and sat at the right side of God. [20]The disciples went and preached everywhere, and the Lord worked with them and proved that their preaching was true by the miracles that were performed.]

ANOTHER OLD ENDING[a]
[[9]The women went to Peter and his friends and gave them a brief account of all they had been told. [10]After this, Jesus himself sent out through his disciples from the east to the west the sacred and everliving message of eternal salvation.]

z. *Some manuscripts and ancient translations do not have this ending to the Gospel.*
a.*Some manuscripts and ancient translations have this shorter ending to the Gospel in addition to the longer ending (verses 9–20).*

16:9-20 / As indicated in the discussion of 16:1–8, nearly all scholars believe that the material designated 16:9–20 is not a part of the original text of Mark, and that the same must be said for the material designated in the GNB Another Old Ending. We shall, therefore, discuss all this material here and shall try to summarize what scholars believe about how this material arose and became attached to Mark in many ancient manuscripts.

The material designated Another Old Ending appears in several Greek manuscripts and in other ancient witnesses, and in them is inserted after 16:8 and often followed by the material here designated An Old Ending to the Gospel. It seems likely, however, that the former material began its life as a separate ending of Mark, designed to overcome the somewhat abrupt felling left by 16:8. Then some scribes who were familiar with manuscripts ending with this material and with other manuscripts with the "Old Ending" (vv. 9–20) prepared manuscripts containing both endings in one continuous narrative.

The essential point of the material called here Another Old Ending is to show the women overcoming their fear (mentioned in 16:8) and announcing to the disciples what they had been told. That is, this material relieves the tension created by 16:8 and describes the disciples as beginning the preaching of the church. The vocabulary used in the material and other evidence, however, make it almost certain that these lines were added in some early copies of Mark (perhaps in the second century) to give the book a more pleasing ending.

As for the material called An Old Ending (vv. 9–20), this appears to have arisen as an independent attempt to give Mark a suitable ending (suitable to the tastes of the writer of the passage!). These verses appear to be a collection of incidents and references from other NT writings and are somewhat clumsily attached to 16:8, for they make no mention of the group of women of 16:8 or the appearance in Galilee promised 16:7. Instead, verse 9 begins a series of appearances of the risen Jesus, probably based on other accounts, by giving an appearance to Mary Magdalene, probably adapted from John 20:11–18. Then follows an appearance to two disciples (probably adapted from Luke 24:13–35), an appearance to the eleven at a meal (freely adapted from Luke 24:36–49; Matt. 28:16–20), and an ascension scene (adapted from Luke 24:50–53). The only distinctive feature of this material is its emphasis upon the signs that are to follow the preaching of the disciples as they go out in the world. Although the parallel accounts in the other Gospels do not mention such things, the traditions of the early church certainly emphasize miraculous signs as a part of the preaching activity of the apostles and others (cf. Acts 2:43; 4:30; 5:12; Heb. 2:4). So, the writer of these verses was familiar with this basic tradition and with specific miracles to which he seems to allude (cf. v. 17, **they will speak with strange tongues,** with Acts 2:4; v. 18, **if they pick up snakes,** with Acts 28:1–6).

Nearly all scholars think that verses 9–20 also began to be attached to Mark, sometime in the second century or later, by scribes trying to make Mark read more like the other Gospels. In the course of time, these verses became the ending to Mark in the great mass of Greek manuscripts and were popularly regarded as a genuine part of the Gospel. The earliest and best Greek manuscripts do not, however, contain these verses, and the testimony of the earliest "fathers" of the church (in the first four centuries) indicates that these verses were known only in a few copies of Mark and were not regarded as original with the book.

In addition to these verses and the material designated here Another Old Ending, one Greek manuscript of the fifth century (Codex W) has another block of material describing a conversation between Jesus and the eleven disciples about the course of the present age and the appearance of the kingdom of righteousness (see a discussion of this material in Lane, pp. 606–611). This likewise seems to be evidence of there having been various attempts to provide an ending to Mark that would improve upon the harshness of 16:8. No doubt most readers will still be dissatisfied with 16:8 as the ending of Mark and will be somewhat distressed to realize that there is disagreement among scholars as to what might have been Mark's original way of ending his book. Two things need to be kept in mind.

First, 16:1–8 clearly presents the resurrection of Jesus as having happened and as a real event. The empty tomb (16:6) means that Jesus' resurrection was not seen as an event in the minds of the disciples but as a real event in its own right. Similarly, 16:1–8 demonstrates that Mark knew and approved of the tradition that Jesus appeared to his disciples after his resurrection, whether Mark recorded such an appearance or not. Thus, the essential point that Jesus is risen and powerfully alive, the Lord of his followers again, but in transcendent glory, is unambiguously presented in a passage about which there is no textual uncertainty.

Secondly, the uncertainty about the ending of Mark demonstrates how very much the Christian Scriptures are a part of the history of the world, written by human beings on this earth, copied and transmitted down the ages in the same way as any document from ancient times, and subject to the same dangers of mutilation, faulty copying, and scribal changes. The volume and the antiquity of the manuscripts of the NT writings make it possible to detect these kinds of effects upon the text of the writings and to prepare editions of the Greek NT and modern translations that can be received with great confidence. These same manuscripts show that such things as accidental damage, faulty copying, and even deliberate scribal changes did happen. But how else could it have been? The Christian who regards the Bible as the Word of God at the same time recognizes that this Word was transmitted through time by human agents who, though they were not always perfect in their work, have placed all subsequent students of the Bible in their debt. We are in no position to complain about their work, for we are wholly dependent upon them for any direct contact with the biblical documents, and we owe them gratitude for their labors.

Additional Notes

16:9 / **Seven demons:** in Luke 8:2, this Mary is described as one of the women whom Jesus healed of various illnesses and demonic afflictions. It is there also that the reference to "seven demons" appears, and this is probably the source for the statement in 16:9.

16:11 / **They did not believe:** This theme of not believing the witnesses appears also in vv. 13–14, in which the disciples refuse to believe the report of the two to whom Jesus appeared. This theme is reflected in Luke 24:22–27; 37–39.

16:17 / **Belivers will be given the power to perform miracles:** Properly translated "These signs shall follow those who believe" the phrase emphasizes the miracles as signs of God's favor upon their message.

16:18 / **If they pick up snakes or drink any poison:** Readers may know of the "snake handlers" of West Virginia, small pockets of Christians who believe that spirituality is demonstrated by handling rattlesnakes in their church services and who point to this verse as the basis for their practice. The writer of the passage here, however, seems to have had in mind such an incident as is described in Acts 28:1–6, in which Paul is accidentally bitten by a creature of some sort and survives, impressing his host as a bearer of divine power.

Place their hands on sick people: The Gospel accounts show Jesus being asked to touch the sick (e.g., Mark 7:32), and the NT indicates that this was a frequent part of the ministry of early church (cf. James 5:14–15).

Abbreviations

GNB	Good News Bible
IDB	*Interpreters Dictionary of the Bible.* Edited by G. A. Buttrick. 4 vols. Nashville: Abingdon, 1962.
IDBSup	*Supplementary Volume: Interpreters Dictionary of the Bible.* Edited by K. Crim. Nashville: Abingdon, 1976.
KJV	King James Version (Authorized Version, 1611)
Lane	W. L. Lane. *The Gospel According to Mark.* Grand Rapids: Eerdmans, 1974.
MBA	*Macmillan Bible Atlas.* By Y. Aharoni and M. Avi-Yonah. New York: Macmillan, 1968.
NEB	New English Bible
NIDNTT	*New International Dictionary of New Testament Theology.* 3 vols. Edited by C. Brown. Grand Rapids: Zondervan, 1975–78.
Nineham	D. E. Nineham. *Saint Mark. Pelican New Testament Commentaries.* Baltimore: Penguin, 1969.
NIV	New International Version
NT	New Testament
OT	Old Testament
RSV	Revised Standard Version

For Further Reading

I provide here a brief selection of helpful publications, first giving general reference works, then books on Mark.

Reference Aids

Aharoni, Y., and Avi-Yonah, M. *The Macmillan Bible Atlas*. New York: Macmillan, 1968. There are several good atlases of the Bible available, but this is probably the most interesting in format.

Brown, C., ed. *New International Dictionary of New Testament Theology*. 3 vols. Grand Rapids: Zondervan, 1975–78. This work deals with the usage and meaning of terms used in the NT with theological significance. There are excellent bibliographies for the advanced student as well.

Buttrick, G. A., ed. *The Interpreters Dictionary of the Bible*. 4 vols. Nashville: Abingdon, 1962. Crim, K., ed. *Supplementary Volume*. Nashville: Abingdon, 1976. This is a well-known and scholarly reference set, useful for information on almost any item in the Bible. There are other multivolume dictionaries and several one-volume ones as well.

Throckmorton, B. H., ed. *Gospel Parallels*. Nashville: Thomas Nelson, 1967. This gives the text of the Gospels of Matthew, Mark, and Luke in parallel columns, making it easy to compare the same or similar sayings and incidents in the Synoptics. The translation is the Revised Standard Version.

Books on Mark

Achtemeier, P. J. *Mark: Proclamation Commentaries*. Philadelphia: Fortress, 1975. A discussion of major themes in Mark by an important scholar whose critical views I do not always share.

Cole, A. *The Gospel According to St. Mark: Tyndale New Testament Commentaries*. Grand Rapids: Eerdmans, 1961. A reverent treatment of Mark by a British Evangelical, written for the general reader.

Kealy, Sean. *Mark's Gospel: A History of Its Interpretation*. New York: Paulist Press, 1982. A readable and well-documented account covering ancient and modern times.

Kee, H. C. *Community of the New Age*. Philadelphia: Westminster, 1977. By a major scholar, this book is for the advanced student and shows the attempt to reconstruct the church lying behind the Gospel of Mark.

Lane, W. L. *The Gospel According to Mark: The New International Commentary on The New Testament*. Grand Rapids: Eerdmans,

1974. A scholarly study for the advanced student, especially good in its documentation of both primary sources and scholarly literature.

Martin, R. *Mark: Evangelist and Theologian*. Grand Rapids: Zondervan, 1972. For the advanced student. A discussion of scholarly work on Mark, emphasizing attempts to describe the theological emphases of the book.

Nineham, D. E. *Saint Mark: Pelican New Testament Commentaries*. Baltimore: Penguin, 1969. For the general reader, by a front-rank scholar who introduces the reader to the concerns of form-criticism of the Gospels.

Schweizer, E. *The Good News According to Mark*. Atlanta: John Knox, 1970. Written by a major Swiss scholar for the general reader.

Subject Index

Scripture Index

SCRIPTURE INDEX

APOCRYPHA

NONCANONICAL BOOKS